Artificial Intelligence and Cognitive Computing

Artificial Intelligence and Cognitive Computing: Methods, Technologies, Systems, Applications and Policy Making

Editors

Miltiadis D. Lytras
Anna Visvizi

MDPI • Basel • Beijing • Wuhan • Barcelona • Belgrade • Manchester • Tokyo • Cluj • Tianjin

Editors
Miltiadis D. Lytras
Effat College of Business
Effat University
Jeddah
Saudi Arabia

Anna Visvizi
Effat College of Engineering
Effat University
Jeddah
Saudi Arabia

Editorial Office
MDPI
St. Alban-Anlage 66
4052 Basel, Switzerland

This is a reprint of articles from the Special Issue published online in the open access journal *Sustainability* (ISSN 2071-1050) (available at: www.mdpi.com/journal/sustainability/special_issues/ artificial_intelligence_sustainability).

For citation purposes, cite each article independently as indicated on the article page online and as indicated below:

LastName, A.A.; LastName, B.B.; LastName, C.C. Article Title. *Journal Name* **Year**, *Volume Number*, Page Range.

ISBN 978-3-0365-1161-0 (Hbk)
ISBN 978-3-0365-1160-3 (PDF)

© 2021 by the authors. Articles in this book are Open Access and distributed under the Creative Commons Attribution (CC BY) license, which allows users to download, copy and build upon published articles, as long as the author and publisher are properly credited, which ensures maximum dissemination and a wider impact of our publications.

The book as a whole is distributed by MDPI under the terms and conditions of the Creative Commons license CC BY-NC-ND.

Contents

Preface to "Artificial Intelligence and Cognitive Computing: Methods, Technologies, Systems, Applications and Policy Making" vii

Miltiadis D. Lytras and Anna Visvizi
Artificial Intelligence and Cognitive Computing: Methods, Technologies, Systems, Applications and Policy Making
Reprinted from: *Sustainability* **2021**, *13*, 3598, doi:10.3390/su13073598 1

Ahmed Abdulhamid Mahmoud, Salaheldin Elkatatny and Dhafer Al Shehri
Application of Machine Learning in Evaluation of the Static Young's Modulus for Sandstone Formations
Reprinted from: *Sustainability* **2020**, *12*, 1880, doi:10.3390/su12051880 5

Amjed Hassan, Salaheldin Elkatatny and Abdulazeez Abdulraheem
Application of Artificial Intelligence Techniques to Predict the Well Productivity of Fishbone Wells
Reprinted from: *Sustainability* **2019**, *11*, 6083, doi:10.3390/su11216083 21

Amjed Hassan, Salaheldin Elkatatny and Abdulazeez Abdulraheem
Intelligent Prediction of Minimum Miscibility Pressure (MMP) During CO_2 Flooding Using Artificial Intelligence Techniques
Reprinted from: *Sustainability* **2019**, *11*, 7020, doi:10.3390/su11247020 35

Ahmed Abdulhamid Mahmoud, Salaheldin Elkatatny, Abdulwahab Z. Ali, Mohamed Abouelresh and Abdulazeez Abdulraheem
Evaluation of the Total Organic Carbon (TOC) Using Different Artificial Intelligence Techniques
Reprinted from: *Sustainability* **2019**, *11*, 5643, doi:10.3390/su11205643 51

Ahmed Gowida, Tamer Moussa, Salaheldin Elkatatny and Abdulwahab Ali
A Hybrid Artificial Intelligence Model to Predict the Elastic Behavior of Sandstone Rocks
Reprinted from: *Sustainability* **2019**, *11*, 5283, doi:10.3390/su11195283 67

Salaheldin Elkatatny
Real-Time Prediction of the Rheological Properties of Water-Based Drill-In Fluid Using Artificial Neural Networks
Reprinted from: *Sustainability* **2019**, *11*, 5008, doi:10.3390/su11185008 89

Huijie Zhang, Ke Ren, Yiming Lin, Dezhan Qu and Zhenxin Li
AirInsight: Visual Exploration and Interpretation of Latent Patterns and Anomalies in Air Quality Data
Reprinted from: *Sustainability* **2019**, *11*, 2944, doi:10.3390/su11102944 107

Wenbing Chang, Xinglong Yuan, Yalong Wu, Shenghan Zhou, Jingsong Lei and Yiyong Xiao
Decision-Making Method based on Mixed Integer Linear Programming and Rough Set: A Case Study of Diesel Engine Quality and Assembly Clearance Data
Reprinted from: *Sustainability* **2019**, *11*, 620, doi:10.3390/su11030620 135

Tao Han, Seyed Mostafa Bozorgi, Ayda Valinezhad Orang, Ali Asghar Rahmani Hosseinabadi, Arun Kumar Sangaiah and Mu-Yen Chen
A Hybrid Unequal Clustering Based on Density with Energy Conservation in Wireless Nodes
Reprinted from: *Sustainability* **2019**, *11*, 746, doi:10.3390/su11030746 157

Recep Sinan Arslan and Necaattin Barışçı
Development of Output Correction Methodology for Long Short Term Memory-Based Speech Recognition
Reprinted from: *Sustainability* **2019**, *11*, 4250, doi:10.3390/su11154250 . . . . **183**

Alessandro Crivellari and Euro Beinat
LSTM-Based Deep Learning Model for Predicting Individual Mobility Traces of Short-Term Foreign Tourists
Reprinted from: *Sustainability* **2020**, *12*, 349, doi:10.3390/su12010349 . . . . **199**

Jie Gao, Xinping Huang and Lili Zhang
Comparative Analysis between International Research Hotspots and National-Level Policy Keywords on Artificial Intelligence in China from 2009 to 2018
Reprinted from: *Sustainability* **2019**, *11*, 6574, doi:10.3390/su11236574 . . . . **217**

Yanfang Zhang and Mushang Lee
A Hybrid Model for Addressing the Relationship between Financial Performance and Sustainable Development
Reprinted from: *Sustainability* **2019**, *11*, 2899, doi:10.3390/su11102899 . . . . **235**

Francisco A. Pujol, María José Pujol, Carlos Rizo-Maestre and Mar Pujol
Entropy-Based Face Recognition and Spoof Detection for Security Applications
Reprinted from: *Sustainability* **2019**, *12*, 85, doi:10.3390/su12010085 . . . . **251**

Preface to "Artificial Intelligence and Cognitive Computing: Methods, Technologies, Systems, Applications and Policy Making"

Artificial intelligence (AI) is a subject garnering increasing attention in both academia and the industry today. The understanding is that AI-enhanced methods and techniques create a variety of opportunities related to improving basic and advanced business functions, including production processes, logistics, financial management and others. As this collection demonstrates, AI-enhanced tools and methods tend to offer more precise results in the fields of engineering, financial accounting, tourism, air-pollution management and many more. The objective of this collection is to bring these topics together to offer the reader a useful primer on how AI-enhanced tools and applications can be of use in today's world. In the context of the frequently fearful, skeptical and emotion-laden debates on AI and its value added, this volume highlights AI's positive applications. Certainly, as AI is a part of a broader ecosystem of sophisticated tools, techniques and technologies, it is not immune to developments in that ecosystem. It is thus imperative that inter- and multidisciplinary research on AI and its ecosystem is encouraged. This collection contributes to that. We thank all contributing authors as well as the MDPI team for their professionalism.

Miltiadis D. Lytras, Anna Visvizi
Editors

Editorial

Artificial Intelligence and Cognitive Computing: Methods, Technologies, Systems, Applications and Policy Making

Miltiadis D. Lytras [1,2] and Anna Visvizi [3,4,*]

1 Effat College of Business, Effat University, Jeddah P.O. Box 34689, Saudi Arabia; mlytras@acg.edu
2 King Abdulaziz University, Jeddah 21589, Saudi Arabia
3 Effat College of Engineering, Effat University, Jeddah P.O. Box 34689, Saudi Arabia
4 SGH Warsaw School of Economics, Al. Niepodległości 162, 02-554 Warsaw, Poland
* Correspondence: avisvizi@gmail.com

Abstract: Artificial intelligence (AI) and cognitive computing (CC) are subject of increased attention of both academia and industry today. The understanding is that AI- and CC-enhanced methods and techniques create a variety of opportunities relating to improving basic and advanced business functions, including production processes, logistics, financial management and others. AI-enhanced tools and methods tend to offer more precise results in the field of engineering, financial accounting, tourism, air-pollution management and many more. The objective of this special issue was to bring together diverse communities of scholars and engage in a broad discussion on the role of AI and CC in today's society, including the process of policy-making.

Keywords: artificial intelligence (AI); cognitive computing (CC); AI-enhanced methods; AI-enhanced applications; policy-making

Citation: Lytras, M.D.; Visvizi, A. Artificial Intelligence and Cognitive Computing: Methods, Technologies, Systems, Applications and Policy Making. *Sustainability* **2021**, *13*, 3598. https://doi.org/10.3390/su13073598

Received: 18 March 2021
Accepted: 20 March 2021
Published: 24 March 2021

Publisher's Note: MDPI stays neutral with regard to jurisdictional claims in published maps and institutional affiliations.

Copyright: © 2021 by the authors. Licensee MDPI, Basel, Switzerland. This article is an open access article distributed under the terms and conditions of the Creative Commons Attribution (CC BY) license (https://creativecommons.org/licenses/by/4.0/).

1. Introduction

Artificial intelligence (AI) and cognitive computing (CC) are subject of increased attention of both academia and industry today [1] The understanding is that AI- and CC-enhanced methods and techniques create a variety of opportunities relating to improving basic and advanced business functions, including production processes, logistics, financial management and others. AI-enhanced tools and methods tend to offer more precise results in the field of engineering, financial accounting, tourism, air-pollution management and many more. The objective of this special issue was to bring together diverse communities of scholars and engage in a broad discussion on the role of AI and CC in today's society, including the process of policy-making. A great number of submissions was received in response to the initial call for papers. Out of these, 14 papers were eventually selected for inclusion in this volume. These papers have been organized in three thematic groups: focusing on the use of AI-enhanced tools in the broadly understood field of engineering; exploring the value of AI- and CC-based techniques in the assembly line, internet of things (IoT), etc.; and querying the uses of AI-enhanced methods in the fields of tourism, safety and security, and policy-making.

2. The Content of the Volume

In their paper titled "Application of Machine Learning in Evaluation of the Static Young's Modulus for Sandstone Formations" [2] the authors showcase how machine learning can be useful in predicting the mechanical characteristics of reservoir formations, especially of sandstone formations. This includes the evaluation of the wellbore stability. Remaining in the field of engineering, the following paper [3] applies advanced AI-based methods to study and enhance the productivity of wells. By focusing on the case of fishbone multilateral wells, the authors develop and apply several AI methods to estimate the performance of fishbone wells. In a similar context, the authors of the next paper [4] examine the problem of carbon dioxide (CO_2) injections as a method for improving hydrocarbon recovery. As the authors explain, the minimum miscibility pressure (MMP) has a great effect on the performance of CO_2 flooding. While several methods exist to determine the MMP, they are costly and time-consuming, and may still produce estimation errors. AI-enhanced methods to determine the MMP are highlighted as more efficient in this context. In the same vein, the following paper [5] elaborates on the value added of AI-enhanced methods in estimating total organic carbon (TOC) content in unconventional shale resources evaluation. Always in the same context, the next paper [6] included in this volume discusses in which ways hybrid AI models can effectively predict the elastic behavior of sandstone rocks. The author of the following paper [7] provides insights into the use of AI in predicting the rheological properties of water-based drill-in fluid. AI-enhanced methods and application in the domain of air quality analysis, visualization and response generation are discussed in the paper that follows [8]. To this end, the authors develop an interactive visual analytic system for recognizing, exploring and summarizing regular patterns, as well as detecting, classifying and interpreting abnormal cases.

Papers included in the second part of the volume address different aspects of AI application. For instance, Chang et al. [9] apply advanced AI-enhanced methods to establish an accurate decision-making method between the quality level of the diesel engine and the parameters of assembly clearance. Han et al. [10] focus on the challenge of energy conservation in context of the internet of things (IoT). The authors stress, on the one hand, the salience of wireless nodes in enabling communication among devices, and on the other hand, the caveats pertaining to recharging the batteries of these wireless nodes. To navigate the problem, the authors propose a novel hybrid unequal multi-hop clustering based on density (HCD) designed to increase the network lifetime. The value of AI-based methods is further evidenced in the following paper [11] that proposes a correction methodology for Long Short-Term Memory (LSTM) based speech recognition.

The third group of papers included in this volume takes the discussion to fields more closely related to social science. For instance, Crivellari and Beinat [12] demonstrate how neural networks can be employed to address the trajectory prediction problem, especially in context of large-scale mobility traces of short-term foreign tourists. As the authors argue, these trajectories, short and non-repetitive, lack spatial and temporal regularity, which makes predictions based on individual historical motion data unreliable. The approach introduced in their paper promises higher reliability and predictive capacity than those offered by traditional approaches. The value added of these findings rests in their applicability in the decision-making process. Looking at the issue of decision-makers taking advantage of research, Gao et al. [13] examine the relationship between academic research and policy making, especially with regards to research on AI and the emulation of the research findings in the policy-making domain. Zhang et al. [14] make a compelling case for the use of AI-enhanced methods to examine companies' financial performance. As the authors argue, even a fraction of accuracy improvement can result in considerable future savings to a firm and investors. The discussion in the special issue closes with a paper that explores the connection between machine learning and safety and security in modern societies [15]. The authors focus explicitly on the problem of identity spoofing, that is, actions by which a person impersonates a third party to carry out a series of illegal activities such as committing fraud, cyberbullying, sextortion, etc., and ways of mitigating it. In this context, a face recognition system is proposed that, while based on the Histogram of Oriented Gradients (HOG), has the capacity of preventing spoofing.

3. Conclusions

The inroads of AI and CC in contemporary society create a number of opportunities across issues and domains. This special issue attests to that. At the same time, as AI and AI-enhanced tools proliferate a cognitive gap emerges where substantial parts of societies worldwide remain ignorant as to the nature, thrust and application of AI. A two-fold problem arises: on the one hand, large parts of the societies are suspicious of AI and

AI-enhanced tools, while on the other hand, a great number of citizens is unaware that AI-based solutions are already present in their lives. The same applies to CC and CC-based tools and solutions. The implicit imperative behind this special issue is to encourage a multidisciplinary debate on AI and CC that would allow us to gradually close the gap. The challenge here rests with governments and effective policy responses [16].

Funding: This research received no external funding.

Conflicts of Interest: The authors declare no conflict of interest.

References

1. Lytras, M.D.; Visvizi, A.; Zhang, X.; Aljohani, N.R. Cognitive computing, Big Data Analytics and data driven industrial marketing. *Ind. Mark. Manag.* **2020**. [CrossRef]
2. Mahmoud, A.A.; Elkatatny, S.; Al Shehri, D. Application of Machine Learning in Evaluation of the Static Young's Modulus for Sandstone Formations. *Sustainability* **2020**, *12*, 1880. [CrossRef]
3. Hassan, A.; Elkatatny, S.; Abdulraheem, A. Application of Artificial Intelligence Techniques to Predict the Well Productivity of Fishbone Wells. *Sustainability* **2019**, *11*, 6083. [CrossRef]
4. Hassan, A.; Elkatatny, S.; Abdulraheem, A. Intelligent Prediction of Minimum Miscibility Pressure (MMP) During CO2 Flooding Using Artificial Intelligence Techniques. *Sustainability* **2019**, *11*, 7020. [CrossRef]
5. Mahmoud, A.A.; Elkatatny, S.; Ali, A.Z.; Abouelresh, M.; Abdulraheem, A. Evaluation of the Total Organic Carbon (TOC) Using Different Artificial Intelligence Techniques. *Sustainability* **2019**, *11*, 5643. [CrossRef]
6. Gowida, A.; Moussa, T.; Elkatatny, S.; Ali, A. A Hybrid Artificial Intelligence Model to Predict the Elastic Behavior of Sandstone Rocks. *Sustainability* **2019**, *11*, 5283. [CrossRef]
7. Elkatatny, S. Real-Time Prediction of the Rheological Properties of Water-Based Drill-In Fluid Using Artificial Neural Networks. *Sustainability* **2019**, *11*, 5008. [CrossRef]
8. Zhang, H.; Ren, K.; Lin, Y.; Qu, D.; Li, Z. AirInsight: Visual Exploration and Interpretation of Latent Patterns and Anomalies in Air Quality Data. *Sustainability* **2019**, *11*, 2944. [CrossRef]
9. Chang, W.; Yuan, X.; Wu, Y.; Zhou, S.; Lei, J.; Xiao, Y. Decision-Making Method based on Mixed Integer Linear Programming and Rough Set: A Case Study of Diesel Engine Quality and Assembly Clearance Data. *Sustainability* **2019**, *11*, 620. [CrossRef]
10. Han, T.; Bozorgi, S.M.; Orang, A.V.; Hosseinabadi, A.A.R.; Sangaiah, A.K.; Chen, M.-Y. A Hybrid Unequal Clustering Based on Density with Energy Conservation in Wireless Nodes. *Sustainability* **2019**, *11*, 746. [CrossRef]
11. Arslan, R.S.; Barışçı, N. Development of Output Correction Methodology for Long Short Term Memory-Based Speech Recognition. *Sustainability* **2019**, *11*, 4250. [CrossRef]
12. Crivellari, A.; Beinat, E. LSTM-Based Deep Learning Model for Predicting Individual Mobility Traces of Short-Term Foreign Tourists. *Sustainability* **2020**, *12*, 349. [CrossRef]
13. Gao, J.; Huang, X.; Zhang, L. Comparative Analysis between International Research Hotspots and National-Level Policy Keywords on Artificial Intelligence in China from 2009 to 2018. *Sustainability* **2019**, *11*, 6574. [CrossRef]
14. Zhang, Y.; Lee, M. A Hybrid Model for Addressing the Relationship between Financial Performance and Sustainable Development. *Sustainability* **2019**, *11*, 2899. [CrossRef]
15. Pujol, F.A.; Pujol, M.J.; Rizo-Maestre, C.; Pujol, M. Entropy-Based Face Recognition and Spoof Detection for Security Applications. *Sustainability* **2020**, *12*, 85. [CrossRef]
16. Visvizi, A.; Lytras, M.D. Government at risk: Between distributed risks and threats and effective policy-responses. *Transform. Gov. People Process. Policy* **2020**, *14*, 333–336. [CrossRef]

Article

Application of Machine Learning in Evaluation of the Static Young's Modulus for Sandstone Formations

Ahmed Abdulhamid Mahmoud, Salaheldin Elkatatny *, and Dhafer Al Shehri

College of Petroleum Engineering and Geosciences, King Fahd University of Petroleum & Minerals, Dhahran 31261, Saudi Arabia; g201205160@kfupm.edu.sa (A.A.M.); alshehrida@kfupm.edu.sa (D.A.S.)
* Correspondence: elkatatny@kfupm.edu.sa; Tel.: +966-5-9466-3692

Received: 17 January 2020; Accepted: 28 February 2020; Published: 2 March 2020

Abstract: Prediction of the mechanical characteristics of the reservoir formations, such as static Young's modulus (E_{static}), is very important for the evaluation of the wellbore stability and development of the earth geomechanical model. E_{static} considerably varies with the change in the lithology. Therefore, a robust model for E_{static} prediction is needed. In this study, the predictability of E_{static} for sandstone formation using four machine learning models was evaluated. The design parameters of the machine learning models were optimized to improve their predictability. The machine learning models were trained to estimate E_{static} based on bulk formation density, compressional transit time, and shear transit time. The machine learning models were trained and tested using 592 well log data points and their corresponding core-derived E_{static} values collected from one sandstone formation in well-A and then validated on 38 data points collected from a sandstone formation in well-B. Among the machine learning models developed in this work, Mamdani fuzzy interference system was the highly accurate model to predict E_{static} for the validation data with an average absolute percentage error of only 1.56% and R of 0.999. The developed static Young's modulus prediction models could help the new generation to characterize the formation rock with less cost and safe operation.

Keywords: static Young's modulus; sandstone formations; machine learning

1. Introduction

Prediction of the mechanical characteristics of the reservoir formations, such as Young's modulus (E), is necessary for the evaluation of the wellbore stability, reservoir compaction, hydraulic fracturing, and formation control [1]. E is a mechanical parameter that gives an indication of the resistance of the rock samples when exposed to a uniaxial load [2]. On the other hand, static Young's modulus (E_{static}) is a critical parameter needed to build the earth geomechanical model [3]. It is also used for fractures' designing and mapping [4,5]. While drilling hydrocarbon wells, E_{static} is also needed with other mechanical and petrophysical properties to make a full description of the in-situ stresses to ensure wellbore stability [6].

E_{static} varies significantly with the change in lithology [2,7]. E_{static} for shale ranges from 0.69 to 6.89 GPa. For limestone, it is between 55.16 and 82.74 GPa, and for sandstone, it is between 13.79 and 68.95 GPa [7]. These ranges confirm the wide difference in E_{static} from one formation type to another and the huge change within the same lithology. Therefore, it is necessary to estimate E_{static} along the whole drilled hydrocarbon well.

Two methods for rock elastic parameters' estimation are currently available. These are the experimental laboratory method or the use of empirical correlations. The experimental laboratory method is based on conducting laboratory experiments on the rock samples using static or dynamic testing techniques. In the static technique, the sample is subjected to a uniaxial or triaxial load and the deformation of the sample is measured, while in the dynamic technique, shear and compressional wave velocities along the tested sample are measured and then the sample's elastic parameters are calculated based on the shear wave (V_s) and compressional wave (V_p) velocity [8]. In the field, wireline logging tools are used to measure V_s and V_p. The dynamic Young's modulus ($E_{dynamic}$) can then be evaluated based on V_s and V_p and using Equation (1).

$$E_{dynamic} = \frac{\rho V_S^2 (3V_P^2 - 4V_S^2)}{V_P^2 - V_S^2} \quad (1)$$

where ρ denotes the formation's bulk density in g/cm^3, V_S and V_P are in km/s, and $E_{dynamic}$ is in GPa.

Several previous studies confirmed that the laboratory-measured $E_{dynamic}$ for the same rock sample is significantly greater than E_{static} [9–11]. $E_{dynamic}$ could be 1.5 to 3 times greater than E_{static} [12] and some recent studies reported that $E_{dynamic}$ could be ten times greater than E_{static} [13,14]. The strain amplitude between the two experimentally testing methods is the main reason for this huge difference, which decreases as the rock strength increase [15].

The static elastic parameters are actually representative of the in-situ stress–strain conditions of the reservoir [16]. Accurate determination of the static elastic parameters requires conducting a time consuming and costly experimental tests on real core samples [17]. The common practice to decrease this high cost is to select core samples at specific intervals and conduct the experimental tests of these cores only. Then an empirical correlation between the laboratory-derived parameters and the conventional well log data will be developed based on the results of laboratory tests. The static moduli throughout the whole reservoir depths can then be predicted by calibrating the dynamic moduli using the developed correlations [4]. Because of the heterogeneity of the reservoir formations, the developed well log-based empirical equations are usually not generalized to all formation types. Therefore, different correlations need to be developed for every formation type to track the changes in the static parameters along the whole reservoir.

The correlation in Equation (2) was developed by Fei et al. [18] for the evaluation of E_{static} for sandstone formations; this correlation evaluates E_{static} as a function of $E_{dynamic}$, which was developed based on 22 triaxial tests results.

$$E_{static} = 0.564\, E_{dynamic} - 3.4941 \quad (2)$$

where E_{static} and $E_{dynamic}$ are in GPa.

Mahmoud et al. [19] developed a set of equations to estimate E_{static} for different types of formations. The main advantage of the correlations developed by Mahmoud et al. [19] is the ability to implement these correlations directly to evaluate E_{static} without the need for $E_{dynamic}$, these correlations are only a function of the bulk formation density (RHOB), compressional transit time (DT_c), and shear transit time data (DT_s).

Different recent studies confirmed the ability of machine learning techniques to accurately estimate rock mechanical properties. Abdulraheem et al. [20] optimized three machine learning models of the artificial neural networks (ANN), fuzzy logic model, and functional neural networks (FNN) for estimation of E_{static} and the static Poison's ratio for the hydrocarbon reservoirs. The authors did not specify the reservoir rock formation type. The developed models confirmed their ability to estimate the reservoir rock mechanical properties.

In another study, Tariq et al. [21] developed three machine learning models of ANN, fuzzy logic, and support vector machine (SVM) to estimate E_{static} for limestone formation. The ANN model overperformed the other machine learning models and the currently available empirical correlation for E_{static} estimation.

Tariq et al. [22] developed empirical correlations for the estimation of the mechanical properties of E_{static}, Poisson's ratio, and unconfined compressive strength based on the application of the artificial neural networks (ANN) and the use of the conventional well log data, the authors also did not specify the type of the formation they used in this study. The developed correlations improved their ability to accurately estimate the rock mechanical properties.

In 2017, Parapuram et al. [23] developed an ANN model to estimate the geomechanical properties of the upper Bakken shale based on well log data. The results of this study confirmed the ability of the ANN model to accurately estimate the rock mechanical properties.

Recently, in our previous study, Mahmoud et al. [24], we evaluated the use of the ANN in estimating E_{static} for sandstone formations. Mahmoud et al. [24] reported that ANN is able to predict E_{static} with very high accuracy, and it overperformed all available empirical equations currently in use.

Sustainable development can be defined as development that meets the needs of the present without compromising the ability of future generations. This study is aimed at evaluating the ability of four machine learning techniques namely ANN, SVM, FNN, and the Mamdani fuzzy interference system (M-FIS) in estimating E_{static} for sandstone formations as a function of RHOB, DT_s, and DT_c. The new systems of static Young's modulus prediction are examples of the new development which will help the new generation to discover and extract the oil and gas at lower cost and with safer operation. The developed method depends on taking the reading from the well logging tools and applying the artificial neural network models to predict the static Young's modulus and provide a continuous profile of the elastic property through the whole reservoir. This will improve the time necessary for the decision on the required action based on given information.

2. Theory of Machine Learning Techniques Considered in This Study

The first machine learning technique used in this work was the ANN, which is a computing system that is designed to mimic the way the biological systems, such as the human or animal brains, behave. ANN is developed to identify, estimate, classify, or make a decision by using a machine program. ANN is available in different structures; the simplest ANN structure, which was used in this study, is called multi-layered perceptron (MLP) which consists of one input layer, one or several hidden (learning) layers, and one output layer, as shown in Figure 1 [25]. The ANN systems are trained originally using training data (supervised learning) to perform the needed tasks [26].

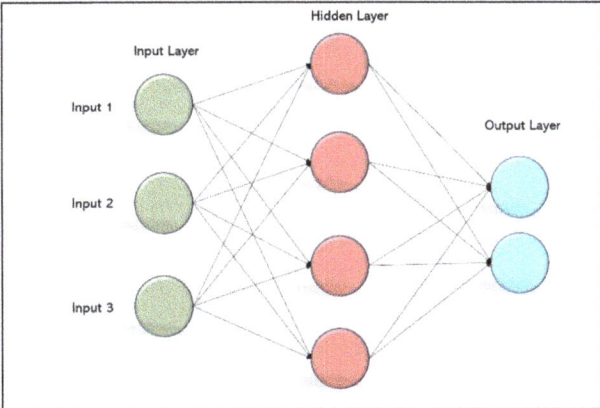

Figure 1. Artificial neural networks model with input layers of three inputs, one hidden layer, and an output layer.

M-FIS was the second machine learning technique used in this study, which combines the adaptive neuro-fuzzy inference system (ANFIS) and subtractive clustering, where ANFIS is a multilayer feed-forward adaptive network in which the incoming signal will be subjected to a particular function performed by each training node where every node has its own parameters pertaining (Figure 2). The hybrid learning procedure was performed in two steps; the first step was the forward pass in which the functional signals representing the input data go forward and the least square formula was used to identify the parameters in the output layer (layer 5). The second step was the backward pass, in which the error rates propagate, in the opposite way, and the gradient method was implemented to update the parameters in the input layer (layer 1) [27].

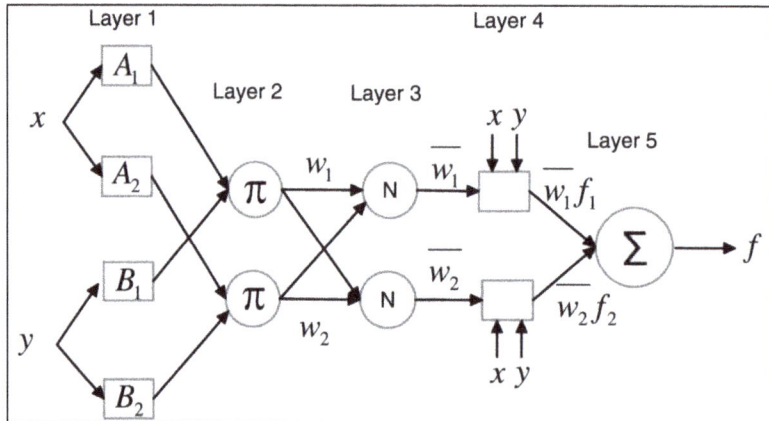

Figure 2. Adaptive neuro-fuzzy inference system architecture of a model using two inputs layers and one output parameter.

The subtractive clustering is an unsupervised clustering algorithm that aims to examine the density of the available input data. Then it defines the point surrounded by the highest number of neighbors as the cluster's center. It then subtracts (removes) the other data points within a pre-specified fuzzy radius, and the subtractive clustering algorithm considers only the point defined as the cluster's center. This process is repeated to examine all input data points. Subtractive clustering generates the rules that approximate a function [28].

The third machine learning technique used in this study was the FNN model, compared to the ANN which uses the sigmoidal common model. The FNN model works with the generalized functional models. In FNN, the neuron's function is learned from the existing data, which means they are not constant. Therefore, the weights related to links are not needed because the neuron functions include the effect of weights [29]. FNN contains an input layer, an output layer and layers of computing units that are related to each other. In FNN, there are different arguments in neural functions instead of one argument, such as in ANN [30].

The fourth machine learning model considered in this study was the SVM, which is one of the most famous classifying algorithms developed by Vapnik [31] in the framework of statistical learning theory. It performs classification of the data optimally into two or more divisions by applying a multidimensional hyperplane; this hyperplane is set to classify the data based on the tuning parameters (design parameters) of the kernel, regularization parameter (C), gamma, and margin. In its nature, SVM is very similar to a neural network, where the use of SVM with sigmoid kernel function is almost identical to the use of the perceptron neural network, having two hidden layers. Although it was originally developed in the statistical learning theory, the SVM technique is applicable in regression and classification problems, and it is also suitable for solving non-linear problems [32].

3. Applications of Machine Learning in Petroleum Engineering

Machine learning techniques are used in several scientific and engineering fields since the early 1990s to solve complicated non-linear problems. Petroleum engineers and petroleum geologists use different machine learning techniques to solve problems related to petroleum industry, such as the characterization of the heterogeneous hydrocarbon reservoirs [33,34], evaluation of the reserve of unconventional reservoirs [35–38], estimation of the rock mechanical parameters, such as the static Poisson's ratio in carbonate reservoirs [39] and the static Young's modulus for sandstone reservoirs [24,40], evaluation of the integrity of wellbore casing [41,42], optimization of drilling hydraulics [43], evaluation of pore pressure and fracture pressure [44,45], hydrocarbon recovery factor estimation [46,47], determination of the alteration in the drilling fluids rheology in real-time [48,49], optimization of rate of penetration [50,51], prediction of the formation tops [52], and others.

4. Application to the Well Log Data

The predictability of the machine learning models depends on the amount of training data points and the design parameters of every model. In this work, the machine learning model's design parameters and the selection of the optimum training data points were conducted based on the optimization process of all combinations of the design parameters, as will be discussed in the following sections.

4.1. Data Preparation

The machine learning models are trained in this study to predict E_{static} based on the RHOB, DT_s, and DT_c as inputs. In this study, core-derived E_{static} and their corresponding well log data collected from two different sandstone wells (598 collected from Well-A and 38 from Well-B) were used. The data of Well-A was used to build and test the machine learning models, and Well-B data (unseen data) was used to validate the trained machine learning models. Both formations considered in wells A and B were sandstone formations.

Before training the machine learning models, the data were studied statistically to remove all noise, unreal values, and outliers from the training data. The standard deviation (SD) was considered for removing the outliers; based on this, all data points without the range of ± 3.0 SD were considered as outliers and removed from the input dataset. This preprocessing is very important to ensure accurate estimation of the targeted parameter by applying the machine learning techniques [53]. Out of the 598 data points collected from Well-A, 6 data points were considered as outliers, these data points were removed from the data before the start of the training process.

Since the core derived E_{static} was estimated based on well log data, it was very important to perform depth matching between the well log input data and core derived E_{static}. Although the gamma-ray log was not considered as input in this study, it was considered at this step to perform the depth matching.

4.2. Training the Machine Learning Models

After data preprocessing, 592 well log data points and their corresponding core derived E_{static} were considered valid for machine learning models training. Four hundred and fourteen, 178, 355, and 444 well log data points (out of the 592) were considered to train ANN, M-FIS, FNN, and SVM models, respectively. The number of the training data was selected based on the optimization process, where the optimum number of the training data that optimize the predictability of the different machine learning models was selected in every case. The statistical characteristics for the training datasets for the different machine learning models are summarized in Table 1. The data of Table 1 is very important when the machine learning models are to be used for evaluating E_{static} for a new dataset; the new testing data should be within the ranges in Table 1.

Table 1. The statistical characteristics for the training data set.

	RHOB, g/cm³	DT$_c$, µs/ft	DT$_s$, µs/ft	E$_{static}$, GPa
Artificial Neural Networks.				
Minimum	2.32	44.4	73.2	7.50
Maximum	2.98	78.9	136	92.8
Range	0.66	34.6	62.4	85.3
Standard Deviation	0.114	5.06	8.91	14.9
Sample Variance	0.013	25.6	79.4	221
Mamdani Fuzzy Interference System				
Minimum	2.33	44.6	73.2	8.63
Maximum	2.98	78.7	133	92.8
Range	0.66	34.1	60.0	84.2
Standard Deviation	0.114	5.45	9.47	15.2
Sample Variance	0.013	29.7	89.6	232
Functional Neural Networks				
Minimum	2.31	44.5	73.6	7.50
Maximum	2.98	78.9	136	92.6
Range	0.67	34.4	62.5	85.1
Standard Deviation	0.112	5.27	9.20	14.9
Sample Variance	0.013	27.7	84.7	222
Support Vector Machine				
Minimum	2.31	44.3	73.2	7.50
Maximum	2.98	78.9	136	92.8
Range	0.67	34.6	62.9	85.3
Standard Deviation	0.113	5.21	8.99	14.5
Sample Variance	0.013	27.1	80.8	210

The input training well logs data were selected based on their relative importance on the actual E$_{static}$ which was determined in this study based on the correlation coefficient (R), Figure 3 compares R for the input well log data used to train the different machine learning model. As indicated in Figure 3, all well log parameters used to train the machine learning models are strongly related to E$_{static}$ with high Rs of >0.7 for the bulk density, >0.8 for the compressional transit time, and >0.95 for the shear transit time.

Figure 4 shows the inputs used to learn the machine learning models. Inserted *for* loops were designed using MATLAB software to optimize all combinations of the machine learning model's design parameters for E$_{static}$ estimation; every single *for* loop represents one design parameter. Sensitivity analysis was conducted to evaluate the effect of changing every single design parameter on the predictability of E$_{static}$ by the different machine learning models considered in this study. The sensitivity analysis is a critical step in optimizing the design parameters of the machine learning models and several previous studies considered it as a crucial step in optimizing the performance of different mathematical models [54–56]. Based on the sensitivity analysis results, the combinations of the variables in Table 2 were found to optimize E$_{static}$ estimation using the different machine learning models; these parameters predicted E$_{static}$ with the lowest average absolute percentage error (AAPE) and the highest R; the AAPE was calculated using Equation (3).

$$AAPE = \frac{1}{N}\sum_{i=1}^{N}\left(\left|\frac{(E_{statica})_i - (E_{staticm})_i}{(E_{statica})_i}\right| \times 100\right) \quad (3)$$

where N represents the number of the data points, a and m denote the actual and estimated E_{static}, respectively.

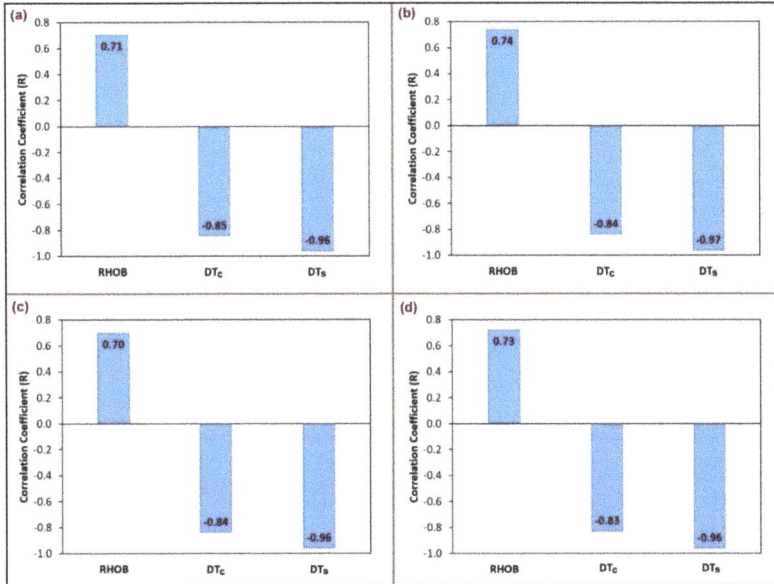

Figure 3. Comparison of the relative importance of the training parameters used to develop (**a**) ANN, (**b**) the Mamdani fuzzy interference system (M-FIS), (**c**) functional neural networks (FNN), and (**d**) support vector machine (SVM) models.

Table 2. Optimized design parameters for the machine learning models.

Artificial Neural Networks	
Training Data (out of total data from Well-A)	70%
Testing Data (out of total data from Well-A)	30%
Learning Function	Trainbr
Transfer Function	Logsig
Number of Training Layers	Single Layer
Neurons per Training Layer	20
Mamdani Fuzzy Interference System	
Training Data (out of total data from Well-A)	30%
Testing Data (out of total data from Well-A)	70%
Cluster Radius	0.3
Number of Iterations	180
Functional Neural Networks	
Training Data (out of total data from Well-A)	60%
Testing Data (out of total data from Well-A)	40%
Training Method	Forward Selection Method
Function Type	Non-linear Function with No Iteration Terms
Support Vector Machine	
Training Data (out of total data from Well-A)	75%
Testing Data (out of total data from Well-A)	25%
Verbose	0.7
C	3000
Epsilon	0.5
Lambda	1×10^{-7}
Kernel	gaussian
Kerneloption	9

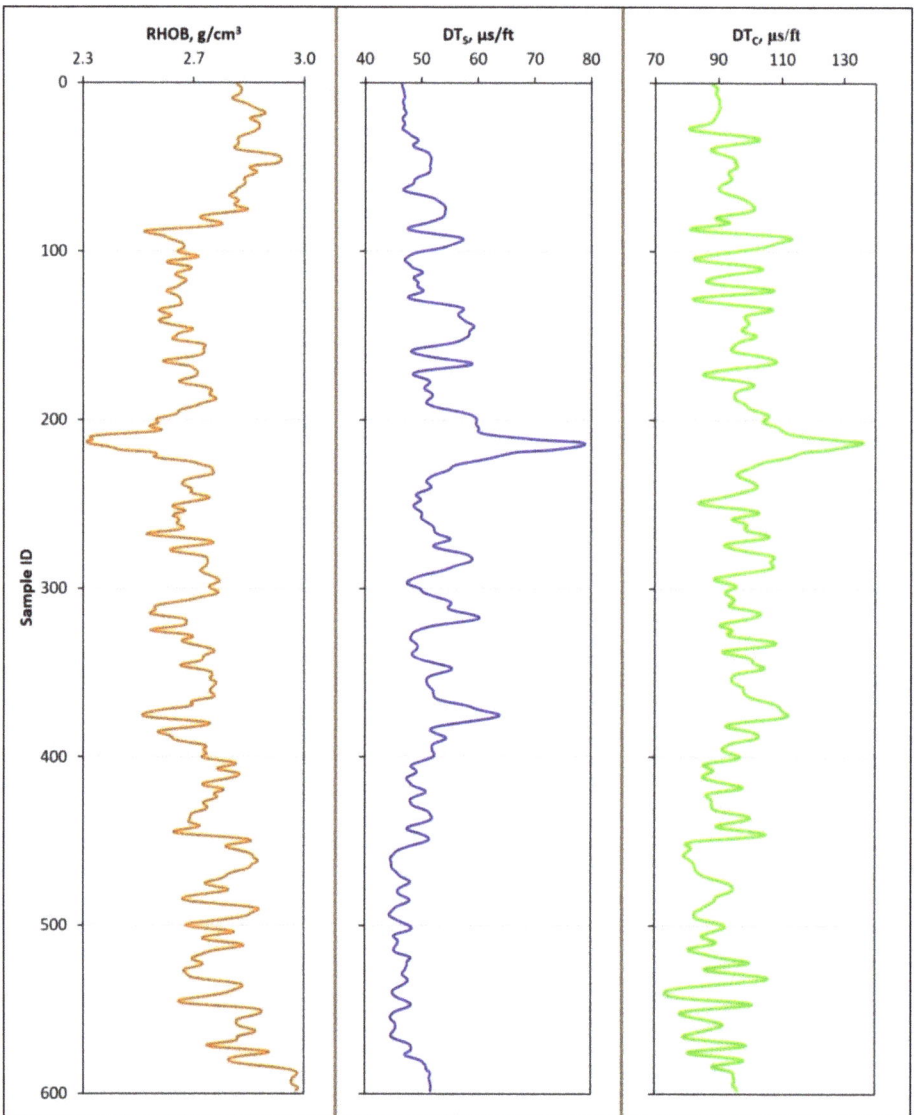

Figure 4. The training input well log data collected from Well-A.

4.3. Evaluation of the Developed Machine Learning Models

After training, the developed machine learning models were then tested using the remaining data collected from the same training sandstone formation in Well-A and then validated using 38 data points (unseen data) collected from a sandstone formation in Well-B.

Uncertainty quantification is at the heart of decision making, especially in subsurface applications. Uncertainty about the geological structures, rocks, and fluids is because of the lack of access to the subsurface geological medium [57,58]. The uncertainty in the prediction results of all machine learning models developed in this study was directly controlled by the uncertainty on the well log data used to develop these models which were highly controlled by the depth of investigation and vertical resolution of every logging tool.

5. Results and Discussion

5.1. Machine Learning Models Development

The machine learning models were trained to predict E_{static} as a function of the RHOB, DT_s, and DT_c. The training data were collected from Well-A. Figure 5 compares the actual and estimated E_{static} for the training dataset.

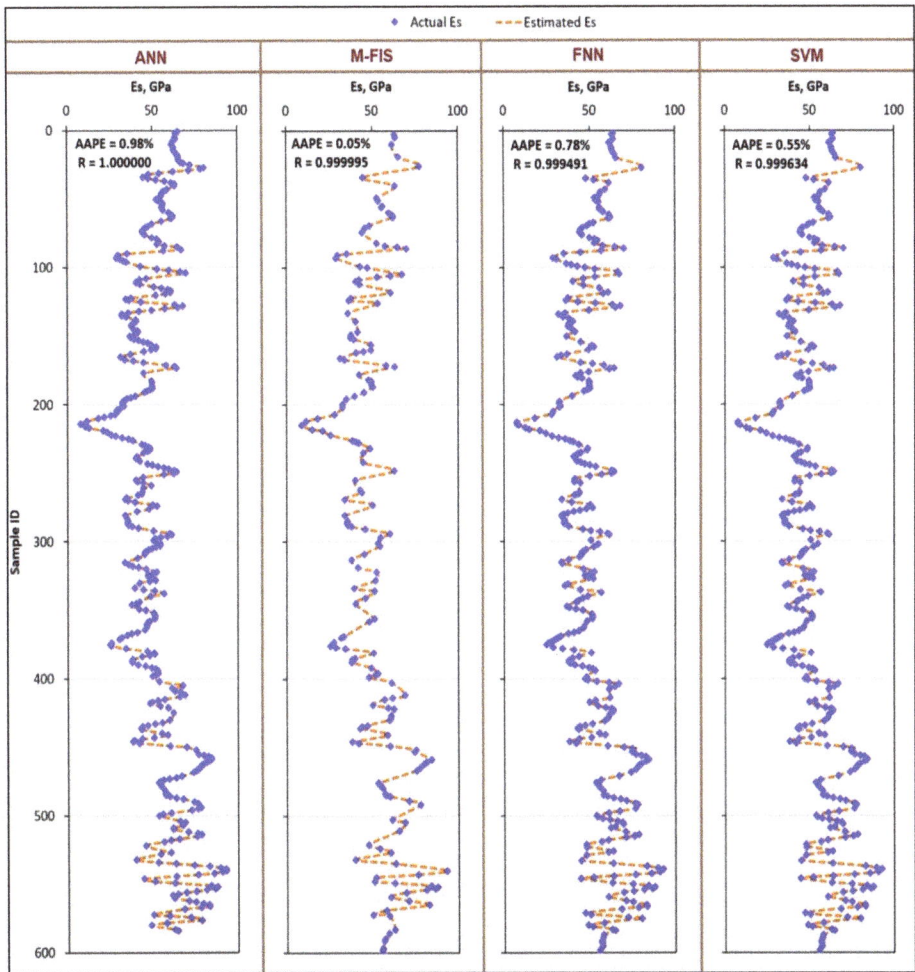

Figure 5. Actual and estimated static Young's modulus (E_{static}) for the training dataset collected from Well-A.

Figure 5 shows that all machine learning models predicted E_{static} with very high accuracy. M-FIS predicted E_{static} with AAPE of only 0.05% and R of 0.999995. FNN model estimated the E_{static} with AAPE and R of 0.78% and 0.999491, respectively, while SVM model estimated E_{static} with AAPE of 0.55% and R of 0.999634, and the ANN model predicted E_{static} with AAPE of 0.98% and R of 1.000000.

The good matching between the actual and estimated E_{static} for the training dataset shown in Figure 5 proves the high accuracy of the machine learning models in evaluating E_{static}.

5.2. Testing the Developed Machine Learning Models

The performance of the developed machine learning models in evaluating the E_{static} for the testing dataset, which was collected from the same training formation used to developed machine learning models (i.e., from Well-A), was evaluated. As indicated in Figure 6, all machine learning models predicted E_{static} with very high accuracy. M-FIS predicted E_{static} for the testing dataset with AAPE and R of 0.09% and 0.999992, respectively, FNN model predicted E_{static} with AAPE of 0.85% and R of 0.999311, then SVM model which estimated E_{static} with an AAPE and R of 0.62% and 0.999813, respectively, and the ANN estimated E_{static} with AAPE of 1.46% and R of 1.000000. Visual check of the actual and estimated E_{static} of the testing data set also confirmed the high accuracy of the machine learning models, as indicated by the good matching between the actual and estimated E_{static}.

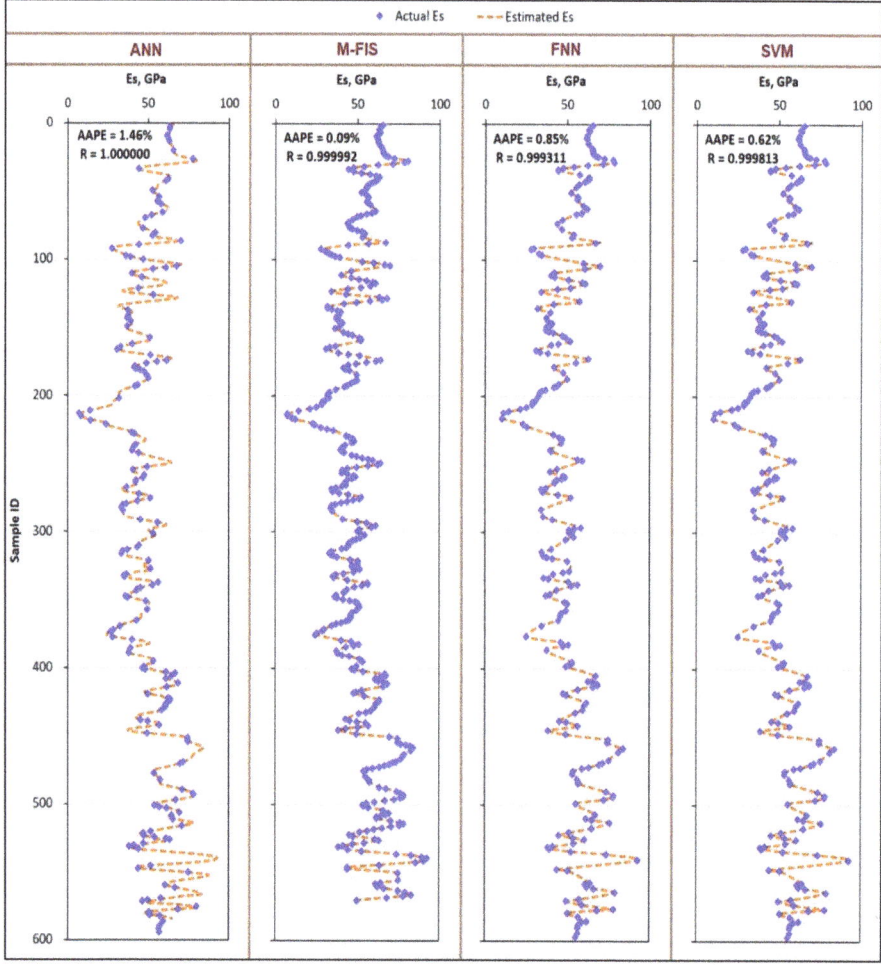

Figure 6. Actual and estimated E_{static} for the testing dataset collected from Well-A.

5.3. Validation of the Developed Machine Learning Models

The machine learning models' accuracy was finally validated using 38 data points collected from another sandstone formation in Well-B. Figure 7 compares the actual core derived and estimated E_{static} using the developed machine learning for the validation data set. The results in Figure 7 confirmed that all machine learning models predicted E_{static} with very high accuracy. This figure also confirmed that M-FIS technique is the best among the others on estimating E_{static} for the validation data set, where the developed M-FIS predicted E_{static} with AAPE of 1.56% and R of 0.999, followed by SVM model which predicted E_{static} with AAPE of 2.03% and R of 0.999, then FNN model which estimated E_{static} with AAPE of 2.54% and R of 0.997, and the least accurate model was the ANN which predicted E_{static} with AAPE of 3.80% and R of 0.991.

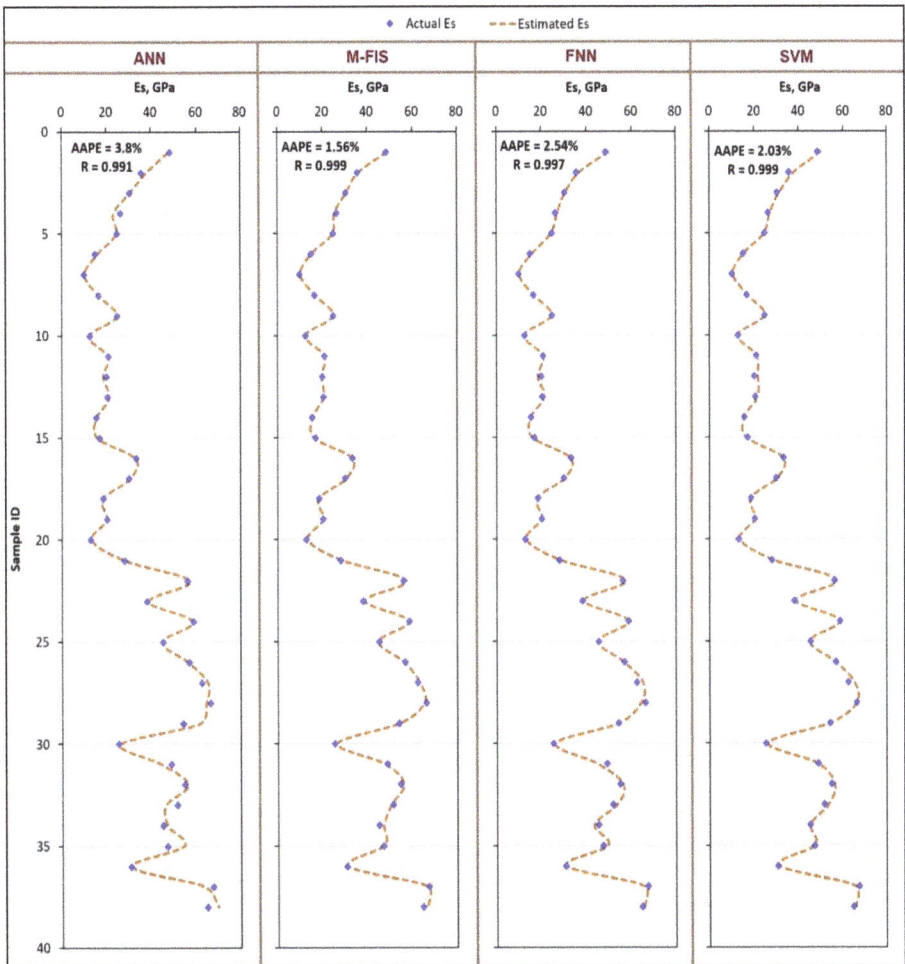

Figure 7. Core-derived and predicted E_{static} for the validation dataset collected from Well-B.

A visual check of the actual and estimated E_{static} of the validation data set also confirmed the high accuracy of all machine learning models considered in this work, as confirmed by the good matching between the estimated and core derived E_{static}. A continuous profile of E_{static} along the drilled sections of Well-B was obtained using the machine learning models. This is not possible to achieve by conducting laboratory work only. The confidence intervals for the validation data were ± 0.574, ± 0.804, ± 0.843, and ± 0.877, with a confidence level of 99% for M-FIS, SVM, ANN, and FNN models, respectively.

Figure 8 compares the AAPE for the calculated E_{static} for training, testing, and validation datasets using the different machine learning models. This figure confirms that the developed M-FIS model overperformed the other machine learning models in predicting E_{static} for the training, testing, and validation datasets in terms of AAPE. M-FIS predicted E_{static} with the lowest AAPE of 1.56 %, while the AAPE for the SVM, FNN, and ANN were 2.03, 2.54, and 3.80, respectively.

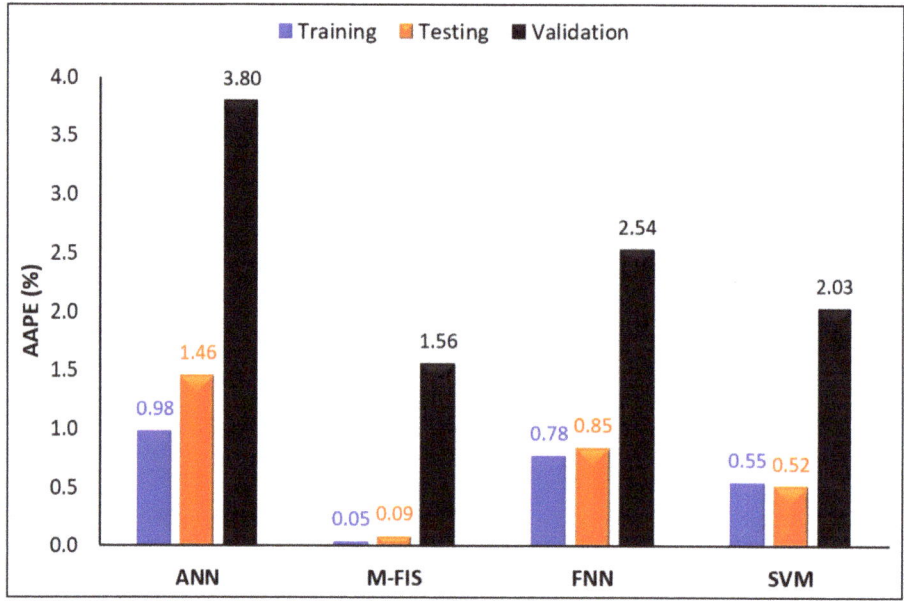

Figure 8. Comparison of the AAPE for the training, testing, and validation datasets for all machine learning models.

Out of the results of training, testing, and validation data and considering the similarity of the results of the evaluation parameters (AAPE and R) and taking into consideration that adding or omitting a few points may change the highest-to-lowest order of the models accuracy, we conclude that the four models are equally adequate to estimate E_{static} using only the conventional well log used in this study. Nevertheless, we recommend using the M-FIS model as it is the best-performed model for estimating E_{static} for the training, testing, and validation data.

The machine learning models developed in this work are very helpful for the petroleum engineers and petroleum industry since they could positively improve E_{static} estimation, therefore, enabling petroleum engineers and geoscientists to construct the earth geomechanical map and to evaluate the wellbore stability condition, the reservoir compaction, hydraulic fracturing, and the formation control [1,3].

6. Conclusions

Four machine learning techniques were applied in this study to develop models for estimating E_{static} for sandstone formations, these machine learning techniques were ANN, FNN, M-FIS, and SVM. The machine learning models were trained to evaluate E_{static} based on conventional well log data of the $RHOB$, DT_s, and DT_c. The machine learning models were trained and tested based on data gathered from sandstone formation in Well-A and then the developed models were validated on unseen data collected from a sandstone formation in Well-B. The outcomes of this work confirmed the high accuracy of all machine learning models, and M-FIS models overperformed all others in estimating E_{static} for training, testing, and validation data sets. For the validation data, M-FIS predicted E_{static} with a very low AAPE of 1.56% and R of 0.999. The high accuracy of the developed machine learning models was also confirmed by visual comparison of the estimated and actual E_{static}.

Author Contributions: Conceptualization, S.E; data preparation, S.E., and A.A.M.; models development, A.A.M.; results analysis, A.A.M.; writing—original draft preparation, A.A.M.; writing—review and editing, S.E., and D.A.S.; supervision, S.E. All authors have read and agreed to the published version of the manuscript.

Conflicts of Interest: The authors declare no conflict of interest.

Nomenclature

AAPE	Average absolute percentage error
ANN	Artificial neural networks
DT_c	Compressional transit time
DT_s	Shear transit time
$E_{dynamic}$	Dynamic Young's modulus
E_{static}	Static Young's modulus
FNN	Functional neural networks
M-FIS	Mamdani fuzzy interference system
SVM	Support vector machine
R	Correlation coefficient
RHOB	Formation bulk density

References

1. Britt, L.K.; Smith, M.B.; Haddad, Z.; Reese, J.; Kelly, P. Rotary Sidewall Cores—A Cost Effective Means of Determining Young's Modulus. Proceeding of the SPE Annual Technical Conference and Exhibition, Houston, TX, USA, 26–29 September 2004. [CrossRef]
2. Fjaer, E.; Horsrud, H.P.; Raaen, A.M.; Risnes, R. *Petroleum Related Rock Mechanics*, 2nd ed.; Elsevier Science: Amsterdam, The Netherlands, 2008; Volume 53, ISBN 9780080557090.
3. Chang, C.; Zoback, M.D.; Khaksar, A. Empirical relations between rock strength and physical properties in sedimentary rocks. *J. Pet. Sci. Eng.* **2006**, *51*, 223–237. [CrossRef]
4. Gatens, J.M.; Harrison, C.W.; Lancaster, D.E.; Guldry, F.K. In-situ stress tests and acoustic logs determine mechanical properties and stress profiles in the Devonian shales. *SPE Form. Eval.* **1990**, *5*, 248–254. [CrossRef]
5. Meyer, B.R.; Jacot, R.H. Impact of Stress-Dependent Young's Moduli on Hydraulic Fracture Modeling. In Proceedings of the 38th U.S. Symposium on Rock Mechanics, Washington, DC, USA, 7–10 July 2001.
6. Nes, O.M.; Fjaer, E.; Tronvoll, J.; Kristiansen, T.G.; Horsrud, P. Drilling time reduction through an integrated rock mechanics analysis. *J. Energy Resour. Technol.* **2012**, *134*, 032802. [CrossRef]
7. Howard, G.C.; Fast, C.R. Hydraulic Fracturing. In *Doherty Memorial Fund of AIME, Society of Petroleum Engineers of AIME*; Henry L.: New York, NY, USA, 1970; Volume 2, ISBN 10.
8. Barree, R.D.; Gilbert, J.V.; Conway, M.W. Stress and Rock Property Profiling for Unconventional Reservoir Stimulation. In Proceedings of the SPE Hydraulic Fracturing Technology Conference, The Woodlands, TX, USA, 19–21 January 2009. [CrossRef]
9. Rinehart, J.S.; Fortin, J.-P.; Burgin, L. Propagation Velocity of Longitudinal Waves in Rock. Effect of State of Stress, Stress Level of the Wave, Water Content, Porosity, Temperature Stratification and Texture. In Proceedings of the 4th Symposium on Rock Mechanics, University Park, PA, USA, 30 March–1 April 1961.
10. Simmons, G.; Brace, W.F. Comparison of Static and Dynamic Measurements of Compressibility of Rocks. *J. Geophys. Res.* **1965**, *70*, 5649–5656. [CrossRef]
11. King, M.S. Wave Velocities in Rocks as a Function of Changes in over burden Pressure and Pore Fluid Saturants. *Geophysics* **1966**, *31*, 50–73. [CrossRef]
12. Larsen, I.; Fjær, E.; Renlie, L. Static and Dynamic Poisson's Ratio of Weak Sandstones. In Proceedings of the 4th North American Rock Mechanics Symposium, Seattle, WA, USA, 31 July–3 August 2000.

13. Hui, C.; Lian-Ku, X.; Li-Jie, G.; Hu-Xin, W.; Biao, C. Rock mechanics study on the safety and efficient extraction for deep moderately inclined medium-thick orebody. *Electron. J. Geotech. Eng.* **2015**, *20*, 11073–11082.
14. Peng, L.; Xinrong, L.; Zuliang, Z. Mechanical Property Experiment and Damage Statistical Constitutive Model of Hongze Rock Salt in China. *Electron. J. Geotech. Eng.* **2015**, *20*, 81–94.
15. King, M.S. Static and Dynamic elastic moduli of rocks under pressure. In Proceedings of the 11th U.S. Symposium on Rock Mechanics (USRMS), Berkeley, CA, USA, 16–19 June 1969.
16. Canady, W.J. A Method for Full-Range Young's Modulus Correction. In Proceedings of the North American Unconventional Gas Conference and Exhibition, The Woodlands, TX, USA, 14–16 June 2011. [CrossRef]
17. Khaksar, A.; Taylor, P.G.; Fang, Z.; Kayes, T.J.; Salazar, A.; Rahman, K. Rock Strength from Core and Logs, Where We Stand and Ways to Go. In Proceedings of the EUROPEC/EAGE Conference and Exhibition, Amsterdam, The Netherlands, 8–11 June 2009. [CrossRef]
18. Fei, W.; Huiyuan, B.; Jun, Y.; Yonghao, Z. Correlation of Dynamic and Static Elastic Parameters of Rock. *Electronic J. Geotech. Eng.* **2016**, *21*, 1551–1560.
19. Mahmoud, M.A.; Elkatatny, S.A.; Ramadan, E.; Abdulraheem, A. Development of Lithology-Based Static Young's Modulus Correlations from Log Data Based on Data Clustering Technique. *J. Pet. Sci. Eng.* **2016**, *146*, 10–20. [CrossRef]
20. Abdulraheem, A.; Ahmed, M.; Vantala, A.; Parvez, T. Prediction of Rock Mechanical Parameters for Hydrocarbon Reservoirs Using Different Artificial Intelligence Techniques. In Proceedings of the SPE Saudi Arabia Section Technical Symposium, Al-Khobar, Saudi Arabia, 9–11 May 2009. [CrossRef]
21. Tariq, Z.; Elkatatny, S.; Mahmoud, M.; Abdulraheem, A. A New Artificial Intelligence Based Empirical Correlation to Predict Sonic Travel Time. In Proceedings of the International Petroleum Technology Conference, Bangkok, Thailand, 14–16 November 2016. [CrossRef]
22. Tariq, Z.; Elkatatny, S.M.; Mahmoud, M.A.; Abdulraheem, A.; Abdelwahab, A.Z.; Woldeamanuel, M. Estimation of Rock Mechanical Parameters Using Artificial Intelligence Tools. In Proceedings of the 51st U.S. Rock Mechanics/Geomechanics Symposium, San Francisco, CA, USA, 25–28 June 2017.
23. Parapuram, G.K.; Mokhtari, M.; Hmida, J.B. Prediction and Analysis of Geomechanical Properties of the Upper Bakken Shale Utilizing Artificial Intelligence and Data Mining. In Proceedings of the SPE/AAPG/SEG Unconventional Resources Technology Conference, Austin, TX, USA, 24–26 July 2017. [CrossRef]
24. Mahmoud, A.A.; Elkatatny, S.; Ali, A.; Moussa, T. Estimation of Static Young's Modulus for Sandstone Formation Using Artificial Neural Networks. *Energies* **2019**, *12*, 2125. [CrossRef]
25. Mahmoud, A.A.A.; Elkatatny, S.; Mahmoud, M.; Abouelresh, M.; Abdulraheem, A.; Ali, A. Determination of the total organic carbon (TOC) based on conventional well logs using artificial neural network. *Int. J. Coal Geol.* **2017**, *179*, 72–80. [CrossRef]
26. Gurney, K. *An Introduction to Neural Networks*; UCL Press Limited: London, UK, 1997; ISBN 0-203-45151-1.
27. Jang, R. ANFIS Adaptive Network Based Fuzzy Inference System. *IEEE Trans. Syst. Man Cybern.* **1993**, *23*, 665–685. [CrossRef]
28. Jang, J.S.R.; Sun, C.T.; Mizutani, E. *Neuro-Fuzzy and Soft Computing*; Prentice Hall: Bergen, NJ, USA, 1997; ISBN 0132610663.
29. Bello, O.; Asafa, T. A Functional Networks Softsensor for Flowing Bottomhole Pressures and Temperatures in Multiphase Production Wells. In Proceeding of the SPE Intelligent Energy Conference & Exhibition, Utrecht, The Netherlands, 1–3 April 2014. [CrossRef]
30. Anifowose, F.; Abdulraheem, A. Fuzzy logic-driven and SVM-driven hybrid computational intelligence models applied to oil and gas reservoir characterization. *J. Natl. Gas Sci. Eng.* **2011**, *3*, 505–517. [CrossRef]
31. Vapnik, V. *Statistical Learning Theory*; Wiley: New York, NY, USA, 1998; ISBN 978-0471030034.
32. Rui, J.; Zhang, H.; Zhang, D.; Han, F.; Guo, Q. Total organic carbon content prediction based on support-vector-regression machine with particle swarm optimization. *J. Pet. Sci. Eng.* **2019**, *180*, 699–706. [CrossRef]
33. Mohaghegh, S.; Arefi, R.; Ameri, S.; Hefner, M.H. A Methodological Approach for Reservoir Heterogeneity Characterization Using Artificial Neural Networks. In Proceedings of the SPE Annual Technical Conference and Exhibition, New Orleans, LA, USA, 25–28 September 1994. [CrossRef]
34. Barman, I.; Ouenes, A.; Wang, M. Fractured Reservoir Characterization Using Streamline-Based Inverse Modeling and Artificial Intelligence Tools. In Proceedings of the SPE Annual Technical Conference and Exhibition, Dallas, TX, USA, 1–4 October 2000. [CrossRef]

35. Mahmoud, A.A.; Elkatatny, S.; Abdulraheem, A.; Mahmoud, M.; Ibrahim, M.O.; Ali, A. New Technique to Determine the Total Organic Carbon Based on Well Logs Using Artificial Neural Network (White Box). In Proceedings of the SPE Kingdom Saudi Arabia Annual Technical Symposium and Exhibition, Dammam, Saudi Arabia, 24–27 April 2017. [CrossRef]
36. Mahmoud, A.A.; Elkatatny, S.; Ali, A.; Abouelresh, M.; Abdulraheem, A. Evaluation of the Total Organic Carbon (TOC) Using Different Artificial Intelligence Techniques. *Sustainability* **2019**, *11*, 5643. [CrossRef]
37. Mahmoud, A.A.; Elkatatny, S.; Ali, A.; Abouelresh, M.; Abdulraheem, A. New Robust Model to Evaluate the Total Organic Carbon Using Fuzzy Logic. In Proceedings of the SPE Kuwait Oil & Gas Show and Conference, Mishref, Kuwait, 13–16 October 2019. [CrossRef]
38. Mahmoud, A.A.; Elkatatny, S.; Abouelresh, M.; Abdulraheem, A.; Ali, A. Estimation of the Total Organic Carbon Using Functional Neural Networks and Support Vector Machine. In Proceedings of the 12th International Petroleum Technology Conference and Exhibition, Dhahran, Saudi Arabia, 13–15 January 2020. [CrossRef]
39. Elkatatny, S. Application of Artificial Intelligence Techniques to Estimate the Static Poisson's Ratio Based on Wireline Log Data. *J. Energy Resour. Technol.* **2018**, *140*, 072905. [CrossRef]
40. Mahmoud, A.A.; Elkatatny, S.; Ali, A.; Moussa, T. A Self-adaptive Artificial Neural Network Technique to Estimate Static Young's Modulus Based on Well Logs. Proceedings of Oman Petroleum & Energy Show, Muscat, Oman, 9–11 March 2020. [CrossRef]
41. Al-Shehri, D.A. Oil and Gas Wells: Enhanced Wellbore Casing Integrity Management through Corrosion Rate Prediction Using an Augmented Intelligent Approach. *Sustainability* **2019**, *11*, 818. [CrossRef]
42. Salehi, S.; Hareland, G.; Dehkordi, K.K.; Ganji, M.; Abdollahi, M. Casing collapse risk assessment and depth prediction with a neural network system approach. *J. Petrol. Sci. Eng.* **2009**, *69*, 156–162. [CrossRef]
43. Wang, Y.; Salehi, S. Application of real-time field data to optimize drilling hydraulics using neural network approach. *J. Energy Resour. Technol.* **2015**, *137*, 062903. [CrossRef]
44. Ahmed, A.S.; Mahmoud, A.A.; Elkatatny, S. Fracture Pressure Prediction Using Radial Basis Function. In Proceedings of the AADE National Technical Conference and Exhibition, Denver, CO, USA, 9–10 April 2019.
45. Ahmed, A.S.; Mahmoud, A.A.; Elkatatny, S.; Mahmoud, M.; Abdulraheem, A. Prediction of Pore and Fracture Pressures Using Support Vector Machine. In Proceedings of the 2019 International Petroleum Technology Conference, Beijing, China, 26–28 March 2019. [CrossRef]
46. Mahmoud, A.A.; Elkatatny, S.; Abdulraheem, A.; Mahmoud, M. Application of Artificial Intelligence Techniques in Estimating Oil Recovery Factor for Water Drive Sandy Reservoirs. In Proceedings of the SPE Kuwait Oil & Gas Show and Conference, Kuwait City, Kuwait, 15–18 October 2017. [CrossRef]
47. Mahmoud, A.A.; Elkatatny, S.; Chen, W.; Abdulraheem, A. Estimation of Oil Recovery Factor for Water Drive Sandy Reservoirs through Applications of Artificial Intelligence. *Energies* **2019**, *12*, 3671. [CrossRef]
48. Abdelgawad, K.Z.; Elzenary, M.; Elkatatny, S.; Mahmoud, M.; Abdulraheem, M.; Patil, S. New approach to evaluate the equivalent circulating density (ECD) using artificial intelligence techniques. *J. Petrol. Explor. Prod. Technol.* **2019**, *9*, 1569. [CrossRef]
49. Elkatatny, S.M. Real Time Prediction of Rheological Parameters of KCl Water-Based Drilling Fluid Using Artificial Neural Networks. *Arab. J. Sci. Eng.* **2017**, *42*, 1655–1665. [CrossRef]
50. Al-AbdulJabbar, A.; Elkatatny, S.; Mahmoud, A.A.; Moussa, T.; Al-Shehri, D.; Abughaban, M.; Al-Yami, A. Prediction of the Rate of Penetration while Drilling Horizontal Carbonate Reservoirs Using the Self-Adaptive Artificial Neural Networks Technique. *Sustainability* **2020**, *12*, 1376. [CrossRef]
51. Al-AbdulJabbar, A.; Elkatatny, S.M.; Mahmoud, M.; Abdelgawad, K.; Abdulaziz, A. A Robust Rate of Penetration Model for Carbonate Formation. *J. Energy Resour. Technol.* **2018**, *141*, 042903. [CrossRef]
52. Elkatatny, S.; Al-AbdulJabbar, A.; Mahmoud, A.A. New Robust Model to Estimate the Formation Tops in Real-Time Using Artificial Neural Networks (ANN). *Petrophysics* **2019**, *60*, 825–837. [CrossRef]
53. Al-Anazi, A.F.; Gates, I.D. A support vector machine algorithm to classify lithofacies and model permeability in heterogeneous reservoirs. *Eng. Geol.* **2010**, *114*, 267–277. [CrossRef]
54. Daniel, C. One-at-a-Time plans. *J. Am. Stat. Assoc.* **1973**, *68*, 353–360. [CrossRef]
55. Sobol', I.M. Global sensitivity indices for nonlinear mathematical models and their Monte Carlo estimates. *Math. Comput. Simul.* **2001**, *55*, 271–280. [CrossRef]
56. Yin, Z.; Feng, T.; MacBeth, C. Fast assimilation of frequently acquired 4D seismic data for reservoir history matching. *Comput. Geosci.* **2019**, *128*, 30–40. [CrossRef]

57. Hermans, T.; Nguyen, F.; Klepikova, M.; Dassargues, A.; Caers, J. Uncertainty Quantification of Medium-Term Heat Storage from Short-Term Geophysical Experiments Using Bayesian Evidential Learning. *Water Resour. Res.* **2018**, *54*, 2931–2948. [CrossRef]
58. Yin, Z.; Strebelle, S.; Caers, J. Automated Monte Carlo-based Quantification and Updating of Geological Uncertainty with Borehole Data (AutoBEL v1.0). *Geosci. Model. Dev.* **2019**, *13*. [CrossRef]

© 2020 by the authors. Licensee MDPI, Basel, Switzerland. This article is an open access article distributed under the terms and conditions of the Creative Commons Attribution (CC BY) license (http://creativecommons.org/licenses/by/4.0/).

Article

Application of Artificial Intelligence Techniques to Predict the Well Productivity of Fishbone Wells

Amjed Hassan, Salaheldin Elkatatny *[ID] and Abdulazeez Abdulraheem

College of Petroleum Engineering and Geosciences, King Fahd University of Petroleum & Minerals, 31261 Dhahran, Saudi Arabia; g201205100@kfupm.edu.sa (A.H.); aazeez@kfupm.edu.sa (A.A.)
* Correspondence: elkatatny@kfupm.edu.sa; Tel.: +96-659-466-3692

Received: 25 August 2019; Accepted: 29 October 2019; Published: 1 November 2019

Abstract: Fishbone multilateral wells are applied to enhance well productivity by increasing the contact area between the bottomhole and reservoir region. Fishbone wells are characterized by reduced operational time and a competitive cost in comparison to hydraulic fracturing operations. However, limited models are reported to determine the productivity of fishbone wells. In this paper, several artificial intelligence methods were applied to estimate the performance of fishbone wells producing from a heterogeneous and anisotropic gas reservoir. The well productivity was determined using an artificial neural network, a fuzzy logic system and a radial basis network. The models were developed and validated utilizing 250 data sets, with the inputs being the permeability ratio (K_h/K_v), flowing bottomhole pressure and lateral length. The results showed that the artificial intelligence models were able to predict the fishbone well productivity with an acceptable absolute error of 7.23%. Moreover, a mathematical equation was extracted from the artificial neural network, which is able to provide a simple and direct estimation of fishbone well productivity. Actual flow tests were used to evaluate the reliability of the developed model, and a very acceptable match was obtained between the predicted and actual flow rates, wherein an absolute error of 6.92% was achieved. This paper presents effective models for determining the well performance of complex multilateral wells producing from heterogeneous reservoirs. The developed models will help to reduce the uncertainty associated with numerical methods, and the extracted equation can be inserted into commercial software, thereby significantly reducing deviation between the actual data and simulated results.

Keywords: fishbone multilateral wells; artificial intelligence; predictive models; well productivity

---

1. Introduction

A multilateral well is defined as a well with multiple branches in the lower bore-hole targeting the pay zone in the same layer or different layers. Depending on the main well bore, a multilateral well can be classified as a root well or a fishbone well. For a root well, the main well bore is vertical, while for a fishbone well the laterals are drilled out from a horizontal well bore [1]. Fishbone wells are applied to enhance well productivity by increasing the contact area between the bottomhole and reservoir region. The productivities of vertical, horizontal and fishbone wells are depicted in Figure 1. Fishbone wells are characterized by larger drainage area; consequently, higher production rates can be achieved compared to vertical and horizontal wells [2]. In comparison to hydraulic fracturing operations, fishbones require less operational time and incur less expense [3]. Furthermore, fishbone wells have shown better performance than fractured horizontal wells in producing from tight reservoirs [2].

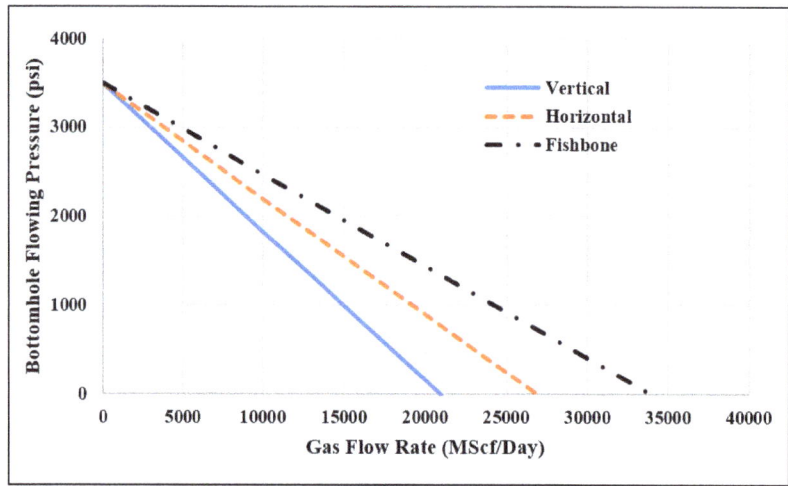

Figure 1. Hydrocarbon productivity for vertical, horizontal and fishbone wells.

Predicting the well productivity is an essential factor in designing and completing a production well, as well as selecting the artificial lift and stimulation processes [4]. Several techniques have been reported to estimate the well performance for multilateral wells. Different correlations and analytical models have been developed to determine the inflow performance relationship (IPR), with the most popular equations being Fetkovitch's and Vogel's correlations [5,6]. Recently, numerical simulators have been utilized to estimate well productivity, which resulted in a significant reduction in estimation errors.

Fishbone wells can be considered a combination of different types of wells, such as horizontal, directional and multilateral. They have a complicated geometry and require complex models to predict their inflow performance. Therefore, several assumptions are generally applied to predict the performance of a fishbone well, such as neglecting the number of laterals or assuming constant pressure in all laterals. This leads to considerable estimation errors and significant deviations between the actual production data and predicted results.

This paper presents a new approach to determine the productivity of fishbone wells. Artificial intelligence techniques were utilized to develop predictive models and avoid the uncertainty of numerical methods. The developed models require the permeability ratio (K_h/K_v), flowing bottomhole pressure and lateral length to determine well productivity. The reliability of the developed models was verified using actual field data, wherein an absolute error of 6.92% was achieved for an ANN-based equation.

1.1. Inflow Performance Relationship

Borisov [7] proposed an analytical model to estimate the inflow performance relationship (IPR) for single phase multilateral wells. This model assumes steady state conditions, leading to impractical predictions. Therefore, Economides et al. [8] modified Borisov's model by including pseudo steady state conditions. Furthermore, Salas et al. [9] investigated the impact of nearby damage (skin factor) on well productivity using different multilateral configurations. Furui et al. [5] developed an analytical model for fishbone multilateral wells. They concluded that the productivity can be expressed as a function of skin factor, drainage distance, permeability ratio and reservoir dimensions.

Yildiz [10] upgraded Salas and colleagues' equation to model multilateral wells producing from extremely heterogeneous reservoirs. Guo et al. [4] reported that multilateral wells are involved with several flow regimes, including linear horizontal flow, radial flow, and vertical radial flow. Also, they mentioned that two different regions exist in the reservoir, the outer undrilled region and inner drilled region, with each region having a certain flow regime.

Yu et al. [11] used the net present value (NPV) concept to compare the performance of fishbone wells with that of fractured horizontal wells. They found that fishbone wells performed better than fractured horizontal wells, especially in tight reservoirs. The first attempt to couple the inflow performance with out-flow performance was reported by Lian et al. [12]. They developed a model by assuming uniform flow rate distribution, which is applicable in pseudo steady or unsteady flow state conditions.

In addition, different numerical models have been developed to simulate well productivity by treating each branch as a fracture with dimensions similar to the lateral dimensions. Several reservoir models have been evaluated to simulate dual porosity systems, triple porosity systems, and isotropic and anisotropic permeability conditions [13]. Moreover, computational fluid dynamics (CFD) analysis has been utilized to model the performance of fishbone wells in depleted reservoirs under water flooding operations. Fishbone multilateral wells have shown a productivity improvement of 25% in comparison with conventional horizontal wells during water flooding treatments [14].

Abdulazeem and Alnuaim [15] developed a new empirical model to determine the performance of a fishbone well in a homogeneous oil reservoir. Their model investigated the effects of reservoir permeability, porosity and fluid properties on the well's productivity. They used Vogel's model to validate the developed IPR fishbone model, and found that the developed model had a lower estimation error compared to Vogel's model. Moreover, Ahmed et al. [6] extended the model proposed by Abdulazeem and Alnuaim in order to predict the performance of fishbone wells producing from gas reservoirs. They reported that their extended model was able to determine the gas production rate for a wide range of reservoir and well parameters. Also, they used real field data to verify their model's reliability, with an acceptable match obtained between the actual data and predicted gas flow rates.

Al-Mashhad et al. [16] evaluated the performance of multilateral wells using an artificial neural network (ANN). Their ANN model was able to determine the oil production rate for multilateral wells based on reservoir and well parameters. They compared the developed model with several analytical models and empirical correlations. They found that the developed ANN model was capable of outperforming the other models, with strong matching between the actual and predicted flow rates achieved. Specifically, the model had an average absolute percentage error of 7.9%.

In this work, three artificial intelligence methods were utilized to predict the performance of fishbone wells. An artificial neural network, fuzzy logic system and radial basis function were used. The inputs to the models included the permeability ratio, flowing bottomhole pressure and lateral length. The developed models showed a strong predictive performance, with an acceptable absolute error of 7.23%. Also, a mathematical equation was extracted using the optimized ANN model. This extracted correlation provides a simple and direct estimation of the fishbone productivity. The ANN-based equation was verified using actual field data, wherein an absolute error of 6.92% was achieved.

1.2. Artificial Intelligence Techniques

The concept of artificial networks was introduced into engineering research in the 1940s [17,18]. In the early stages, artificial intelligence was used to solve complex equations and mimic the nervous system [19,20]. Artificial intelligence (AI) techniques include artificial neural networks, fuzzy logic systems, support vector machines and radial basis networks. Artificial neural networks (ANNs) are considered effective AI tools; therefore, they have been widely applied in several fields, such as in classification and optimization tasks [21,22]. An ANN model is a system of neurons and hidden layers [23]. Usually the whole data is grouped into two sets, namely the training and testing data sets. The training set is used to train the network and capture the relationship between the input and output parameters, while the testing data are used to measure the reliability of the developed ANN system. During the training stage, the testing data remain unseen by the model, which increases confidence in the model's reliability [24–26]. A fuzzy logic model is an integrated network that combines a neural network with fuzzy logic. The most common model of fuzzy logic is an adaptive neuro-fuzzy inference system (ANFIS), which has the ability to extract the benefits of AI techniques in (a) single or multi-framework(s) [27]. Another kind of AI method is the radial basis function (RBF), which consists of linear and nonlinear functions [28].

Recently, artificial intelligence techniques have been extensively applied in the petroleum industry, especially in predicting well or field performance. Alajmi et al. [29] made predictions about choke performance using an ANN. Alarifi et al. [30] estimated the productivity index for horizontal oil wells using an ANN, a functional network and fuzzy logic. Chen et al. [31] applied a neural network and fuzzy logic to evaluate the performance of an inflow control device (ICD) in a horizontal well. Their model investigated the influence of reservoir parameters, such as reservoir size, thickness, heterogeneity and permeability ratio, on ICD completion performance.

Elkatatny et al. [32,33] comprehensively applied artificial neural networks (ANNs) to determine the permeability of a heterogeneous reservoir, and to estimate the rheological properties of drilling fluids based on real-time measurements. They developed robust models that can be used by petroleum engineers to obtain highly accurate predictions in less time. Van and Chon [34,35] evaluated the performance of CO_2 flooding using artificial neural network techniques. Specifically, they developed ANN models to determine the oil production rate, CO_2 production and gas oil ratio (GOR).

2. Data Acquisition and Analysis

In this work, the used data were generated by a commercial well performance software, with more than 250 runs performed. Real reservoir and well data were utilized as inputs for the commercial software. The minimum and maximum limits for each parameter were accurately selected. Then, the software outputs were carefully reviewed by a production consultant with over 30 years' experience in the petroleum industry. Thereafter, the most practical results were used to develop the proposed models. The reservoir model was constructed in a 3D Cartesian grid system (62 × 21 × 11) with a fishbone well placed at the center. The dimensions of the reservoir were set to 20,000 ft (length) by 10,000 ft (width), with a depth of 750 ft. The reservoir was single layer, dry gas and anisotropic, and had produced for 20 years. The generated data, which comprised of more than 250 data sets, were sufficient to train and validate the artificial intelligence models. The data sets included simulation results for flowing bottomhole pressure (P_{wf}), well production rate, distances between laterals, length of each lateral, number of laterals, and permeability ratio (K_h/K_v).

A randomization function was utilized to divide the whole data into two sets: training and testing groups. The training data, which was 70% of the total data, was used to train the networks to capture the relationship between the inputs and flow rate. The testing data, which was data that was unseen during the training stage, was utilized to evaluate the reliability of the models. Before running the AI models, statistical analyses were conducted to determine their minimum, maximum, mean, mode and other statistical parameters, the results of which are summarized in Table 1. As shown in the table, the permeability ratio (K_h/K_v) ranged from 1 to 1000, while the flowing bottomhole pressure (P_{wf}) varied between 14.7 and 4800 psia. The statistical dispersion for flow rate results was measured by calculating the skewness and kurtosis, with the data showing huge spread over a wide range of values.

In addition, statistical distributions were obtained for all of the data to get a rough sense of the density of the underlying distributions, wherein the data set was found to represent a multimodal pattern. Figure 2 shows the distributions for input and output parameters against the number of samples. In general, the data showed typical trends for reservoir properties. For example, a hydrocarbon reservoir usually has one average permeability value, but it can produce using several bottomhole pressures. Therefore, one value can be used to represent the reservoir's permeability, while a wide range of flowing pressures can be applied. Finally, correlation coefficients were determined to measure the impact of the input parameters on the well flow rate, as shown in Figure 3. Strong relationships were observed between the production rate and the flowing bottomhole pressure (P_{wf}), permeability ratio (K_h/K_v) and lateral length (L), with correlation coefficient values of −0.831, 0.292 and 0.230, respectively. The results of the correlation coefficient analysis indicate that the flow rate can be increased by reducing the flowing pressure or by increasing the lateral length. Also, increased hydrocarbon production can be obtained from a hydrocarbon reservoir with a higher permeability ratio. However, the number of laterals (N) and distance between laterals (D) showed very small correlation coefficient values (0.171 and −0.035, respectively). The same observation was reported by Ahmed et al. [6], who found that increasing the number of laterals or the distance between the laterals only had a minor effect on improving the fishbone productivity. Therefore, the number of laterals and the distance between laterals were excluded from further research as input parameters.

Table 1. A statistical analysis of the input/output data.

Parameter	K_h/K_v	No. of Laterals	Length (ft)	Distance (ft)	P_{wf} (psia)	Flow Rate (scf/D)
Minimum	1	2	700	1300	14.7	0
Maximum	1000	14	3100	5200	4800	197,903.226
Mean	61	6.667	2759.523	2723.809	2359.558	81,860.474
Mode	10	6	3100	2600	14.7	0
Range	999	12	2400	3900	4785.3	197,903.226
Standard Deviation	211.275	2.499	693.099	685.121	1551.738	48,712.516
Skewness	4.192	1.412	−1.9159	2.0689	0.09535	−0.118
Kurtosis	18.73	5.358	5.3081	9.503	1.7184	2.216
Coefficient of variation	346.352	37.491	25.116	25.153	65.763	59.507

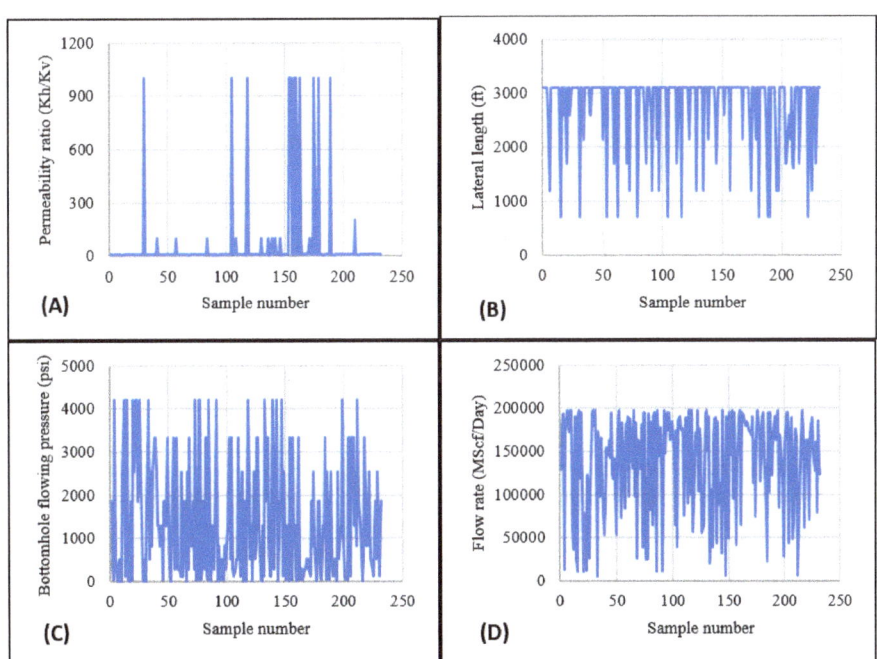

Figure 2. Distributions of input and output data, including (A) permeability ratio (K_h/K_v), (B) lateral length (L), (C) flowing bottomhole pressure (P_{wf}) and (D) flow rate.

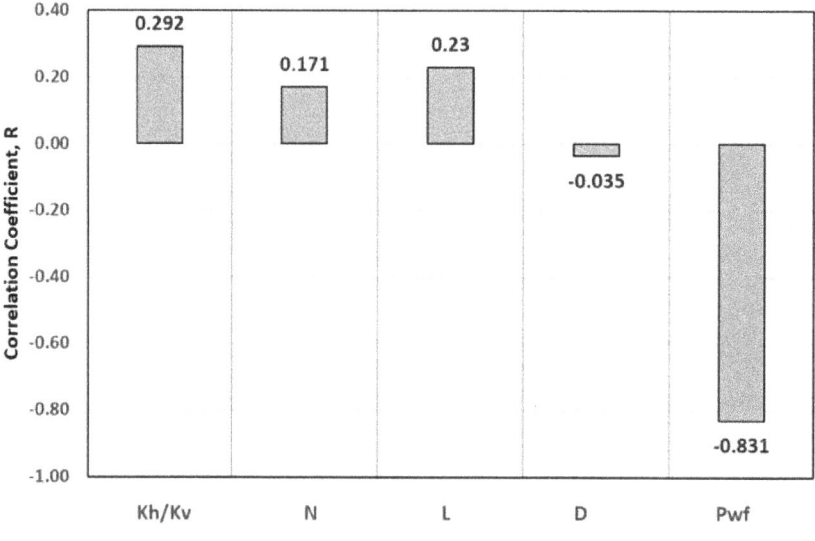

Figure 3. The relative importance of production rate with input parameters used to train the artificial neural network (ANN) model.

In summary, the statistical distribution plots indicated that most of the data set was represented by a multimodal pattern, while the correlation coefficient analysis revealed that the production rate was in a moderate positive linear relationship with the permeability ratio, in a weak positive linear relationship with the lateral length, and in a strong negative linear relationship with the flowing bottomhole pressure.

3. Results and Discussion

Several artificial intelligence models were investigated to obtain the model with the lowest average absolute percentage error (AAPE) and maximum correlation coefficient (CC) value. A sensitivity analysis was performed for each AI technique in order to optimize the model parameters. Evaluating the fishbone performance using the original data showed significant deviations between the predicted results and the target values, with an error of 28.12% and correlation coefficient of 0.290 obtained for the ANN model. To reduce these deviations, data processing techniques were implemented, and the number of inputs was reduced from five to three. The model inputs considered were the flowing bottomhole pressure, permeability ratio and lateral length. As a result, the prediction performance was improved significantly, with the error decreasing from 28.12% to around 12.65% and the correlation coefficient increasing from 0.290 to 0.982 for the ANN model. In the following sections, the results from several AI techniques in determining fishbone productivity are discussed.

3.1. Artificial Neural Network

The neural network model was developed to evaluate the fishbone performance by determining the flow rate based on the well bore configurations and reservoir parameters. The model inputs were the permeability ratio, lateral length and flowing bottomhole pressure. The developed ANN model consisted of three layers: input, hidden and output. The optimum number of neurons was found to be 5 (see Figure 4). The ANN model was trained using 70% of the data, after which the model became ready to predict the flow rate for the testing or unseen data. Different cases were investigated in order to optimize the model parameters, the results of which are summarized in Table 2. Four cases were investigated, each with a different number of neurons (from 1 to 20 in each layer) or a different number of hidden layers (between 1 and 3). From this, optimum values for the number of neurons and layers were able to be defined. A minimum average absolute error of 7.23% and a relatively high correlation coefficient of 0.979 were obtained using 1 hidden layer with 20 neurons. Figure 5 shows the predicted results against the actual values for the training and testing data.

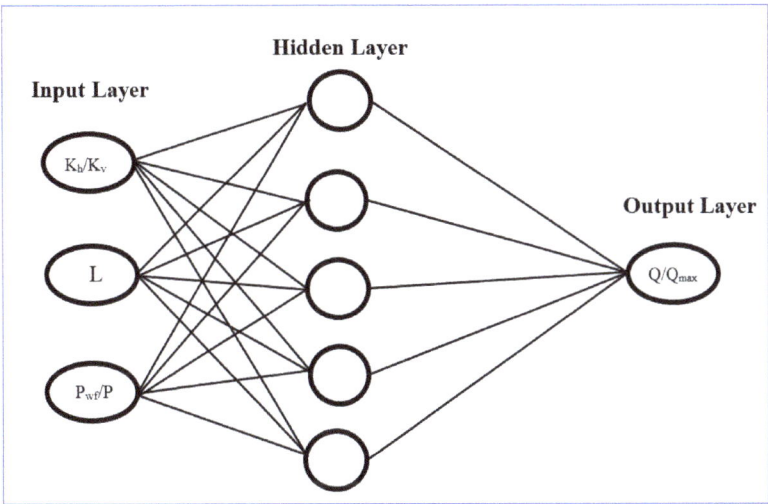

Figure 4. Artificial neural network model architecture with input, hidden, and output layer.

Table 2. Artificial neural network results.

Case No.	No. of Hidden Layers	Number of Neurons in Layer	CorrCoef_Test	AAPE_Test
1	1	10	0.9849	15.7040
2	1	20	0.9796	7.2327
3	2	20	0.9547	14.4647
4	3	20	0.9868	11.6491

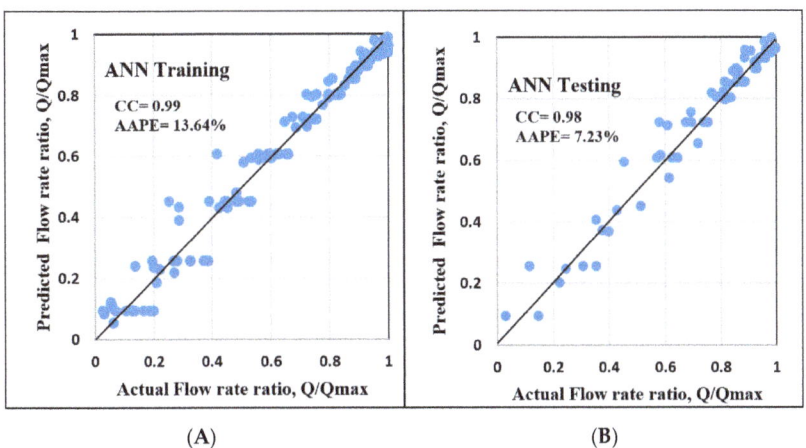

Figure 5. Comparison between the predicted and the target flow rate ratio (Q/Qmax) using the ANN model for the (**A**) training and (**B**) testing data sets.

3.2. Fuzzy Logic System

Fishbone productivity was estimated using an adaptive neuro-fuzzy inference system (ANFIS). Several scenarios were studied to fine tune the model parameters in order to minimize the estimation error and maximize the correlation coefficient, and Table 3 summarizes the ANFIS results. The optimum model was selected based on the absolute error, correlation coefficients and visualization check. Usually, better results can be obtained by increasing the cluster radius; or increasing the number of iterations. In this study, the best scenario was achieved by using five membership functions, a linear output membership function, a cluster radius of 0.8 and an iteration number of 200 (Case 3), for which the AAPE was 13.92% and the correlation coefficient was 0.985. Figure 6 shows the actual values against the predicted flow rates using the fuzzy logic model.

Table 3. Adaptive neuro-fuzzy inference system (ANFIS) results.

Case No	Cluster Radius	Number of Iterations	CorrCoef_Test	AAPE_Test
1	0.1	200	0.9822	14.4962
2	0.3	200	0.9838	14.1589
3	**0.8**	**200**	**0.9845**	**13.9187**
4	0.7	200	0.9845	13.9242
5	1	200	0.9845	13.9208
6	0.6	100	0.9848	14.0791

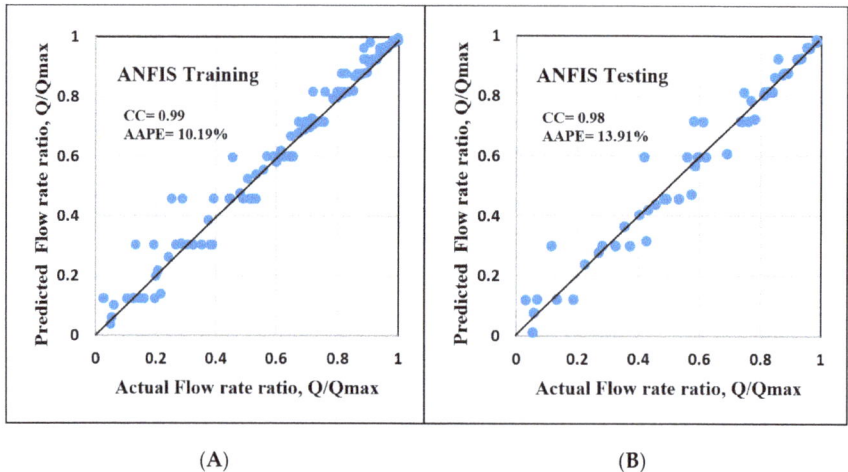

Figure 6. Comparison between the predicted and the target flow rate ratio (Q/Qmax) using the ANFIS model for the (**A**) training and (**B**) testing data sets.

3.3. Radial Basis Function (RBF) Network

Finally, an RBF network was utilized to predict the fishbone production rate, and the impact of the model parameters on improving the model prediction was investigated. Different values of goal, spread and maximum number of neurons were examined to optimize the model parameters, with the results of this examination summarized in Table 4. It may be observed that increasing the goal or spread values led to worse results (higher AAPE and lower CC values), which could be due to increasing the model's tolerance. In this work, changing the goal value showed insignificant effect in improving the prediction performance, while reducing the model's spread led to considerable improvements in the prediction performance. Also, no further improvement was observed by increasing the maximum number of neurons (MN) above 20. The optimum case (case 4) was obtained using a goal value of 0.0, a spread value of 50, an MN of 20 and a DF (number of neurons to be added between displays) of 1.

For this case, the correlation coefficient was 0.985 and the absolute error was 11.14%. Figure 7 shows the actual flow rate against the predicted flow rate using this optimal RBF model.

Table 4. Radial basis function network (RBF) results.

Case No.	GOAL	SPREAD	MN, Maximum Number of Neurons	CorrCoef_Test	AAPE_Test
1	0	100	10	0.8786	19.3701
2	0	100	15	0.9830	11.4670
3	0	100	20	0.9851	11.1697
4	0	50	20	0.9851	11.1464
5	0.5	10	20	0.8614	32.8188

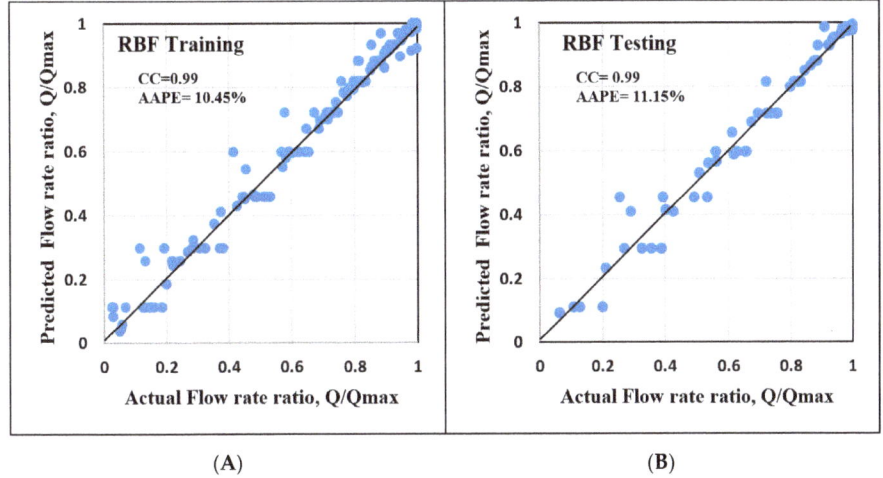

Figure 7. Comparison between the predicted and the target flow rate ratio (Q/Qmax) using the RBF model for the (**A**) training and (**B**) testing data sets.

Figure 8 compares the fishbone productivity obtained using the artificial neural network (ANN), fuzzy logic system (ANFIS) and radial basis function (RBF), for which the absolute errors are 7.23%, 13.92% and 11.15%, respectively, and the correction coefficients are between 0.98 and 0.99 for all methods. The model developed using an artificial neural network showed the best prediction performance, with the absolute error of 7.23% indicating that the ANN model may be the preferred model for determining the flow rate of a fishbone well.

3.4. New Empirical Correlation for Fishbone Productivity

An empirical equation was extracted from the optimized neural network model (Equation (2)). This extracted equation can predict the flow rate based the weights and biases of the ANN model. Table 5 lists the values of weights and biases used in Equation (2). The proposed model to predict the fishbone productivity is given by the following equations:

$$\frac{q}{q_{max}} = \left[\sum_{i=1}^{N} w_{2i} \tan \text{sig}\left(\sum_{j=1}^{J} w_{1i,j} x_j + b_{1i}\right)\right] + b_2 \qquad (1)$$

$$\frac{q}{q_{max}} = \left[\sum_{i=1}^{N} w_{2i}\left(\frac{2}{1 + e^{-2(w_{1i,1}(\frac{K_h}{K_v})_j + w_{1i,2}L_j + w_{1i,3}(P_{wf}/P_{avg})_j + b_{1i})}}\right)\right] + b_2 \qquad (2)$$

where N is the total number of neurons, w1 is the weights of the hidden layer, w$_2$ is the weights of the output layer, K_h/K_v is the permeability ratio, L is the lateral length, P_{wf} is the flowing bottomhole pressure, and P_{avg} is the average reservoir pressure. Note that the ANN model automatically normalizes the input into a range between −1 and 1.

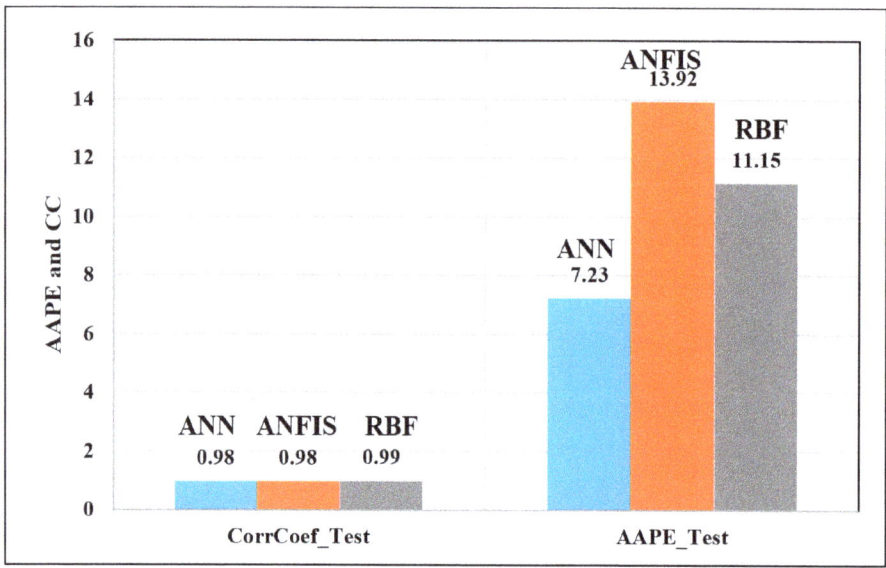

Figure 8. Comparison of different artificial intelligence (AI) techniques.

Table 5. The values of weights and biases extracted from the ANN model.

Neurons (N)	Weights between Input and Hidden Layer (W$_1$)			Weights between Hidden and Output Layer (W$_2$)	Hidden Layer Bias (b$_1$)	Output Layer Bias (b$_2$)
	K$_h$/K$_v$	Length	P$_{wf}$			
1	−3.84692	0.617902	−2.26283	−2.819227146	0.752135	
2	3.358502	−2.56259	−1.34471	−2.498195347	0.232057	
3	3.162647	−3.3314	1.433747	−0.682675154	0.430348	
4	2.595679	−3.26074	−1.83961	0.666775968	−0.9063	
5	−2.19077	2.3777	1.716382	−2.423948008	0.130544	
6	−1.74031	2.608322	2.778165	−0.581621184	0.281862	
7	1.455491	−2.75341	−2.49005	0.699240526	−0.74851	
8	−1.01596	1.755128	1.831094	−2.721731367	−0.23775	
9	−0.51291	2.085212	1.655426	−2.701708506	−0.15973	
10	−0.30873	3.380575	−1.66117	0.602113511	0.173508	−0.28498
11	0.169321	−1.10784	−3.44826	−1.33129177	0.285198	
12	−0.35496	−1.95086	−2.1071	2.340221069	−0.05304	
13	1.08924	2.348532	1.9611	−2.136881713	0.191233	
14	1.407857	0.420195	2.554844	2.696650854	0.15787	
15	−1.74964	−1.27965	−0.31507	3.224532039	−0.16893	
16	−2.24378	−1.25899	1.524934	−3.236788256	−0.11517	
17	−2.61158	−2.64587	−2.30505	1.377837678	−0.07059	
18	3.316892	3.350453	0.264872	−1.109735463	−0.12635	
19	3.298386	1.357587	−3.4066	−0.837658734	0.641118	
20	3.717023	0.598516	−3.12083	1.403728747	0.227681	

3.5. Model Verification

Our developed correlation was used to determine the fishbone productivity for the unseen data. More than 70 data sets with different conditions of reservoir parameters and well bore configurations were used. This correlation achieved an average absolute error of 7.23% and a relatively high correlation coefficient of 0.979. Moreover, the developed correlation was compared with different numerical and analytical models proposed in the literature. Ahmed et al. [6] proposed an empirical IPR correlation based on Vogel's productivity model. Ahmed's correlation (Equation (3)) can be used to determine the productivity of a fishbone well drilled into a dry gas reservoir. Based on a literature review, Ahmed's correlation is considered one of the most accurate models that can be used to estimate the gas flow rate for fishbone wells. Therefore, the reliability of the developed ANN-based correlation was compared with that of Ahmed's model. Figure 9 shows a comparison between the gas flow rate predicted using Ahmed's correlation and the ANN-based correlation proposed in this work. It is clear that the flow rates predicted using the developed ANN correlation are a better match with the actual flow rate data than Ahmed's model. Also, at low pressure, the Vogel-form equation overestimates the production rate, while the developed ANN correlation has excellent predictions. The developed empirical equation based on the optimized ANN model predicted the flow rate with an average absolute error of 6.92%.

$$\frac{q}{q_{max}} = 1.00756 + 1.154379 * \left(\frac{P_{wf}}{P_{wfmax}}\right)^{1.35} - 2.15268 * \left(\frac{P_{wf}}{P_{wfmax}}\right)^{1.7} \quad (3)$$

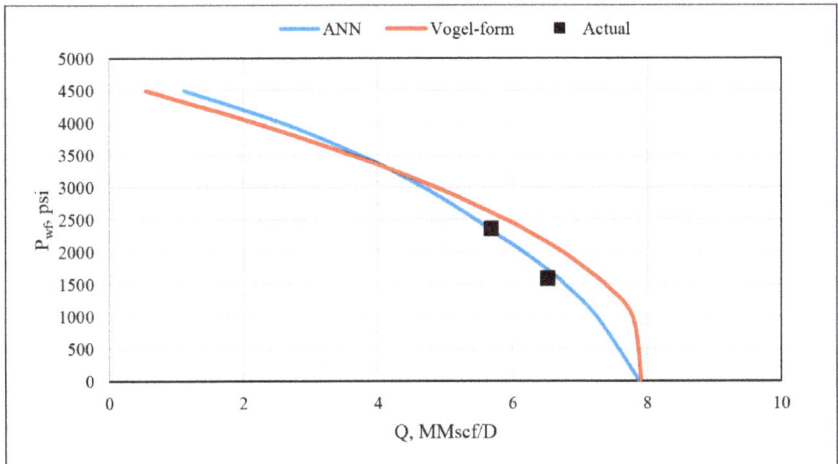

Figure 9. Comparison between the gas flow rate predicted by the ANN model and the Vogel-form equation alongside the actual gas rate.

Overall, this work can increase the confidence of decision makers in deciding to drill more fishbone wells, instead of drilling vertical or horizontal wells. The main issue with drilling fishbone wells is that most of the available production models are inaccurate, which leads to significant deviations between the models' results and the actual production data. As a consequence, most of the petroleum engineering industry prefer to drill vertical or horizontal wells in order to reduce the drilling cost and avoid the risk of fishbone wells, as it is easier to estimate the production rate for a vertical or horizontal well compared to a fishbone well. However, developing accurate models for determining fishbone well productivity can add to the credibility of such complex wells. The AI models presented in this paper can be used to provide an accurate estimation for the hydrocarbon production of multilateral fishbone wells, which will help in designing and optimizing production plans. Ultimately, this work can help

4. Conclusions

In this study, the productivity of fishbone wells was determined using three artificial intelligence techniques. The fishbone performance was estimated using a neural network model, fuzzy logic system and radial basis network. The models were developed and validated using more than 250 data sets. The following conclusions can be drawn from this work;

- The developed models showed very acceptable matches between the predicted and actual flow rates for fishbone wells.
- Only three parameters are required as inputs to the models for determining the production rate of fishbone wells: flowing bottomhole pressure, permeability ratio and lateral length.
- The developed models are able to estimate the fishbone productivity without introducing the uncertainty present in numerical models.
- The ANN model outperforms all of the artificial intelligence methods in predicting the fishbone productivity. Absolute errors of 7.23%, 13.92%, and 11.14% were obtained using the neural network, fuzzy logic and radial basis function models, respectively.
- An empirical equation was extracted from the ANN model which can provide a direct and simple determination of fishbone productivity.
- The extracted ANN-based equation can be inserted into commercial production software to provide more accurate predictions for fishbone productivity.
- The proposed models can help production engineers in designing and optimizing their production plans for complex wells.

Author Contributions: Conceptualization, A.H., S.E. and A.A.; methodology, A.H. and S.E.; software, A.H.; validation, A.H. and S.E.; formal analysis, A.H.; data curation, A.H. and S.E.; writing—original draft preparation, A.H.; writing—review and editing, S.E.; visualization, A.H., A.A. and S.E.; supervision, A.A., and S.E.

Funding: This research received no external funding.

Acknowledgments: The authors wish to acknowledge King Fahd University of Petroleum and Minerals (KFUPM) for utilizing the various facilities in carrying out this research. Many thanks are due to the anonymous referees for their detailed and helpful comments.

Conflicts of Interest: The authors declare no conflict of interest.

Abbreviations

AAPE	Average absolute percentage error
AAPE_Test	Average absolute percentage error for testing data set
ANFIS	Adaptive neuro-fuzzy inference system
ANN	Artificial neural network
b_1	Bias for hidden layer neuron j
b_2	Bias for output layer of ANN model
CC	Correlation coefficient
CorrCoef_Test	Correlation coefficient for testing data set
D	Distance between laterals in ft
i	Index for input parameters
j	Index for hidden layer neurons
K_h	Horizontal permeability in md
K_h/K_v	Permeability ratio
K_v	Vertical permeability in md
L	Length of lateral in ft
N	Number of lateral or branches
N_i	Total number of input parameters

P_{wf}	Flowing bottomhole pressure in psia
P_{wfmax}	Average reservoir pressure in psia.
Q	Flow rate in Mscf/D
Q_{max}	Absolute open flow in Mscf/day.
w_{1i}	Weights vector between input and hidden layer for ANN model
w_{2i}	Weights vector between hidden and output layer for ANN model
x_i	Input parameters

References

1. Bosworth, X.; El-Sayed, H.S.; Ismail, G.; Ohmer, H.; Stracke, M.; West, C.; Retnanto, A. Key Issues in Multilateral Technology. *Oilfield Rev.* **1998**, *10*, 14–28.
2. Guangyu, X.; Guo, F.; Cheng, S.; Sun, Y.; Yu, J.; Wang, G. Fishbone Well Drilling and Completion Technology in Ultra-Thin Reservoir. In Proceedings of the IADC/SPE Asia Pacific Drilling Technology Conference and Exhibition (Paper IADC/SPE 155958), Tianjin, China, 9–11 July 2012.
3. Filho, J.C.; Yifei, X.; Sepehrnoori, K. Modeling Fishbones Using the Embedded Discrete Fracture Model Formulation: Sensitivity Analysis and History Matching. In Proceedings of the SPE Annual Technical Conference and Exhibition (SPE-175124-MS), Houston, TX, USA, 28–30 September 2015.
4. Guo, B.; Sun, K.; Ghalambo, A. *Well Productivity Hand Book*; Gulf Publishing Company: Houston, TX, USA, 2008; pp. 226–230.
5. Furui, K.; Zhu, D.; Hill, A.D. A Comprehensive Model of Horizontal Well Completion Performance. In Proceedings of the SPE Annual Technical Conference and Exhibition (Paper SPE 84401), Denver, CO, USA, 5–8 October 2003.
6. Ahmed, M.E.; Alnuaim, S.; Abdulazeem, A. New Algorithm to Quantify Productivity of Fishbone Type Multilateral Gas Well. In Proceedings of the SPE Annual Technical Conference and Exhibition (SPE-181888-MS), Dubai, UAE, 26–28 September 2016.
7. Borisov, J.P. *Oil Production Using Horizontal and Multiple Deviation Wells*; Joshi, S.D., Ed.; Strauss, J., Translator; Phillips Petroleum Co.: Bartlesville, OK, USA, 1984.
8. Economides, M.J.; Hill, A.D.; Economides, C. *Petroleum Production Systems*; Prentice Hall PTR: Upper Saddle River, NJ, USA, 1994.
9. Salas, J.R.; Clifford, P.J.; Jenkins, D.P. Multilateral Well Performance. In Proceedings of the Western Regional Meeting (Paper SPE 35711), Anchorage, AK, USA, 22–24 May 1996.
10. Yildiz, T. Multilateral Horizontal Well Productivity. In Proceedings of the SPE Europec/EAGE Annual Conference (Paper SPE 94223), Madrid, Spain, 13–16 June 2005.
11. Xiance, Y.; Guo, B.; Ai, C.; Bu, Z. A comparison between multi-fractured horizontal and fishbone wells for development of low-permeability fields. In Proceedings of the Asia Pacific Oil and Gas Conference and Exhibition (Paper SPE 120579), Jakarta, Indonesia, 4–6 August 2009.
12. Lian, P.; Cheng, L.; Tan, X.; Li, L. A model for coupling reservoir inflow and wellbore flow in fishbone wells. *Pet. Sci. J.* **2012**, *9*, 336–342. [CrossRef]
13. Ding, Z.; Liu, Y.; Gong, Y.; Xu, N. A new technique: Fishbone well injection. *Pet. Sci. Technol.* **2012**, *30*, 2488–2493. [CrossRef]
14. Freyer, R.; Shaoul, J.R. Laterals stimulation method. In *Brasil Offshore Conference and Exhibition*; SPE-143381-MS; Society of Petroleum Engineers: Macae, Brazil, 2011. [CrossRef]
15. Abdulazeem, A.; Alnuaim, S. New Method to Estimate IPR for Fishbone Oil Multilateral Wells in Solution Gas Drive Reservoirs. In Proceedings of the SPE Kingdom of Saudi Arabia Annual Technical Symposium and Exhibition (SPE-182757-MS), Dammam, Saudi Arabia, 25–28 April 2016.
16. Al-Mashhad, A.S.; Al-Arifi, S.A.; Al-Kadem, M.S.; Al-Dabbous, M.S.; Buhulaigah, A. Multilateral Wells Evaluation Utilizing Artificial Intelligence. In Proceedings of the Abu Dhabi International Petroleum Exhibition and Conference (SPE-183508-MS), Abu Dhabi, UAE, 7–10 November 2016.
17. McCullock, W.S.; Pitts, W. A logical calculus of the ideas immanent in nervous activity. *Bull. Math. Biophys.* **1943**, *5*, 115–133. [CrossRef]
18. Bailey, D.; Thompson, D. How to Develop Neural Network. *AI Expert* **1990**, *5*, 38–47.

19. Rosenblatt, F. *The Perceptron, A Perceiving and Recognizing Automaton*; Project Para Report No. 85-460-1; Cornell Aeronautical Laboratory (CAL): Buffalo, NY, USA, 1957.
20. Fausett, L. *Fundamentals of Neural Networks, Architectures, Algorithms, and Applications*; Prentice-Hall Inc.: Eaglewood Cliffs, NJ, USA, 1994.
21. Ali, J.K. Neural Networks: A new Tool for the Petroleum Industry. In Proceedings of the European Petroleum Computer Conference, Aberdeen, UK, 15–17 March 1994.
22. Russell, S.J.; Norvig, P. *Artificial Intelligence: A Modern Approach*, 3rd ed.; Prentice Hall: Upper Saddle River, NJ, USA, 2009; ISBN 0-13-604259-7.
23. Sargolzaei, J.; Saghatoleslami, N.; Mosavi, S.M.; Khoshnoodi, M. Comparative Study of Artificial Neural Networks (ANN) and statistical methods for predicting the performance of Ultrafiltration Process in the Milk Industry. *Iran. J. Chem. Eng.* **2006**, *25*, 67–76.
24. Lippmann, R. An introduction to computing with neural nets. *IEEE ASSP Mag.* **1987**, *4*, 4–22. [CrossRef]
25. Jain, A.K.; Mao, J.; Mohiuddin, K.M. Artificial neural networks: A tutor. *Computer* **1996**, *29*, 31–44. [CrossRef]
26. MathWorks, Inc. Neural Network Toolbox 6, User's Guide. 2008. Available online: http://128.174.199.77/matlab_pdf/nnet.pdf (accessed on 30 June 2019).
27. Tahmasebi, P. A hybrid neural networks-fuzzy logic-genetic algorithm for grade estimation. *Comput. Geosci.* **2012**, *42*, 18–27. [CrossRef] [PubMed]
28. Broomhead, D.S.; David, L. Radial basis functions, multi-variable functional interpolation and adaptive networks. 1988. Available online: https://pdfs.semanticscholar.org/b08b/a914037af6d88d16e2657a65cd9dc5cf5da1.pdf (accessed on 30 June 2019).
29. AlAjmi, M.D.; Alarifi, S.A.; Mahsoon, A.H. Improving Multiphase Choke Performance Prediction and Well Production Test Validation Using Artificial Intelligence: A New Milestone. In Proceedings of the SPE Digital Energy Conference and Exhibition (SPE-173394-MS), The Woodlands, TX, USA, 3–5 March 2015.
30. Alarifi, S.A.; AlNuaim, S.; Abdulraheem, A. Productivity Index Prediction for Oil Horizontal Wells Using Different Artificial Intelligence Techniques. In Proceedings of the SPE Middle East Oil & Gas Show and Conference (SPE-172729-MS), Manama, Bahrain, 8–11 March 2015.
31. Chen, F.; Duan, Y.; Zhang, J.; Wang, K.; Wang, W. Application of neural network and fuzzy mathematic theory in evaluating the adaptability of inflow control device in horizontal well. *J. Pet. Sci. Eng.* **2015**, *134*, 131–142.
32. Elkatatny, S.; Mahmoud, M.; Tariq, Z.; Abdulraheem, A. New insights into the prediction of heterogeneous carbonate reservoir permeability from well logs using artificial intelligence network. *Neural Comput. Appl.* **2018**, *30*, 2673–2683. [CrossRef]
33. Elkatatny, S.; Tariq, Z.; Mahmoud, M. Real time prediction of drilling fluid rheological properties using Artificial Neural Networks visible mathematical model (white box). *J. Pet. Sci. Eng.* **2016**, *146*, 1202–1210. [CrossRef]
34. Van, S.L.; Chon, B.H. Effective Prediction and Management of a CO_2 Flooding Process for Enhancing Oil Recovery using Artificial Neural Networks. *ASME J. Energy Resour. Technol.* **2018**, *140*, 032906. [CrossRef]
35. Van, S.L.; Chon, B.H. Evaluating the critical performances of a CO_2–Enhanced oil recovery process using artificial neural network models. *J. Pet. Sci. Eng.* **2017**, *157*, 207–222. [CrossRef]

© 2019 by the authors. Licensee MDPI, Basel, Switzerland. This article is an open access article distributed under the terms and conditions of the Creative Commons Attribution (CC BY) license (http://creativecommons.org/licenses/by/4.0/).

Article

Intelligent Prediction of Minimum Miscibility Pressure (MMP) During CO_2 Flooding Using Artificial Intelligence Techniques

Amjed Hassan, Salaheldin Elkatatny * and Abdulazeez Abdulraheem

College of Petroleum Engineering and Geosciences, King Fahd University of Petroleum & Minerals, Dhahran 31261, Saudi Arabia; g201205100@kfupm.edu.sa (A.H.); toazeez@gmail.com (A.A.)
* Correspondence: elkatatny@kfupm.edu.sa; Tel.: +966594663692

Received: 28 October 2019; Accepted: 5 December 2019; Published: 9 December 2019

Abstract: Carbon dioxide (CO_2) injection is one of the most effective methods for improving hydrocarbon recovery. The minimum miscibility pressure (MMP) has a great effect on the performance of CO_2 flooding. Several methods are used to determine the MMP, including slim tube tests, analytical models and empirical correlations. However, the experimental measurements are costly and time-consuming, and the mathematical models might lead to significant estimation errors. This paper presents a new approach for determining the MMP during CO_2 flooding using artificial intelligent (AI) methods. In this work, reliable models are developed for calculating the minimum miscibility pressure of carbon dioxide (CO_2-MMP). Actual field data were collected; 105 case studies of CO_2 flooding in anisotropic and heterogeneous reservoirs were used to build and evaluate the developed models. The CO_2-MMP is determined based on the hydrocarbon compositions, reservoir conditions and the volume of injected CO_2. An artificial neural network, radial basis function, generalized neural network and fuzzy logic system were used to predict the CO_2-MMP. The models' reliability was compared with common determination methods; the developed models outperform the current CO_2-MMP methods. The presented models showed a very acceptable performance: the absolute error was 6.6% and the correlation coefficient was 0.98. The developed models can minimize the time and cost of determining the CO_2-MMP. Ultimately, this work will improve the design of CO_2 flooding operations by providing a reliable value for the CO_2-MMP.

Keywords: minimum miscibility pressure (MMP); CO_2 flooding; artificial intelligence; new models

---

1. Introduction

Enhanced oil recovery (EOR) processes are used to create favorable conditions for producing oil, through interfacial tension (IFT) reduction, wettability alteration or decreasing the oil viscosity [1]. CO_2 injection is one of the most practical and effective EOR methods because it significantly reduces the oil viscosity and improves the sweep efficiency [2,3]. The minimum miscibility pressure (MMP) plays a significant role in designing the gas flooding operations. The minimum miscibility pressure can be measured using slim tube tests [4]. However, the laboratory measurements are costly and time-consuming [5]. MMP can also be determined using empirical correlations, but these correlations can lead to significant deviations, where the absolute error can reach up to 25% [6–10]. Several empirical correlations were proposed to estimate the MMP based on the reservoir condition and the fluids compositions. The empirical correlations were developed utilizing regression approaches. The common correlations are the Glaso correlation, Sebastian et al. correlation and Khazam et al. correlation [6,8,9]. Generally, the accuracy of the empirical correlations is increasing as the mathematical complexity of the equation increases. Most of the empirical correlations are used mainly for the fast screening applications [10].

In addition, analytical methods have been coupled with the equation of state (EOS) to estimate the MMP, and an average absolute percentage error of 15.7% is reported. The main advantage of analytical methods is that they can determine the MMP without introducing uncertainties associated with the condensing or vaporizing displacement (CV) process. Since the displacement processes are associated with complex miscibility mechanisms and then reduce the reliability of MMP prediction [11–13], Yuan et al. [14,15] applied the analytical gas theory to estimate the CO_2-MMP. They used more than 180 data sets to build and evaluate the proposed semi-empirical model. They concluded that the developed model is more accurate and reliable than the empirical correlations, with a maximum average absolute percentage error of 9%. Furthermore, numerical approaches are used to determine the MMP. Fine-grid compositional simulations are utilized to solve the equation of state for particular grid sizes. The advantage of this approach is that it can be applied for heterogenous system of different pressure and temperature distributions as well as various fluid compositions. However, the numerical models can suffer from stability problems and may require a significantly small time-step in order to obtain stable solutions [10,15].

The use of artificial intelligence (AI) has proved to be an effective tool for prediction tasks because AI can capture the complex relationships between the output and input parameters [16]. Artificial neural network (ANN) is the most famous technique applied in the petroleum industry [17–20]. ANN technique has been utilized to predict the drilling fluids rheology, estimate the reservoir permeability and characterize the unconventional reservoirs [21–26]. AI also has been used for predicting the performance of several enhanced oil recovery (EOR) processes, such as steam-assisted gravity drainage (SAGD) process in heavy oil reservoirs [27–29].

Edalat et al. [30] presented a new ANN model to determine the MMP during hydrocarbon injection operations. Multi-layer perceptron (MLP) with two-layer feed-forward backpropagation were used. A total of 52 data points from an Iranian oil reservoir was employed with 20% for testing and 80% for training. They compared their results with a slim tube test and correlations, the maximum error of 18.58% and R-squared (R^2) of 0.938 is reported. They concluded that their ANN model can determine the MMP for different fluid compositions.

Dehghani et al. [31] combined a genetic algorithm with an ANN technique (GA–ANN) to determine the minimum miscibility pressure for gas injection operations. A total of 46 data points of MMP experiments were utilized, and back propagation with two hidden layers was used. The GA–ANN model predicts the MMP using the reservoir parameters and the injected-gas composition. They concluded that the developed model can afford a high level of dependability and accuracy for determining the MMP.

Shokrollahi et al. [32] utilized a support vector machine technique to determine the MMP for CO_2-injection operations. A total of 147 data points from experimental CO_2-MMP was used to developed and validate the model reliability, and the values of coefficient of determination (R^2) and average absolute percentage error were 0.90% and 9.6%, respectively. They mentioned that the proposed model shows high performance and good matching with the experimental data.

Liu et al. [33] suggested an improved method for estimating the CO_2-MMP utilizing magnetic resonance imaging (MRI). The obtained results showed good agreements with the experimental measurements. Khazam et al. [9] developed a simple correlation to determine the CO_2-MMP using a regression tool. A total of 100 PVT measurements from Libyan oilfields were used with a wide range of conditions, and a CO_2-MMP between 1544 and 6244 psia. The developed correlation requires the values of the oil properties and system condition (pressure and temperature) to estimate the CO_2-MMP with a high degree of accuracy, R^2 is 0.95 and AAPE is 5.74%. However, the model was developed based on limited data and from one region, and all samples were collected from Libyan oilfields. Czarnota et al. [5] presented a new approach to estimate the CO_2-MMP using an acoustic separator by taking images for the CO_2/oil system as a function of system pressure. They mentioned that the proposed approach can minimize the time required to obtain the CO_2-MMP.

Rostami et al. [34] applied the support vector machine (SVM) technique to estimate the CO_2-MMP during CO_2 flooding. SVM was used to determine the CO_2-MMP for live and dead crude oil systems. The developed model showed an accurate prediction with the average absolute relative deviation (AARD) of less than 3% and minimum coefficient of determination (R^2) of 0.99. However, no direct equation is reported and the developed SVM model is considered as a black box model. Alfarge et al. [35] used laboratory measurements and field studies to characterize the CO_2-flooding in shale reservoirs; more than 95 case studies were used. They constructed a proxy system to predict the incremental oil recovery based on the affecting parameters. The relationship between rock properties and incremental oil recovery were explained; the effect of permeability, porosity, total organic carbon content and fluid saturations on oil production was investigated. They mentioned that their findings could help to understand the complex recovery mechanisms during CO_2-EOR operations.

Based on an intensive literature review, significant deviations between the measured and predicted CO_2-MMP was observed. Analytical and empirical models can lead to considerable estimation errors. Artificial intelligence methods can improve the prediction performance for CO_2-MMP. However, the available AI models were developed based on the hydrocarbon's injection, not CO_2 flooding data, which may lead to unreliable predictions. The difference between hydrocarbons injection and CO_2-flooding is significant in terms of system disturbance and miscibility mechanisms [10,14,15]. Usually, hydrocarbons injection was implemented by injecting the same reservoir composition, while CO_2-flooding introduces new components into the reservoir system which results in disturbing the reservoir system. First contact miscibility (FCM) is usually associated with hydrocarbon injection while injecting non-hydrocarbon fluids (such as CO_2 and N_2) leads to multiple contact miscibility (MCM) [10,15]. Considerable errors could be generated when hydrocarbons injection models are used to predict the CO_2-flooding performance [34,35]. Therefore, looking for a reliable model to estimate the CO_2-MMP based on actual CO_2-flooding data is highly needed.

In this paper, a reliable approach is presented to determine the MMP during the CO_2 miscible flooding. Several artificial intelligence (AI) methods were studied, such as neural network, radial basis function, generalized neural network and fuzzy logic. The studied models investigate the significance of reservoir temperature, oil gravity, hydrocarbon composition and the injected-gas composition on the CO_2-MMP. More than 100 data sets belonging to actual CO_2-MMP experiments were used to develop and investigate the model reliability. This work introduces an effective approach for estimating the MMP during CO_2-flooding, which could be used to refine the current numerical or analytical models and result in a better determination of the CO_2-MMP.

2. Methodology

The data used were gathered from several published papers [7,10,14,15,36,37]. The minimum miscibility pressures (MMP) were measured using slim tube tests. The used dataset covers a wider range of reservoir conditions and hydrocarbon compositions; the main inputs are fluid composition, reservoir temperature and molecular weights. The dataset was randomly categorized into two divisions, training group (70% of the total data set) and testing group (30% of the total data). Before developing the AI models, statistical analysis was conducted by determining the minimum, maximum, mean, mode and other parameters, as listed in Table 1. The temperature data is changing in a range of 229 °F with a minimum value of 71 °F, maximum of 330 °F and arithmetic mean of 185.67 °F. The MMP values are changing between 1100 psia to 5000 psia with an arithmetic mean of 2583.49 psia. The statistical dispersion for MMP results was measured by calculating the standard deviation, skewness and kurtosis, and values of 876.98, 0.21 and 2.20 were obtained, respectively, which indicates that the data points are spread out over a wider range of values.

Table 1. A statistical analysis of the input and output data used in this study.

Parameter	Temperature, °F	Mole % of C_2–C_6	MW of C_{7+}	MMP, psia
Minimum	71.00	2.00	139.00	1100.00
Maximum	300.00	43.50	319.70	5000.00
Arithmetic Mean	185.67	22.06	204.85	2583.49
Range	229.00	41.50	180.70	3900.00
Variation	3630.62	73.64	1550.35	769,100.02
Standard deviation	60.25	8.58	39.37	876.98
Skewness	0.23	0.16	−0.11	0.21
Kurtosis	2.00	2.54	2.53	2.20
Coefficient of variation	32.45	38.90	19.22	33.95

In addition, the frequency histograms were obtained for all data to give a rough estimation for the distribution density. The data set showed a multimodal pattern as shown in Figure 1. Finally, the correlation coefficient was determined to measure the strength and direction of the linear relationship between the input data and MMP data, Figure 2. Values of 0.7481, −0.493 and 0.1626 were obtained for temperature, mole fractions, and molecular weight, respectively, which indicates a weak linear relationship for both the mole fractions and molecular weight. Histogram plots indicate that most of the data set can be represented by the multimodal pattern. The correlation coefficient analysis reveals that the MMP has a weak relationship with the molecular weight, moderate relationship with the mole fractions, and a strong relationship with the system temperature.

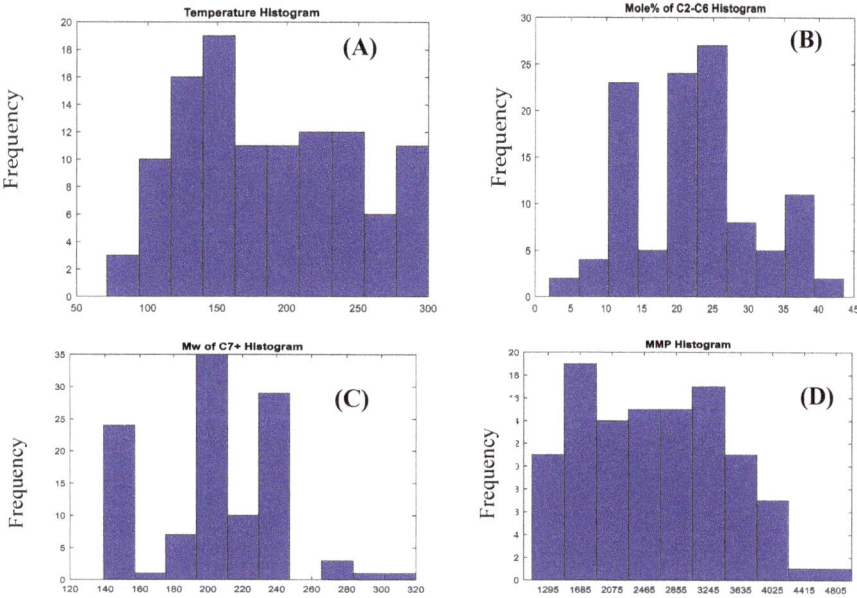

Figure 1. Histograms of input and output data. (**A**) Reservoir temperature, (**B**) Mole % of C2–C6, (**C**) MW of C_{7+} and (**D**) CO_2-MMP (MMP = minimum miscibility pressure).

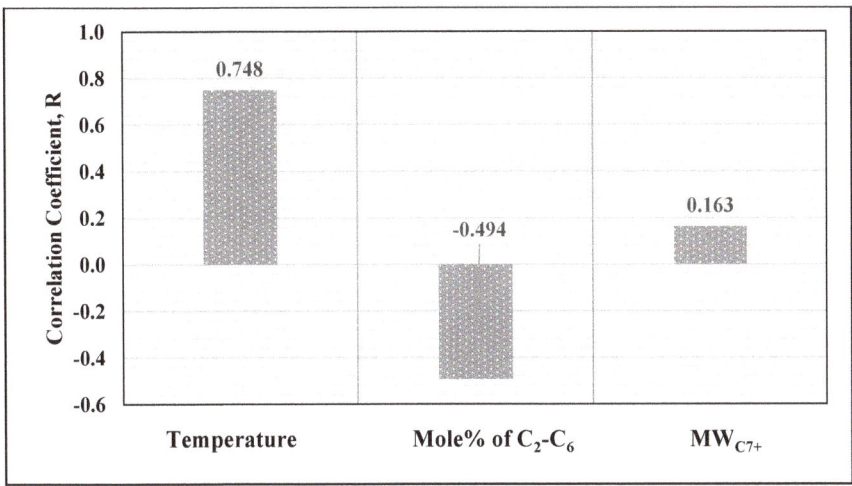

Figure 2. Correlation coefficient analysis: the effect of input parameters on CO_2-MMP.

The correlation coefficient analysis showed that the molecular weight of C_{7+} and the mole fractions of C_2–C_6 have a small effect on the MMP; however, those parameters are playing a significant role in controlling the MMP. Therefore, to improve these relationships the input data was transformed to different domains using different approaches (i.e., log, power, sigmoidal, etc.) until the best relationships, that have the highest correlation coefficient values, were obtained. Using the power model with power values of −1 and −0.5 for the molecular weight and the mole fraction, respectively, showed the best relationships between the input and output parameters (results are listed in Table 2).

Table 2. Correlation coefficient analysis for original and power transformed data.

Input Parameters	Correlation Coefficient	
	Original Data	Power Transformed
Temperature	0.7481	0.7481
C_2–C_6%	−0.4935	0.6682
MW_{C7+}	0.1626	0.4982

3. Results and Discussion

Different artificial intelligence methods were used to obtain the optimum model that has the lowest average absolute percentage error (AAPE) for both the training and testing data and has the maximum correlation coefficient (R) value. Appendix A illustrates the equations used to calculate the AAPE and R. Sensitivity analysis was performed to fine tune the model parameters; the most suitable models are reported in this paper.

Initially, the original data were used to predict the MMP; however, significant errors were observed for all AI models. For example, the ANN model gave an error of 41.39%, and fuzzy logic system showed an error of 26.14%. Therefore, data processing techniques were implemented, by filtering the data to remove the outlier based on the average values and standard deviation (SD). The input data were also transformed into another domain using a power model. Trial and error technique was used to determine the best combination for the input parameters. Mainly, the fluid composition was categized into two groups: the first group is the mole percentage of ethane to hexane (C_2 to C_6%) and the second group is the molecular weight of heptane plus (MW C_{7+}). Then, the square root of the first group (C_2 to C_6%) and the reciprocal of the second group (MW C_7) were used as input parameters. As results of that, the error was reduced significantly, for example, in the ANN model the error decreased from 41.392% to 9.682%. The results from the artificial intelligence techniques are discussed below. Moreover, the problem of local minima was avoided by running the AI models several times using different model parameters. The profile of the error for the training and the testing data sets were also monitored during the phase of model development and validation. The error profiles were used to avoid the model memorization and the local minima problems.

3.1. Artificial Neural Network

Figure 3 illustrates a schematic of the ANN model developed for estimating the CO_2-MMP. The model inputs are reservoir temperature (Temp.), the molecular weight of the heptane plus (MWC_{7+}) and the mole fraction of ethane to hexane (C_2–C_6%). The ANN model was trained using the seen data (training dataset), then the model becomes ready to determine the MMP for the testing data (unseen data). The model parameters were fine-tuned to minimize the AAPE and maximize the correlation coefficient. The ANN parameters were fine-tuned by changing the number of hidden layers and the number of neurons per each layer, and the best predictive models listed in Table 3. Three cases were reported, the number of hidden layers and neuron per each layer were varied to find the best ANN model. A minimum error of 7.22% and a relatively high correlation coefficient of 0.974 were obtained by using one hidden layer with 20 neurons. Figure 4 shows the predicted results against the actual values for training and testing data for visual validation.

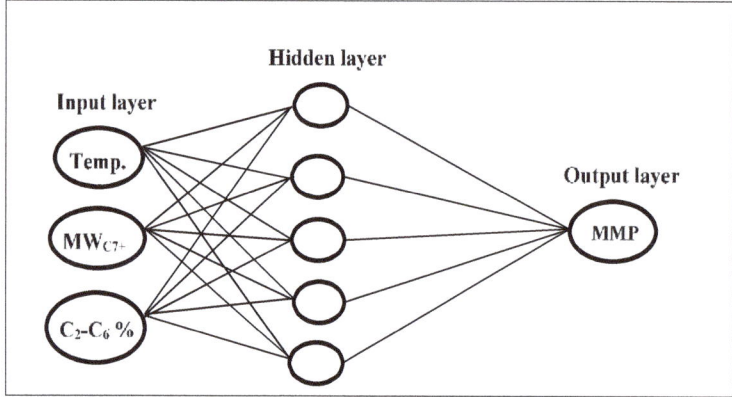

Figure 3. Artificial neural network (ANN) model architecture with input, hidden and output layers.

Table 3. Artificial neural network (ANN) for testing results.

No. of Hidden Layers	No. of Neurons in Each Layer	R	AAPE, %
1	20	0.95	7.61
2	20	0.94	10.42
3	20	0.93	12.45

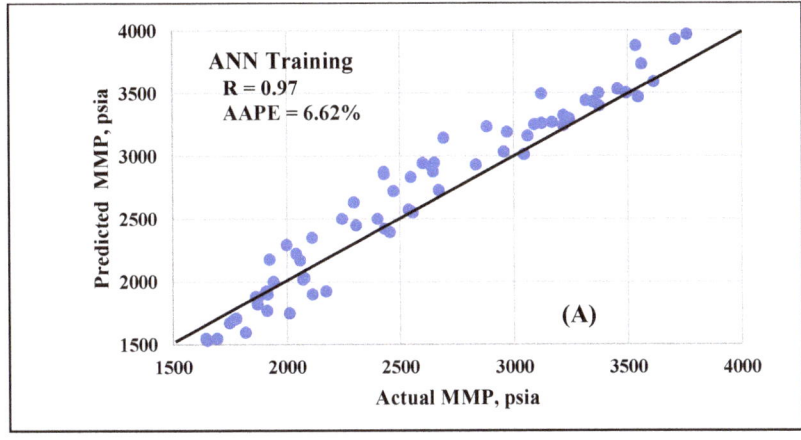
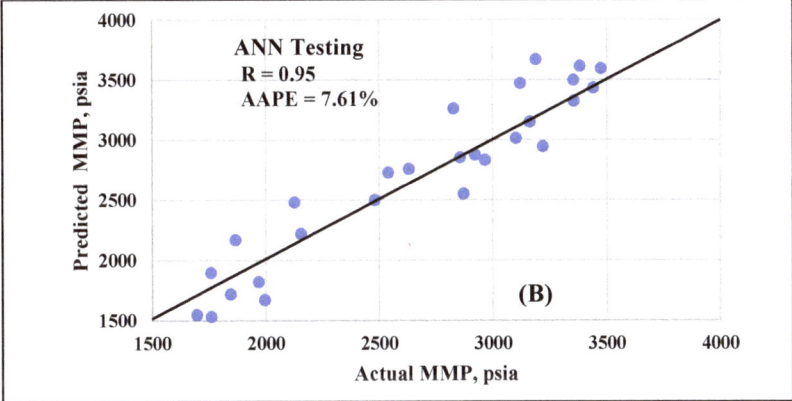

Figure 4. Cross plot of actual against predicted CO_2-MMP using the ANN model for (**A**) the training data set and (**B**) the testing data.

3.2. Fuzzy Logic System

Different cases were investigated to optimize the model parameters and achieve the best possible model, and the results are represented in Table 4 and Figure 5. Correlation coefficients (R) and absolute error (AAPE) for testing data were used to select the optimum model. Increasing the cluster radius led to better results, i.e., increase the R-values and decrease AAPE for the testing data. Increasing the number of iterations led to worse results that could be due to memorization, i.e., decreasing the R-values for testing data; 50 was selected as the optimum value for the iteration number. Case 7 has the lowest AAPE of 9.54%, and can be considered as the best possible model.

Table 4. Results of using the fuzzy logic system for testing results.

Case No.	Cluster Radius	Number of Iterations	R	AAPE, %
1	0.1	200	0.76	17.09
2	0.3	200	0.86	14.65
3	0.6	200	0.89	10.77
4	0.7	200	0.87	11.61
5	1	200	0.83	13.80
6	0.6	100	0.89	10.58
7	**0.6**	**50**	**0.89**	**9.86**
8	0.6	10	0.84	13.47

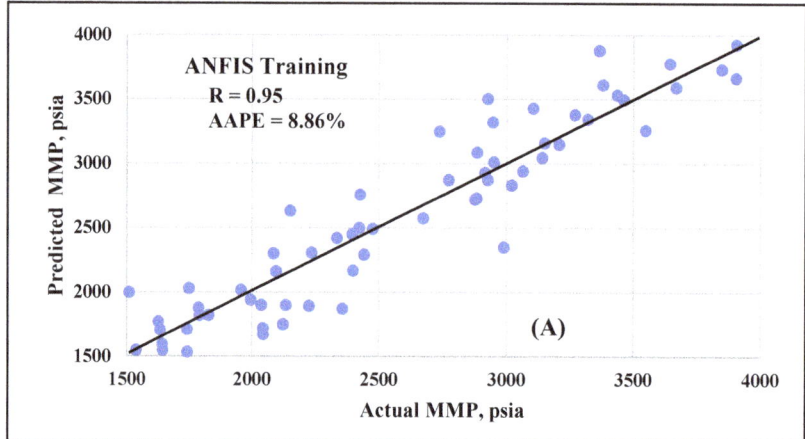

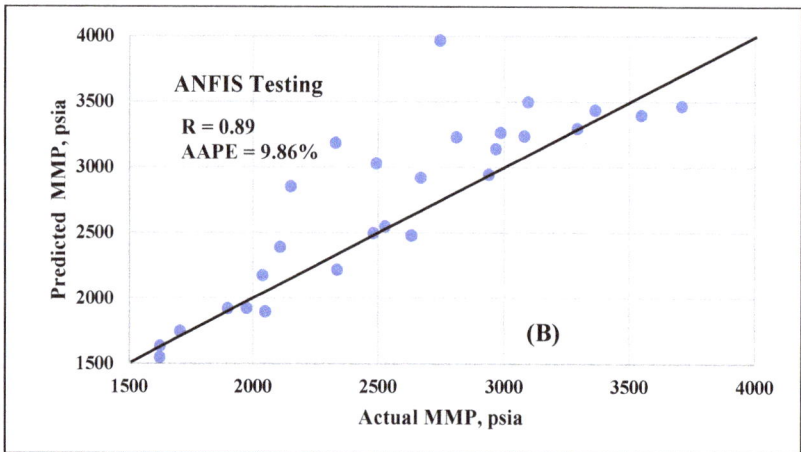

Figure 5. Cross plot of actual against predicted CO_2-MMP using the adaptive neuro-fuzzy inference system (ANFIS) model, for A) Training data set, B) Testing data.

3.3. Generalized Neural Network

A generalized neural network (GRNN) was used to determine the CO_2-MMP based on the reservoir temperature and the hydrocarbon composition. This network showed a good performance for predicting the minimum miscibility pressure. Table 5 and Figure 6 summarize the results obtained using the GRNN method. Several cases were investigated to optimize the model parameters. It was found that increasing the spread from 1 to 50 led to improving the R-value from 0.96 to 0.98. Different training functions were also tested, with "newgrnn" showing the highest performance among the others. The best GRNN model (Case 2) showed an error of 7.02% and R-value of 0.98.

Table 5. Generalized regression neural network (GRNN) results for the testing data.

Case No.	Training Function	Spread	R	AAPE, %
1	newgrnn	1	0.96	9.69
2	newgrnn	10	0.97	8.79
3	newgrnn	50	0.98	16.14
4	newrbe	1	0.97	18.07
5	newrbe	10	0.48	19.76

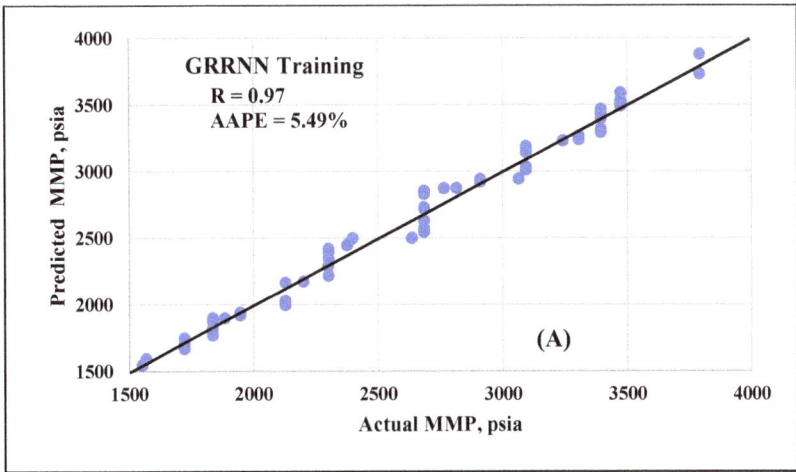

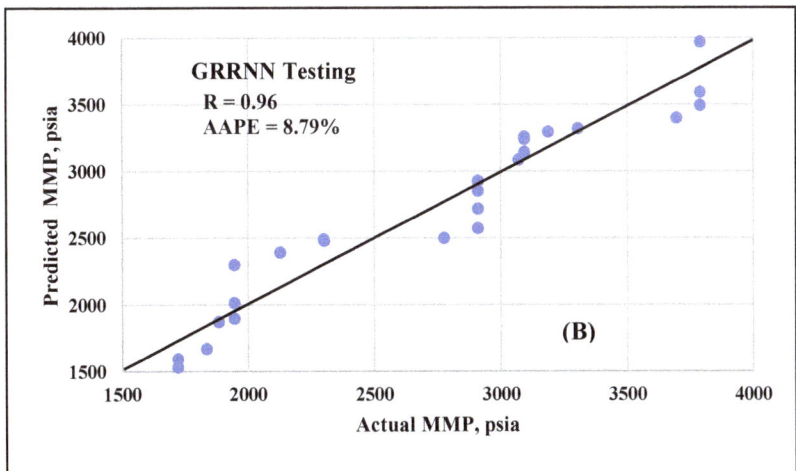

Figure 6. Cross plot of actual against predicted CO_2-MMP using the GRNN model for (A) the training data set and (B) testing data.

3.4. Radial Basis Function

Different model parameters (goal, spread, the maximum number of neurons and number of neurons) were studied to achieve the optimum values. Generally, increasing the goal values mean increasing the model tolerance, leading to increases in the AAPE and a decreased R-value; the same trend was observed for the spread. Table 6 summarizes the obtained results for 5 cases. For this data set, the goal showed a minor effect in obtaining a better solution, and the value of 0.5 is selected for the goal. Reducing the spread has a positive effect in improving the solution, spread of 10 is selected. Increasing the MN (maximum number of neurons) led to memorization and then reduced the R-value, and 20 MN is selected as an optimum value. The number of neurons to add between displays (DF) has a small effect in improving the model accuracy; a DF of 1 is selected. Based on the previous analysis, the optimum case could be obtained by using the goal of 0.5, the spread of 10, MN of 10 and DF of 1, the obtained R is 0.98 and the AAPE is 6.56% (Case 4); the obtained results are shown in Figure 7.

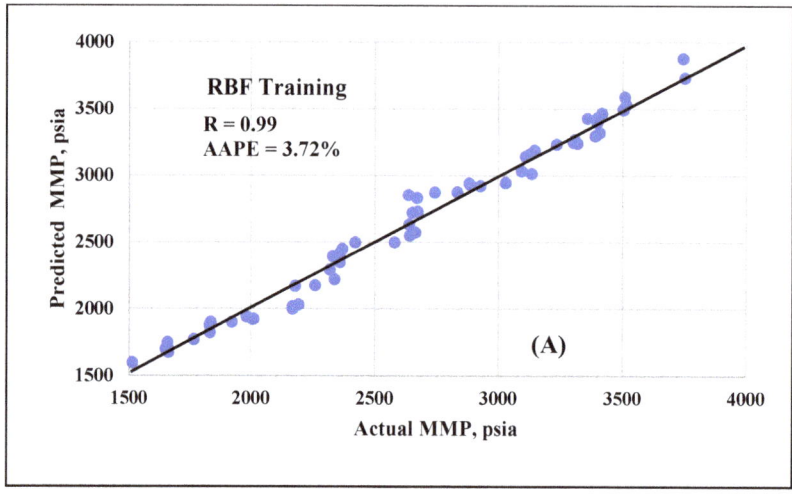

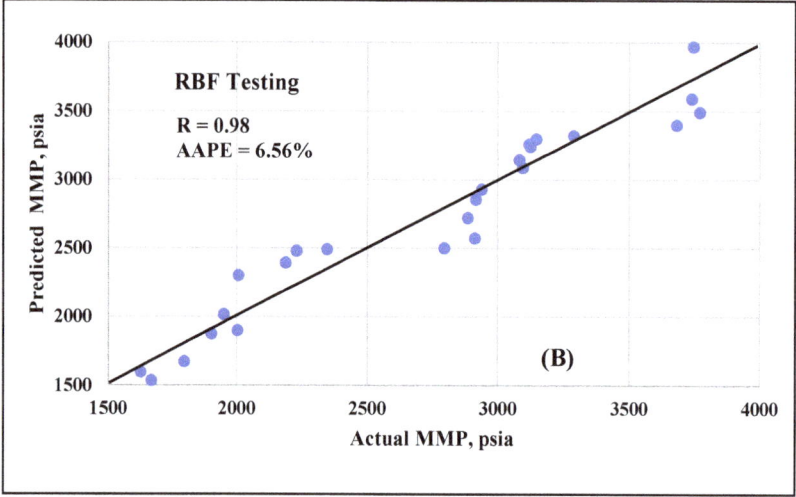

Figure 7. Cross plot of actual against predicted CO_2-MMP using the radial basis function (RBF) model for (**A**) the training data set and (**B**) testing data.

Table 6. Radial basis function network (RBF) results for unseen data.

Case No.	Goal	Spread	MN	DF	R	AAPE, %
1	0	100	10	1	0.96	8.98
2	0.5	100	10	1	0.96	8.98
3	1	100	10	1	0.96	8.98
4	0.5	10	20	1	0.98	6.56
5	0.5	100	20	1	0.95	9.84

3.5. Validation of the Developed Model

The radial basis network was utilized to extract an empirical correlation, the weights of the hidden layer (w_1) and the output layer (w_2) were used to derive the empirical equation, and the values are listed in Table 7. The proposed model to predict the CO_2-MMP is given by the following equations:

$$MMP = \left[\sum_{i=1}^{N} w_{2i} tansig\left(\sum_{j=1}^{J} w_{1i,j} x_j + b_{1i}\right)\right] + b_2, \quad (1)$$

$$MMP = \left[\sum_{i=1}^{N} w_{2i}\left(\frac{2}{1 + e^{-2(w_{1i,1}(x1)_j + w_{1i,2}(x2)_j + w_{1i,3}(x3)_j + b_{1i})}}\right)\right] + b_2. \quad (2)$$

Table 7. The developed RBF-based weights and biases for CO_2-MMP determinations for Equation (2).

No. of Neurons	Input Layer				Output Layer	
	Weights (W_1)			Biases (b_1)	Weights (W_2)	Bias (b_2)
	x_1	x_2	x_3			
i = 1	300	2.0145	4.6110	0.0023	1.191E+11	
i = 2	71	0.3679	2.1756	0.0023	−6.700E+08	
i = 3	88	0.3667	1.9069	0.0023	−3.196E+10	
i = 4	280	1.4368	3.7815	0.0023	7.492E+10	
i = 5	110	0.3873	1.5902	0.0023	−9.397E+09	
i = 6	250	0.8993	4.5083	0.0023	9.049E+11	−3,966,379.393
i = 7	260	1.3342	3.6439	0.0023	−5.683E+11	
i = 8	250	1.0348	4.9060	0.0023	−8.044E+11	
i = 9	90	0.4369	1.8974	0.0023	4.042E+10	
i = 10	300	1.5394	3.9142	0.0023	−4.105E+11	
i = 11	260	1.7459	4.2926	0.0023	4.109E+11	
i = 12	300	1.2435	3.4496	0.0023	2.750E+11	

Equation (2) is an empirical equation extracted from the optimized radial basis model; this equation can be used to estimate the MMP during CO_2 flooding. Similar equations were developed before based on the weights and biases for determining several parameters as reported by Elkatatny et al., Moussa et al., Mahmoud et al. and Rammay and Abdulraheem [23–25,38]. In Equations (1) and (2), N is the total neurons number, j is the input index, x1, x2, x3 are the reservoir temperature, the mole fraction of C_2 to C_6, and the molecular weight of heptane plus a fraction, respectively. The weights (w) and biases (b) are listed in Table 7. The developed model normalizes the input data automatically into a range between −1 and 1 based on the two-points method. Equations (3) and (4) are used to calculate the normalized values:

$$\frac{Y - Y_{min}}{Y_{max} - Y_{min}} = \frac{X - X_{min}}{X_{max} - X_{min}}, \quad (3)$$

$$Y = Y_{min} + (Y_{max} - Y_{min})\left(\frac{X - X_{min}}{X_{max} - X_{min}}\right). \quad (4)$$

Furthermore, a comparison study was performed between the different MMP determination approaches. CO_2-MMP was determined using the Glaso [8] empirical correlation, the Yuan et al. [15] analytical method and the developed AI model. Figure 8 and Table 8 summarize the obtained CO_2-MMP. The absolute error and correlation coefficient were used to select the best determination approach. Yuan et al.'s [15] analytical equation showed the highest error (16.7%) and the lowest correlation coefficient (0.60) among all approaches. Absolute error of 16.4% and correlation coefficient of 0.67 were obtained using the Glaso [8] empirical correlation, which indicates that those equations (Yuan et al. and Glaso 1985) were developed based on limited experimental results and several assumptions were applied. The AI model of radial basis function showed the best prediction performance, the absolute error and the correlation coefficients are 6.6% and 0.98 respectively. Based on this study, the recommended approach for predicting the CO_2-MMP is an AI model with a radial basis function.

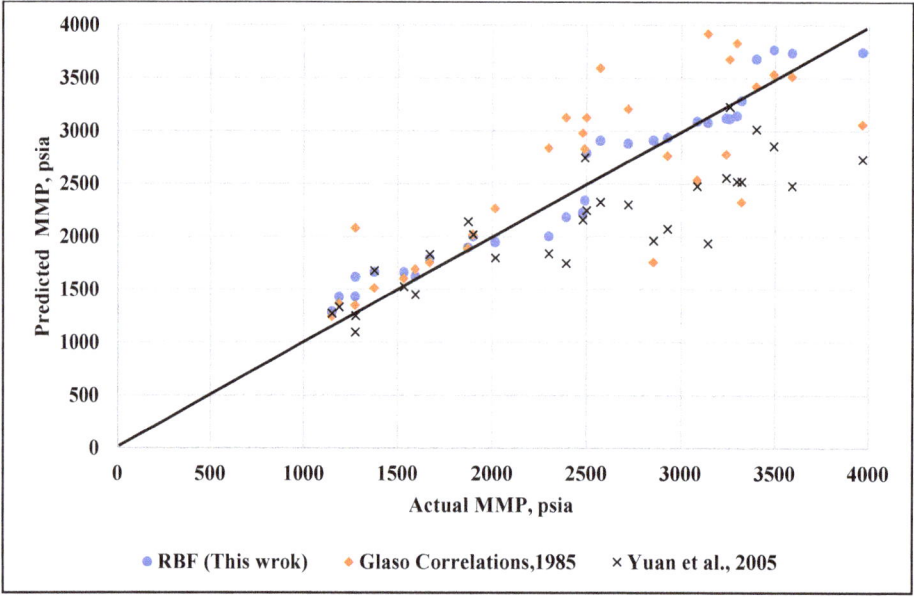

Figure 8. Comparison between different CO_2-MMP determination approaches; numerical, analytical and the developed RBF model.

Table 8. Determination of CO_2-MMP using different approaches.

Determination Approach	R	AAPE, %
Correlation	0.67	16.4
Analytical	0.60	16.7
RBF model (this work)	0.98	6.6

In addition, real case studies for the flooding of hydrocarbon reservoirs with carbon dioxide were used. The data were collected from Kanatbayev et al. and Alomair et al. [39,40]. The CO_2 minimum miscibility pressure was determined using the developed AI model, numerical simulation and regression techniques. Numerical approach (in Eclipse 300) was utilized to determine the CO_2-MMP, the reservoir system was segmented into 2000 grid blocks, and the numerical dispersion was corrected using the infinite cell solution [39]. Alternating conditional expectation (ACE) regression algorithm was used to predict the CO_2-MMP, the regression algorithm was proposed by Alomair et al., 2015 [40]. The predicted MMP values were compared with the actual values that were measured using slim tube tests. The actual minimum miscibility pressures and the predicted values were calculated by different methods and, in addition to the error values, are listed in Table 9. Average absolute error of 10.2% was obtained using the regression approach, and errors between 8.7% to 17.3% were obtained using the numerical approach (Eclipse 300). The developed AI model in this study showed an acceptable prediction performance, with the absolute error varying between 6.4% to 9%.

Table 9. Actual and predicted values of the minimum miscibility pressures.

Case Number	Actual MMP, Psi	Regression Approach		Numerical Approach		The Developed AI Model	
		MMP, Psi	Error, %	MMP, psi	Error, %	MMP, psi	Error, %
1	3974.0	3319.3	16.5	3556.9	10.5	4264.7	7.3
2	2407.6	2203.3	8.5	2010.8	16.5	2605.9	8.2
3	4728.2	3810.6	19.4	3909.4	17.3	5138.6	8.7
4	4351.1	3531.1	18.8	3752.1	13.8	4674.5	7.4
5	4380.1	4122.3	5.9	4993.4	14.0	4720.8	7.8
6	2860.1	2637.4	7.8	3342.5	16.9	3064.2	7.1
7	4677.5	4519.6	3.4	5485.6	17.3	5077.0	8.5
8	4890.7	4730.3	3.3	4083.3	16.5	5311.8	8.6
9	4496.2	3619.5	19.5	5126.8	14.0	4892.1	8.8
10	4278.6	3682.6	13.9	4995.9	16.8	4553.8	6.4
11	4496.2	3763.0	16.3	5193.4	15.5	4903.0	9.0
12	4322.1	3926.4	9.2	4989.6	15.4	4662.8	7.9
13	4119.1	3788.7	8.0	3737.0	9.3	4457.5	8.2
14	4612.2	3771.1	18.2	5141.2	11.5	4953.3	7.4
15	4554.2	4511.1	0.9	5117.8	12.4	4865.6	6.8
16	4844.3	3973.1	18.0	4190.9	13.5	5221.1	7.8
17	4960.3	4866.0	1.9	4465.9	10.0	5338.9	7.6
18	4568.7	4468.9	2.2	5003.9	9.5	4891.7	7.1
19	2523.7	2477.1	1.8	2875.9	14.0	2734.2	8.3
20	3190.8	2847.2	10.8	2912.6	8.7	3397.2	6.5

4. Conclusions

This paper presents an intelligent model for determining the minimum miscibility pressure (MMP) during CO_2 flooding. Artificial intelligence (AI) techniques were used to build a new MMP model. A neural network, radial basis function, generalized network and fuzzy logic system were used. The best predictive model was selected based on the absolute error and the correlation coefficient for the testing data set. Based on this work, the following points can be drawn:

- The proposed AI models are quick, rigorous and outperforms the current CO_2-MMP methods. The developed models can minimize the time and cost of determining the CO_2-MMP.
- The developed models investigate the effect of hydrocarbon component and the injected gas composition on the MMP during CO_2-flooding.
- A new equation was extracted using the optimized radial basis function, the developed equation showed a good performance for determining the CO_2-MMP, and the absolute error is 6.6% and the correlation coefficient is 0.98.
- Ultimately, this work will improve the design of CO_2 flooding operations by providing a reliable value for the CO_2-MMP.

Author Contributions: Conceptualization, A.H., S.E and A.A.; methodology, A.H. and S.E.; software, A.H.; validation, A.H. and S.E.; formal analysis, A.H.; data curation, A.H. and S.E; writing—original draft preparation, A.H.; writing—review and editing, S.E.; visualization, A.H., A.A. and S.E.; supervision, A.A., and S.E.

Funding: This research received no external funding.

Acknowledgments: The authors wish to acknowledge King Fahd University of Petroleum and Minerals (KFUPM) for utilizing the various facilities in carrying out this research.

Conflicts of Interest: The authors declare no conflict of interest.

Appendix A. Mathematical Formulas

This appendix presents the formulas used in this study for the error calculation, Glaso [8] empirical correlation and Yuan et al. [15] analytical equation.

Average Absolute Percentage Error (AAPE):

$$AAPE = \frac{100}{N} \sum_{i=1}^{N} \left| \frac{(MMP_m)_i - (MMP_a)_i}{(MMP_a)_i} \right|. \tag{A1}$$

Coefficient of Determination:

$$R^2 = \frac{\sum_{i=1}^{N} \left[\left((MMP_a)_i - \overline{MMP_a} \right) - \left((MMP_m)_i - \overline{MMP_m} \right) \right]}{\sqrt{\sum_{i=1}^{N} \left[(MMP_a)_i - \overline{MMP_a} \right]^2 \sum_{i=1}^{N} \left[(MMP_m)_i - \overline{MMP_m} \right]^2}}, \tag{A2}$$

where, N = Total number of samples, MMP_m = Estimated MMP, MMP_a = Actual MMP, $\overline{MMP_m}$ = Average estimated MMP, $\overline{MMP_a}$ = Average actual MMP.

Yuan et al. [15] analytical equation:

$$MMP = a_1 + a_2 M_{C7+} + a_3 P_{C2-6} + \left(a_4 + a_5 M_{C7+} + \frac{a_6 P_{C2-6}}{M_{C7+}} \right) T + \left(a_7 + a_8 M_{C7+} + a_9 M_{C7+}^2 + a_{10} P_{C2-6} \right) T^2 \tag{A3}$$

where MMP is the predicted minimum miscibility pressure for CO_2 injection, M_{C7+} is the molecular weight of C_{7+}, P_{C2-6} is the percentage of C_2 to C_6 and a_1 to a_{10} are fitting coefficients.

$$a_1 = -1463.4, a_2 = 6.612, a_3 = -44.979, a_4 = 2.139, a_5 = 0.11667, a_6 = 8166.1,$$
$$a_7 = -0.12258, a_8 = 0.0012283, a_9 = -4.0152\text{E-}6, \text{ and } a_{10} = -9.2577\text{E-}4. \tag{A4}$$

The Glaso [8] empirical correlation is given by:

For $C_{2-6} > 18\%$,

$$MMP = 810 - 3.404 M_{C7+} + 1.700 * 10^{-9} M_{C7+}^{3.730} e^{786.8 M_{C7+}^{-1.058}} T; \tag{A5}$$

For $C_{2-6} < 18\%$,

$$MMP = 2947.9 - 3.404 M_{C7+} + 1.700 * 10^{-9} M_{C7+}^{3.730} e^{786.8 M_{C7+}^{-1.058}} T - 121.2\, C_{2-6}, \tag{A6}$$

where MMP is the estimated minimum miscibility pressure in psia, C_{2-6} is the mole fraction of C_2 to C_6 and MW_{C7+} is the molecular weight of heptane plus fraction.

References

1. Cronquist, C. Carbon dioxide dynamic displacement with light reservoir oils. In Proceedings of the Fourth Annual US DOE Symposium, Tulsa, OK, USA, 28 August 1978; pp. 18–23.
2. Yellig, W.F.; Metcalfe, R.S. Determination and Prediction of CO_2 Minimum Miscibility Pressures (includes associated paper 8876). *J. Pet. Technol.* **1980**, *32*, 160–168. [CrossRef]
3. Shi, Q.; Jing, L.; Qiao, W. Solubility of n-alkanes in supercritical CO_2 at diverse temperature and pressure. *J. CO_2 Util.* **2015**, *9*, 29–38. [CrossRef]
4. Holm, L.W.; Josendal, V.A. Effect of oil composition on miscible-type displacement by carbon dioxide. *Soc. Pet. Eng. J.* **1982**, *22*, 87–98. [CrossRef]
5. Czarnota, R.; Janiga, D.; Stopa, J.; Wojnarowski, P. Determination of minimum miscibility pressure for CO_2 and oil system using acoustically monitored separator. *J. CO_2 Util.* **2017**, *17*, 32–36. [CrossRef]
6. Sebastian, H.M.; Wenger, R.S.; Renner, T.A. Correlation of minimum miscibility pressure for impure CO_2 streams. *J. Pet. Technol.* **1985**, *37*, 2–076. [CrossRef]

7. Alston, R.B.; Kokolis, G.P.; James, C.F. CO_2 minimum miscibility pressure: A correlation for impure CO_2 streams and live oil systems. *Soc. Pet. Eng. J.* **1985**, *25*, 268–274. [CrossRef]
8. Glaso, O. Generalized minimum miscibility pressure correlation. *SPE J.* **1985**, *25*, 927–934.
9. Khazam, M.; Arebi, T.; Mahmoudi, T.; Froja, M. A new simple CO_2 minimum miscibility pressure correlation. *Oil Gas Res.* **2016**, *2*. [CrossRef]
10. Yuan, H.; Johns, R.T.; Egwuenu, A.M.; Dindoruk, B. Improved MMP correlation for CO_2 floods using analytical theory. *SPE Reserv. Eval. Eng.* **2005**, *8*, 418–425. [CrossRef]
11. Johns, R.T.; Dindoruk, B.; Orr, F.M., Jr. Analytical theory of combined condensing/vaporizing gas drives. *SPE Adv. Technol. Ser.* **1993**, *1*, 7–16. [CrossRef]
12. Dindoruk, B.; Orr, F.M., Jr.; Johns, R.T. Theory of multi-contact miscible displacement with nitrogen. *SPE J.* **1997**, *2*, 268–279. [CrossRef]
13. Jessen, K.; Michelsen, M.L.; Stenby, E.H. Global approach for calculation of minimum miscibility pressure. *Fluid Phase Equilibria* **1998**, *153*, 251–263. [CrossRef]
14. Yuan, H. Application of Miscibility Calculation to Gas Floods. Ph.D. Thesis, The University of Texas at Austin, Austin, TX, USA, 2003.
15. Yuan, H.; Johns, R.T.; Egwuenu, A.M.; Dindoruk, B. Improved MMP correlations for CO_2 floods using analytical gas flooding theory. Presented at the 2004 SPE Symposium on Improved Oil Recovery, Tulsa, OK, USA, 17–21 April 2004. SPE 89359.
16. Venkatraman, V.; Alsberg, B.K. Predicting CO_2 capture of ionic liquids using machine learning. *J. CO_2 Util.* **2017**, *21*, 162–168. [CrossRef]
17. Sargolzaei, J.; Saghatoleslami, N.; Mosavi, S.M.; Khoshnoodi, M. Comparative Study of Artificial Neural Networks (ANN) and statistical methods for predicting the performance of Ultrafiltration Process in the Milk Industry. *Iran. J. Chem. Eng.* **2006**, *25*, 67–76.
18. Sedghamiz, M.A.; Rasoolzadeh, A.; Rahimpour, M.R. The ability of artificial neural network in prediction of the acid gases solubility in different ionic liquids. *J. CO_2 Util.* **2015**, *9*, 39–47. [CrossRef]
19. Al-Shehri, D.A. Oil and Gas Wells: Enhanced Wellbore Casing Integrity Management through Corrosion Rate Prediction Using an Augmented Intelligent Approach. *Sustainability* **2019**, *11*, 818. [CrossRef]
20. Mahmoud, A.A.; Elkatatny, S.; Ali, A.; Moussa, T. Estimation of Static Young's Modulus for Sandstone Formation Using Artificial Neural Networks. *Energies* **2019**, *12*, 2125. [CrossRef]
21. Elkatatny, S. Real-time prediction of rheological parameters of KCL water-based drilling fluid using artificial neural networks. *Arab. J. Sci. Eng.* **2017**, *42*, 1655–1665. [CrossRef]
22. Elkatatny, S.; Mahmoud, M.; Tariq, Z.; Abdulraheem, A. New insights into the prediction of heterogeneous carbonate reservoir permeability from well logs using artificial intelligence network. *Neural Comput. Appl.* **2018**, *30*, 2673–2683. [CrossRef]
23. Elkatatny, S.; Tariq, Z.; Mahmoud, M. Real time prediction of drilling fluid rheological properties using Artificial Neural Networks visible mathematical model (white box). *J. Pet. Sci. Eng.* **2016**, *146*, 1202–1210. [CrossRef]
24. Moussa, T.; Elkatatny, S.; Mahmoud, M.; Abdulraheem, A. Development of new permeability formulation from well log data using artificial intelligence approaches. *J. Energy Resour. Technol.* **2018**, *140*, 072903. [CrossRef]
25. Mahmoud, A.A.; Elkatatny, S.; Mahmoud, M.; Abouelresh, M.; Abdulraheem, A.; Ali, A. Determination of the total organic carbon (TOC) based on conventional well logs using artificial neural network. *Int. J. Coal Geol.* **2017**, *179*, 72–80. [CrossRef]
26. Ali, H.; Choi, J.H. A Review of Underground Pipeline Leakage and Sinkhole Monitoring Methods Based on Wireless Sensor Networking. *Sustainability* **2019**, *11*, 4007. [CrossRef]
27. Amirian, E.; Leung, J.Y.; Zanon, S.; Dzurman, P. Integrated cluster analysis and artificial neural network modeling for steam-assisted gravity drainage performance prediction in heterogeneous reservoirs. *Expert Syst. Appl.* **2015**, *42*, 723–740. [CrossRef]
28. Amirian, E.; Fedutenko, E.; Yang, C.; Chen, Z.; Nghiem, L. Artificial Neural Network Modeling and Forecasting of Oil Reservoir Performance. In *Applications of Data Management and Analysis*; Springer: Cham, Switzerland, 2018; pp. 43–67.
29. Malo, S.; McNamara, J.; Volkmer, N.; Amirian, E. Eagle Ford—Introducing the Big Bad Wolf. Presented at the Unconventional Resources Technology Conference, Denver, CO, USA, 22–24 July 2019; pp. 4733–4743.

30. Edalat, M.; Dinarvand, N.; Shariatpanahi, S.F. Development of a new artificial neural network model for predicting minimum miscibility pressure in hydrocarbon gas injection. Presented at the 15th SPE Middle East Oil & Gas Show and Conference, Bahrain International Exhibition Centre, Manama, Bahrain, 11–14 March 2007; SPE 105407.
31. Dehghani, S.M.; Sefti, M.V.; Ameri, A.; Kaveh, N.S. Minimum miscibility pressure prediction based on a hybrid neural genetic algorithm. *Chem. Eng. Res. Des.* **2008**, *86*, 173–185. [CrossRef]
32. Shokrollahi, A.; Arabloo, M.; Gharagheizi, F.; Mohammadi, A.H. Intelligent model for prediction of CO_2–reservoir oil minimum miscibility pressure. *Fuel* **2013**, *112*, 375–384. [CrossRef]
33. Liu, Y.; Jiang, L.; Song, Y.; Zhao, Y.; Zhang, Y.; Wang, D. Estimation of minimum miscibility pressure (MMP) of CO_2 and liquid n-alkane systems using an improved MRI technique. *Magn. Reson. Imaging* **2016**, *34*, 97–104. [CrossRef]
34. Rostami, A.; Arabloo, M.; Lee, M.; Bahadori, A. Applying SVM framework for modeling of CO_2 solubility in oil during CO_2 flooding. *Fuel* **2018**, *214*, 73–87. [CrossRef]
35. Alfarge, D.; Wei, M.; Bai, B. Data analysis for CO_2-EOR in shale-oil reservoirs based on a laboratory database. *J. Pet. Sci. Eng.* **2018**, *162*, 697–711. [CrossRef]
36. Rathmell, J.J.; Stalkup, F.I.; Hassinger, R.C. A laboratory investigation of miscible displacement by carbon dioxide. Presented at the Fall Meeting of the Society of Petroleum Engineers of AIME, New Orleans, LA, USA, 3–6 October 1971. SPE 3483.
37. Shokir, E.M. CO_2–oil minimum miscibility pressure model for impure and pure CO_2 streams. *J. Pet. Sci. Eng.* **2007**, *58*, 173–185. [CrossRef]
38. Rammay, M.H.; Abdulraheem, A. PVT correlations for Pakistani crude oils using artificial neural network. *J. Pet. Explor. Prod. Technol.* **2017**, *7*, 217–233. [CrossRef]
39. Kanatbayev, M.; Meisingset, K.K.; Uleberg, K. Comparison of MMP estimation methods with proposed workflow. Presented at the SPE Bergen One Day Seminar, Bergen, Norway, 22 April 2015; SPE 173827.
40. Alomair, O.; Malallah, A.; Elsharkawy, A.; Iqbal, M. Predicting CO_2 minimum miscibility pressure (MMP) using alternating conditional expectation (ACE) algorithm. *Oil Gas Sci. Technol. Rev. d'IFP Energ. Nouv.* **2015**, *70*, 967–982. [CrossRef]

© 2019 by the authors. Licensee MDPI, Basel, Switzerland. This article is an open access article distributed under the terms and conditions of the Creative Commons Attribution (CC BY) license (http://creativecommons.org/licenses/by/4.0/).

Article

Evaluation of the Total Organic Carbon (TOC) Using Different Artificial Intelligence Techniques

Ahmed Abdulhamid Mahmoud [1], Salaheldin Elkatatny [1,*], Abdulwahab Z. Ali [2], Mohamed Abouelresh [3] and Abdulazeez Abdulraheem [1]

[1] College of Petroleum Engineering and Geosciences, King Fahd University of Petroleum & Minerals, Dhahran 31261, Saudi Arabia; eng.ahmedmahmoud06@gmail.com (A.A.M.); aazeez@kfupm.edu.sa (A.A.)
[2] Center of Integrative Petroleum Research, King Fahd University of Petroleum & Minerals, Dhahran 31261, Saudi Arabia; awali@kfupm.edu.sa
[3] Center of Environment and Water, King Fahd University of Petroleum & Minerals, Dhahran 31261, Saudi Arabia; abouelresh@kfupm.edu.sa
* Correspondence: elkatatny@kfupm.edu.sa; Tel.: +966-594663692

Received: 16 September 2019; Accepted: 11 October 2019; Published: 13 October 2019

Abstract: Total organic carbon (TOC) is an essential parameter used in unconventional shale resources evaluation. Current methods that are used for TOC estimation are based, either on conducting time-consuming laboratory experiments, or on using empirical correlations developed for specific formations. In this study, four artificial intelligence (AI) models were developed to estimate the TOC using conventional well logs of deep resistivity, gamma-ray, sonic transit time, and bulk density. These models were developed based on the Takagi-Sugeno-Kang fuzzy interference system (TSK-FIS), Mamdani fuzzy interference system (M-FIS), functional neural network (FNN), and support vector machine (SVM). Over 800 data points of the conventional well logs and core data collected from Barnett shale were used to train and test the AI models. The optimized AI models were validated using unseen data from Devonian shale. The developed AI models showed accurate predictability of TOC in both Barnett and Devonian shale. FNN model overperformed others in estimating TOC for the validation data with average absolute percentage error (AAPE) and correlation coefficient (R) of 12.02%, and 0.879, respectively, followed by M-FIS and SVM, while TSK-FIS model showed the lowest predictability of TOC, with AAPE of 15.62% and R of 0.832. All AI models overperformed Wang models, which have recently developed to evaluate the TOC for Devonian formation.

Keywords: total organic carbon; artificial intelligence; barnett shale; devonian shale

1. Introduction

Recently, due to the advances in horizontal drilling and multi-stage fracturing, the possibility of producing hydrocarbon from unconventional hydrocarbon resources, such as shale oil and shale gas is significantly increased. The total organic carbon (TOC) is an essential parameter for unconventional shale resource characterization and evaluation. It expresses the amount of organic carbon present in the formation, thus, indicates the hydrocarbon reserve in these unconventional resources [1,2].

TOC is dependent on many factors, such as gas adsorption, maturity, and carbon content because these factors affect the reservoir organic porosity [2–4]. TOC is also significantly affected by the pore structure and wettability of the shale [2,5,6]. Thus, reserve prediction of unconventional reservoirs needs an accurate method to predict the TOC [5,6].

Currently, several empirical correlations, which were developed based on different assumptions, are used to evaluate the TOC for specific formation types, based on the available well logs. Schmoker [7] developed the first correlation for TOC prediction based on the formation bulk density (RHOB).

His correlation in Equation (1) is developed initially for Devonian shale, this correlation estimates the TOC as volume percentage, which could then be converted to weight percentage as explained in Schmoker [7],

$$TOC(vol.\%) = \frac{(\rho_B - \rho)}{1.378} \tag{1}$$

where ρ_B and ρ denote the organic matter free rock density and the rock bulk density both in g/cm³.

Schmoker [8] revised his first model to be applicable for Bakken shale formation and he came up with the revised model in Equation (2),

$$TOC(wt.\%) = \frac{[(100\rho_o) - (\rho - 0.9922\rho_{mi} - 0.039)]}{[(R\rho)(\rho_o - 1.135\rho_{mi} - 0.675)]} \tag{2}$$

where ρ_o denotes the density of the organic matter in g/cm³, R is the ratio of the organic matter to organic carbon as the weight percentage, ρ_{mi} denotes the grain and pore fluid average density in g/cm³.

Passey et al. [9] developed a simple model for TOC prediction, based on the deep resistivity (DR) and sonic transit time (DT) logs, this model is named $\Delta logR$ model, which is summarized in Equations (3) and (4). $\Delta logR$ model is currently widely used for evaluating the unconventional resources reserve,

$$\Delta logR = log_{10}\left(\frac{R}{R_{baseline}}\right) + 0.02 \times (\Delta t - \Delta t_{baseline}) \tag{3}$$

$$\Delta logR = log_{10}\left(\frac{R}{R_{baseline}}\right) + 0.02 \times (\Delta t - \Delta t_{baseline}) \tag{4}$$

where $\Delta logR$ is the logs separation, R and $R_{baseline}$ denote the evaluated formation and the base formation resistivity in ohm.m, Δt and $\Delta t_{baseline}$ represent the evaluated formation and base formation sonic transit times both in µs/ft, and LOM is the level of maturity.

The Schmoker and $\Delta logR$ models were evaluated by Charsky and Herron [10] into various formations in four different wells. The authors found that these models are not accurate, where TOC is predicted with an average absolute difference (ADD) of 1.6 wt%, forming the core derived TOC for Schmoker model and 1.7 wt% for $\Delta logR$ method.

The most recent and current studies focus on estimating the TOC by improving the accuracy of $\Delta logR$ model [11–13] or by applying machine learning techniques [14–16].

Wang et al. [12] revised the $\Delta logR$ models and developed new empirical correlations for TOC estimation in Devonian shale formation as a function of the DR, DT, RHOB, and gamma-ray (GR). In their models, Wang et al. [12] suggested to include GR log to enhance TOC estimation, and they used more common thermal indicators such as vitrinite reflectance (R_o) or T_{max} instead of LOM, which simplify the use of Wang et al. [12] models, since the conversion between (T_{max} or R_o) and LOM is not required. Therefore, it reduces the practical problems [17]. Equations (5) and (6) are the revised $\Delta logR$ models based on sonic and density logs, respectively. Equation (7) could be used to estimate the TOC using $\Delta logR$ and gamma-ray log:

$$\Delta logR = log_{10}\left(\frac{R}{R_{baseline}}\right) + \frac{1}{\ln 10}\frac{m}{(\Delta t - \Delta t_m)} \times (\Delta t - \Delta t_{baseline}) \tag{5}$$

$$\Delta logR = log_{10}\left(\frac{R}{R_{baseline}}\right) + \frac{1}{\ln 10}\frac{m}{(\rho_m - \rho)} \times (\rho - \rho_{baseline}) \tag{6}$$

$$TOC = [\alpha \Delta logR + \beta(GR - GR_{baseline})] \times 10^{(\delta - \eta T_{max})}. \tag{7}$$

where Δt_m denotes the matrix sonic transit time (µs/ft), m represents the cementation exponent, ρ_m and $\rho_{baseline}$ are the matrix and baseline densities (g/cm³), where the baseline density corresponds to $R_{baseline}$

value, α, β, δ and η are the matrix constants, which are different for different formations and must be determined, T_{max} is the maturity indicator (°C), $GR_{baseline}$ is the baseline value of shale (API).

Applying the revised $\Delta logR$ models into the Devonian shale formation showed an improvement in TOC evaluation with a coefficient of determination (R^2) of more than 0.92 compared with R^2 of 0.82 when the original $\Delta logR$ model is used.

Applying any of the previously discussed correlations to evaluate TOC in formations different than the one developed leads to inaccurate predictions. Recently, Mahmoud et al. [18,19] suggested an artificial neural network (ANN)-based correlation for TOC estimation in Barnett formation using conventional well logs. Later on, Elkatatny [20] applied the self-adaptive differential evolution algorithm to optimize Mahmoud et al.'s [18,19] ANN model and he was able to improve the model predictability.

In this study, four artificial intelligence (AI) models were developed to estimate TOC based on the application of the Takagi-Sugeno-Kang fuzzy interference system (TSK-FIS), Mamdani fuzzy interference system (M-FIS), functional neural network (FNN), and support vector machine (SVM). These models use conventional well logs of DR, GR, DT, and RHOB, collected from the Barnett shale formation.

Different Applications of Artificial Intelligence Techniques

Since the early 1990s, AI techniques had been extensively applied in many scientific and engineering fields, including in the petroleum industry. Nowadays, AI has been used by petroleum engineers and geologists to solve problems related to unconventional hydrocarbon resources evaluation [18–20], reservoir characterization [21,22], bubble point pressure evaluation [23], prediction of real-time change in the rheological parameters of the drilling fluids [24,25], optimization of rate of penetration [26], estimation of rock mechanical parameters [27,28], prediction of pore pressure and fracture pressure [29,30], evaluation of the wellbore casing integrity [31,32], hydrocarbon recovery factor estimation [33,34] optimization of the drilling hydraulics [35], and others. AI techniques have also been applied successfully in other fields like social media [36,37].

2. Methodology

2.1. Experimental Testing Using Rock-Eval 6

The core samples collected from Barnett shale (Fort Worth Basin (FWB), North Texas, USA) and Devonian Duvernay shale (Western Canada Sedimentary Basin (WCSB)) were analyzed for TOC estimation. The collected samples were crushed to less than 63 μm, the weight percentage of the pyrolyzable carbon and pyrolyzable mineral-carbon in every sample were first determined by thermally decomposing the sample using the pyrolysis oven. During pyrolysis, the temperature was kept constant at 300°C for three minutes then increased by 25 °C/min to reach 650 °C, the flame ionization detector and infrared cells are used to simultaneously detect the hydrocarbons, CO_2, and CO. After that, the weight percentages of the residual carbon and oxidized mineral-carbon in every sample were determined by burning them in the oxidation oven at 300 °C for 30 seconds, then increasing the temperature up to 850 °C at a rate of 25 °C/min, and finally keeping the temperature at 850 °C for five minutes. More details about sample preparation procedures and considerations for TOC measurement by Rock-Eval 6 were reported by different authors [38–40].

2.2. Proposed Methodology

In this study, conventional well logs of DR, GR, DT, and RHOB, collected from Barnett shale, are used to train TSK-FIS, M-FIS, FNN, and SVM models to predict the corresponding laboratory-measured TOC. These AI models were used in this study to estimate the TOC because of their already proven high accuracy in evaluating petroleum- and geology-related parameters. A total of 838 data points of core and log data were collected from Barnett shale. Figure 1 shows the log data collected from Barnett shale which is used to develop the models. Different combinations of the design parameters of the AI models were optimized using inserted for loops built-in Matlab. The optimization process of the AI models was continued until the minimum average absolute percentage error (AAPE), and the highest coefficient of determination (R^2) and correlation coefficient (R) between the predicted and the core measured TOC are obtained. The trained and optimized AI models were then tested using another set of data from the same well, and validated using data points collected from the Devonian shale formation. TOC predictability of the developed AI models for the validation data collected from Devonian formation was then compared with that of Wang et al. [12] sonic- and density-based models summarized in Equations (5)–(7).

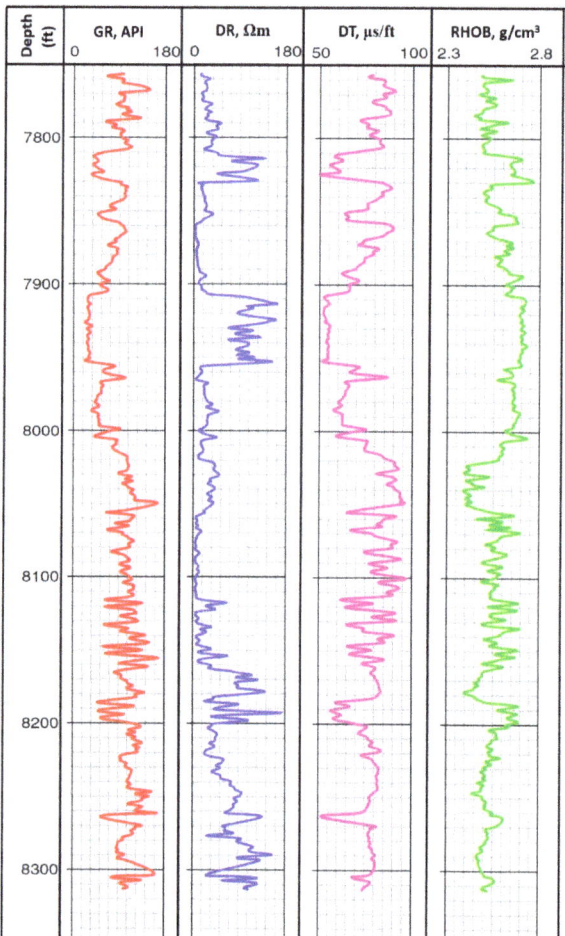

Figure 1. Well log data collected from Barnett shale formation to develop the AI models.

2.3. Data Description and Preprocessing

Conventional log data of DR, GR, DT, and RHOB and the corresponding actual (laboratory-measured) TOC values collected from Barnett shale formation were used to train the four AI models considered in this study. Before training, all the data was pre-processed to remove unrealistic values and outliers. After data pre-processing, 838 data points of the different well logs and their corresponding actual TOC values were found to be valid for model buildup. The use of 545, 545,

587, and 671 of the data to train TSK-FIS, M-FIS, FNN, and SVM models, respectively, were found to optimize the performance of the AI models in predicting the TOC. The number of training data was selected based on the optimization process, as discussed later in this paper.

Table 1 compares the different statistical features of the training data that are used to learn the four AI models developed in this study. These statistical parameters are very important for consideration when the AI models are applied to estimate the TOC using new data. In this study, before testing and validating the developed AI models, the statistical parameters of the testing and validation data were determined to ensure that these data (i.e., testing and validation data) are within the range of the training data used to develop the AI models which are summarized in Table 1.

Table 1. Statistical features of the data used to train the Takagi-Sugeno-Kang fuzzy interference system (TSK-FIS), Mamdani fuzzy interference system (M-FIS), functional neural network (FNN), and support vector machine (SVM) models.

	Takagi-Sugeno-Kang Fuzzy Inference System				
Data points = 545	DR, Ωm	DT, µs/ft	GR, API	RHOB, g/cm^3	TOC, wt%
Minimum	4.97	50.95	23.73	2.39	0.75
Maximum	163.3	97.1	146.9	2.7	5.1
Range	158.3	46.1	123.2	0.3	4.4
Standard Deviation	40.86	9.27	24.91	0.07	1.03
Sample Variance	1670	86	621	0.0055	1.061
	Mamdani Fuzzy Inference System				
Data points = 545	DR, Ωm	DT, µs/ft	GR, API	RHOB, g/cm^3	TOC, wt%
Minimum	4.97	53.78	28.07	2.39	0.76
Maximum	163.3	95.0	146.9	2.7	5.0
Range	158.3	41.2	118.9	0.3	4.2
Standard Deviation	38.95	8.24	22.31	0.07	0.98
Sample Variance	1517	68	498	0.0053	0.953
	Functional Neural Network				
Data points = 587	DR, Ωm	DT, µs/ft	GR, API	RHOB, g/cm^3	TOC, wt%
Minimum	4.97	52.00	26.16	2.40	0.84
Maximum	163.6	97.1	146.9	2.7	5.1
Range	158.6	45.1	120.8	0.3	4.3
Standard Deviation	42.12	7.52	20.73	0.06	0.85
Sample Variance	1774	57	430	0.0040	0.731
	Support Vector Machine				
Data points = 671	DR, Ωm	DT, µs/ft	GR, API	RHOB, g/cm^3	TOC, wt%
Minimum	4.97	50.95	27.37	2.39	0.76
Maximum	163.6	97.1	146.9	2.7	5.1
Range	158.6	46.1	119.6	0.3	4.4
Standard Deviation	39.81	8.20	21.63	0.07	0.96
Sample Variance	1585	67	468	0.0044	0.916

The relative importance of the selected training well log data on the predictability of the TOC values was then studied. Figure 2 compares the relative importance between the different conventional well logs used to train the four AI models and the laboratory-measured TOC values. As indicated in Figure 2 and for the data used to train all AI models, TOC is strongly dependent on the RHOB, while it is moderately related to DR, DT, and GR.

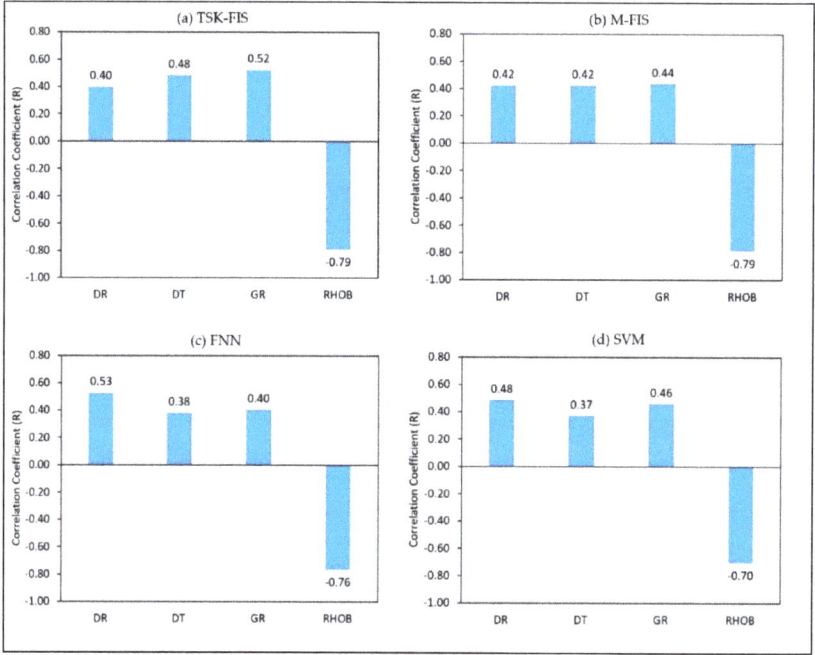

Figure 2. The relative importance of the data used to train (**a**) Takagi-Sugeno-Kang fuzzy interference system (TSK-FIS), (**b**) Mamdani fuzzy interference system (M-FIS), (**c**) functional neural network (FNN), and (**d**) support vector machine (SVM) models.

2.4. AI Model's Development

Four AI models namely: TSK-FIS, M-FIS, FNN, and SVM models were developed in this study to estimate the TOC using conventional well logs of DR, DT, GR, and RHOB. The four conventional well logs, used to train the AI models, were selected based on their relative importance to the core measured TOC, as discussed earlier and shown in Figure 2. However, the selection conforms to their published reported relationship with TOC. For example, DR is believed to be affected by the presence of kerogen in the source rock [41]; DT decreases with the increase in the TOC [42]; several studies have confirmed that GR could significantly enhance TOC prediction [41,43], but the relationship is controversial to others [44,45]; and RHOB decreases with the increase in the kerogen content, and hence, organic matter in the formation increases [7]. Because of the above-listed reasons, the four conventional well logs of DR, DT, GR, and RHOB are considered to develop the TOC models in this study.

All AI models were optimized for their design parameters and the training-to-testing data ratio. Table 2 summarizes the optimized design parameters of the AI models.

Table 2. The optimum design parameters for TSK-FIS, M-FIS, FNN, and SVM models to estimate the TOC.

Takagi-Sugeno-Kang Fuzzy Inference System	
Training/Testing Data Ratio	65/35
Number of Membership Functions	2
Input Membership Function	Gaussian Membership Function
Output Membership Function	Linear Function
Mamdani Fuzzy Inference System	
Training/Testing Data Ratio	65/35
Cluster Radius	0.35
Number of Iterations	300
Functional Neural Network	
Training/Testing Data Ratio	70/30
Training Method	Backward-Forward Selection Method
Function Type	Non-linear Function with Iteration Terms
Support Vector Machine	
Training/Testing Data Ratio	80/20
Kernel	gaussian
Kerneloption	9
Lambda	1×10^{-7}
Epsilon	0.5
Verbose	0.7
C	3000

2.5. Evaluation Criterion

The predictability of the developed AI models, used to estimate the TOC for the training, testing, and validation data sets, was evaluated based on the absolute average percentage error "Equation (8)", correlation coefficient "Equation (9)", coefficient of determination "Equation (10)", and the visual check of the actual and predicted TOC.

$$AAPE = \frac{1}{N}\sum_{i=1}^{N}\left(\left|\frac{(RF_a)_i - (RF_m)_i}{(RF_a)_i}\right| \times 100\right) \qquad (8)$$

$$R = \frac{\sum_{i=1}^{N}\left[((RF_a)_i - \overline{RF_a}) \times ((RF_m)_i - \overline{RF_m})\right]}{\sqrt{\sum_{i=1}^{N}\left[(RF_a)_i - \overline{RF_a}\right]^2 \sum_{i=1}^{N}\left[(RF_m)_i - \overline{RF_m}\right]^2}} \qquad (9)$$

$$R^2 = \left[\frac{\sum_{i=1}^{N}\left[((RF_a)_i - \overline{RF_a}) \times ((RF_m)_i - \overline{RF_m})\right]}{\sqrt{\sum_{i=1}^{N}\left[(RF_a)_i - \overline{RF_a}\right]^2 \sum_{i=1}^{N}\left[(RF_m)_i - \overline{RF_m}\right]^2}}\right]^2 \qquad (10)$$

where in all previous equations a and m denote the actual and estimated RF, respectively.

2.6. Application Examples to Barnett and Devonian Shale

The predictability of the four AI models considered in this study was evaluated using data of two different depositional environments. The first formation is the Mississippian Barnett shale, which was considered earlier by the United States Energy Information Administration as the main source rock of hydrocarbon in FWB [3,46]. In 2011, the proven reserve of this formation was more than 31 trillion cubic feet (TCF) with a cumulative gas production rate of 8.0 TCF. Several studies, such as Pollastro et al. [46], Romero-Sarmiento et al. [47], and Thomas [48] reported the general geologic information about Barnett shale. The second formation is the Devonian shale in WCSB, which is an organic-rich source rock in the Devonian conventional hydrocarbon system [49]. The oil and gas in place in this formation are 61.7 Billion barrels, and 443 Tcf, respectively. According to recent production data, this shale is rich in liquid [50].

3. Results and Discussion

3.1. Training the AI Models

The AI models considered in this work (TSK-FIS, M-FIS, FNN, and SVM) were trained to optimize their design parameters, the optimum design parameters of the AI models are summarized earlier in Table 2. Figure 3 compares the predictability of the four optimized AI models for the training data sets, as shown in Figure 3. The number of data used to train every AI model are different. As explained earlier, the training to testing data ratio is considered during the models optimization process, and based on this optimization, the number of training data that maximize predictability of every model is selected.

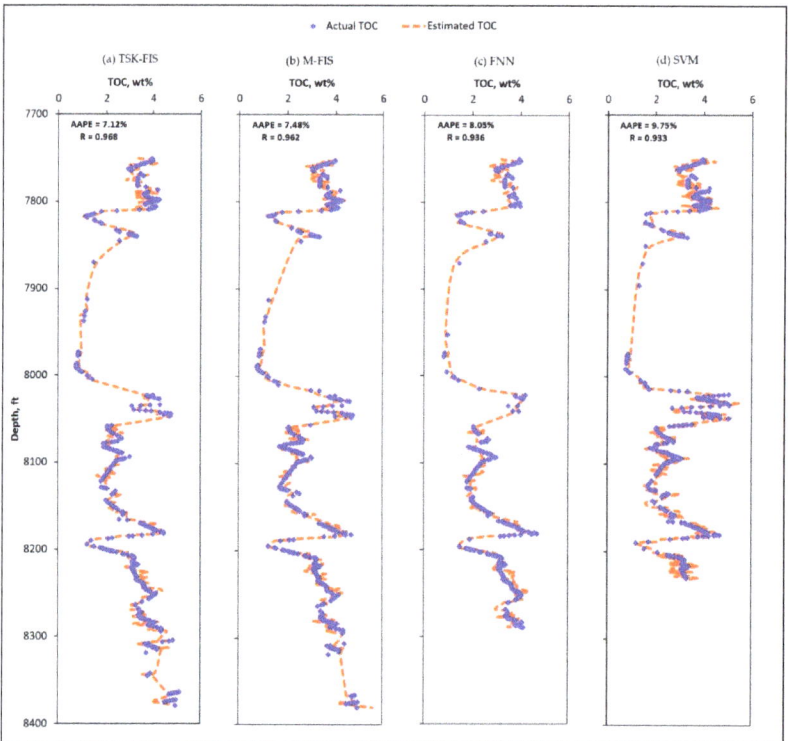

Figure 3. Comparison of measured and estimated TOC using (**a**) TSK-FIS, (**b**) M-FIS, (**c**) FNN, and (**d**) SVM for the training data sets.

Figure 3 shows that the TSK-FIS model predicted the TOC for the training data set with the highest accuracy compared to other models, with AAPE of 7.12% and R of 0.968. M-FIS comes second with AAPE and R of 7.48% and 0.962, followed by the FNN model with AAPE of 8.05% and R of 0.936, and finally the SVM model with AAPE and R of 9.75%, and 0.933, respectively. The visual check of the plots confirms a high accuracy of the four AI models in estimating the TOC for the training data set.

Cross-plot of Figure 4 compares the measured and estimated TOC for the training data set. The narrow scattering of the points indicates the predictability of the models; TSK-FIS model is the highest with $R^2 = 0.937$, then M-FIS model with $R^2 = 0.926$, followed by FNN model with $R^2 = 0.876$, and finally SVM with the lowest R^2 of 0.871.

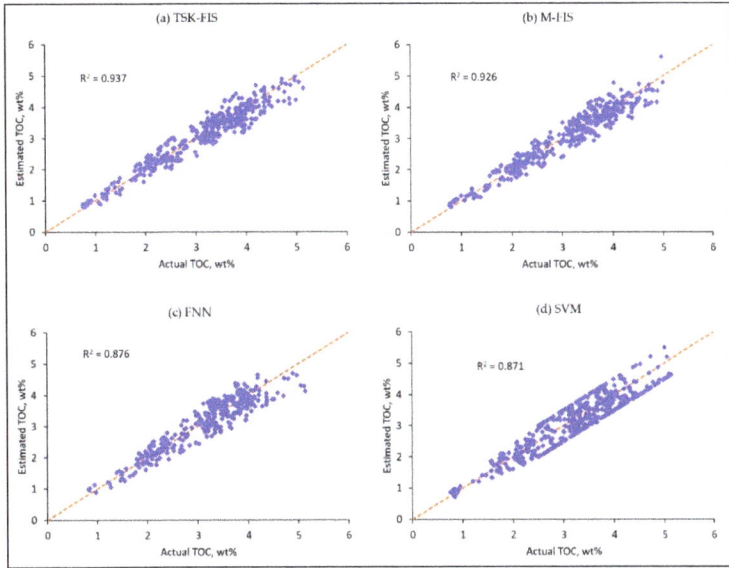

Figure 4. Cross-plot of the measured and estimated TOC using (**a**) TSK-FIS, (**b**) M-FIS, (**c**) FNN, and (**d**) SVM for the training data set.

3.2. Testing the AI Models

The predictability of the four AI models, developed in this study, is then tested using data collected from the Barnett shale formation. The number of the testing data points is selected based on the optimization process as mentioned earlier.

Figure 5 compares the predictability of the AI models to evaluate the TOC for the testing data sets. Visually, the four plots indicate similar predictability for the four models, with minor differences. Considering the AAPE and R M-FIS model is the highest with 11.10% and 0.933, followed by TSK-FIS model with 11.20% and 0.918, then FNN model with 11.29% and 0.905, and finally SVM model with 11.45%, and 0.931 respectively.

The cross-plot in Figure 6 presents the correlation between measured and estimated TOC for the testing data set. The plots indicate high correlation with R^2 equal 0.870, 0.867, 0.842, and 0.818 for M-FIS, SVM, TSK-FIS, and FNN models, respectively.

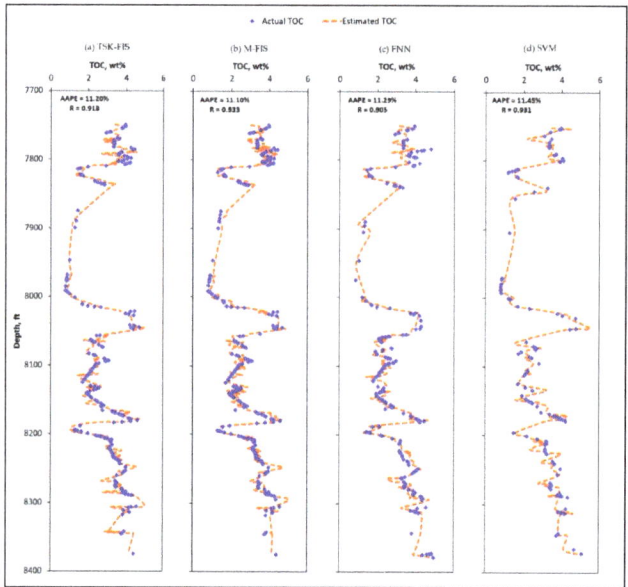

Figure 5. Comparison of measured and estimated TOC using (**a**) TSK-FIS, (**b**) M-FIS, (**c**) FNN, and (**d**) SVM for the testing data sets.

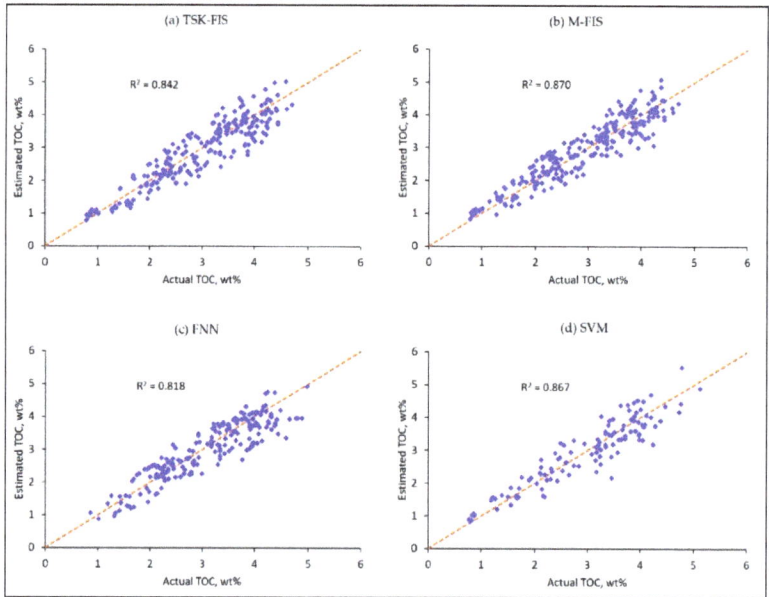

Figure 6. Cross-plot of the measured and estimated TOC using (**a**) TSK-FIS, (**b**) M-FIS, (**c**) FNN, and (**d**) SVM for the testing data sets.

3.3. Validating the AI Models

The AI model's validation was completed using unseen data collected from the Devonian shale formation. The total number of core derived TOC data collected from Devonian shale are 22 data points, out of these data, only 20, 19, 19, and 15 were found to fit within the range of the training data that is used to develop TSK-FIS, M-FIS, FNN, and SVM models, respectively. The range for the training data are summarized in Table 1. Based on the AAPE and R results as indicated in Figure 7, FNN model was the best model with AAPE of 12.02% and R of 0.879, followed by M-FIS model with AAPE and R of 13.18 and 0.875, then SVM with AAPE and R of 14.52% and 0.860, and finally TSK-FIS model with AAPE of 15.62% and R of 0.832 respectively. As shown in Figure 7, all AI models are highly accurate compared to Wang et al. [12] sonic- and density-based models, Wang sonic-based model (WSBM) predicted the TOC with AAPE of 34.58% and R of 0.806, while Wang density-based model (WDBM) predicted TOC with AAPE, and R of 49.04% and 0.469, respectively.

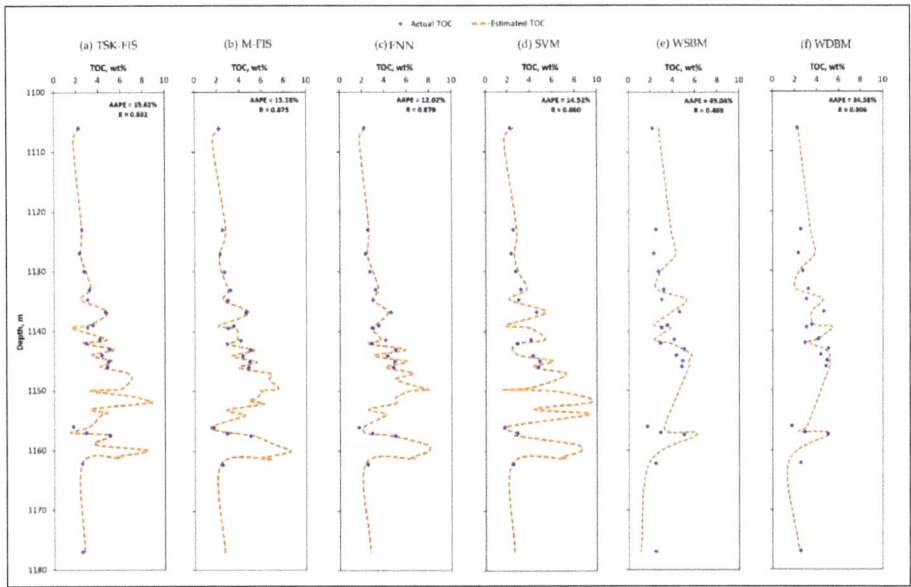

Figure 7. Comparison of measured and estimated TOC using (a) TSK-FIS, (b) M-FIS, (c) FNN, (d) SVM, (e) WSBM, and (f) WDBM for the validation data sets.

From the the results of training, testing, and validation data, considering the similarity of the results of the evaluation parameters (AAPE and R), and taking into consideration that adding or omitting a few points may change the highest-to-lowest order of the parameters, we conclude that the four models are equally adequate to estimate the TOC using only the conventional well log used in this study. Nevertheless, we recommend using the FNN model as it is the best-performed model on the validation data.

4. Conclusions

In this study, four artificial intelligence (AI) models based on Takagi-Sugeno-Kang fuzzy interference system, Mamdani fuzzy interference system, functional neural network, and support vector machine are developed to estimate the total organic carbon (TOC) using conventional well logs of deep resistivity, gamma-ray, sonic transit time, and bulk density. The models are developed and tested using data collected from Barnett shale and then validated using unseen data from Devonian shale. The optimized AI models showed a high predictability of TOC for both formations evaluated in this study. The four models are equally adequate to estimate the TOC using the well log used in this study. Nevertheless, for the validation (unseen) data considered in this study, the FNN model overperformed other models in predicting the TOC, with the lowest AAPE and the highest R, compared with other techniques. All AI models over-performed Wang models, which are recently developed to evaluate the TOC for Devonian formation.

Author Contributions: Conceptualization, S.E., A.A. and A.A.M; methodology, A.A.M. and M.A.; validation, A.A.M., S.E. and M.A.; formal analysis, A.A.M. and A.Z.A; data preparation, A.A.M.; models preparation, A.A.M., A.A. and A.Z.A; writing—original draft preparation, A.A.M.; writing—review and editing, S.E., A.Z.A. and M.A.; visualization, A.Z.A. and A.A.; supervision, S.E. and A.A.

Funding: This research received no external funding.

Conflicts of Interest: The authors declare no conflict of interest.

Nomenclature

AI	Artificial Intelligence
AAPE	Average Absolute Percentage Error
DR	Deep Resistivity
DT	Sonic Transit Time
FNN	Functional Neural Network
FWB	Fort Worth Basin
GR	Gamma Ray
M-FIS	Mamdani Fuzzy Inference System
RHOB	Formation Bulk Density
SVM	Support Vector Machine
TCF	Trillion Cubic Feet
TSK-FIS	Takagi-Sugeno-Kang Fuzzy Inference System
WCSB	Western Canada Sedimentary Basin

References

1. Passey, Q.R.; Bohacs, K.; Esch, W.L.; Klimentidis, R.; Sinha, S. From oil-prone source rock to gas-producing shale reservoir-geologic and petrophysical characterization of unconventional shale gas reservoirs. In Proceedings of the International Oil and Gas Conference and Exhibition in China, Beijing, China, 8–10 June 2010.
2. Sondergeld, C.H.; Ambrose, R.J.; Rai, C.S.; Moncrieff, J. Micro-structural studies of gas shales. In Proceedings of the SPE Unconventional Gas Conference, Pittsburgh, PA, USA, 23–25 February 2010.
3. Montgomery, S.L.; Jarvie, D.M.; Bowker, K.A.; Pollastro, R.M. Mississippian Barnett Shale, Fort Worth basin, North-Central Texas: Gas-shale Play with Multi-trillion Cubic Foot Potential. *Am. Assoc. Pet. Geol. Bull.* **2005**, *89*, 155–175. [CrossRef]
4. Ross, D.J.; Bustin, R.M. Impact of mass balance calculations on adsorption capacities in microporous shale gas reservoirs. *Fuel* **2007**, *86*, 2696–2706. [CrossRef]
5. Ding, J.; Xiaozhi, C.; Xiudi, J.; Bin, W.; Jinmiao, Z. Application of AVF Inversion on Shale Gas Reservoir TOC Prediction. In Proceedings of the SEG Annual Meeting: Society of Exploration Geophysicists, New Orleans, LA, USA, 18–23 October 2015.
6. Zhang, T.; Ellis, G.S.; Ruppel, S.C.; Milliken, K.; Yang, R. Effect of organic-matter type and thermal maturity on methane adsorption in shale-gas systems. *Org. Geochem.* **2012**, *47*, 120–131. [CrossRef]
7. Schmoker, J.W. Determination of Organic Content of Appalachian Devonian Shales from Formation-Density Logs. *Am. Assoc. Pet. Geol. Bull.* **1979**, *63*, 1504–1509. [CrossRef]
8. Schmoker, J.W. Organic content of Devonian shale in Western Appalachian Basin. *Am. Assoc. Pet. Geol. Bull.* **1980**, *64*, 2156–2165.
9. Passey, Q.R.; Creaney, S.; Kulla, J.B.; Moretti, F.J.; Stroud, J.D. A practical model for organic richness from porosity and resistivity logs. *Am. Assoc. Pet. Geol. Bull.* **1990**, *74*, 1777–1794.
10. Charsky, A.; Herron, S. Accurate, direct Total Organic Carbon (TOC) log from a new advanced geochemical spectroscopy tool: Comparison with conventional approaches for TOC estimation. In Proceedings of the AAPG Annual Convention and Exhibition, Pittsburg, PA, USA, 19–22 May 2013.

11. Wang, J.; Gu, D.; Guo, W.; Zhang, H.; Yang, D. Determination of Total Organic Carbon Content in Shale Formations With Regression Analysis. *J. Energy Resour. Technol.* **2019**, *141*, 012907. [CrossRef]
12. Wang, P.; Chen, Z.; Pang, X.; Hu, K.; Sun, M.; Chen, X. Revised models for determining TOC in shale play: Example from Devonian Duvernay Shale, Western Canada Sedimentary Basin. *Mar. Pet. Geol.* **2016**, *70*, 304–319. [CrossRef]
13. Zhu, L.; Zhang, C.; Zhang, Z.; Zhou, X.; Liu, W. An improved method for evaluating the TOC content of a shale formation using the dual-difference $\Delta logR$ method. *Mar. Pet. Geol.* **2019**, *102*, 800–816. [CrossRef]
14. Wang, H.; Wu, W.; Chen, T.; Dong, X.; Wang, G. An improved neural network for TOC, S1 and S2 estimation based on conventional well logs. *J. Pet. Sci. Eng.* **2019**, *176*, 664–678. [CrossRef]
15. Zhu, L.; Zhang, C.; Zhang, C.; Zhang, Z.; Nie, X.; Zhou, X.; Liu, W.; Wang, X. Forming a new small sample deep learning model to predict total organic carbon content by combining unsupervised learning with semisupervised learning. *Appl. Soft Comput.* **2019**, *83*, 105596. [CrossRef]
16. Zhu, L.; Zhang, C.; Zhang, C.; Zhou, X.; Wang, J.; Wang, X. Application of Multiboost-KELM algorithm to alleviate the collinearity of log curves for evaluating the abundance of organic matter in marine mud shale reservoirs: A case study in Sichuan Basin, China. *Acta Geophys.* **2018**, *66*, 983. [CrossRef]
17. Crain, E.R. Petrophysical Handbook. 2000. Available online: https://spec2000.net/11-vshtoc.htm (accessed on 20 July 2019).
18. Mahmoud, A.A.A.; Elkatatny, S.; Mahmoud, M.; Abouelresh, M.; Abdulraheem, A.; Ali, A. Determination of the total organic carbon (TOC) based on conventional well logs using artificial neural network. *Int. J. Coal Geol.* **2017**, *179*, 72–80. [CrossRef]
19. Mahmoud, A.A.; Elkatatny, S.; Abdulraheem, A.; Mahmoud, M.; Ibrahim, M.O.; Ali, A. New Technique to Determine the Total Organic Carbon Based on Well Logs Using Artificial Neural Network (White Box). In Proceedings of the SPE Kingdom Saudi Arabia Annual Technical Symposium and Exhibition, Dammam, Saudi Arab, 24–27 April 2017.
20. Elkatatny, S. A Self-Adaptive Artificial Neural Network Technique to Predict Total Organic Carbon (TOC) Based on Well Logs. *Arab. J. Sci. Eng.* **2018**, *44*, 6127–6137. [CrossRef]
21. Mohaghegh, S.; Arefi, R.; Ameri, S.; Hefner, M.H. A Methodological Approach for Reservoir Heterogeneity Characterization Using Artificial Neural Networks. In Proceedings of the SPE Annual Technical Conference and Exhibition, New Orleans, LA, USA, 25–28 September 1994.
22. Barman, I.; Ouenes, A.; Wang, M. Fractured Reservoir Characterization Using Streamline-Based Inverse Modeling and Artificial Intelligence Tools. In Proceedings of the SPE Annual Technical Conference and Exhibition, Dallas, TX, USA, 1–4 October 2000.
23. Elkatatny, S.A.; Mahmoud, M.A. Development of a New Correlation for Bubble Point Pressure in Oil Reservoirs Using Artificial Intelligent Technique. *Arab. J. Sci. Eng.* **2018**, *43*, 2491–2500. [CrossRef]
24. Elkatatny, S.M. Real Time Prediction of Rheological Parameters of KCl Water-Based Drilling Fluid Using Artificial Neural Networks. *Arab. J. Sci. Eng.* **2017**, *42*, 1655–1665. [CrossRef]
25. Abdelgawad, K.; Elkatatny, S.; Moussa, T.; Mahmoud, M.; Patil, S. Real Time Determination of Rheological Properties of Spud Drilling Fluids Using a Hybrid Artificial Intelligence Technique. *J. Energy Resour. Technol.* **2018**. [CrossRef]
26. Al-AbdulJabbar, A.; Elkatatny, S.M.; Mahmoud, M.; Abdelgawad, K.; Abdulaziz, A. A Robust Rate of Penetration Model for Carbonate Formation. *J. Energy Resour. Technol.* **2019**, *141*, 042903. [CrossRef]
27. Elkatatny, S. Application of Artificial Intelligence Techniques to Estimate the Static Poisson's Ratio Based on Wireline Log Data. *J. Energy Resour. Technol.* **2018**, *140*, 072905. [CrossRef]
28. Mahmoud, A.A.; Elkatatny, S.; Ali, A.; Moussa, T. Estimation of Static Young's Modulus for Sandstone Formation Using Artificial Neural Networks. *Energies* **2019**, *12*, 2125. [CrossRef]
29. Ahmed, A.S.; Mahmoud, A.A.; Elkatatny, S. Fracture Pressure Prediction Using Radial Basis Function. In Proceedings of the AADE National Technical Conference and Exhibition, Denver, CO, USA, 9–10 April 2019.
30. Ahmed, A.S.; Mahmoud, A.A.; Elkatatny, S.; Mahmoud, M.; Abdulraheem, A. Prediction of Pore and Fracture Pressures Using Support Vector Machine. In Proceedings of the 2019 International Petroleum Technology Conference, Beijing, China, 26–28 March 2019.

31. Al-Shehri, D.A. Oil and Gas Wells: Enhanced Wellbore Casing Integrity Management through Corrosion Rate Prediction Using an Augmented Intelligent Approach. *Sustainability* **2019**, *11*, 818. [CrossRef]
32. Salehi, S.; Hareland, G.; Dehkordi, K.K.; Ganji, M.; Abdollahi, M. Casing collapse risk assessment and depth prediction with a neural network system approach. *J. Pet. Sci. Eng.* **2009**, *69*, 156–162. [CrossRef]
33. Mahmoud, A.A.; Elkatatny, S.; Abdulraheem, A.; Mahmoud, M. Application of Artificial Intelligence Techniques in Estimating Oil Recovery Factor for Water Drive Sandy Reservoirs. In Proceedings of the SPE Kuwait Oil & Gas Show and Conference, Kuwait City, Kuwait, 15–18 October 2017.
34. Mahmoud, A.A.; Elkatatny, S.; Chen, W.; Abdulraheem, A. Estimation of Oil Recovery Factor for Water Drive Sandy Reservoirs through Applications of Artificial Intelligence. *Energies* **2019**, *12*, 3671. [CrossRef]
35. Wang, Y.; Salehi, S. Application of real-time field data to optimize drilling hydraulics using neural network approach. *J. Energy Resour. Technol.* **2015**, *137*. [CrossRef]
36. Amato, F.; Moscato, V.; Picariello, A.; Sperl, G. Recommendation in Social Media Networks. In Proceedings of the 2017 IEEE Third International Conference on Multimedia Big Data (BigMM), Laguna Hills, CA, USA, 19–21 April 2017.
37. Su, X.; Sperli, G.; Moscato, V.; Picariello, A.; Esposito, C.; Choi, C. An Edge Intelligence Empowered Recommender System Enabling Cultural Heritage Applications. *IEEE Trans. Ind. Inform.* **2019**, *15*, 4266–4275. [CrossRef]
38. Carvajal-Ortiz, H.; Gentzis, T. Critical considerations when assessing hydrocarbon plays using Rock-Eval pyrolysis and organic petrology data: Data quality revisited. *Int. J. Coal Geol.* **2015**, *152*, 113–122. [CrossRef]
39. Chen, Z.; Jiang, C.; Lavoie, D.; Reyes, J. Model-assisted Rock-Eval data interpretation for source rock evaluation: Examples from producing and potential shale gas resource plays. *Int. J. Coal Geol.* **2016**, *165*, 290–302. [CrossRef]
40. Hazra, B.; Dutta, S.; Kumar, S. TOC calculation of organic matter rich sediments using Rock-Eval pyrolysis: Critical consideration and insights. *Int. J. Coal Geol.* **2016**, *169*, 106–115. [CrossRef]
41. Heslop, K.A. Generalized Method for the Estimation of TOC from GR and Rt. In Proceedings of the AAPG Annual Convention and Exhibition, New Orleans, LA, USA, 11–14 April 2010.
42. Liu, Y.; Chen, Z.; Hu, K.; Liu, C. Quantifying Total Organic Carbon (TOC) from Well Logs Using Support Vector Regression. GeoConvention 2013, Calgary, Canada. Available online: https://www.geoconvention.com/archives/2013/281_GC2013_Quantifying_Total_Organic_Carbon.pdf (accessed on 15 July 2019).
43. Zhao, T.; Verma, S.; Devegowda, D. TOC estimation in the Barnett Shale from Triple Combo logs Using Support Vector Machine. In Proceedings of the 85th Annual International Meeting of the SEG, New Orleans, LA, USA, 18–23 October 2015; pp. 791–795.
44. Gonzalez, J.; Lewis, R.; Hemingway, J.; Grau, J.; Rylander, E.; Pirie, I. Determination of Formation Organic Carbon Content Using a New Neutron-Induced Gamma Ray Spectroscopy Service that Directly Measures Carbon. In Proceedings of the SPWLA 54th Annual Logging Symposium, New Orleans, LA, USA, 22–26 June 2013.
45. Luning, S.; Kolonic, S. Uranium Spectral Gamma-Ray Response as a Proxy for Organic Richness in Black Shales: Applicability and Limitations. *J. Pet. Geol.* **2003**, *26*, 153–174. [CrossRef]
46. Pollastro, R.M.; Jarvie, D.M.; Hill, R.J.; Adams, C. Geologic Framework of the Mississippian Barnett Shale, Barnett-Paleozoic Total Petroleum System, Bend Arch-Fort Worth Basin, Texas. *Am. Assoc. Pet. Geol. Bull.* **2007**, *91*, 405–436. [CrossRef]
47. Romero-Sarmiento, M.F.; Ducros, M.; Carpentier, B.; Lorant, F.; Cacas, M.C.; Pegaz-Fiornet, S.; Wolf, S.; Rohais, S.; Moretti, I. Quantitative Evaluation of TOC, Organic Porosity and Gas Retention Distribution in a Gas Shale Play Using Petroleum System Modeling: Application to the Mississippian Barnett Shale. *Mar. Pet. Geol.* **2013**, *45*, 315–330. [CrossRef]
48. Thomas, J.D. Integrating Synsedimentary Tectonics with Sequence Stratigraphy to Understand the Development of the Fort Worth Basin. In Proceedings of the AAPG Southwest Section Meeting, Ruidoso, NM, USA, 6–8 June 2002.

49. Creaney, S.; Allan, J.; Cole, K.S.; Fowler, M.G.; Brooks, P.W.; Osadetz, K.G.; Riediger, C.L. Petroleum Generation and Migration in the Western Canada Sedimentary Basin. In *Geological Atlas of the Western Canada Sedimentary Basin*; Canadian Society of Petroleum Geologists: Calgary, AB, Canada, 1994; pp. 455–468.
50. Rokosh, C.D.; Lyster, S.; Anderson, S.D.A.; Beaton, A.P.; Berhane, H.; Brazzoni, T.; Chen, D.; Cheng, Y.; Mack, T.; Pana, C.; et al. *Summary of Alberta's Shale-and Siltstone-Hosted Hydrocarbon Resource Potential*; Energy Resources Conservation Board: Edmonton, AB, Canada, 2012.

© 2019 by the authors. Licensee MDPI, Basel, Switzerland. This article is an open access article distributed under the terms and conditions of the Creative Commons Attribution (CC BY) license (http://creativecommons.org/licenses/by/4.0/).

Article

A Hybrid Artificial Intelligence Model to Predict the Elastic Behavior of Sandstone Rocks

Ahmed Gowida [1], Tamer Moussa [1], Salaheldin Elkatatny [1,*] and Abdulwahab Ali [2]

[1] College of Petroleum Engineering and Geosciences, King Fahd University of Petroleum & Minerals, 31261 Dhahran, Saudi Arabia; g201708730@kfupm.edu.sa (A.G.); g201105270@kfupm.edu.sa (T.M.)
[2] Center of Integrative Petroleum Research, King Fahd University of Petroleum & Minerals, Dhahran 31261, Saudi Arabia; awali@kfupm.edu.sa
* Correspondence: elkatatny@kfupm.edu.sa; Tel.: +966-594-663-692

Received: 8 August 2019; Accepted: 17 September 2019; Published: 25 September 2019

Abstract: Rock mechanical properties play a key role in the optimization process of engineering practices in the oil and gas industry so that better field development decisions can be made. Estimation of these properties is central in well placement, drilling programs, and well completion design. The elastic behavior of rocks can be studied by determining two main parameters: Young's modulus and Poisson's ratio. Accurate determination of the Poisson's ratio helps to estimate the in-situ horizontal stresses and in turn, avoid many critical problems which interrupt drilling operations, such as pipe sticking and wellbore instability issues. Accurate Poisson's ratio values can be experimentally determined using retrieved core samples under simulated in-situ downhole conditions. However, this technique is time-consuming and economically ineffective, requiring the development of a more effective technique. This study has developed a new generalized model to estimate static Poisson's ratio values of sandstone rocks using a supervised artificial neural network (ANN). The developed ANN model uses well log data such as bulk density and sonic log as the input parameters to target static Poisson's ratio values as outputs. Subsequently, the developed ANN model was transformed into a more practical and easier to use white-box mode using an ANN-based empirical equation. Core data (692 data points) and their corresponding petrophysical data were used to train and test the ANN model. The self-adaptive differential evolution ($SADE$) algorithm was used to fine-tune the parameters of the ANN model to obtain the most accurate results in terms of the highest correlation coefficient (R) and the lowest mean absolute percentage error (MAPE). The results obtained from the optimized ANN model show an excellent agreement with the laboratory measured static Poisson's ratio, confirming the high accuracy of the developed model. A comparison of the developed ANN-based empirical correlation with the previously developed approaches demonstrates the superiority of the developed correlation in predicting static Poisson's ratio values with the highest R and the lowest MAPE. The developed correlation performs in a manner far superior to other approaches when validated against unseen field data. The developed ANN-based mathematical model can be used as a robust tool to estimate static Poisson's ratio without the need to run the ANN model.

Keywords: elastic parameters; Poisson's ratio; sandstone; artificial neural network; self-adaptive differential evolution

---

1. Introduction

Rock characterization is a crucial aspect in the oil and gas industry, with a major impact on the exploration and production processes [1]. It requires a high level of efficiency and accuracy as minor errors in the identification of the rock characteristics incur significant losses in time and money. On the other hand, improvements in the prediction accuracy of these characteristics result in a significant positive impact in the economic and technical optimization of a range of processes [2,3]. Even though recently developed models for rock characterization meet the basic requirements of the oil and gas industry, the enormous impact of even minor improvements in the prediction accuracy on the optimization process makes further enhancement of prediction worthwhile [4].

Geo-mechanical earth models are one of the tools used to represent the in-situ state of rock [5]. The development of such models depends on the in-situ stresses encountered within a formation, which can be estimated using the values of its elastic parameters, Poisson's ratio, and Young's modulus [6,7]. These parameters are very important in describing the elastic behavior of rock [8]. These parameters are crucial for avoiding many problems and minimizing the risks associated with well drilling operations [5,9–11]. An accurate estimation of these parameters helps to solve wellbore instability issues, identify the safe mud-weight window while drilling, and optimize the fracture geometry and orientation, etc. [12,13]. On the other hand, the inaccurate determination of the elastic parameters of formations may cause critical problems affecting the strategies of field development negatively from both technical and financial points of view [5,14–16].

The most commonly used reliable tool for estimating the mechanical properties of formations is conducting laboratory measurements. This approach requires retrieving core samples representing the area of interest under in-situ conditions to accurately simulate the formation conditions. However, this approach has some drawbacks due to its high cost and time-consuming nature [17,18]. Hence, an alternate approach in which the experimentally-determined elastic parameters are correlated with the available log data, which are normally collected during drilling, is used [5,19] These petrophysical log data comprise bulk density (RHOB), porosity logs, and the measurements of the P-wave and S-wave transit times (Δt_{comp} and Δt_{shear}, respectively) [19–21].

The correlations derived from the well log data can provide a real-time, continuous profile of static Poisson's ratio (PR_{static}) values. However, the applicability of the developed profile is limited to the section from which the core samples are collected, limiting the feasibility of the application of these correlations due to their accuracy and reliability [5,16]. Alternatively, the profiles of dynamic Poisson's ratio ($PR_{dynamic}$) are estimated using sonic log data, which are calibrated by determining the difference between $PR_{dynamic}$ and PR_{static} of the measured core data using Equation (1). All dynamic Poisson's ratio values can then be adjusted by adding this difference, resulting in a shift in the $PR_{dynamic}$ profile towards the actual values of PR_{static} [11,15,17,21]. However, the accuracy of this technique is limited to the interval which the core samples represent [5,14]. Also, a large scatter in the data is observed, making it difficult to establish a reasonable relationship, especially in heterogeneous reservoirs [11,17].

When core data and direct downhole rock strength measurements are unavailable, PR_{static} values are estimated using empirical correlations of the petrophysical log data. D'Andrea et al. [22] have found that PR_{static} values for different rock samples decrease with increasing transit time (Δt). Also, higher PR_{static} values are associated with rocks containing larger pores, and a new correlation was developed to predict PR_{static} values using porosity values [23,24]. Kumar [23] introduced an empirical correlation to predict PR_{static} values using the velocities of the P-wave and S-wave (V_P and V_S, respectively) stated in Equation (2). Kumar et al. [25] have presented a new correlation relating PR_{static} values to V_P and V_S using a non-linear regression technique, but it is only limited to isotropic rocks. Al-Shayea [26] showed that PR_{static} values are dependent on the microcracks within a rock and correlated them with confining pressure. Singh and Singh [27] developed a predictive model to estimate PR_{static} values for different rocks using unified compressive strength (UCS) and tensile strength (T). Shalabi et al. [28] applied linear regression to correlate PR_{static} values with rock hardness and UCS. Al-Anazi and Gates [29] have presented different correlations using the support vector regression (SVR) technique relating PR_{static} values for limestone formations with different parameters, such as V_P, V_S, Young's modulus (E_s), and the rigidity modulus. They also developed a model to predict PR_{static} values using several input parameters such as rock porosity, RHOB, V_P, V_S, overburden stress (σ_v), and minimum horizontal stress (σ_h). Abdulraheem [30] developed new models to predict PR_{static} values of carbonate rocks from well log data using fuzzy logic and an artificial neural network.

$$PR_{dynamic} = \frac{V_p^2 - 2V_s^2}{2(V_p^2 - V_s^2)} \quad (1)$$

$$PR_{static} = 1.316 - 1.5313 \frac{V_s}{V_p} \quad (2)$$

The literature survey indicates that there have been no significant studies performed to estimate PR_{static} values from well log data for sandstone rocks using empirical formulations. Most of the correlations reported in the literature for predicting PR_{static} values have been developed using datasets representing carbonate rocks. Thus, in this study a new model to predict PR_{static} values of sandstone rocks has been developed based on petrophysical well log data, i.e., RHOB, Δt_{comp}, and Δt_{shear} using artificial neural networks (ANN). The model is presented in a white-box mode by developing a new empirical equation to estimate PR_{static} values of sandstone rocks directly from the log data without running the ANN model.

The rest of the paper is structured as follows: Section 2 contains materials and methods used for developing the new approach, Section 3 includes the obtained results from the optimization process of the developed model in addition to the procedure required to be followed to use the developed model, performance analysis and the validation process. Finally, Section 4 comprises a summary of the findings of this study listed as conclusions.

2. Materials and Methods

2.1. Data Description

The data used for developing the proposed ANN model comprises both core data and wire-lined log data, which are described in the following subsections.

2.1.1. Wire-Lined Log Data Analysis

The selected log dataset represents sandstone rocks for the same sections from which the core samples were also retrieved for experimental measurements. The log dataset included RHOB, Δt_{comp}, and Δt_{shear} measurements. Based on the statistical analysis, the obtained data were found to represent a wide range of sandstone rocks, which is highly recommended for boosting the accuracy of the ANN models. The ranges of the obtained log data are: RHOB from 2.24 to 2.98 g/cm³, Δt_{comp} from 44.34 to 80.49 µs/ft, and Δt_{shear} from 73.19 to 145.6 µs/ft. Table 1 lists different statistical parameters for describing the core and well log data used for building the artificial intelligence (AI) models.

Table 1. Statistical parameters of the obtained core data and well-log data. RHOB: formation bulk density; Δt_{comp}: P-wave transit time; Δt_{shear}: S-wave transit time.

Parameter	RHOB, g/cm³	Δt_{comp}, µs/ft.	Δt_{shear}, µs/ft.	PR_{static}
Minimum	2.24	44.34	73.19	0.20
Maximum	2.98	80.49	145.60	0.46
Range	0.74	36.15	72.42	0.26
Standard deviation	0.13	7.59	11.80	0.05
Variance	0.02	57.63	139.35	0.00

2.1.2. Core Data Generation

After retrieving core samples representing sandstone sections from the drilled wells, static mechanical properties of the core samples were experimentally determined. These properties (E_S and PR_{static}) were determined using triaxial compressional tests. Triaxial tests were performed under room temperature and an increasing applied confining pressure from 500 to 1500 psi. The triaxial compression test was conducted according to the recommended practice of the American Society of Testing and Materials (ASTM D 2664-86, ASTM D 3148-93) [31]. Figure 1 shows a stress–strain curve for a retrieved sandstone sample using the triaxial compression test. The values of E_S and PR_{static} were determined by drawing a tangent straight-line at 50% of the maximum stress value (y-axis) and calculating the slope of this straight line. The slope of the straight-line tangent of the axial stress-strain curve (on the right section) is used to determine E_S and the slope of the straight-line tangent of the radial stress-strain curve (on the left section) is used to determine PR_{static}.

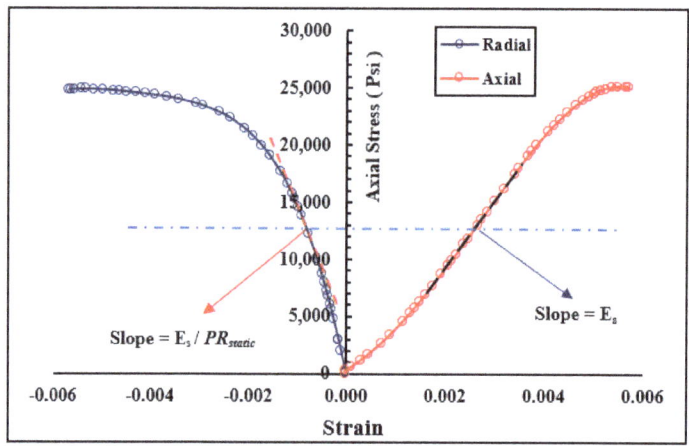

Figure 1. A typical axial and radial stress–strain curve obtained from the triaxial test of a sandstone sample.

2.2. Quality Check and Data Filtration

The higher the quality of the training data is, the better the accuracy of AI models [32]. This can be accomplished using technical and statistical approaches. First, any unrealistic values such as negative values and zero values were filtered from the data using MATLAB. Then the quality of the obtained data using the values of P-wave and S-wave velocities was checked by calculating $PR_{dynaimc}$ values using Equation (1). The values of P-wave and S-wave velocities are the reciprocals of Δt_{comp} and Δt_{shear}, respectively. For typical rocks Poisson's ratio has positive values; thereafter, any data points yielding negative values of $PR_{dynaimc}$ should be removed [30,32]. Subsequently, any outlier values which significantly deviated from the normal trend were removed. The outliers were removed using a box and whisker plot, in which top whisker represents the upper limit of the data and the bottom whisker represents the lower limit of the data. Any value beyond these limits was considered an outlier and removed [33]. These limits are determined by dividing the data into four equal divisions (quartiles) using the minimum, maximum, mean, and median parameters [34] obtained from the results of statistical analysis of the data listed in Table 1.

2.3. Correction for the Depth Shifting Between Wireline-Logged Depth and Core Depth

The depth of the wireline-logged data are usually measured depending on the length of the wireline used during the logging operation while the recorded depths of core data are based on the length of the drill string. Therefore, it is common to have some mismatch between core and log data. The main reasons for this discrepancy between the two depths are drill pipe stretch, cable stretch, tidal changes, incomplete core recovery, and core expansion [35]. Hence, this difference should be accounted while correlating log data with core measurements. To identify this shift, density-log data are plotted in the same plot with density-data obtained from the core obtained from the same interval [36]. Then, both data are correlated by taking the shift-correction value into account using Equation (3).

$$Log_{depth} = Core_{depth} \pm Shift_{depth} \qquad (3)$$

2.4. Inputs/Output Relative Importance

The accuracy of prediction using artificial intelligence (AI) techniques depends on the selected input parameters and their effect on the predicted output. The relative importance of these input parameters with respect to the output can be indicated in terms of the correlation coefficient (R) between them. The correlation coefficient (R) is bounded between −1 and 1. When R equals one, it indicates that the two selected variables are strongly and directly dependent on each other, while for R equals −1, it indicates that they are inversely dependent on each other. When R equals to zero, a linear relationship between these variables does not exist [37]. The mathematical formula used to calculate R is given in Appendix A. Studying the relative importance of the input parameters (RHOB, Δt_{comp} and Δt_{shear}) with the output (PR_{static}) resulted in reasonable R values of 0.32, −0.57, −0.21 between PR_{static} and the inputs RHOB, Δt_{comp}, and Δt_{shear} respectively, as shown in Figure 2.

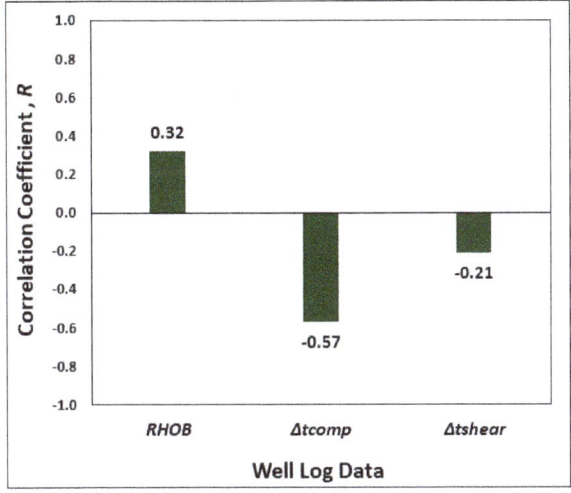

Figure 2. Relative importance between the input parameters and the output, the static Poisson's ratio (PR_{static}).

2.5. The Proposed Prediction Approach

Both artificial neural network (ANN) and self-adaptive differential evolution (SADE) algorithm are implemented in this study to predict PR_{static}.

2.5.1. Artificial Neural Network (ANN)

Artificial intelligence (AI) and machine learning have become very effective tools for handling complex engineering problems with high accuracy. Many studies have been reported for utilizing AI tools in rock characterization [38–44]. Among these tools, ANN is considered one of the most effective and applicable AI techniques, especially in the petroleum industry [45]. Based on the literature, there are many applications of ANN in the field of formation evaluation, such as mechanical property prediction of carbonate rocks [5,21], and reservoir characterization [19,46]. ANN can characterize a system under analysis without the need for any physical phenomenon [47]. There is a significant similarity between the performance of biological neural networks and ANN in processing the input signals to get output responses [48]. The ANN elementary units are called neurons. The minimum number of layers composing the ANN architecture is three; namely input layer, hidden layer, and output layer. These layers are linked using transfer functions and trained using appropriate algorithms representing the nature of the problem [47]. The connections between the neurons are associated with weights and biases [49]. The output layer is commonly assigned to the activation function "pure linear", while there are many available options for the transfer functions assigned to input/hidden layers, such as the log-sigmoidal and tan-sigmoidal types [50]. The backpropagation feedforward neural network is recommended as an effective tool in preference to multilayer perceptron (MLP) [15,51]. The number of neurons should be optimized as a large number of neurons may cause over-fitting and negatively affect the prediction process, while using few neurons may yield under-fitting [52].

2.5.2. The Self-Adaptive Differential Evolution (SADE) Algorithm

Differential evolution (*DE*) is a population-based search technique introduced by Storn and Price [53]. The technique is an outstanding tool used to handle stochastic global optimization problems, which requires tuning and varying a few parameters to get the optimized results. The governing parameters of *DE* depend significantly on the nature of the problem to be optimized. However, the optimization process, in which the controlling parameters are tuned using different strategies, is excessively time consuming, making the technique computationally expensive [54]. Qin and Suganthan [55] developed the self-adaptive differential evolution (*SADE*) technique to overcome this drawback. *SADE* is capable of self-adapting the controlling parameters in a much shorter time compared to *DE*. *SADE* is also superior to other optimization algorithms such as particle swarm optimization (PSO), especially for solving numerical problems with medium dimensions [56]. Detailed information on the workflow and the mathematical formulations used in this algorithm have been obtained by many researchers [54,55,57]. *SADE* has been successfully implemented in many application in the petroleum industry, such as oil production optimization [58] and prediction of spud mud rheology [59].

2.5.3. Building and Implementing of ANN to Predict PR_{static} Values

In this study, a new ANN model is developed then optimized using *SADE* to get the best predictions with the highest possible accuracy. Using such hybrid system increases the performance of the developed network, as indicated in the reviewed studies. The developed approach with the learning algorithm is applied using MATLAB. At first, data are used to train the network and then the results are tested. The evaluation of the network performance in this study depends on the accuracy degree between the actual and the predicted results in terms of three main factors:

- Correlation coefficient (*R*)
- Mean absolute percentage error (MAPE)
- Coefficient of determination (R^2)

The formulas used for *R*, MAPE, and R^2 are listed in Appendix A. MAPE and R^2 are considered the most commonly measures used for evaluating the prediction accuracy. More details on MAPE and R^2 can be found in [60].

The dataset, including input and output parameters, is used to train the network. Then the network parameters are randomly selected to an optimum choice through iterations. Once the learning algorithm is converged, the determined weights and biases are used to estimate the results using feed forward network structure (FFN) with back propagation learning. This structure contains three layers (input, hidden, and output layers). The number of neurons in the hidden layer are usually estimated using a trial and error technique based on the nature of the problem. The input data are processed through the neurons and their assigned weights and biases; then, the selected transfer function between input/hidden layers is applied to get the response of the hidden layer. Thereafter, the transfer function between hidden/output layers is applied to get the desired output. The network performance is tested based on the results accuracy. Afterwards the error is estimated and propagated back (using back propagation learning) to the earlier layers and *SADE* is applied to optimize the network parameters based on the obtained results to get more precise results. A simplified flowchart for the developed hybrid approach is shown in Figure 3.

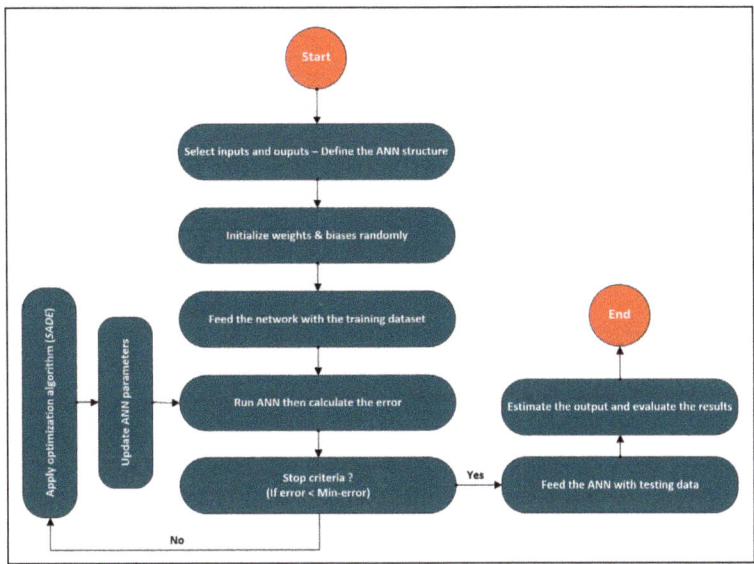

Figure 3. Flowchart describing the workflow of the hybrid approach ANN-*SADE*. ANN: artificial neural network; *SADE*: self-adaptive differential evolution.

The dataset used for building the ANN model was obtained from drilled wells in the Middle East Region. This set comprises 692 data points representing core data and their corresponding wire-lined log data measurements was used to build the ANN model to estimate the static Poisson's ratio for sandstone formations. In this study, The ANN model was trained using log data, namely $RHOB$, Δt_{comp}, and Δt_{shear} as input parameters to predict PR_{static}. The collected data were randomly divided using MATLAB into two partitions. In total, 631 data points, representing 90% of the selected dataset, were used for training the proposed model and 10% of the dataset (61 data points) was used for testing the model. The dataset was divided in the way that testing data points are within the range of the training data as shown in Figure 4. The input parameters should be fed to the ANN model in the following order: $RHOB$, Δt_{comp}, and then Δt_{shear}. The varying ANN parameters in the optimization process are the number of neurons in the hidden layers, learning rate, training algorithms, number of hidden layers, and transfer functions. Several options of these parameters are used to optimize the model. The optimization process involves tracking the error in the predicted results during training, testing processes through runs of the model for different scenarios. For each scenario, different combinations of these varying parameters are selected and used to train the network. The developed ANN model was optimized using the *SADE* algorithm, which was described earlier to identify the optimized choices of these parameters which result in the most accurate results. Thereafter, the ANN parameters yielding the lowest possible error in the predicted results are selected as the optimized values. The tested options of ANN parameters are listed in Table 2.

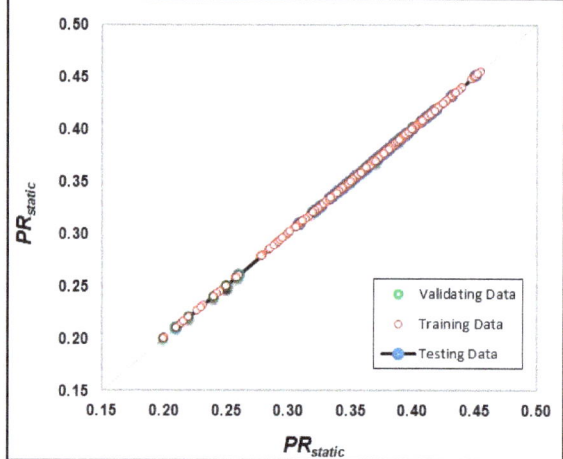

Figure 4. Testing data ranges with respect to the training data used for developing the ANN model.

Table 2. Summary of the tested options of different ANN parameters during the optimization process. trainbr: Bayesian regularization backpropagation training algorithm; elliotsig: Elliot symmetric sigmoid; tansig: hyperbolic tangent sigmoid transfer function; tribas: triangular basis transfer function; pure-linear: linear transfer function; trainlm: Levenberg–Marquardt backpropagation; trainscg: scaled conjugate gradient backpropagation; trainbfg: BFGS quasi-Newton.

Parameter	Ranges		
Number of Neurons	5–25		
Inputs Number	3		
Output Number	1		
Number of Hidden Layers	1–3		
Learning Rate	0.01–0.9		
Input Layer Transfer Function	tansig elliotsig tribas		
Output Layer Transfer Function	pure-linear		
Training Algorithm	trainlm trainbr		trainscg trainbfg

3. Results and Discussion

3.1. Sensitivity Analysis

The *SADE*-based approach starts initially with a randomly selected population from the obtained dataset. Then, they are processed using an objective function moving through several trials and error by implementing different sets of the aforementioned ANN parameters till reaching the termination criterion of the minimum possible error. Thereafter, ANN is continued with the optimized choices obtained by *SADE*.

In this study, 20 independent runs are applied to develop the best ANN model in terms of highest R and lowest MAPE between the predicted and actual values. Figure 5 shows the sensitivity of ANN to the varying number of neurons in the hidden layer. The four performance indicators considered in this case are R and MAPE for both the training and testing datasets. The figure demonstrates that 13 neurons leads to the best fit as it could be shown from the highest values of R of 0.96 and 0.95 for training and testing, respectively, as well as the lowest values of MAPE of 2.4 and 2.1% for training and testing, respectively. The figure shows that although different configurations of ANN lead to almost similar fitness results on the training dataset, there is a significant variance on the testing dataset. This confirms the importance of validating ANN on unseen testing dataset to compare the different ANN models.

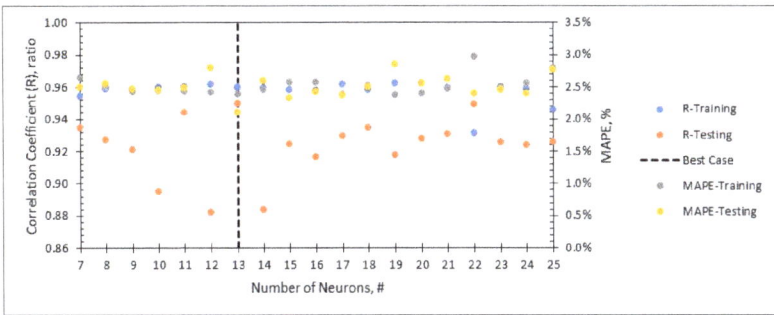

Figure 5. Sensitivity analysis of the ANN performance for varying number of neurons.

Another governing parameter is the learning algorithm. The Bayesian regularization backpropagation training algorithm (trainbr) shows the best performance as a training function for the developed ANN. Out of 20 independent runs, the performance of the trainbr was superior compared to other training functions in 60% of the runs as shown in Figure 6. This outperformance is due to the fact that that unlike other training functions, the trainbr minimizes a combination of squared errors and weights, and then it identifies the best combination in order to produce an ANN that is able to generalize better (prevent overfitting) than other algorithms. This also can be demonstrated by the high testing R achieved by trainbr, as shown in Figure 7.

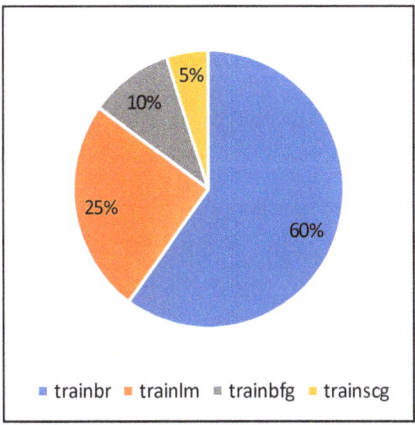

Figure 6. Success rate of each of the training functions out of the 20 independent runs.

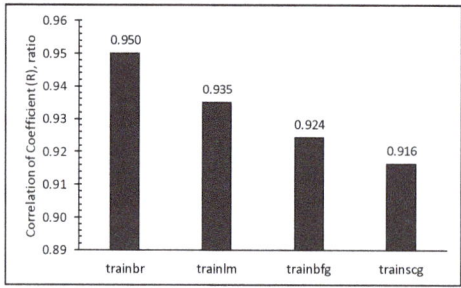

Figure 7. Comparison analysis between the tested training functions.

3.2. Optimization Process Findings

Consequently, the optimized network would use certain parameters, summarized as follows:

- Only one hidden layer with 13 neurons
- A Bayesian regularization backpropagation (trainbr) training algorithm
- An optimized learning rate of 0.12
- An input/hidden layer transfer function that is Elliot symmetric sigmoid (elliotsig)
- A hidden/output layer transfer function that is pure-linear

Figure 8 shows a schematic diagram of the architecture of the developed ANN model used to estimate the PR_{static} values for sandstone formations. The results obtained from the developed ANN model show a significant match between the measured and predicted PR_{static} values from the ANN model. This is indicated by high values of R of 0.96 and MAPE of 2.39% between the measured and predicted PR_{static} values for the training process as shown in Figures 9 and 10. Also, the results showed R of 0.95 and MAPE of 2.10% between the measured and predicted PR_{static} values for the testing process as depicted in Figures 11 and 12. These findings are only guaranteed if the new input data are within the same range of the dataset used to train the network in order to get accurate predictions of PR_{static}, otherwise a large error may be encountered. If the new data are out of that range, the network should be re-trained from the beginning to be updated and to get the new optimized parameters for the new dataset.

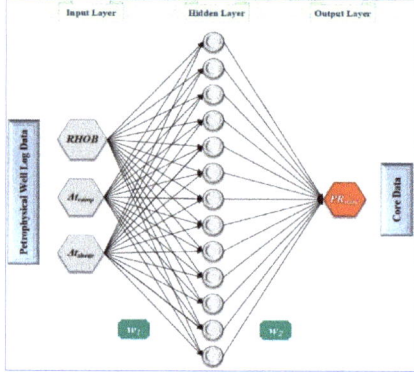

Figure 8. Schematic diagram of the architecture of the developed ANN model showing the input and output parameters with the optimized number of neurons (13 neurons) and assigned weights and biases between the model layers.

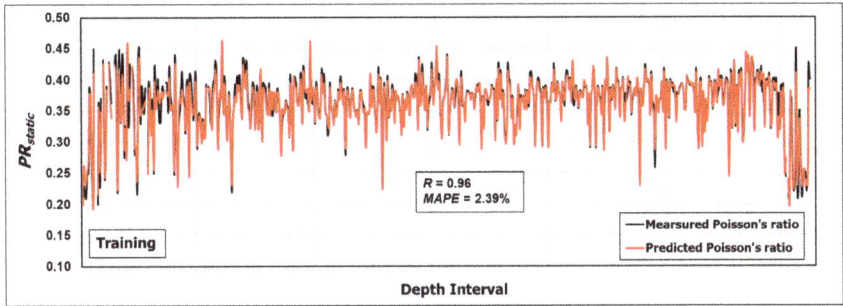

Figure 9. Comparison profile between predicted PR_{static} vs. measured PR_{static} during the training process showing a high match between the predicted and measured values with a correlation coefficient (R) of 0.96 and mean absolute percentage error (MAPE) of 2.39%.

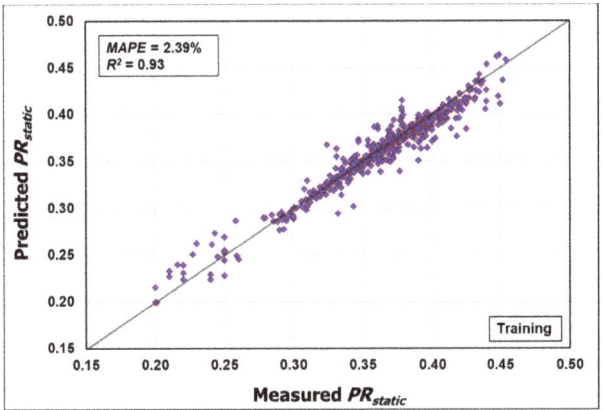

Figure 10. Cross plot between predicted PR_{static} vs. measured PR_{static} for the training process with an R^2 of 0.9 between the predicted and measured values.

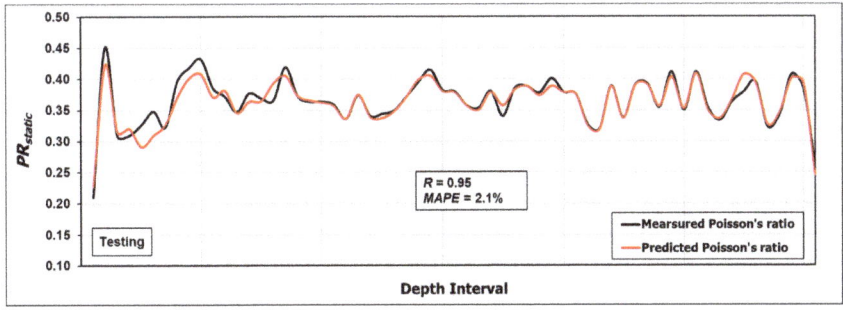

Figure 11. Comparison profile between predicted PR_{static} vs. measured PR_{static} during the testing process, showing a significant match between the predicted and measured values with R of 0.95 and MAPE of 2.10%.

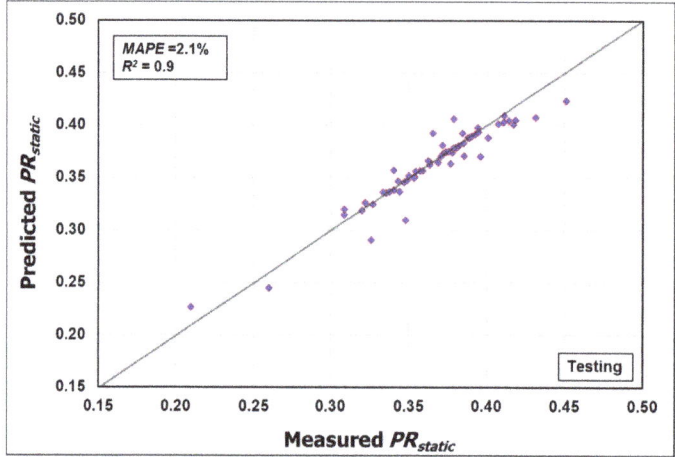

Figure 12. Cross plot between predicted PR_{static} vs. measured PR_{static} for the testing process with R^2 of 0.90 between the predicted and measured values.

3.3. Development of an ANN-Based Mathematical Model

The developed ANN model can be mathematically expressed by Equation (4), which includes the linking weights and biases of the aforementioned three layers of the ANN model (input layer, hidden layer, and output layer).

$$PR_{static,n} = \sum_{i=1}^{N} w_{2_i} \frac{w_{1_{i,1}} RHOB_n + w_{1_{i,2}} \Delta t_{comp,n} + w_{1_{i,3}} \Delta t_{shear,n} + b_{1_i}}{1 + |w_{1_{i,1}} RHOB_n + w_{1_{i,2}} \Delta t_{comp,n} + w_{1_{i,3}} \Delta t_{shear,n} + b_{1_i}|} + b_2 \quad (4)$$

where $PR_{static,n}$ is the normalized value, N is the optimized number of neurons in the hidden layer ($n = 13$), i is the index of each neuron in the hidden layer, w_1 is a matrix of weights linking the input and hidden layers, b_1 is a vector of biases linking the input and hidden layers, w_2 is a matrix of the weight linking the hidden and output layers, b_2 is a bias (scalar) between the hidden and output layers ($b_2 = 0.544$), $w_{1_{i,1}}$ represents the weight (associated with neuron of index (i) in the hidden layer) which will be multiplied by the normalized value of the first input ($RHOB_n$), $w_{1_{i,2}}$ represents the weight (associated with neuron of index (i) in the hidden layer) which will be multiplied by the normalized value of the second input ($\Delta t_{comp,n}$), and $w_{1_{i,3}}$ represents the weight (associated with neuron of index (i) in the hidden layer) which will be multiplied by the normalized value of the third input ($\Delta t_{shear,n}$).

The development of this empirical equation converts the developed ANN model from a black-box mode into a white-box mode. This provides the ability to predict PR_{static} values for sandstone formations using Equation (4) by only substituting the required input parameters ($RHOB$, Δt_{comp}, Δt_{shear}) and the optimized weights and biases listed in Table 3, without the need to run the ANN model. Hence, the feasibility of practical implementation of the developed ANN model is high.

Table 3. The optimized weights and biases for the developed ANN model.

Neuron Index	Input Layer Weights			Hidden Layer Weights	Input Layer Biases
i	$w_{1_{i,1}}$	$w_{1_{i,2}}$	$w_{1_{i,3}}$	$b_{1,i}$	$w_{2,i}$
1	−2.020	−4.310	3.000	1.551	−5.071
2	4.057	1.753	2.032	−0.689	4.269
3	−1.519	−4.775	3.168	1.309	4.943
4	−5.682	−2.829	−1.652	1.235	3.583
5	−0.388	−1.805	1.971	0.088	1.466
6	0.165	−1.357	3.607	−1.041	−4.866
7	2.678	−4.758	2.102	1.225	−4.560
8	1.961	−2.012	−4.199	1.508	−5.459
9	−2.979	3.590	−1.195	−1.485	−6.104
10	−1.352	3.028	6.392	−1.405	−3.564
11	0.982	2.406	−3.062	1.549	−3.602
12	3.043	−1.423	0.093	2.899	−3.161
13	−3.225	−1.833	1.484	−2.479	−2.090

3.4. Procedure to Use the Developed Empirical Equation to Predict PRstatic Values

The developed empirical equation can be used to estimate PR_{static} values for sandstone formations according to the steps described below.

First, the input parameters (RHOB, Δt_{comp} and Δt_{shear}) should be normalized using Equations (5)–(7). The normalized values ($RHOB_n$, $\Delta t_{comp,n}$ and $\Delta t_{shear,n}$) are substituted in Equation (4) to calculate the normalized value of the static Poisson's ratio ($PR_{static,n}$) with the optimized weights and biases listed in Table 3.

$$RHOB_n = 2.994(RHOB - 2.312) - 1 \quad (5)$$

$$\Delta t_{comp,n} = 0.0578(\Delta t_{comp} - 44.341) - 1 \quad (6)$$

$$\Delta t_{shear,n} = 0.0318(\Delta t_{shear} - 73.187) - 1 \quad (7)$$

Then, the actual value of the static Poisson's ratio (PR_{static}) can be obtained by denormalizing its normalized value ($PR_{static,n}$) using Equation (8). Figure 13 shows a summary of the procedure needed for applying the developed correlation.

$$PR_{static} = \frac{PR_{static,n} + 1}{7.1174} + 0.2 \quad (8)$$

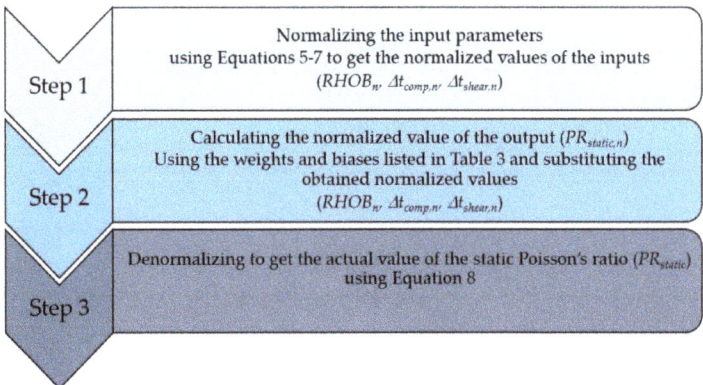

Figure 13. Procedure to apply the developed ANN-based correlation.

3.5. Validation of the Developed ANN Model and the Extracted Equation

The validation process of the developed ANN model is conducted in two main phases:

Phase 1: includes using unseen data from other drilled wells within the same area to predict PR_{static} and comparing the results with the actual values.

Phase 2: validates the developed model vs. common previous approaches.

3.5.1. Phase: Validation Using Field Data

For validating the developed ANN model, actual field data from two other wells are used. These data are not included in building the ANN model (training and testing).

Case Number 1

The data collected from well number 1 comprise a continuous profile of petrophysical log data including $RHOB$, Δt_{comp}, and Δt_{shear} measurements of an interval of 550 ft of the sandstone formation, in addition to five core data points representing core samples of the formation within this interval. The log data of these three parameters were used as the inputs to estimate PR_{static} using the ANN-based empirical equation expressed in Equation (4). Then, the results obtained from the ANN model are compared with the laboratory measured PR_{static} core data. Figure 14 shows that the model estimates PR_{static} values within this 550 ft-interval with good match, indicated by R of 0.93 and an MAPE of 4.2% between the predicted and the actual values.

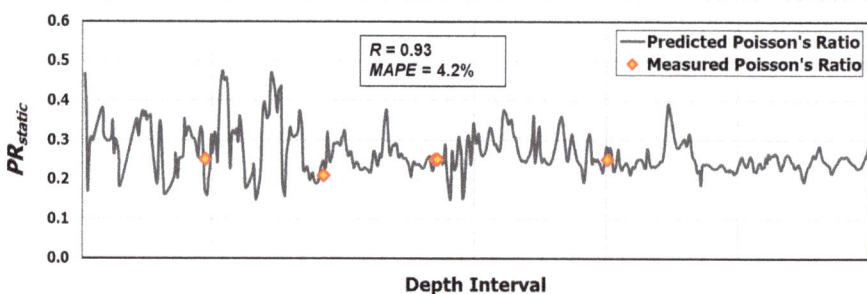

Figure 14. Comparison of the predicted PR_{static} values by the ANN model with the measured values for cores from well number 1 ($R = 0.93$, MAPE = 4.2%).

Case Number 2

For this well, wire-lined log data ($RHOB$, Δt_{comp}, and Δt_{shear}) for an interval of 300 ft of sandstone formation are used as inputs. In addition, five experimentally measured core data points of PR_{static} are available from the same interval to compare with the results obtained from the ANN model. Figure 15 shows very good agreement between the values measured in the laboratory and predicted PR_{static} values, with R of 0.92 and an MAPE of 2.53% between the predicted and the actual values.

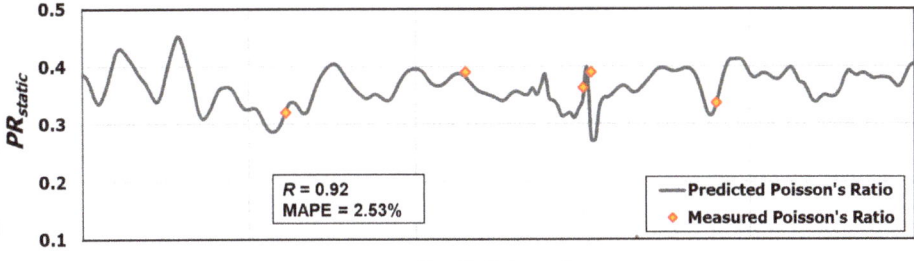

Figure 15. Comparison of the PR_{static} values predicted by the ANN model with the measured values for cores from well number 2 ($R = 0.92$, MAPE = 2.53%).

3.5.2. Phase 2: Validation by Comparing the Predictions of the ANN Model with Common Previous Approaches

As mentioned before the most reliable measurements of PR_{static} values are provided by the lab measurements of core samples representing the desired interval. However, due to the difficulty and complexity to get samples for the depth interval of interest, it is common in the oil and gas industry to use correlations to predict PR_{static} values via a standard workflow. These correlations are normally obtained by relating the PR_{static} values measured in the laboratory to the calculated $PR_{dynamic}$ from well logs. The dynamic Poisson's ratio values can be estimated using V_p and V_s via Equation (1). Then PR_{static} values can be related to $PR_{dynamic}$ values by plotting PR_{static} vs. $PR_{dynamic}$. In this study, the correlation between the actual PR_{static} and the calculated $PR_{dynamic}$ is developed using the same dataset used for building the ANN model resulting in Equation (9) which relates PR_{static} with $PR_{dynamic}$. Thereafter this correlation can be then used to predict PR_{static} for other datasets.

Equations (9) is determined by identifying the best fit equation when plotting PR_{static} vs. $PR_{dynamic}$, as shown in Figure 16. The extracted equation shows low coefficient of determination (R^2) between PR_{static} and $PR_{dynamic}$ of 0.58.

$$PR_{static} = 1.3 \times PR_{dynmic} - 0.006 \tag{9}$$

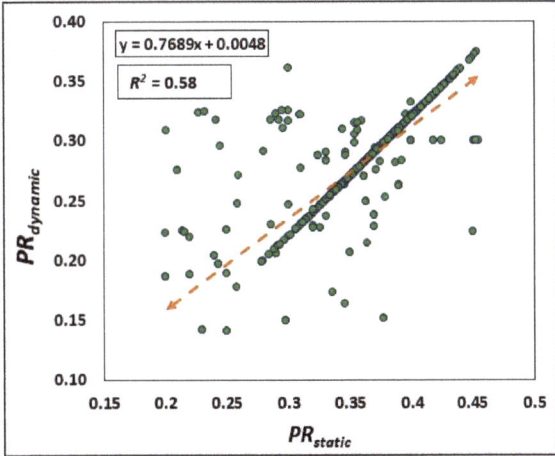

Figure 16. Relationship between PR_{static} vs. $PR_{dynamic}$ using well log data (V_p and V_s) for sandstone sections in the same area.

After that another (unseen) dataset representing sandstone sections within the same area is then used to estimate PR_{static} using the developed ANN model and Equation (9) and compare the accuracy of the results relative to the actual PR_{static} values. Figure 17a,b show comparison between the actual PR_{static} and those estimated using the developed ANN model and Equation (9). The developed ANN is found to outperform with R^2 of 0.96 compared to R^2 of 0.5 using Equation (9). More details about this standard workflow to predict PR_{static} can be found in [61–63].

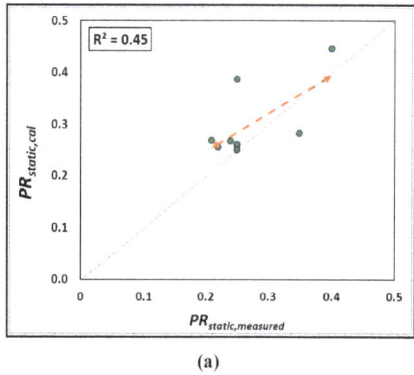
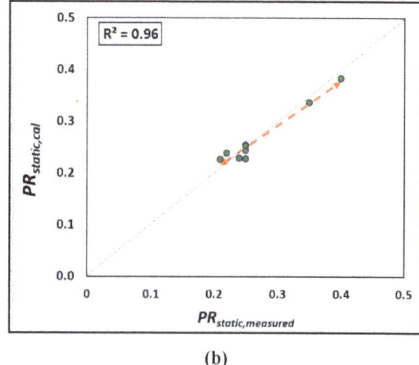

Figure 17. Comparison between the measured values of PR_{static} vs. the estimated values using (a) $PR_{dynamic}$ values via Equation (9) (b) the developed ANN model.

For further confirmation on the superiority of the developed ANN model to predict PR_{static}, it is compared with the model developed by Kumar [25]. Kumar developed a correlation relating PR_{static} with V_p and V_s stated in Equation (2). Then, PR_{static} values are estimated using Kumar's model (using the same dataset used for validating the ANN model vs. the aforementioned standard workflow) and the results are compared to actual PR_{static} values. The performance of the developed ANN model, the standard workflow, and Kumar's model is evaluated in terms of R, MAPE, and R^2 between the estimated and measured PR_{static} values, as listed in Table 4 and shown in Figure 18.

Table 4. The optimized weight and biases for the developed ANN model.

Model	R	MAPE, %	R^2
ANN_SADE	0.97	4.88	0.96
Standard Workflow	0.67	53.5	0.45
Kumar's Model	0.94	16.13	0.88

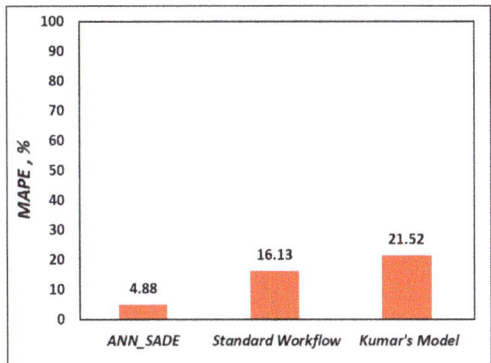

Figure 18. Comparison between the prediction efficiency of PR_{static} values using previous approaches vs. the developed ANN model in terms of MAPE.

4. Conclusions

The self-adaptive differential evolution ($SADE$) algorithm was implemented to determine the best combination of ANN parameters to predict the static Poisson's ratio with a high accuracy. Comparing the results obtained from the developed ANN model with the PR_{static} values measured in the laboratory demonstrates the following:

- The developed ANN model has the leading predictive efficiency for the static Poisson's ratio compared with other approaches.
- Petrophysical log data, namely $RHOB$, Δt_{comp}, and Δt_{shear}, are used as input parameters for the developed model to produce a continuous profile of PR_{static} values whenever these log data are available.
- The extracted ANN-based empirical equation makes the implementation of the developed ANN model easier and more practical, without the need to run the ANN model using any software.
- The developed ANN model allows the estimation of PR_{static} values of retrieved sandstone samples without destroying them, which makes them available for more tests.
- The developed ANN-based equation is considered a timely and economically effective tool to estimate PR_{static} values, especially when core data are not available.

Author Contributions: Conceptualization, S.E., A.A. and T.M.; methodology, T.M., A.G.; software, T.M.; validation, S.E., A.G. and A.A.; formal analysis, S.E. A.G.; investigation, A.A.; resources, S.E.; data curation, S.E., A.A.; writing—original draft preparation, A.G.; writing—review and editing, A.A., S.E.; visualization, T.M., A.A.; supervision, S.E.

Funding: This research received no external funding.

Acknowledgments: The authors wish to acknowledge King Fahd University of Petroleum and Minerals (KFUPM) for use of various facilities in carrying out this research. Many thanks are due to the anonymous referees for their detailed and helpful comments.

Conflicts of Interest: The author declares no conflict of interest.

Nomenclature

AI	Artificial intelligence
MAPE	Mean absolute percentage error
UCS	Unconfined compressive strength
ANN	Artificial neural network
SADE	self-adaptive differential evolution
Tansig	Hyperbolic tangent sigmoid transfer function
Hardlim	Hard-limit transfer function
Logsig	Log-sigmoid transfer function
Pure-linear	Linear transfer function
Elliotsig	Elliot symmetric sigmoid transfer function
Tribas	Triangular basis transfer function
Satlin	Saturating linear transfer function
Radbas	Radial basis transfer function
Trainlm	Levenberg–Marquardt backpropagation
Trainbfg	BFGS quasi-Newton
Trainbr	Bayesian regularization backpropagation
Trainscg	Scaled conjugate gradient backpropagation

List of Symbols

R^2	Coefficient of determination
PR_{static}	Static Poisson's ratio
$PR_{dynamic}$	Dynamic Poisson's ratio
RHOB	Formation bulk density
P-wave	Compressional wave
S-wave	Shear wave
Δt_{comp}	P-wave transit time
Δt_{shear}	S-wave transit time
T	Tensile strength
σ_v	Overburden stress
σ_h	Horizontal stress
V_p	P-wave velocity
V_s	S-wave velocity
E_s	Static Young's modulus
b_1	Input layer biases
b_2	Output layer bias
N	Number of neurons in the hidden layer
R	Correlation coefficient
w_1	Weights linking inputs and hidden layer
w_2	Weights linking output and hidden layer

Subscripts

i	Index of each neuron in the hidden layer
n	Normalized value

Appendix A

The formula of correlation coefficient (R) between any two variables (x, y) used in this study is expressed as:

$$R = \frac{k\sum_{i=1}^{k} xy - \left(\sum_{i=1}^{k} x\right)\left(\sum_{i=1}^{k} y\right)}{\sqrt{k\left(\sum_{i=1}^{k} x^2\right) - \left(\sum_{i=1}^{k} y\right)^2} \sqrt{k\left(\sum_{i=1}^{k} y^2\right) - \left(\sum_{i=1}^{k} y\right)^2}}$$

where K is the number of dataset points.

Mean absolute percentage error (MAPE) is expressed as:

$$MAPE = \frac{\sum \left|\frac{PR_{static,measured} - PR_{static,predicted}}{PR_{static,measured}}\right| \times 100\%}{m}$$

where m is the number of dataset points.

Coefficient of determination (R^2)

$$R^2 = \left(\frac{k\sum_{i=1}^{k} xy - (\sum_{i=1}^{k} x)(\sum_{i=1}^{k} y)}{\sqrt{k\left(\sum_{i=1}^{k} x^2\right) - \left(\sum_{i=1}^{k} y\right)^2} \sqrt{k\left(\sum_{i=1}^{k} y^2\right) - \left(\sum_{i=1}^{k} y\right)^2}}\right)^2$$

References

1. Anifowose, F.; Adeniye, S.; Abdulraheem, A.; Al-Shuhail, A. Integrating seismic and log data for improved petroleum reservoir properties estimation using non-linear feature-selection based hybrid computational intelligence models. *J. Pet. Sci. Eng.* **2016**, *145*, 230–237. [CrossRef]
2. Anifowose, F.A.; Labadin, J.; Abdulraheem, A. Ensemble model of non-linear feature selection-based extreme learning machine for improved natural gas reservoir characterization. *J. Nat. Gas Sci. Eng.* **2015**, *26*, 1561–1572. [CrossRef]
3. Helmy, T.; Hossain, M.I.; Adbulraheem, A.; Rahman, S.M.; Hassan, M.R.; Khoukhi, A.; Elshafei, M. Prediction of non-hydrocarbon gas components in separator by using hybrid computational intelligence models. *Neural Comput. Appl.* **2017**, *28*, 635–649. [CrossRef]
4. Al-Bulushi, N.I.; King, P.R.; Blunt, M.J.; Kraaijveld, M. Artificial neural networks workflow and its application in the petroleum industry. *Neural Comput. Appl.* **2012**, *21*, 409–421. [CrossRef]
5. Tariq, Z.; Elkatatny, S.; Mahmoud, M.; Ali, A.Z.; Abdulraheem, A. A new technique to develop rock strength correlation using artificial intelligence tools. In *SPE Reservoir Characterisation and Simulation Conference and Exhibition*; Society of Petroleum Engineers: Calgary, AB, Canada, 2017. [CrossRef]
6. Nes, O.M.; Fjær, E.; Tronvoll, J.; Kristiansen, T.G.; Horsrud, P. Drilling time reduction through an integrated rock mechanics analysis. In Proceedings of the SPE/IADC Drilling Conference, Amsterdam, The Netherlands, 23–25 February 2005.
7. Zhang, H.; Qiu, K.; Fuller, J.; Yin, G.; Yuan, F.; Chen, S. Geomechanical Evaluation Enabled Successful Stimulation of a HPHT Tight Gas Reservoir in Western China. In Proceedings of the International Petroleum Technology Conference, Kuala Lumpur, Malaysia, 19–22 January 2014.
8. Tutuncu, A.N.; Sharma, M.M. Relating Static and Ultrasonic Laboratory Measurements to Acoustic Log Measurements in Tight Gas Sands. In Proceedings of the SPE Annual Technical Conference and Exhibition, Washington, DC, USA, 4–7 October 1992. [CrossRef]
9. Gatens, J.M., III; Harrison, C.W., III; Lancaster, D.E.; Guidry, F.K. In-situ stress tests and acoustic logs determine mechanical propertties and stress profiles in the devonian shales. *SPE Formation Eval.* **1990**, *5*, 248–254. [CrossRef]
10. Najibi, A.R.; Ghafoori, M.; Lashkaripour, G.R.; Asef, M.R. Empirical relations between strength and static and dynamic elastic properties of Asmari and Sarvak limestones, two main oil reservoirs in Iran. *J. Pet. Sci. Eng.* **2015**, *126*, 78–82. [CrossRef]
11. Tariq, Z.; Mahmoud, M.; Abdulraheem, A. Core log integration: A hybrid intelligent data-driven solution to improve elastic parameter prediction. *Neural Comput. Appl.* **2019**, 1–21. [CrossRef]
12. Nawrocki, P.A.; Dusseault, M.B. Modelling of Damaged Zones around Boreholes Using a Radius Dependent Young's Modulus. *J. Can. Pet. Technol.* **1996**, *35*, 31–35. [CrossRef]
13. Wang, C.; Wu, Y.S.; Xiong, Y.; Winterfeld, P.H.; Huang, Z. Geomechanics coupling simulation of fracture closure and its influence on gas production in shale gas reservoirs. In Proceedings of the SPE Reservoir Simulation Symposium, Houston, TA, USA, 23–25 February 2015.

14. Ameen, M.S.; Smart, B.G.; Somerville, J.M.; Hammilton, S.; Naji, N.A. Predicting rock mechanical properties of carbonates from wireline logs (a case study: Arab-D reservoir, Ghawar field, Saudi Arabia). *Mar. Pet. Geol.* **2009**, *26*, 430–444. [CrossRef]
15. Elkatatny, S.; Mahmoud, M.; Mohamed, I.; Abdulraheem, A. Development of a new correlation to determine the static Young's modulus. *J. Pet. Explor. Prod. Technol* **2018**, *8*, 17–30. [CrossRef]
16. Spain, D.R.; Gil, I.R.; Sebastian, H.M.; Smith, P.; Wampler, J.; Cadwallader, S.; Graff, M. Geo-engineered completion optimization: An integrated, multi-disciplinary approach to improve stimulation efficiency in unconventional shale reservoirs. In Proceedings of the SPE Middle East Unconventional Resources Conference and Exhibition, Muscat, Oman, 26–28 January 2015.
17. Mahmoud, M.; Elkatatny, S.; Ramadan, E.; Abdulraheem, A. Development of lithology-based static Young's modulus correlations from log data based on data clustering technique. *J. Pet. Sci. Eng.* **2016**, *146*, 10–20. [CrossRef]
18. Tariq, Z.; Elkatatny, S.; Mahmoud, M.; Abdulraheem, A. A new artificial intelligence based empirical correlation to predict sonic travel time. In Proceedings of the International Petroleum Technology Conference, Bangkok, Thailand, 14–16 November 2016.
19. Tariq, Z.; Elkatatny, S.; Mahmoud, M.; Ali, A.Z.; Abdulraheem, A. A new technique to develop rock strength correlation using artificial intelligence tools. In Proceedings of the SPE Reservoir Characterisation and Simulation Conference and Exhibition, Abu Dhabi, UAE, 8–10 May 2017.
20. Tariq, Z.; Elkatatny, S.M.; Mahmoud, M.A.; Abdulraheem, A.; Abdelwahab, A.Z.; Woldeamanuel, M. *Estimation of Rock Mechanical Parameters Using Artificial Intelligence Tools*; American Rock Mechanics Association: San Francisco, CA, USA, 2017.
21. Elkatatny, S.; Tariq, Z.; Mahmoud, M.; Abdulraheem, A.; Mohamed, I. An integrated approach for estimating static Young's modulus using artificial intelligence tools. *Neural Comput. Appl.* **2018**. [CrossRef]
22. D'Andrea, D.V.; Fischer, R.L.; Fogelson, D.E. *Prediction of Compressive Strength from Other Rock Properties*; US Department of the Interior, Bureau of Mines: Washington, DC, USA, 1965; Volume 6702.
23. Kumar, J. The effect of Poisson's ratio on rock properties. In Proceedings of the SPE Annual Fall Technical Conference and Exhibition, New Orleans, LA, USA, 3–6 October 1976.
24. Edimann, K.; Somerville, J.M.; Smart, B.G.D.; Hamilton, S.A.; Crawford, B.R. Predicting rock mechanical properties from wireline porosities. In Proceedings of the SPE/ISRM Rock Mechanics in Petroleum Engineering, Trondheim, Norway, 8–10 July 1998.
25. Kumar, A.; Jayakumar, T.; Raj, B.; Ray, K.K. Correlation between ultrasonic shear wave velocity and Poisson's ratio for isotropic solid materials. *Acta Mater.* **2003**, *51*, 2417–2426. [CrossRef]
26. Al-Shayea, N.A. Effects of testing methods and conditions on the elastic properties of limestone rock. *Eng. Geol.* **2004**, *74*, 139–156. [CrossRef]
27. Singh, V.; Singh, T.N. A Neuro-Fuzzy Approach for Prediction of Poisson's Ratio and Young's Modulus of Shale and Sandstone. In Proceedings of the 41st US Symposium on Rock Mechanics (USRMS), Golden, CO, USA, 17–21 June 2006.
28. Shalabi, F.I.; Cording, E.J.; Al-Hattamleh, O.H. Estimation of rock engineering properties using hardness tests. *Eng. Geol.* **2007**, *90*, 138–147. [CrossRef]
29. Al-Anazi, A.; Gates, I.D. A support vector machine algorithm to classify lithofacies and model permeability in heterogeneous reservoirs. *Eng. Geol.* **2010**, *114*, 267–277. [CrossRef]
30. Abdulraheem, A. Prediction of Poisson's Ratio for Carbonate Rocks Using ANN and Fuzzy Logic Type-2 Approaches. In Proceedings of the International Petroleum Technology Conference, Beijing, China, 26 March 2019.
31. ASTM D2664-04. Standard Test Method for Triaxial Compressive Strength of Undrained Rock Core Specimens without Pore Pressure Measurements. 2005. Available online: https://www.astm.org/Standards/D2664.htm (accessed on 3 April 2019).
32. Gercek, H. Poisson's ratio values for rocks. *Int. J. Rock Mech. Min. Sci.* **2007**, *44*, 1–13. [CrossRef]
33. Dawson, R. How Significant Is A Boxplot Outlier? *J. Stat. Educ.* **2011**, *19*. [CrossRef]
34. Thirumalai, C.S.; Manickam, V.; Balaji, R. Data analysis using Box and Whisker Plot for Lung Cancer. In Proceedings of the 2017 Innovations in Power and Advanced Computing Technologies, Vellore, Tamil Nadu, India, 21–22 April 2017. [CrossRef]

35. Fontana, E.; Iturrino, G.J.; Tartarotti, P. Depth-shifting and orientation of core data using a core–log integration approach: A case study from ODP–IODP Hole 1256D. *Tectonophysics* **2010**, *494*, 85–100. [CrossRef]
36. Nadezhdin, O.; Zairullina, E.; Efimov, D.; Savichev, V. *Algorithms of Automatic Core-Log Depth-Shifting In Problems of Petrophysical Model Construction, Proceedings of the SPE Russian Oil and Gas Exploration & Production Technical Conference and Exhibition*; Society of Petroleum Engineers: Moscow, Russia, 16 October 2014.
37. Benesty, J.; Chen, J.; Huang, Y.; Cohen, I. Pearson correlation coefficient. In *Noise Reduction in Speech Processing*; Springer: Berlin, Genmany, 2009; pp. 1–4.
38. Sudakov, O.; Burnaev, E.; Koroteev, D. Driving Digital Rock towards Machine Learning:predicting permeability with Gradient Boosting and Deep Neural Networks. *Comput. Geosci.* **2018**, *127*, 91–98. [CrossRef]
39. Chauhan, S.; Rühaak, W.; Anbergen, H.; Kabdenov, A.; Freise, M.; Wille, T.; Sass, I. Phase segmentation of X-ray computer tomography rock images using machine learning techniques: An accuracy and performance study. *Solid Earth* **2016**, *7*, 1125–1139. [CrossRef]
40. Chauhan, S.; Rühaak, W.; Khan, F.; Enzmann, F.; Mielke, P.; Kersten, M.; Sass, I. Processing of rock core microtomography images: Using seven different machine learning algorithms. *Comput. Geosci.* **2016**, *86*, 120–128. [CrossRef]
41. Tahmasebi, P.; Javadpour, F.; Sahimi, M. Data mining and machine learning for identifying sweet spots in shale reservoirs. *Expert Syst. Appl.* **2017**, *88*, 435–447. [CrossRef]
42. Mousavi Nezhad, M.; Gironacci, E.; Rezania, M.; Khalili, N. Stochastic modelling of crack propagation in materials with random properties using isometric mapping for dimensionality reduction of nonlinear data sets. *Int. J. Numer. Methods Eng.* **2017**, *113*, 656–680. [CrossRef]
43. Keller, L.M.; Schwiedrzik, J.J.; Gasser, P.; Michler, J. Understanding anisotropic mechanical properties of shales at different length scales: In situ micropillar compression combined with finite element calculations. *J. Geophys. Res. Solid Earth* **2017**, *122*. [CrossRef]
44. Sone, H.; Zoback, M.D. Mechanical properties of shale-gas reservoir rocks—Part 1: Static and dynamic elastic properties and anisotropy. *Geophysics* **2013**, *78*, 381–392. [CrossRef]
45. Rable, B. The Future is Here: 3 Ways AI Roots Itself in O&G in the Surge Magazine. 2017. Available online: http://thesurge.com/stories/future-artificial-intelligence-roots-oil-gas-industry (accessed on 3 April 2019).
46. Anifowose, F.A.; Labadin, J.; Abdulraheem, A. Ensemble machine learning: An untapped modeling paradigm for petroleum reservoir characterization. *J. Pet. Sci. Eng.* **2017**, *151*, 480–487. [CrossRef]
47. Lippman, R.P. An introduction to computing with neural nets. *IEEE ASSP Mag.* **1987**, *4*, 4–22. [CrossRef]
48. Nakamoto, P. *Neural Networks and Deep Learning: Deep Learning Explained to Your Granny a Visual Introduction for Beginners Who Want to Make Their Own Deep Learning Neural Network (Machine Learning)*; CreateSpace Independent Publishing Platform: Scotts Valley, CA, USA, 2017.
49. Hinton, G.E.; Osindero, S.; Teh, Y.-W. A fast learning algorithm for deep belief nets. *Neural Comput.* **2006**, *18*, 1527–1554. [CrossRef]
50. Niculescu, S. Artificial neural networks and genetic algorithms in Qsar. *J. Mol. Struct.* **2003**, *622*, 71–83. [CrossRef]
51. Yılmaz, I.; Yuksek, A.G. An example of artificial neural network (ANN) application for indirect estimation of rock parameters. *Rock Mech. Rock Eng.* **2008**, *41*, 781–795. [CrossRef]
52. Rao, S.; Ramamurti, V. A hybrid technique to enhance the performance of recurrent neural networks for time series prediction. In Proceedings of the IEEE international conference on neural networks, San Francisco, CA, USA, 28 March–1 April 1993; pp. 52–57.
53. Storn, R.; Price, K. Differential Evolution: A Simple and Efficient Adaptive Scheme for Global Optimization Over Continuous Spaces. *J. Glob. Optim.* **1995**, *23*, 341–359.
54. Goudos, S.K.; Baltzis, K.B.; Antoniadis, K.; Zaharis, Z.D.; Hilas, C.S. A comparative study of common and self-adaptive differential evolution strategies on numerical benchmark problems. *Procedia Comput. Sci.* **2011**, *3*, 83–88. [CrossRef]
55. Qin, A.K.; Suganthan, P.N. Self-adaptive differential evolution algorithm for numerical optimization. In Proceedings of the IEEE Congress on Evolutionary Computation, Edinburgh, UK, 2–4 September 2005; Volume 2, pp. 178–1791.

56. Vesterstrom, J.; Thomsen, R. A comparative study of differential evolution, particle swarm optimization, and evolutionary algorithms on numerical benchmark problems. In Proceedings of the 2004 Congress on Evolutionary Computation, Portland, OR, USA, 19–23 June 2004.
57. Qin, A.K.; Huang, V.L.; Suganthan, P.N. Differential evolution algorithm with strategy adaptation for global numerical optimization. *IEEE Trans. Evol. Comput.* **2009**, *13*, 398–417. [CrossRef]
58. Foroud, T.; Baradaran, A.; Seifi, A. A comparative evaluation of global search algorithms in black box optimization of oil production: A case study on Brugge field. *J. Pet. Sci. Eng.* **2018**, *167*, 131–151. [CrossRef]
59. Abdelgawad, K.; Elkatatny, S.; Moussa, T.; Mahmoud, M.; Patil, S. Real-Time Determination of Rheological Properties of Spud Drilling Fluids Using a Hybrid Artificial Intelligence Technique. *J. Energy Resour. Technol.* **2019**, *141*, 032908. [CrossRef]
60. Smith, G. *Essential Statistics Regression and Econometrics*; Academic Press: Cambridge, MA, USA, 2015.
61. Kim, S.; Kim, H. A new metric of absolute percentage error for intermittent demand forecasts. *Int. J. Forecast.* **2016**, *32*, 669–679. [CrossRef]
62. Yale, D.P. Static and Dynamic Rock Mechanical Properties in the Hugoton and Panoma Fields, Kansas. In Proceedings of the SPE Mid-Continent Gas Symposium, Amarillo, TX, USA, 22–24 May 1994.
63. Montmayeur, H.; Graves, R.M. Prediction of static elastic/mechanical properties of consolidated and unconsolidated sands from acoustic measurements: Correlations. In Proceedings of the SPE Annual Technical Conference and Exhibition, Houston, TX, USA, 3–6 October 1993.

© 2019 by the authors. Licensee MDPI, Basel, Switzerland. This article is an open access article distributed under the terms and conditions of the Creative Commons Attribution (CC BY) license (http://creativecommons.org/licenses/by/4.0/).

Article

Real-Time Prediction of the Rheological Properties of Water-Based Drill-In Fluid Using Artificial Neural Networks

Salaheldin Elkatatny

College of Petroleum Engineering & Geosciences, King Fahd University of Petroleum & Minerals, Dhahran 31261, Saudi Arabia; elkatatny@kfupm.edu.sa; Tel.: +966-594663692

Received: 14 August 2019; Accepted: 11 September 2019; Published: 12 September 2019

Abstract: The rheological properties of drilling fluids are the key parameter for optimizing drilling operation and reducing total drilling cost by avoiding common problems such as hole cleaning, pipe sticking, loss of circulation, and well control. The conventional method of measuring the rheological properties are time-consuming and require a high effort for equipment cleaning, so they are only measured twice a day. There is a need to develop an automated system to measure the rheological properties in real-time based on the frequent measurements of mud density, Marsh funnel time, and solid percent. The main objective of this paper is to apply a modified self-adaptive differential evolution technique to determine the optimum combination of an artificial neural network's variables to precisely predict the rheological properties of water-based drill-in fluid using the frequent measuring of mud density, Marsh funnel time, and solid percent. The second objective is whitening the black box of an artificial neural network by developing five new empirical correlations to determine the rheological properties without the need for the artificial neural network models. Actual field measurements (900 data points) were used to train, test, and validate the artificial neural network models and the developed empirical correlations. The optimization process illustrated that the best training function was Bayesian regularization backpropagation (trainbr), and the best transferring function was Elliot symmetric sigmoid (elliotsig). The optimum number of neurons was 30 for the plastic viscosity and the flow consistency index, while it was 29 for apparent viscosity, yield point, and the flow behavior index. The developed artificial neural network models and empirical correlations predicted the rheological properties with high accuracy. The correlation coefficient (R) was more than 90%, and the average absolute percentage error was less than 8.6%. The new technique for rheological properties estimation is an example of the new development which will help the new generation to discover and extract oil and gas with less cost and with safer operations.

Keywords: empirical correlations; rheological properties; real-time; water-based drill-in fluid; artificial neural network

1. Introduction

Water-based drill-in fluid (WBDIF) is used to drill the reservoir section, which carries the hydrocarbon. WBDIF should be designed to be non-damaging by building an impermeable layer on the face of the formation during the drilling process while this layer should be removed easily before casing and cementing the hole. WBDIF should provide stable rheological properties (RHPs) in order to provide a stable and clean hole and to prevent cutting accumulation, both of which lead to the possibility of pipe sticking, [1–3]. The main function of WBDIF is to support formation pressure and prevent reservoir fluid from entering the wellbore while drilling [4]. In addition, the drill-in fluid should cool and lubricate the bit and the drill string [5,6].

Sodium chloride-water-based drill-in fluid (NaCl-WBDIF) is mainly used while drilling the reservoir section. NaCl salt is used as a weighting material to increase mud density, while the Na+ ions work as shale stabilizers [7]. NaCl polymer mud is characterized as an inhibited, non-dispersed drilling fluid in which the viscosity control and the filtration properties are enhanced by using some types of polymers such as xanthan gum and starch. This helps reduce the possibility of formation damage [8].

RHPs play a key role in the success of the drilling operation. RHPs such as plastic viscosity (PV), yield point (YP), apparent viscosity (AV), flow consistency index (K), and flow behavior index (n) should be determined in real-time to calculate rig hydraulics and determine the required pressure to optimize hole cleaning. Increasing the PV value gives an indication about the increase in solid content, and it can highly affect the rate of penetration [9–11]. Paiaman et al. [12] stated that a lower YP value is preferred in turbulent flow, while a high YP value is required for laminar flow. The ratio of YP/PV is very important for hole cleaning. The YP/PV ratio should be greater than 1.5 [13]. The consistency index of the drilling fluid (k) is the main controlling parameter of the carrying capacity index (CCI) [14].

The common procedure in rig-sites is that the drilling crew usually measures the mud density and Marsh funnel time [15] every 15–20 min, and these measurements are used as indicators for the changes in the fluid properties [16]. Other RHPs (PV, YP, n, and K) are usually measured twice a day, as it requires a long time to heat the fluid, record, analyze the data, and clean the equipment. This process is tedious and time-consuming.

The effect of solid content on drilling fluid RHPs is very obvious, as can be seen throughout the literature. The objective of this study was to develop novel empirical models that are capable of acquiring the RHPs of NaCl polymer mud using one of the powerful artificial intelligence techniques—the artificial neural network (ANN)—using 900 field measurements of mud density (MD), Marsh funnel time (FT), and solid percent (SP). The novelty of this research is getting a real-time prediction (every 10–15 min) of the mud RHPs. Additionally, in this paper, a self-adaptive evolution algorithm was used to optimize the input parameters at the same time, and this was linked with the ANN model. The developed method depends on taking the reading from the automated Marsh funnel system (which contains different sensors) and applying artificial neural network models to predict the rheological properties every 10–20 min, which enable the driller to understand the changes of the drilling fluid properties as well as changes in the rig hydraulics. This make decisions regarding the required action based on given information much faster.

Artificial Neural Network

The concept of artificial networks was introduced into engineering research in the 1940s [17,18]. At early stages, artificial intelligence (AI) was used to solve the complex equations and mimic the nervous system [19,20].

The ANN has been considered as an effective AI tool; therefore, it has been widely applied in several fields such as classification and optimization tasks [21,22]. The ANN model is a system of neurons and hidden layers [23]. Usually, the whole data are grouped into two sets—training and testing data sets. The training group is used to train the network and capture the relationship between the input and output parameters, while the testing data are used to measure the reliability of the developed ANN system. During the training stage, the testing data remain unseen by the model, which provides more confidence regarding model reliability [24–26].

Alajmi et al. [27] predicted choke performance using an ANN. Alarifi et al. [28] estimated the productivity index for oil horizontal wells using an ANN, a functional network and fuzzy logic. Chen et al. [29] applied a NN and fuzzy logic to evaluate the performance of an inflow control device (ICD) in a horizontal well. Their model investigated the influences of reservoir parameters (such as reservoir size, thickness, reservoir heterogeneity, and permeability ratio) on ICD completion performance. Van and Chon [30,31] evaluated the performance of carbon dioxide (CO_2) flooding using

ANN techniques. They developed ANN models for determining oil production rate, CO_2 production, and gas-oil ratio (GOR).

The self-adaptive differential evolution (SaDE) was introduced by Qin et al. [32] to overcome the common issues of the differential evaluation (DE) [33]. The advantage of the SaDE is the ability to self-adapt the controlling parameters and mutation strategies based on the learning experience in the previous algorithm generations to obtain better results. Moussa and Awotunde [34] developed a modified SaDE that can be used for the optimization in different engineering problems.

Al-Khdheeawi and Mahdi [35] applied an ANN to predict the apparent viscosity of water-based drilling fluid using the mud density and Marsh funnel time. They concluded that the developed ANN correlation could predict AV with an average absolute percentage error (AAPE) of 8.6% and a correlation coefficient of 98.8%. Gowida et al. [36] stated that the ANN can be used efficiently to predict the rheological properties of the calcium chloride ($CaCl_2$) water-based drilling fluid based on mud density and Marsh funnel time.

Zhang et al. [37] developed a new technique for breast cancer detection using a combination of rectified linear unit and rank-based stochastic pooling. They concluded that the detection efficiency of the new technique overcomes the known six standard techniques known for breast cancer detection. For abnormal breasts in mammogram images, Wang et al. [38] developed a combined system of a feed-forward neural network with principal computer analysis, a Jaya algorithm, and a weighted-type fractional Fourier transform. They concluded that Jaya was a better algorithm for training the feed-forward neural network than the common know algorithms, and the developed technique was able to detect the abnormal breast with high accuracy (>92.27%).

The main goal of this study was to develop new sets of empirical correlations, optimized using modified self-adaptive differential evolution (MSaDE), to determine the RHPs of NaCl-WBDIF using a hybrid ANN model.

2. Methodology

ANN variables such as percent of training to testing, number of neurons, training and testing functions, and the number of layers should be optimized to develop a robust ANN model, and from this model, empirical correlation can be extracted. In this study, MSaDE was applied to optimize the variable parameters of the ANN for different RHPs. Nine-hundred field measurements were used to train, test, and validate the ANN models. The data were selected randomly to train the model, with 65% of the data being used for training (570 data points), 23% of the data being used for testing (180 data points), and 12% of the data being used (150 data points) for further validation. The ANN models were built using 88% of the available data, including training and testing and based on the optimized models, and the new empirical correlation was developed. The 12% remaining of data were used to validate the developed empirical correlations. The correlation coefficient ®, AAPE, and visualization check were used as criteria to evaluate the developed models and correlations.

The AAPE is a measure of the relative deviation of the predicted data from the real data and can be calculated using Equation (1):

$$AAPE = \frac{1}{n}\sum_{i=1}^{n}|E_i| \qquad (1)$$

where n is the number of data points and E_i is the relative deviation of a predicted value from a real value, Equation (2);

$$E_i = \left(\frac{y_{real} - y_{predict}}{y_{real}}\right) * 100 \qquad (2)$$

For the network training and transferring functions, two pools of 12 different training functions and 7 transferring functions were established, respectively. Each individual training/transferring function was indexed and used as one of the input parameters to the MSaDE optimization algorithm along with the other parameters such as the number of neurons, the percent of training to testing, and the number of hidden layers. Twenty independent optimization runs were performed to optimize the above-mentioned parameters. The optimization run that resulted best fit (in terms of the highest R and the lowest AAPE was considered as the best run, and its results are shown and discussed in this paper.

Data Description

Data were collected from different wells which were drilled using NaCl-WBDIF. Nine-hundred data records of MD, FT, SP, PV, and YP were used to train, test and validate the developed correlations for different RHPs. The data were collected while drilling a different reservoir section in which non-damaging drill-in fluid was used. The rheological properties were measure twice a day, and the mud density, solid percent and Marsh funnel time were measured at the same time.

Table 1 lists the statistical parameters of the nine-hundred data points. The drill-in fluid covered a wide range of fluid density where the MD ranged from 64 to 121 ppg. The FT ranged from 35 to 91 s/quart, and SP ranged from 0 to 32.5%. PV ranged from 7 to 51 cP, and the YP ranged from 19 to 45 lb/100 ft². Figure 1 shows that the PV was a strong function of MD and SP, where the R was 0.76 and 0.70 for MD and SP, respectively. PV was a moderate function of FT, with its R being 0.57. YP was a strong function of MD and moderate function of SP and FT. The R was 0.67, 0.58, and 0.42 for MD, SP, and FT, respectively, as seen in Figure 1.

Table 1. Statistical analysis of the collected field data from the drill-in fluid.

Statistical Parameter	Mud Weight (MD)	Marsh Funnel Time (MT)	Solid Percent (SP)	Plastic Viscosity (PV)	Yield Point (YP)
Minimum	64	35	0	7	19
Maximum	121	91	32.5	51	45
Mean	82.12	59.22	13.79	21.65	27.15
Median	78	58	13	20	27
Standard Deviation	14.33	10.10	7.18	8.15	3.95
Kurtosis	0.50	0.20	−0.39	0.74	1.23
Skewness	1.08	0.59	0.44	0.91	0.87

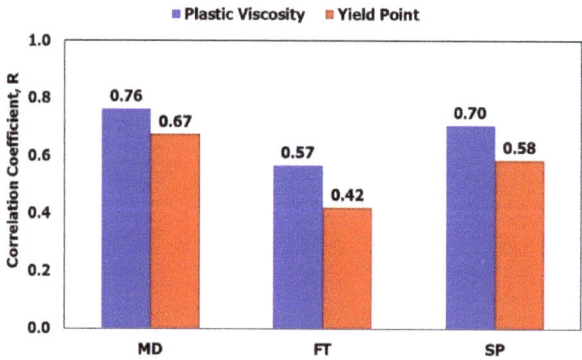

Figure 1. The relative importance of the input parameters to plastic viscosity and yield point.

3. Results and Discussion

3.1. Building Artificial Intelligence Models

The MSaDE technique was applied to optimize the ANN model for the PV. Equations (3)–(6) were used to normalize the input and the output parameters for the model. To train the ANN model, 570 data points were used.

$$MD_n = 0.034 * (MD - 64) - 1 \tag{3}$$

$$FT_n = 0.036 * (FT - 35) - 1 \tag{4}$$

$$SP_n = 0.062 * SP - 1 \tag{5}$$

$$PV_n = 0.044 * (PV - 6) - 1 \tag{6}$$

The optimization process showed that the best training function was Bayesian regularization backpropagation (trainbr) when using three input parameters (MD, FT, SP), and the optimized number of neurons was 30 when only one hidden layer was applied. The optimization process showed that the best transferring function was Elliot symmetric sigmoid (elliotsig).

Figure 2 shows that the R was 0.97 and the AAPE was 7.8% between the actual and predicted PV for the training data. For testing the model, 180 data points were used. Figure 2 shows that the R was 0.95 and the AAPE was 8.4% between the actual and predicted PV for the testing data.

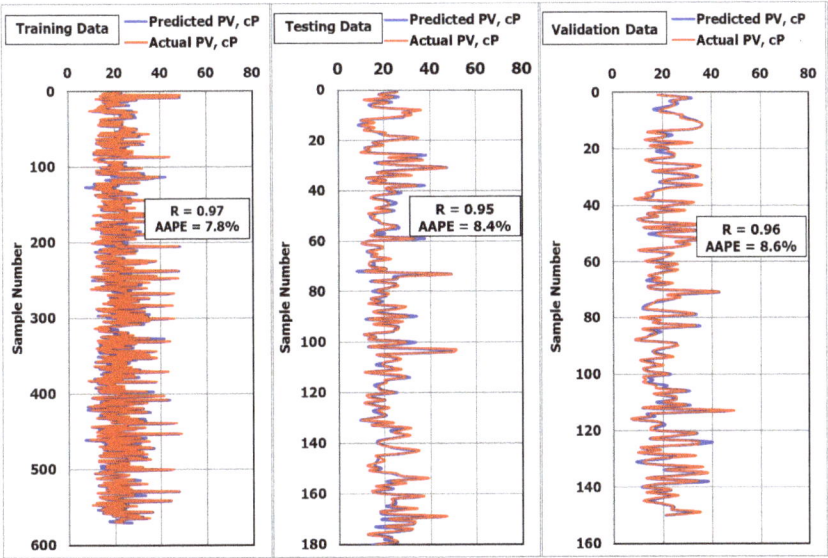

Figure 2. Prediction of plastic viscosity using the modified self-adaptive differential evolution-artificial neural network (MSaDE-ANN) technique.

The above results confirmed the high accuracy of using the MSaDE-ANN technique to predict the PV. For further validation, 150 unseen data points were used to evaluate the developed ANN-PV model. Figure 2 shows that the R was 0.96 and the AAPE was 8.6%, with an excellent match between the actual and predicted PV values for the validation points.

The same procedure was used to estimate the YP values using MD, FT, and SP. Training data (570 data points) were used to build the ANN-YP model. The optimization process after applying the MSaDE technique showed that the optimized number of neurons was 29, the optimum training function was Bayesian regularization backpropagation (trainbr), and the best transferring function was Elliot symmetric sigmoid (elliotsig).

Figure 3 shows that the R was 0.96 and the AAPE was 3.5% when using the MSaDE-ANN model to predict the YP values for the training data set. To test the developed model for YP, another set of data (180 unseen data points) was used. Figure 3 shows that for the unseen data, the R was 0.95 and the AAPE was 3.6. These results confirmed the high accuracy of the MSaDE-ANN model for predicting the YP from the MD, FT, and SP.

The flow behavior index (n) was used to describe the degree of fluid deviation from the standard Newtonian behavior. In other words, n was used to represent the degree of non-Newtonian behavior. For drilling fluids that act according to the pseudoplastic fluids behavior, the standard value of n is between zero and 1 [39], where the value is 1 for Newtonian fluids behavior and less than 1 for dilatant fluids. n also can be used as a representation of the shear-thinning properties of the drilling fluids. A fluid with a low value of n is good for hole cleaning purposes.

The flow behavior index (n) can be calculated through Equation (7) based on the values of PV and YP [40].

$$n = 3.32 * \log\left(\frac{2PV + YP}{PV + YP}\right) \tag{7}$$

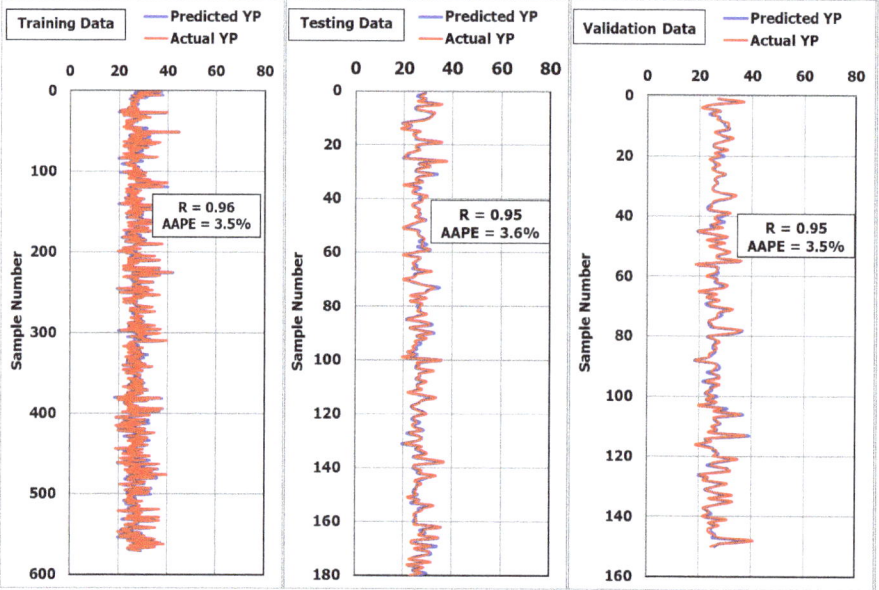

Figure 3. Prediction of yield point using the MSaDE-ANN technique.

The MSaDE technique was applied to optimize the variable parameters of the ANN model for n. The optimization process yielded that the optimized number of neurons was 29, the optimum training function was Bayesian regularization backpropagation (trainbr), and the best transferring function was Elliot symmetric sigmoid (elliotsig).

Figure 4 shows that the MSaDE-ANN predicted n with high accuracy, where the R was 0.94 and the AAPE was 3.96% for the training dataset (570 data points). The same results were obtained when applying the ANN-n model for the unseen data set (180 data points). The R was 0.93 and the AAPE was 4.1% between the actual and predicted values of n, as seen in Figure 4.

A new set of data was used to validate the developed ANN-n model (150 data points). Figure 4 shows the high accuracy of the developed model to calculate n values based on MD, FT, and SP. The R was 0.94 and the AAPE was 4.0% between the calculated and actual values of n.

The flow consistency index (K) can be calculated from the PV and YP values using Equation (8) [39].

$$K = \frac{2PV + YP}{1022^{3.22 \log\left(\frac{2PV+YP}{PV+YP}\right)}} \tag{8}$$

The optimization technique (MSaDE) was applied for the training dataset (570 data points) to determine the best combination of ANN variables to predict the K values based on MD, FT, and SP. The optimization process showed that the optimum number of neurons was 30, the optimum training function was Bayesian regularization backpropagation (trainbr), and the best transferring function was Elliot symmetric sigmoid (elliotsig).

Figure 5 shows that the R was 0.92 and the AAPE was 8.0% when plotting the actual and predicted values of K for the training dataset. For testing the developed ANN-K model, 150 unseen data points were used. Figure 5 shows that the R was 0.90 and the AAPE was 8.6% for the testing data.

For further validation for the developed model for K, a new set of data was used (150 data points). Figure 5 shows that the R was 0.91 and the AAPE was 8.4% when plotting the calculated and actual values of K.

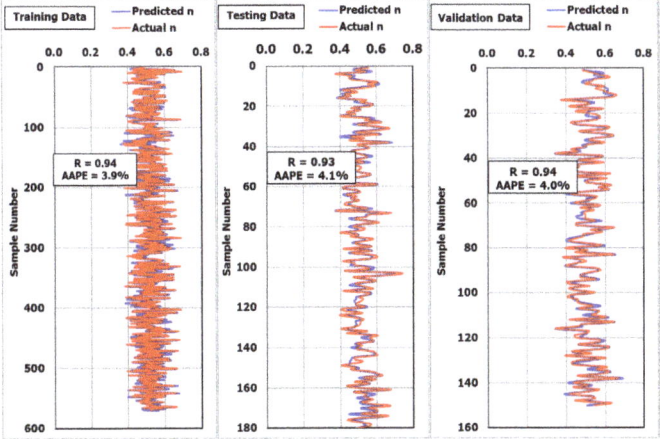

Figure 4. Prediction of the flow behavior index using the MSaDE-ANN technique.

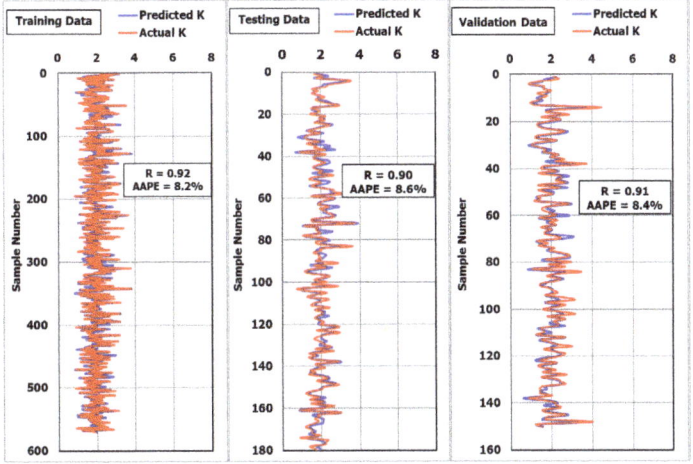

Figure 5. Prediction of the consistency index using the MSaDE-ANN technique.

3.2. Development of Empirical Correlations

Plastic viscosity can be estimated using Equation (9) in normalized form using the weights and biases of the optimized PV-ANN model.

$$PV_n = \sum_{i=1}^{N} w_{2_i} \frac{w_{1_1}MD_n + w_{1_2}FT_n + w_{1_3}SP_n + b_{1_i}}{1 + |w_{1_1}MD_n + w_{1_2}FT_n + w_{1_3}SP_n + b_{1_i}|} + b_2 \tag{9}$$

where PV_n is the PV in the normalized form; N is the optimized number of neurons (30 neurons); w_1 and w_2 are the weights between the input layer and hidden layer and the weights between the hidden layer and the output layer, respectively (see Table 2); b_1 is the biases between the input layer and the hidden layer; $b_2 = 0.073$, which is the bias associated with hidden layer and output layer; and MD_n, FT_n, and SP_n are the normalized value of the MD, FT, and SP, respectively.

Table 2. Weight and biases for the MSaDE- ANN-PV (plastic viscosity) model.

i	$w_{1,1}$	$w_{1,2}$	$w_{1,3}$	$b_{1,i}$	$w_{2,i}$
1	−0.583	1.507	−0.860	0.903	0.908
2	−3.501	−0.904	2.668	0.687	−3.538
3	1.808	−0.951	−1.900	−0.919	−1.791
4	−1.425	−0.233	0.978	0.831	1.730
5	0.694	−0.185	−2.284	−1.747	2.862
6	−0.437	−0.051	−2.132	0.938	2.268
7	−1.859	−0.960	−0.078	1.793	2.691
8	−1.938	0.218	−0.768	1.179	−1.546
9	−0.292	−0.861	1.351	0.265	2.066
10	−1.499	−1.501	−0.483	0.853	−2.594
11	2.684	−1.286	0.365	−0.872	2.682
12	−2.306	−1.507	0.739	0.798	2.175
13	−3.429	0.825	−0.812	0.612	2.935
14	−3.670	−0.562	2.914	0.212	3.500
15	−0.212	2.242	0.215	0.898	0.636
16	−3.783	0.359	−0.924	0.322	−2.874
17	1.841	0.508	−2.393	0.406	2.054
18	0.070	0.416	1.032	0.120	−1.277
19	−1.983	−1.337	−0.348	−1.039	−1.360
20	2.361	0.706	−1.352	0.682	−1.953
21	−0.433	1.532	−1.024	−0.416	0.591
22	3.936	−0.190	−0.664	1.675	2.266
23	−2.621	−0.446	1.632	−1.496	2.190
24	−3.587	−0.179	0.248	−1.957	3.859
25	0.391	2.102	−0.766	−0.486	0.718
26	−1.657	0.513	−1.322	2.493	−2.294
27	3.939	0.095	−0.526	2.303	3.056
28	2.624	−0.271	1.179	3.204	2.736
29	−1.101	0.296	−1.454	−1.872	2.617
30	−0.090	0.159	1.012	0.695	0.595

The de-normalized value of the PV can be obtained using Equation (10).

$$PV = 22.727 * PV_n + 28.727 \tag{10}$$

Using the weights and biases of the optimized MSaDE-ANN model for YP, Equation (9) can be used to calculate the normalized value of YP by changing the PV_n by YP_n. Equation (11) can be used to determine the actual value of YP. Table 3 list the values of w_1, w_2, i, and b_1. The value of b_2 was 1.309.

$$YP = 16.393 * YP_n + 28.393 \tag{11}$$

Table 3. Weight and biases for the MSaDE-ANN-YP model.

i	$w_{1,1}$	$w_{1,2}$	$w_{1,3}$	$b_{1,i}$	$w_{2,i}$
1	−1.221	1.308	2.159	1.233	1.591
2	−0.037	2.097	−0.212	−1.118	1.439
3	0.718	0.232	2.575	−1.190	−2.301
4	4.058	0.842	−0.047	−3.523	−2.752
5	1.106	2.035	1.657	−1.937	−1.485
6	−1.831	1.350	−0.601	0.126	−2.434
7	−0.374	−1.661	0.175	0.694	2.705
8	−0.911	1.444	1.932	0.630	1.460
9	3.782	−2.940	1.792	−0.087	−1.533
10	−2.465	−0.160	2.281	0.814	−2.687
11	−3.233	−0.544	−0.973	1.313	−3.472
12	4.663	0.189	−0.004	−1.128	−3.994
13	−3.581	0.020	−2.615	1.008	−3.412
14	−0.552	−0.904	1.216	−0.231	−0.450
15	0.232	−1.919	−2.035	0.649	−1.958
16	−1.575	−0.279	−2.414	0.708	2.612
17	−1.180	1.007	0.957	−0.032	−1.186
18	3.017	0.111	−2.673	0.428	0.984
19	−1.576	−0.403	1.255	−0.136	2.349
20	0.594	−1.155	−2.862	0.690	1.720
21	1.168	0.259	−3.619	1.469	−2.071
22	1.279	1.252	1.368	1.121	1.375
23	3.282	0.251	3.735	4.043	−2.204
24	1.963	0.661	1.648	1.578	−1.968
25	2.453	−0.114	2.042	2.638	3.704
26	1.825	0.060	1.069	2.281	−3.608
27	−0.513	−1.540	−0.980	1.370	−3.686
28	1.815	0.280	0.012	−1.744	2.755
29	2.985	−0.438	0.644	3.077	1.977

The normalized flow behavior index can be calculated using Equation (9) by changing PV_n by n_n based on the optimized ANN-n model by extracting the weights and biases. To obtain the de-normalized value of n, Equation (12) can be used. Table 4 lists the values of w_1, w_2, b_1, and i. b_2 was 1.209.

$$n = 0.226 * n_n + 0.516 \qquad (12)$$

Table 4. Weight and biases for the MSaDE-ANN-n (artificial neural network-flow behavior index) model.

i	$w_{1,1}$	$w_{1,2}$	$w_{1,3}$	$b_{1,i}$	$w_{2,i}$
1	−0.443	−0.156	0.758	−0.485	−0.994
2	1.141	2.210	−0.648	−2.048	−1.732
3	0.939	1.042	0.370	−1.657	1.965
4	−0.176	1.325	−0.765	0.989	−1.317
5	0.365	−0.246	−2.876	−2.609	3.213
6	0.373	1.195	1.975	2.595	3.107
7	−2.520	−0.795	0.373	1.659	−2.423
8	−1.340	0.991	2.523	1.324	−2.301
9	−0.961	0.901	2.914	−0.831	2.361
10	−2.506	−0.345	4.267	−0.129	−2.154
11	1.981	−0.971	−0.055	−1.641	−2.219
12	−1.794	0.269	−1.606	0.618	1.510

Table 4. Cont.

i	$w_{1,1}$	$w_{1,2}$	$w_{1,3}$	$b_{1,i}$	$w_{2,i}$
13	0.218	−2.321	−1.555	0.361	0.814
14	2.416	0.465	−2.349	−0.419	−2.432
15	−0.614	1.457	1.175	0.794	0.851
16	3.914	0.056	−0.523	1.832	−3.468
17	2.065	0.085	1.889	−0.278	1.808
18	0.401	0.534	−2.224	−0.083	−1.622
19	3.154	−0.414	−0.337	1.019	−2.465
20	−1.901	−1.296	−0.574	−1.033	−1.579
21	2.438	−0.437	−4.073	1.524	2.822
22	4.731	−0.405	−0.561	1.886	3.552
23	−0.986	0.434	−1.951	−2.056	3.097
24	−3.643	−0.243	−0.544	−2.627	−2.013
25	0.342	0.091	−0.593	0.421	0.846
26	1.679	−0.291	−0.439	1.433	−2.427
27	−1.483	−0.556	2.154	−0.003	1.369
28	−2.376	−0.493	0.507	−2.083	3.200
29	−2.915	0.143	−1.838	−3.799	−3.532

The flow consistency index (K) can be estimated as a function of MD, FT, and SP using Equation (9) in a normalized form which was developed using the weights and biases of the optimized ANN-K model. The normal values of K can be calculated using Equation (13). Table 5 lists the values of w_1, w_2, b_1, and i. b_2 was −0.148.

$$k = 2.16 * K_n + 2.90 \qquad (13)$$

Table 5. Weight and biases for the MSaDE-ANN-K (artificial neural network-flow consistency index) model.

i	$w_{1,1}$	$w_{1,2}$	$w_{1,3}$	$b_{1,i}$	$w_{2,i}$
1	−0.543	0.439	2.175	1.330	2.624
2	−1.067	−1.016	1.717	0.141	−1.152
3	−0.288	−0.348	−1.421	1.359	2.115
4	−2.822	−0.325	−0.492	0.816	1.942
5	−0.065	1.376	−0.993	−1.101	1.357
6	−0.462	1.782	0.506	1.347	−1.852
7	−0.952	−1.445	−0.386	1.426	−1.660
8	−2.003	−0.135	3.601	−0.129	2.638
9	−0.583	−1.707	0.477	0.618	1.754
10	0.117	1.851	1.359	−0.358	1.278
11	0.486	−0.749	−2.045	0.623	2.230
12	1.568	0.610	−0.380	−0.357	1.534
13	−2.644	0.202	−1.245	0.768	−2.811
14	1.429	−1.114	−0.571	0.095	−1.969
15	1.465	−2.126	−0.567	−0.087	1.053
16	2.855	−0.573	−0.995	0.830	2.813
17	1.486	0.230	−2.934	0.298	2.534
18	−1.656	−0.036	−2.234	0.405	1.775
19	−2.152	−1.729	−1.419	−1.295	1.239
20	1.276	0.531	2.234	1.557	−1.516
21	−1.246	0.749	−0.784	−1.348	−2.167
22	−3.413	0.427	0.067	−1.320	2.202
23	2.306	0.410	0.193	1.080	3.402
24	−4.026	0.409	2.392	−1.307	3.331
25	1.399	0.202	−2.729	1.177	−2.509
26	−2.946	0.447	2.470	−1.180	2.865
27	−0.856	−1.843	0.506	−1.775	−1.709
28	−3.792	0.467	2.515	−1.314	−3.679
29	−1.587	−0.228	−2.388	−3.075	3.192
30	1.722	−0.022	−0.091	1.562	2.176

AV can be calculated using Equation (9) as a function of MD, FT, and SP, which was developed based on the optimized ANN-AV model by extracting the weights and biases. Equation (14) can be used to calculate the de-normalized values of AV. Table 6 lists the values of w_1, w_2, b_1, and i. b_2 was −0.248.

$$AV = 10.73 * AV_n + 27.23 \tag{14}$$

Table 6. Weight and biases for the MSaDE-ANN-AV (apparent viscosity) model.

i	$w_{1,1}$	$w_{1,2}$	$w_{1,3}$	$b_{1,i}$	$w_{2,i}$
1	0.374	−1.536	0.574	0.882	−1.163
2	−1.408	1.125	−1.291	2.137	−3.658
3	−0.850	0.114	1.787	1.031	−2.843
4	0.062	1.644	0.325	−0.692	1.350
5	1.712	0.026	1.101	−1.484	2.197
6	−0.414	0.927	−1.626	0.997	2.071
7	2.731	0.188	0.132	−1.953	−2.308
8	1.872	−1.064	−0.627	−0.908	−1.324
9	−0.021	1.993	−0.154	0.632	0.597
10	−3.044	0.148	−0.800	0.982	3.794
11	−1.352	0.428	−2.180	−2.010	−1.469
12	−1.044	−0.865	2.198	−0.549	−1.772
13	3.590	0.253	1.442	−0.968	2.094
14	2.952	0.264	−2.643	−0.011	−1.670
15	−3.100	1.961	−0.781	1.463	−2.407
16	−1.318	−0.515	2.887	−0.371	2.183
17	−1.602	−0.282	2.118	−0.310	−2.710
18	−2.679	−0.947	1.475	−0.746	1.870
19	−1.975	0.530	0.362	−0.818	−2.142
20	−2.174	−1.062	0.256	−0.855	−1.848
21	0.285	−1.041	−0.577	0.283	1.225
22	2.634	0.435	−1.599	1.482	−2.305
23	−2.845	−0.052	−0.060	−1.538	2.172
24	−2.066	0.203	−0.763	−2.269	−2.080
25	0.872	−1.133	−0.508	0.858	1.674
26	−1.022	1.391	0.304	1.738	1.591
27	2.455	0.309	−0.406	1.484	2.241
28	2.346	−0.231	0.980	2.353	−2.973
29	0.641	0.218	1.541	1.810	1.331

3.3. Comparison with Previous Models

To compare the new MSaDE-ANN technique for the RHPs, the AV was predicted using the MSaDE-ANN, and the obtained results were compared with Pitt [41] and Almahdawi et al. [42]. The actual values of AV can be calculated based on PV and YP using Equation (15).

$$AV = \frac{2PV + YP}{2} \tag{15}$$

Figure 6 shows the high accuracy of the developed ANN-AV model for the training dataset using the MSaDE technique. The R was 0.97 and the AAPE was 5.1% when plotting the predicted and actual AV values (570 data points). The same results were obtained for the testing data set, where the R was 0.97 and the AAPE was 5.3%, as can be seen in Figure 6.

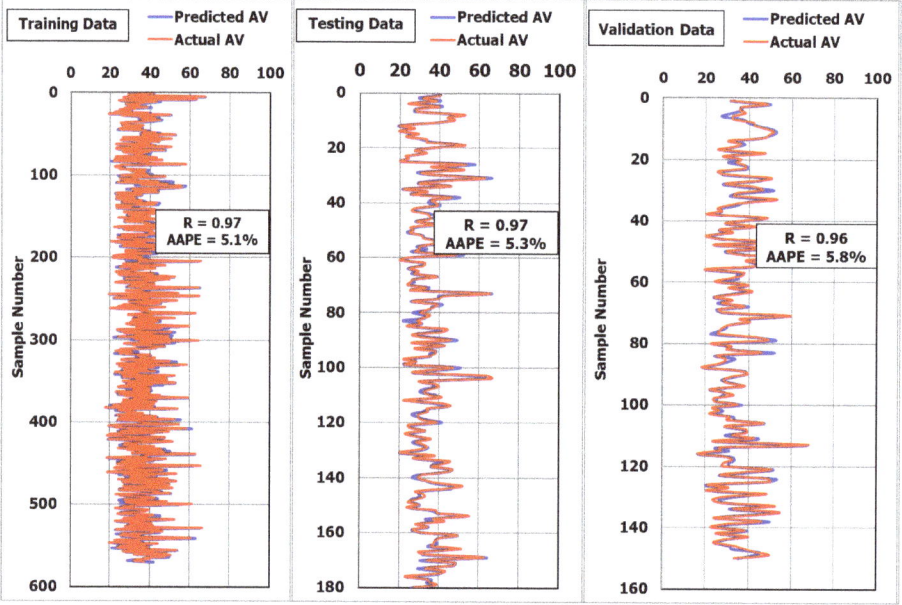

Figure 6. Prediction of apparent viscosity using the MSaDE-ANN technique.

For the further validation of the AV developed ANN-AV model, a new data set was used (150 data points). Figure 6 shows that the R was 0.96 and the AAPE was 5.8% between the calculated and actual values of AV.

Pit [41] illustrated that the AV can be calculated as a function of MD and FT using Equation (16), while Almahdawi et al. [42] stated that AV can be determined using Equation (17).

$$AV = MD * (FT - 25) \tag{16}$$

$$AV = MD * (FT - 28) \tag{17}$$

Applying Equations (16) and (17) using the available data sets (900 data points) showed that the ANN-AV model outperformed these models. Figure 7 shows that the coefficient of determination (R^2) when plotting the calculated and actual valued of AV was 0.94 when the ANN-AV equation was used, 0.65 when Pitt's equation was used, and 0.64 when Almahdawi's equation was used. Figure 8 shows that the ANN-AV equation yielded the lowest AAPE (5.26%) as compared with the Pitt [41] equation (the AAPE was 31.47%) and the Almahdawi et al. [42] equation, where the AAPE was 24.81%.

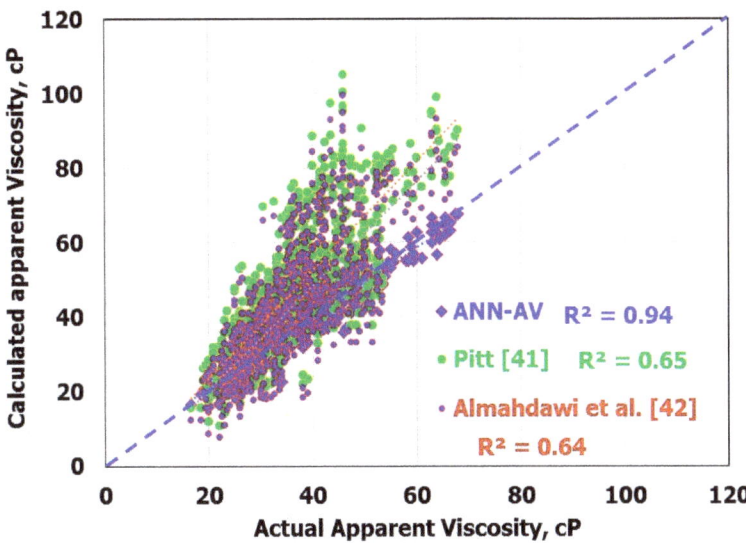

Figure 7. Coefficient of determination for the apparent viscosity using different techniques.

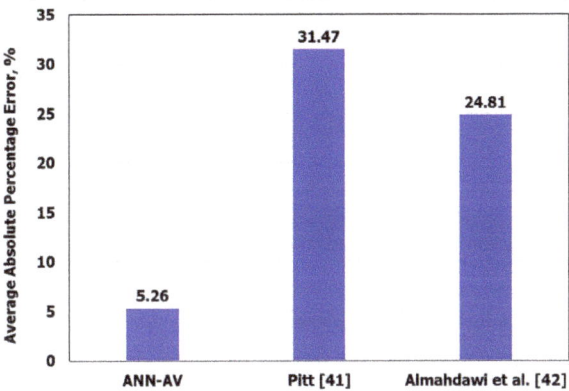

Figure 8. Average absolute percentage error for calculating the apparent viscosity using different techniques.

3.4. Sensitivity Analysis

As mentioned earlier, the methodology of this study involved 20 independent optimization runs. Figure 9 shows that 18 out of the 20 optimization runs showed that the best training algorithm that achieved the best fit was the trainbr. The remaining two optimization runs were distributed equally between trainlm and trainbfg. This shows the consistency of this training function in achieving 90% of the best-fit performance compared to the other training algorithms. Figure 10 shows the best results achieved by each of the three training algorithms. The figure demonstrates that trainbr achieved the highest R and the lowest AAPE. The outperformance of trainbr could be related to its backpropagation capability of minimizing a combination of the squared errors and weights to determine the optimum combination that produces an ANN that is able to generalize well by preventing the overfitting (preventing increasing values of weights).

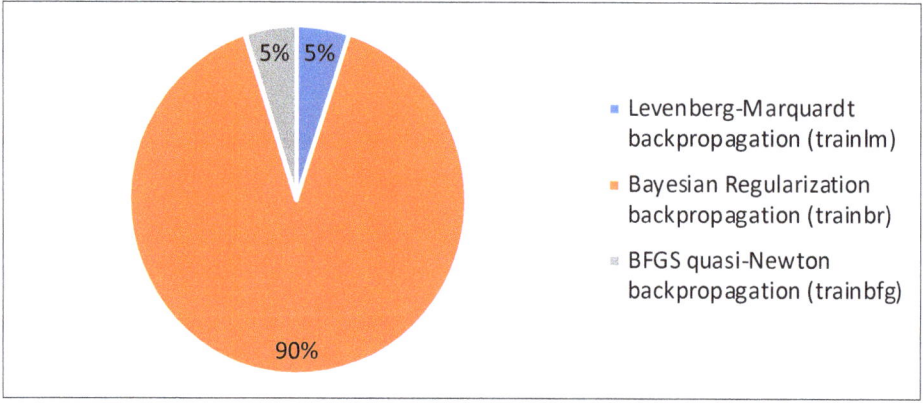

Figure 9. The success percentage for each training algorithm.

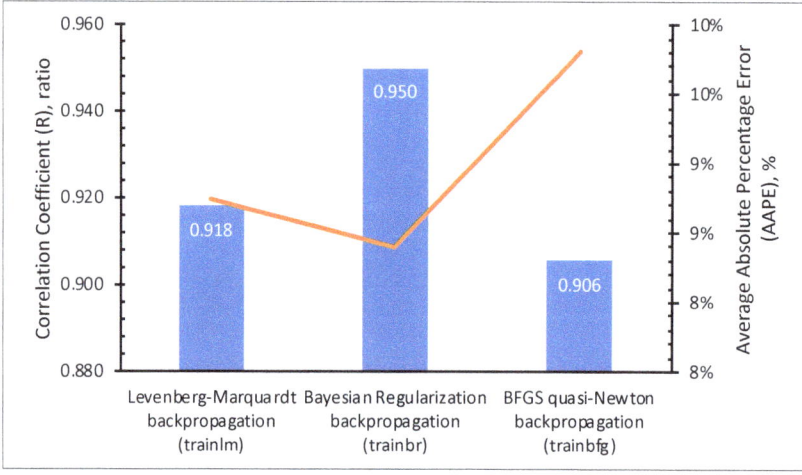

Figure 10. Performance comparison of the training algorithms.

Figure 11 shows the sensitivity of the ANN performance to the number of neurons. The ANN performance indicators were the correlation coefficient (R) and the AAPE for the training and testing datasets. The figure demonstrates that, generally, increasing the number of neurons enhanced the ANN performance in terms of increasing the R of testing until reaching an optimum value of 30 neurons; then, the performance dropped. The reason for this behavior was the overfitting. Increasing the number of neurons to a very large value resulted in the ANN performing well on the training set but performing poorly on the testing set, which indicates overfitting. This is demonstrated by the figure, as it shows when the number of neurons increased more than 30, the R-value of training set generally increased, but the R-value of testing generally decreased. Therefore, the optimum number of neuron, in this case, was determined to be 30 neurons. Figure 12 shows the topography of the ANN with the optimized number of neurons.

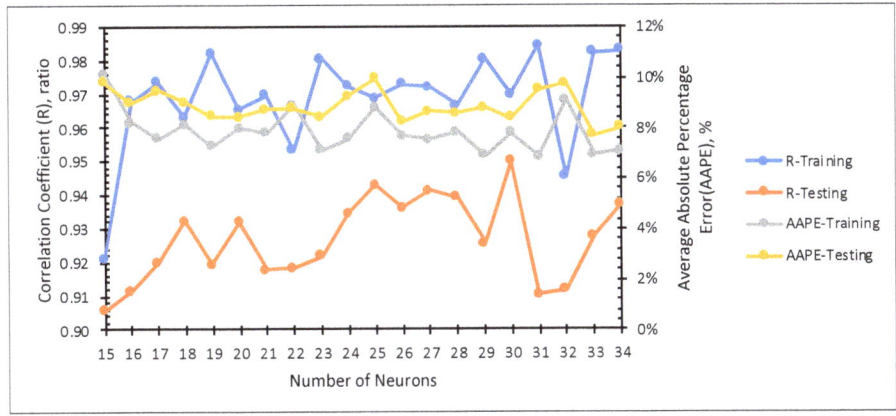

Figure 11. Sensitivity analysis of the model performance to the number of neurons.

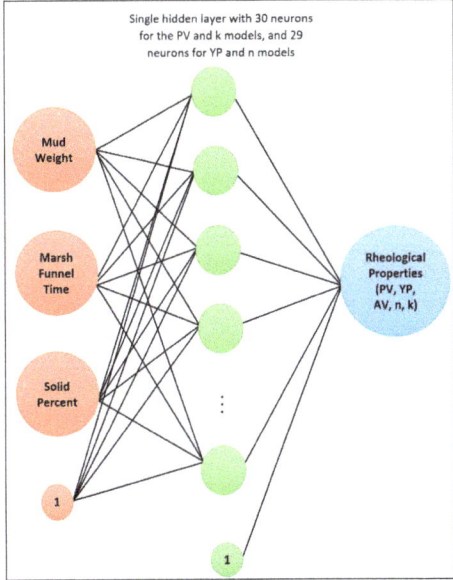

Figure 12. The topography of the artificial neural network.

4. Conclusions

The modified self-adaptive differential evolution technique was implemented to optimize the different variables of an ANN to determine the RHPs of NaCl-WBDIF using actual field measurements (900 data points) of MD, FT, and SP. Based on the obtained results, the following conclusions can be drawn:

1. For all rheological properties, the optimization process showed that the best training function was Bayesian regularization backpropagation (trainbr) and the best transferring function was Elliot symmetric sigmoid (elliotsig).
2. The optimum number of neurons was 30 for PV and K, while it was 29 for n, AV and YP.
3. The developed ANN models predicted the RHPs with high accuracy. The R was more than 90%, and the AAPE was less than 8.6%.

4. The five empirical equations for the RHPs were simple and accurate to be applied in a real-time without the need for ANN models or any special equipment.
5. The AV empirical equations based on the optimized ANN model outperformed the previous AV models.

It is recommended to develop an automated Marsh funnel system that measures the mud density, Marsh funnel time, and solid percent using automated method, and the yielded results can be used as inputs for the developed ANN models, which can be used to estimate the rheological properties every 5–10 min. This will enable the driller to understand the changes in the drilling fluid properties as well as the changes in the rig hydraulics. This make decisions regarding the required action based on given information much faster.

Funding: This research received no external funding.

Acknowledgments: The authors wish to acknowledge King Fahd University of Petroleum and Minerals (KFUPM) for utilizing the various facilities in carrying out this research. Many thanks are due to the anonymous referees for their detailed and helpful comments.

Conflicts of Interest: The author declares no conflict of interest.

Abbreviations

RHPs	Rheological properties
WBDIF	Water-based drill-in fluid
NaCl-WBDIF	Sodium chloride-water-based drill-in fluid
ANN	Artificial neural network
AI	Artificial intelligent
DE	Differential evaluation
SaDE	Self-adaptive differential evolution
MSaDE	Modified self-adaptive differential evolution
MD	Mud density, ppg
FT	Marsh funnel time, s/quart
SP	Solid percent, %
PV	Plastic viscosity, cP
YP	Yield point, 100/ 100 ft^2
n	Flow behavior index
K	Flow consistency index, 100/ 100 ft^2
AV	Apparent viscosity, cP
R	Correlation coefficient
MD_n	Normalized value of mud density
FT_n	Normalized value of Marsh funnel time
SP_n	Normalized value of solid percent
PV_n	Normalized value of plastic viscosity
YP_n	Normalized value of yield point
AV_n	Normalized value of apparent viscosity
n_n	Normalized value of flow behavior index
K_n	Normalized value of flow consistency index
R^2	Coefficient of determination
AAPE	Average absolute percentage error
CCI	Carrying capacity index
ICD	Inflow control device
GOR	Gas-oil ratio
CO_2	Carbon dioxide
$CaCl_2$	Calcium chloride
y_{real}	Actual value for any properties
$y_{predicted}$	Predicted value using any model

elliotsig	Elliot symmetric sigmoid
N	Number of neurons
w_1	Weights between the input layer and hidden layer
w_2	Weights between the hidden layer and the output layer
b_1	Biases between the input layer and the hidden layer
b2	Bias associated with hidden layer and output layer

References

1. Zhang, X.; Jiang, G.; Xuan, Y.; Wang, L.; Huang, X. Associating Copolymer Acrylamide/Diallyldimethylammonium Chloride/Butyl Acrylate/2-Acrylamido-2-methylpropanesulfonic Acid as a Tackifier in Clay-Free and Water-Based Drilling Fluids. *Energy Fuels* **2017**, *31*, 4655–4662. [CrossRef]
2. Zhang, L.-M.; Tan, Y.B.; Li, Z.M. Application of a new family of amphoteric cellulose-based graft copolymers as drilling-mud additives. *Colloid Polym. Sci.* **1999**, *277*, 1001–1004. [CrossRef]
3. Luo, Z.; Pei, J.; Wang, L.; Yu, P.; Chen, Z. Influence of an ionic liquid on rheological and filtration properties of water-based drilling fluids at high temperatures. *Appl. Clay Sci.* **2017**, *136*, 96–102. [CrossRef]
4. Bourgoyne, A.T.; Cheever, M.E.; Mulheim, K.K.; Young, F.S. *Applied Drilling Engineering*; SPE Textbook Series; Society of Petroleum Engineers: Richardson, TX, USA, 1986; Volume 2.
5. Ahmad, H.M.; Kamal, M.S.; Al-Harthi, M.A. Rheological and Filtration Properties of Clay-Polymer Systems: Impact of Polymer Structure. *Appl. Clay Sci.* **2018**, *160*, 226–237. [CrossRef]
6. Sadeghalvaad, M.; Sabbaghi, S. The effect of the TiO_2/polyacrylamide nanocomposite on water-based drilling fluid properties. *Powder Technol.* **2015**, *272*, 113–119. [CrossRef]
7. Lyons, W.C.; Plisga, J. *Standard Handbook of Petroleum and Natural Gas Engineering*, 2nd ed.; Gulf Publishing Company: Houston, TX, USA, 2005.
8. Hossain, M.E.; Al-Majed, A.A. *Fundamentals of Sustainable Drilling Engineering*; Scrivener Publishing LLC: Salem, MA, USA, 2015.
9. Adams, N.J. *Drilling Engineering: A Complete Well Planning Approach*; Penn Well Publishing Company: Tulsa, OK, USA, 1985.
10. Kersten, G.V. Results and Use of Oil-Base Fluids in Drilling and Completing Wells. In *Drilling and Production Practice*; Paper API-46-061; American Petroleum Institute: New York, NY, USA, 1946.
11. Luo, Y.; Bern, P.A.; Chambers, B.D. Simple Charts to Determine Hole Cleaning Requirements in Deviated Wells. In *SPE/IADC Drilling*; Paper SPE 27486; Society of Petroleum Engineers: Houston, TX, USA, 1994.
12. Paiaman, A.M.; Al-Askari, M.K.G.; Salmani, B.; Al-Anazi, B.D.; Masihi, M. Effect of Drilling Fluid Properties on Rate of Penetration. *NAFTA* **2009**, *60*, 129–134.
13. Okrajni, S.; Azar, J. The Effects of Mud Rheology on Annular hole Cleaning in Directional Wells. *SPE Drill. Eng.* **1986**, *1*, 297–308. [CrossRef]
14. Robinson, L.; Morgan, M. Effect of hole cleaning on drilling rate performance. Paper AADE-05-DF-HO-41. In Proceedings of the AADE Drilling Fluid Conference, Houston, TX, USA, 6–7 April 2004.
15. Marsh, H.N. Properties and Treatment of Rotary Mud. *Trans. AIME* **1931**, *92*, 234–251. [CrossRef]
16. Balhoff, M.T.; Lake, L.W.; Bommer, P.M.; Lewis, R.E.; Weber, M.J.; Calderin, J.M. Rheological and yield stress measurements of non-Newtonian fluids using a Marsh Funnel. *J. Pet. Sci. Eng.* **2011**, *77*, 393–402. [CrossRef]
17. McCulloch, W.S.; Pitts, W. A logical calculus of the ideas immanent in nervous activity. *Bull. Math. Biophys.* **1943**, *5*, 115–133. [CrossRef]
18. Rosenblatt, F. *The Perceptron, a Perceiving and Recognizing Automaton*; Project Para Report No. 85-460-1; Cornell Aeronautical Laboratory (CAL): Buffalo, NY, USA, 1957.
19. Bailey, D.; Thompson, D. How to Develop Neural Network. *AI Expert* **1990**, *5*, 38–47.
20. Fausett, L. *Fundamentals of Neural Networks, Architectures, Algorithms, and Applications*; Prentice-Hall Inc.: Eaglewood Cliffs, NJ, USA, 1994.
21. Ali, J.K. Neural Networks: A new Tool for the Petroleum Industry. Paper SPE-27561-MS. In Proceedings of the European Petroleum Computer Conference, Aberdeen, UK, 15–17 March 1994.
22. Russell Stuart, J.; Norvig, P. *Artificial Intelligence: A Modern Approach*, 3rd ed.; Prentice Hall: Upper Saddle River, NJ, USA, 2009; ISBN 0-13-604259-7.

23. Sargolzaei, J.; Saghatoleslami, N.; Mosavi, S.M.; Khoshnoodi, M. Comparative Study of Artificial Neural Networks (ANN) and statistical methods for predicting the performance of Ultrafiltration Process in the Milk Industry. Iranian. *J. Chem. Eng.* **2006**, *25*, 67–76.
24. Lippmann, R. An introduction to computing with neural nets. *IEEE ASSP Mag.* **1987**, *4*, 4–22. [CrossRef]
25. Mao, J.; Mohiuddin, K.; Jain, A. Artificial neural networks: A tutorial. *Computer* **1996**, *29*, 31–44.
26. Demuth, H.B.; Beale, M.H.; Hagan, M.T. *Neural Network Toolbox 6, User's Guide*; MathWorks, Inc.: Natick, MA, USA, 2009.
27. AlAjmi, M.D.; Alarifi, S.A.; Mahsoon, A.H. Improving Multiphase Choke Performance Prediction and Well Production Test Validation Using Artificial Intelligence: A New Milestone. SPE-173394-MS. In Proceedings of the SPE Digital Energy Conference and Exhibition, Woodlands, TX, USA, 3–5 March 2015.
28. Alarifi, S.A.; AlNuaim, S.; Abdulraheem, A. Productivity Index Prediction for Oil Horizontal Wells Using Different Artificial Intelligence Techniques. SPE-172729-MS. In Proceedings of the SPE Middle East Oil & Gas Show and Conference, Manama, Bahrain, 8–11 March 2015.
29. Chen, F.; Duan, Y.; Zhang, J.; Wang, K.; Wang, W. Application of neural network and fuzzy mathematic theory in evaluating the adaptability of inflow control device in horizontal well. *J. Pet. Sci. Eng.* **2015**, *134*, 131–142.
30. Van, S.L.; Chon, B.H. Effective Prediction and Management of a CO_2 Flooding Process for Enhancing Oil Recovery using Artificial Neural Networks. *ASME J. Energy Resour. Technol.* **2017**, *140*, 032906. [CrossRef]
31. Van, S.L.; Chon, B.H. Evaluating the critical performances of a CO_2–Enhanced oil recovery process using artificial neural network models. *J. Pet. Sci. Eng.* **2017**, *157*, 207–222. [CrossRef]
32. Qin, A.K.; Huang, V.L.; Suganthan, P.N. Differential Evolution Algorithm with Strategy Adaptation for Global Numerical Optimization. *IEEE Trans. Evol. Comput.* **2009**, *13*, 398–417. [CrossRef]
33. Storn, R.; Price, K. Differential Evolution—A Simple and Efficient Heuristic for global Optimization over Continuous Spaces. *J. Glob. Optim.* **1997**, *11*, 341–359. [CrossRef]
34. Moussa, T.M.; Awotunde, A.A. Self-adaptive differential evolution with a novel adaptation technique and its application to optimize ES-SAGD recovery process. *Comput. Chem. Eng.* **2018**, *118*, 64–76. [CrossRef]
35. Al-Khdheeawi, E.A.; Mahdi, D.S. Apparent Viscosity Prediction of Water-Based Muds Using Empirical Correlation and an Artificial Neural Network. *Energies* **2019**, *12*, 3067. [CrossRef]
36. Gowida, A.; Elkatatny, S.; Ramadan, E.; Abdulraheem, A. Data-Driven Framework to Predict the Rheological Properties of $CaCl_2$ Brine-Based Drill-in Fluid Using Artificial Neural Network. *Energies* **2019**, *12*, 1880. [CrossRef]
37. Zhang, Y.; Pan, C.; Chen, X.; Wang, F. Abnormal breast identification by nine-layer convolutional neural network. *J. Comput. Sci.* **2018**, *27*, 57–68. [CrossRef]
38. Wang, S.; Rao, R.V.; Chen, P.; Liu, A.; Wei, L. Abnormal Breast Detection in Mammogram Images by Feed-forward Neural Network Trained by Jaya Algorithm. *Fundam. Inform.* **2017**, *151*, 191–211. [CrossRef]
39. Metzner, A.B. Non-Newtonian technology: Fluid mechanics and transfers. *Adv. Chem. Eng.* **1956**, *1*, 77–153.
40. Savins, J.G.; Roper, W.F. A Direct Indicating Viscometer for Drilling Fluids. Paper API-54-007. In Proceedings of the Drilling and Production Practice, New York, NY, USA, 1 January 1954.
41. Pitt, M.J. The Marsh Funnel and Drilling Fluid Viscosity: A New Equation for Field Use. *SPE Drill. Complet.* **2000**, *15*, 3–6. [CrossRef]
42. Almahdawi, F.H.; Al-Yaseri, A.Z.; Jasim, N. Apparent Viscosity Direct from Marsh Funnel Test. *Iraqi J. Chem. Pet. Eng.* **2014**, *15*, 51–57.

© 2019 by the author. Licensee MDPI, Basel, Switzerland. This article is an open access article distributed under the terms and conditions of the Creative Commons Attribution (CC BY) license (http://creativecommons.org/licenses/by/4.0/).

Article

AirInsight: Visual Exploration and Interpretation of Latent Patterns and Anomalies in Air Quality Data

Huijie Zhang [1,2,†], **Ke Ren** [1,2,†], **Yiming Lin** [1,2], **Dezhan Qu** [1,3,*] **and Zhenxin Li** [4,*]

1. School of Information Science and Technology, Northeast Normal University, Changchun 130024, China; zhanghj167@nenu.edu.cn (H.Z.); renk205@nenu.edu.cn (K.R.); linym762@nenu.edu.cn (Y.L.)
2. Key Laboratory of Intelligent Information Processing of Jilin Universities, Changchun 130024, China
3. Library, Northeast Normal University, Changchun 130024, China
4. State Environmental Protection Key Laboratory of Wetland Ecology and Vegetation Restoration, School of Environment, Northeast Normarl University, Changchun 130024, China
* Correspondence: qudz862@nenu.edu.cn (D.Q.); lizx542@nenu.edu.cn (Z.L.)
† These authors contributed equally to this work.

Received: 16 March 2019; Accepted: 15 May 2019; Published: 23 May 2019

Abstract: Nowadays, huge volume of air quality data provides unprecedented opportunities for analyzing pollution. However, due to the high complexity, most traditional analytical methods focus on abstracting data, so these techniques discard the original structure and limit the understanding of the results. Visual analysis is a powerful technique for exploring unknown patterns since it retains the details of the original data and gives visual feedback to users. In this paper, we focus on air quality data and propose the AirInsight design, an interactive visual analytic system for recognizing, exploring, and summarizing regular patterns, as well as detecting, classifying, and interpreting abnormal cases. Based on the time-varying and multivariate features of air quality data, a dimension reduction method Composite Least Square Projection (CLSP) is proposed, which allows appreciating and interpreting the data patterns in the context of attributes. On the basis of the observed regular patterns, multiple abnormal cases are further detected, including the multivariate anomalies by the proposed Noise Hierarchical Clustering (NHC) method, abruptly changing timestamps by Time diversity (TD) indicator, and cities with unique patterns by the Geographical Surprise (GS) measure. Moreover, we combine TD and GS to group anomalies based on their underlying spatiotemporal correlations. AirInsight includes multiple coordinated views and rich interactive functions to provide contextual information from different aspects and facilitate a comprehensive understanding. In particular, a pair of glyphs are designed that provide a visual representation of the temporal variation in air quality conditions for a user-selected city. Experiments show that CLSP improves the accuracy of Least Square Projection (LSP) and that NHC has the ability to separate noises. Meanwhile, several case studies and task-based user evaluation demonstrate that our system is effective and practical for exploring and interpreting multivariate spatiotemporal patterns and anomalies in air quality data.

Keywords: visual analytics; system; air quality; spatiotemporal; multivariate; dimension reduction; clustering; regular patterns; anomalies

1. Introduction

With the rapid development of the social economy and the improvement in public life conditions, urban air pollution has become a hot topic and has attracted progressively more attention [1]. The new Ambient Air Quality Standard of China defines six kinds of major pollutants ($PM_{2.5}$, PM_{10}, SO_2, NO_2, O_3, and CO), which are sufficient to give a more comprehensive evaluation of urban air quality.

Under the new standard, air quality data are collected continuously by monitoring stations throughout the whole country. The gathered data are typically multivariate, temporal, and geographically labeled.

An increasing number of works have been devoted to the analysis of air quality data, but most of them have been limited to analyzing the patterns of only one major pollutant in a specific city or monitoring station because of the complexity, diversity and large volumes of data [2,3]. Determining the best approach to handling complicated air quality data to obtain multivariate temporal patterns and the relationships between different regions is a great challenge. The results of the analysis provide support for the pollution abatement of specific pollutants and areas. For example, AirVis [4] is a web-based visual analytic system that supports a collaborative analysis of spatiotemporal and multivariate features. However, it is implemented using only eight air quality monitoring stations in Beijing and is incapable of managing big data. Moreover, it is rare to find a study that focuses on detecting anomalies in air quality; for example, a particular city has a unique appearance compared with its adjacent locations, even if they have similar topographies and climate conditions. Obtaining divergent air quality data for a region despite other similarities to its neighbors can drive the analysis of air pollution causes and development of prevention measures. Furthermore, most of the previous works have obtained conclusions by computing isolated indicators [5,6], and the lack of meaningful contextual information has limited their further applications. Visual analytics is a new technology that makes up for this flaw. It is dedicated to transforming complex data into concise graphics that not only support the exploration of hidden patterns in the data but also assist in the comprehension of the patterns found. Thus, it is imperative to establish a comprehensive visual analysis platform that can analyze the regular patterns of air quality and potential anomalies. Such a technique helps the departments involved in environmental protection formulate effective policies to improve air quality; it even enables non-professional users to understand the patterns of air pollution.

In this paper, we propose AirInsight, an interactive visual analytic system that supports the interactive visual inspection of multivariate spatiotemporal patterns and anomalies from a variety of perspectives. In order to facilitate users' effective perception of data features, we propose a dimension reduction method called Composite Least Square Projection (CLSP), which generates an explicable layout that maintains both the multivariate data distribution and attribute information. CLSP outperforms the traditional projection solutions by enhancing the observation of preliminary patterns as well as the interpretation of patterns through a layout that embeds the multivariate context. For the purpose of exploring multivariate features more deeply, we propose the Noise Hierarchical Clustering (NHC) algorithm to extract inherent patterns and separate outliers. Considering that there are still some noteworthy anomalies hidden in regular patterns that reflect significant changes among similar timestamps or adjacent cities, we further introduce two indicators called time diversity (TD) and geographical surprise (GS) to quantize the data anomaly strength in these two cases. By utilizing them together, we further define all data by four categories of spatiotemporal anomalies and assist users in finding interesting data items intuitively. Multiple linked views are integrated into AirInsight to visualize the above analysis results. At the same time, a variety of contextual information is provided to help users understand the extracted patterns. Moreover, we design a pair of novel glyphs called R-Shield and A-Shield to summarize the normal and abnormal temporal patterns, respectively, of a specific city. By linking the glyphs in the temporal evolution process, several meaningful transform states can be revealed. The contributions of this work are the following:

1. **A visual analysis framework for exploring patterns of multivariate spatiotemporal data.** We propose a dimension reduction method called CLSP and a clustering algorithm called NHC, which provide two levels of pattern extraction and interpretation in the context of attribute information.
2. **A novel strategy for detecting and classifying anomalies.** We combine two indices to identify and group abnormal cases according to inherent spatiotemporal relationships, which can guide users in the analysis of representative instances for further understanding.

3. **A visual analytic system integrating summarization glyphs and multiple coordinated views for air quality data.** This tool allows analysts to explore and interpret regular patterns and anomalies from different aspects and levels.

2. Literature Review

2.1. Visualization of Air Quality Data

With the extensive use of Internet of Things (IoT), a massive volume of data is being generated and collected [7]. This is a cornerstone of city computing [8], but it renders traditional methods of numerical analysis ineffective. Increasingly more visual analytic methods are being applied to explore and interpret IoT data by combining automated analysis for different fields, such as non-residential building performance analysis [9], public transport optimization using mobile phone data [10], and so on.

As a common type of data collected by sensors, air quality data have attracted the attention of many scholars. Most works have comprised time-varying analysis and regional research. Du et al. [11] proposed an adaptive multiscale trend view that could flexibly reveal the linear and periodical temporal patterns of air quality. Similarly, Li et al. [12] integrated the variations in multiple pollutants. They also studied the various air quality features in time and space and designed Global Distribution View, which jointly visualizes the spatiotemporal and clustering information in a neat form. Through even deeper analysis, Zhou et al. [13] illustrated how spatial clusters changed over different time scales and used a storyline design to depict evolving changes for different locations. Another essential requirement for the visual analysis of air quality consists of correlation detection. The Time-Correlation-Partitioning (TCP) tree [14] presented a novel visual representation that concisely describes both the variable hierarchy and the temporal variation in correlations hidden in air quality data. Qu et al. [15] not only considered the correlation between different kinds of pollutants but also accounted for the influence of weather data on air conditions.

However, few works have paid attention to abnormal cases of air pollution. Li et al. [16] extracted events of air quality data and detected various co-occurrence patterns among them. Although they could find pollution-related urban agglomeration, the lack of extracted temporal variation for the target city limited the determinacy of the discovered events. In this paper, we propose a comprehensive system for air quality data that supports not only regular pattern analysis but also abnormal event detection in time and space.

2.2. Visualization of Multivariate Data

Analysis of multivariate data is an important and challenging research topic. Displaying an abstract data structure and discovering latent features generally rely on visualization.

Two major types of visualization approaches can be summarized as direct display and visual space projection. The parallel coordinate plot [17] and radar chart [18] are common methods of direct display: the attributes are represented as axes and the data items are drawn as lines across the axes. However, it is difficult for users to intuitively determine the relationships among items because tracking all the axes simultaneously is difficult, especially when the number of items increases along with the inevitable clutter. The other type, visual space projection, aims to map items from a high-dimensional space to the visual space while preserving relationships as much as possible. Thus, a poorly understood data structure can be observed and understood intuitively. Principal component analysis (PCA) [19], multidimensional scaling (MDS) [20], and t-distributed stochastic neighbor embedding (t-SNE) [21] are widely used projection methods. In the projection layout, users can quickly discover clusters through the densities of points. However, the lack of attribute information limits the user's understanding. In recent years, Radviz [22] and star coordinates [23] have been proposed. In these methods, the attributes are used as anchor points or axes aligned on a circle, and data are projected into the circle according to the attribute strengths. Nevertheless, these methods are strongly affected by the ordering of the attributes. Moreover, the relationships among the data are not considered, so items with different quantities and the same proportion are projected to the same position. To address this drawback, RadViz++ [24] includes histograms over each attribute cell. The histograms show the data distribution and are linked with brushed data, thereby explaining ambiguity.

The data context map [25] was developed to overcome the above shortcomings by mapping attribute points and data points together on the basis of their integrated similarities. However, its availability is restrained to air quality data whose items greatly outnumber the attributes. Building on this method, we propose CLSP, which can reduce errors and enhance the effectiveness of handling such types of data.

2.3. Visualization of Anomaly Detection

Extensive works have studied anomaly detection by visual analytic approaches in the past several years. Wilkinson presented hdoutliers [26], which was based on a distributional model that could deal with big complex data. It has widespread applications, even for a mixture of categorical and continuous variables. Nevertheless, apart from multivariate features, real-life data sets often have temporal and geographical tags, for which this type of global method is powerless.

In order to assist users in finding temporal anomalies, Muelder et al. [27] portrayed the behaviors of compute nodes over time by applying a force-directed layout that aggregated similar patterns and distinguished abnormal timelines. Similarly, Xu et al. [28] introduced a time-aware outlier-preserving technique to extend Marey's graph and achieved effective anomaly detection in manufacturing processes. Unlike the approaches that focus on a time axis, Shi et al. [29] linked two time-slots in a projection view in a method that supported the analysis of temporal evolution and multivariate features of different items. Cao et al. [30] designed glyphs with a time arc to detect anomalous users in social media data. For a deeper analysis of spatiotemporal anomalies, several visual analytic systems have been developed [31,32]. For example, a visual analytic system named Voila, developed by Cao et al. [33], achieved an interactive anomaly detection performance through a tensor-based unsupervised algorithm that analyzed the current spatiotemporal state by incorporating the historical states.

However, a significant limitation of these existing approaches is that they only consider unidirectional temporal variations while ignoring the periodicity in temporal data. Further, they are restricted to finding items that behave normally individually but abnormally compared with adjacent locations. In this paper, we propose a novel strategy that allows for the detection of abnormal cases from an integral space–time perspective.

3. Overview

3.1. Data Description

The data used in this research are fetched from a weather website (http://www.tianqihoubao.com/aqi) that releases air quality monitoring data in China. The website contains daily data for different cities and records six kinds of major air pollutants, namely, $PM_{2.5}$, PM_{10}, SO_2, NO_2, O_3, and CO. After data cleaning, we compute the Individual Air Quality Index (IAQI) for each pollutant using its concentration. Moreover, the Air Quality Index (AQI) of each piece of data is defined as the max IAQI.

The chosen data are dated from December 2013 to November 2016. We defined an annual period as the time from December of one year to November of the next year. Geographically, our data cover 88 cities in China (Figure 1), and we divide these cities according to their geographical locations into 8 regions: North China, Central China, South China, Southwest, Northwest, Northeast, East China, and East China coastal area.

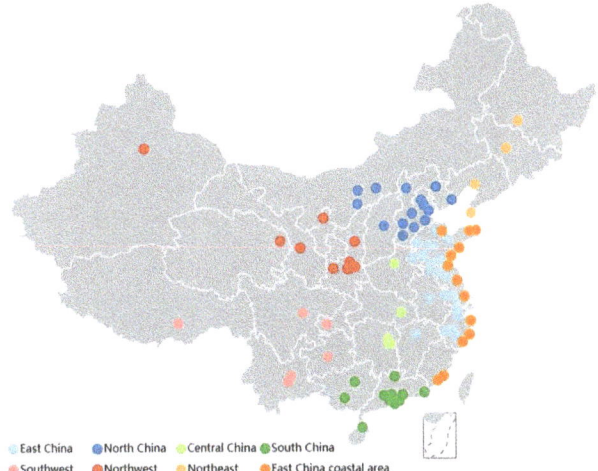

Figure 1. Urban distribution of the research. Each circle represents a city. Color of the circle encodes the geographical division of the city.

3.2. Analytical Tasks

The proposed AirInsight system is designed to satisfy several needs that allow an environmental expert to discover and understand the multivariate regular patterns and anomalies in air quality data. After discussions with an expert and repeated refinements of the requirements, we finally summarize the analytical tasks as follows:

- **T1**: **Multivariate pattern extraction.** Summarize the common pollution patterns in China, show their multivariate features, and compare their spatiotemporal distributions.
- **T2**: **Temporal trend exploration.** Cluster timestamps with similar air quality patterns and reveal the periodic temporal laws of different clusters. For a chosen target location, find abnormal timestamps that change dramatically.
- **T3**: **Geographic feature inspection.** Identify commonalities and difference among cities at levels of temporal trends. For a specific timestamp, detect abnormal cities that have unique multivariate patterns.

3.3. Workflow

To achieve these tasks, we design the analysis pipeline (illustrated in Figure 2), which contains the following modules:

1. **Preliminary exploration of patterns**. We propose a dimension reduction method, CLSP, that generates a composite layout. Data and attribute information are blended to form a composite distance matrix. From the constructed matrix, we perform the projection and obtain the final view from which users can observe and interpret multivariate patterns (T1).
2. **Extraction of inherent patterns**. Using the result of the projection, we define more intuitive patterns using an improved hierarchical clustering method (NHC), which can not only extract clusters but also separate outliers (T1).
3. **Detection of latent anomalies**. To find anomalies that are common in the global distribution but unique for a particular aspect, we calculate TD to detect abruptly changing timestamps (T2). At the same time, GS is introduced to find abnormal cities among their neighboring regions (T3). Furthermore, we combine these two indices and define the different abnormal performances of samples (T2 and T3).

4. **Visual analysis module.** This module consists of three main views: (a) Projection view supports flexible switching between scatter mode and glyph mode to provide an overview of the multivariate data distribution with spatiotemporal information (T2 and T3) or further explore a specific city under the summarization glyphs (T3). (b) Trend view summarizes the distribution of different clusters for each timestamp (T2) and compares the patterns changing with time for different cities (T3). (c) Abnormity classification view exhibits the performance of all data under the anomaly indices (T2 and T3). In addition, we provide rich interaction functions, such as filtering and brushing, to help users explore interesting features with more flexibility.

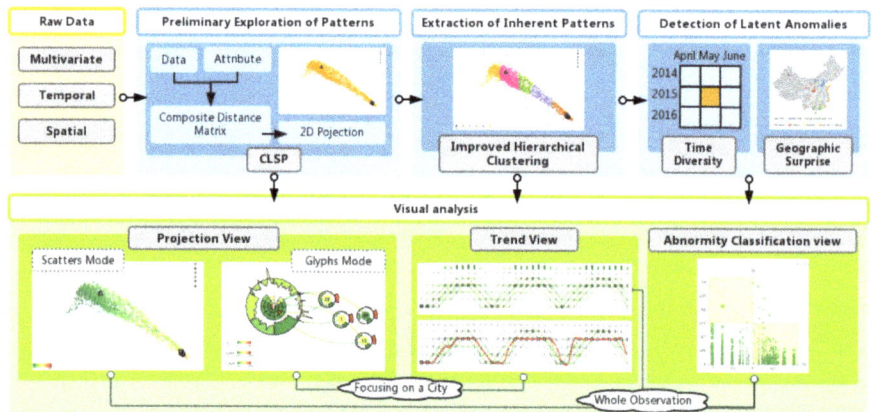

Figure 2. Workflow of AirInsight.

4. Methods

4.1. Preliminary Exploration of Patterns

In this section, we explain the CLSP method, which maps multivariate spatiotemporal data and attributes in visual space.

4.1.1. Vectorized Representation

We let S denote a sample set, A denote an attribute set. One month of data from a city is defined as a sample. Here, $S = \{s_1, s_2, \ldots, s_n\}$, where n is the product of the number of cities and the number of months. For the data studied in this paper, n is 3168. Each sample s_i is a temporally ordered sequence and combines attribute values, $s_i = \{s_{i,j}^k \mid 1 \leq j \leq d_i, 1 \leq k \leq m\}$, where d_i is the number of days that belong to s_i, and m is the number of attributes. Table 1 shows the sample from Chengdu in March 2014.

The attribute set consists of m vectors, $A = \{a^1, a^2, \ldots, a^m\}$. Each attribute vector a^k has n dimensions, and $a^k = \{a_i^k \mid 1 \leq i \leq n\}$, in which each dimension a_i^k is the mean value of s_i^k and can be computed as

$$a_i^k = \frac{\sum_{j=1}^{d_i} s_{i,j}^k}{d_i}. \tag{1}$$

4.1.2. Construction of Composite Distance Matrix

Inspired by the data context map [25], we construct a composite distance matrix that stores the relationships among sample vectors and attribute vectors. As demonstrated in the orange block in Figure 3, the matrix consists of four submatrices: DD stores the pairwise diversities between sample vectors, VV stores the pairwise diversities between attribute vectors, DV stores the diversities between sample vectors and attribute vectors, and VD is the transpose of matrix DV. Since the characteristics of different vectors are distinct, we choose different methods that are suitable to quantify different kinds of diversities.

Table 1. The sample from Chengdu in March 2014.

City	Time	$PM_{2.5}$	PM_{10}	SO_2	NO_2	CO	O_3
Chengdu	2014/3/1	68	70	20	69	26	16
Chengdu	2014/3/2	73	72	15	64	27	15
Chengdu	2014/3/3	65	60	16	54	28	10
Chengdu	2014/3/4	59	61	16	58	30	19
Chengdu	2014/3/5	87	75	21	82	33	11
Chengdu	2014/3/6	63	58	20	64	35	12
Chengdu	2014/3/7	84	71	16	67	36	9
Chengdu	2014/3/8	43	44	10	57	28	26
Chengdu	2014/3/9	94	82	18	83	35	13
Chengdu	2014/3/10	129	104	34	88	40	12
Chengdu	2014/3/11	137	105	39	90	38	23
Chengdu	2014/3/12	115	111	28	90	29	15
Chengdu	2014/3/13	102	118	24	80	24	18
Chengdu	2014/3/14	59	73	10	50	18	31
Chengdu	2014/3/15	100	90	25	88	28	23
Chengdu	2014/3/16	179	136	33	103	39	36
Chengdu	2014/3/17	172	124	46	95	35	31
Chengdu	2014/3/18	163	121	29	109	38	28
Chengdu	2014/3/19	160	131	51	93	38	30
Chengdu	2014/3/20	58	80	13	59	23	23
Chengdu	2014/3/21	53	67	13	53	17	23
Chengdu	2014/3/22	63	62	11	59	23	8
Chengdu	2014/3/23	82	67	11	67	28	12
Chengdu	2014/3/24	158	117	23	97	36	24
Chengdu	2014/3/25	165	120	26	98	40	23
Chengdu	2014/3/26	211	137	29	103	45	22
Chengdu	2014/3/27	211	144	35	110	48	22
Chengdu	2014/3/28	203	139	30	104	45	30
Chengdu	2014/3/29	208	151	36	112	55	18
Chengdu	2014/3/30	113	92	20	57	37	23
Chengdu	2014/3/31	40	50	12	52	26	23

Similar to the data context map, we apply the Pearson correlation coefficient [34] to evaluate the distance between a pair of attribute vectors and construct submatrix VV. With regard to the distance between a sample vector s_i and an attribute vector a^k, "$max - value$" [25] is used as follows:

$$distance(s_i, a^k) = max - a_i^k, \qquad (2)$$

where max is the maximum of the IAQI (500), and it can be thought of as the theoretical maximum of a_i^k. The $distance(s_i, a^k)$ is a significance distance. It is small for s_i when a_i^k is large, so when the mean value of a sample's k-th attribute is high, the relationship between the sample and the k-th attribute is close. Using Equation (2), we can construct the submatrices DV and VD.

Nevertheless, the sample vector s_i in this paper is a multivariate time-series. When we perform a diversity evaluation of submatrix DD, it is vital to take into account the whole temporal trend of the two vectors. In addition, the length of the vectors may not be equal since the number of days in each month is not the same. In order to overcome the above challenges, we apply dynamic time warping (DTW) [35], which can compute the shape similarity of two temporal vectors with unequal lengths. Under certain conditions, DTW extends or shortens two time-series to find the optimal alignment for all timestamps; this sets the accumulated distance of the aligned paths equal to the smallest value. When we compare two timestamps in the process of finding aligned paths, we introduce the structural similarity index (SSIM) [36] for multivariate features.

Since the diversities of the four submatrices are quantified by different means, their value ranges are also diverse. To construct the final composite distance matrix using the same scale, we set the mean values of these submatrices to be the same and fuse them. This matrix can evaluate all three kinds of relationships among samples and attributes and provide a foundation for projection.

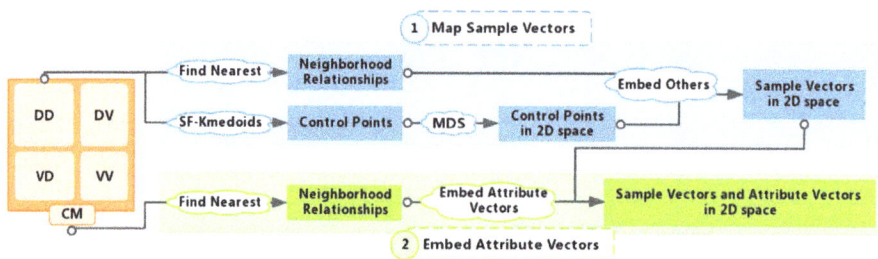

Figure 3. Pipeline of two-step projection.

4.1.3. Projection of Vectors

On the basis of the composite distance matrix, we map samples and attributes into visual space. In contrast to the data sets in the data context map [25], air quality data are characterized by having a sample number that is much larger than the number of attributes, and VV stores less information than DD and DV. To ensure that the accuracy of DD and DV is maintained as much as possible in the projection layout, we adopt two mapping steps: we map the samples first and then embed the attributes into the samples layout. Figure 3 shows the pipeline of the whole projection process.

Step 1: Map sample vectors

In this step, we utilize the Least Square Projection (LSP) [37], which is efficient for large data sets. The core process of LSP is mapping a representative subset first and then efficiently embedding others into the subset layout. To select a subset that best represents the original distribution, we use the SF-Kmedoids algorithm [38] on the basis of submatrix DD to split the samples into multiple clusters and define the centroid of each cluster as a control point. Then, the classical MDS algorithm [20] is applied to map them into 2D space. Since each point is located in the convex hull of its neighboring points, we embed other samples into the layout of the control points according to the neighborhood relationship among all samples. The projection results of samples $s'_i (1 \leq i \leq n)$ are shown in Figure 4a, which was obtained using the air quality data analyzed in this paper. Each orange point represents a sample, and the Chengdu sample in March 2014 is marked in the figure.

Step 2: Embed attribute vectors

To embed attributes into the layout generated in step 1, we regard all samples as new control points. According to submatrices DV, VD, and VV, we build the neighborhood relationship system of attributes. Using the same method as in step 1, we embed the attributes and obtain the final layout containing both samples $s'_i (1 \leq i \leq n)$ and attributes $a'^k (1 \leq k \leq m)$. As shown in Figure 4b, each orange point is a sample, and the gray symbols represent attributes.

Figure 4. Projection results. (**a**) Projection of sample vectors after Step 1. (**b**) Projection of sample vectors and attribute vectors after Step 2.

4.1.4. CLSP Evaluation

The core reason for choosing LSP as the foundation of our method is that it has high computational efficiency and can preserve neighborhood relationships in visual space, as verified by Paulovich et al. [37]. Although our CLSP method has one more step, little extra time is consumed because the attribute set is small. Also, the ability to retain neighborhood relations results in a more compact layout, which achieves the visualization goal of being able to quickly find associated data, and the multivariate patterns can be observed more effectively.

Moreover, the ability to handle multiple kinds of relationships makes CLSP more powerful than LSP. The data mapping in the first step maintains submatrix DD to the greatest extent without any other interference. The second step of embedding attributes ensures that DV and VD are adequately considered. To prove the validity of CLSP, we adopt a commonly used strategy to evaluate the projection quality for each submatrix. For one sample vector or attribute vector, we find the k nearest vectors in the original space and the k nearest points in the projection layout. Furthermore, we can calculate the proportion of repetition between them. For each submatrix, we assess the mean repetition proportions (MRP) of all included vectors. Table 2 shows the MRP of the air quality data we studied, and k is set to 20% of the corresponding vector count.

Table 2. Comparing the MRP of LSP and CLSP.

	MRP_{DD}	MRP_{VD}	MRP_{DV}	MRP_{VV}
LSP	0.445515	0.459782	0.298815	0.722222
CLSP	0.475259	0.645123	0.404991	0.722222
UP	6.68%	40.31%	35.53%	0

We find that MRP_{VD} and MRP_{DV} improve significantly, while MRP_{VV} remains unchanged. This result means that CLSP can better maintain the relationships between the data and attributes without losing the relationships among attributes. MRP_{DD} is also improved, which is also beneficial when the size of the data is large enough.

4.2. Extraction of Inherent Patterns

4.2.1. Clustering

According to the projection results shown in Figure 4, a distinct cluster and some discrete points can be observed. To further examine the patterns in detail, we perform clustering for the sample points. Since there are some extremely separate points, it is not rational to utilize partition clustering methods, such as K-means [39], which assigns labels to every data item and ignores abnormal patterns. Another widely used method, DBSCAN [40], is a kind of incomplete clustering method and can recognize noises. However, it is hard for users to obtain a satisfying result for data with uneven densities since DBSCAN significantly depends on the selection of the two parameters.

In this paper, we propose the Noise Hierarchical Clustering (NHC) algorithm to effectively extract regular patterns and abnormal patterns. Similarly, our method starts by setting each point as a cluster and then merges the two most similar clusters. Contrary to the traditional hierarchical clustering method [41], we set a threshold to additionally control the termination of cluster merging. When the point number of a cluster is larger than the threshold, it will not be merged with any other clusters. The algorithm will be terminated if no clusters can be merged. Hence, we can split a sizable consecutive point cloud into some finer clusters, which can be regarded as general patterns, while the cluster that does not meet the threshold will be disintegrated as noises. We apply NHC to the results of projection in Section 4.1; Algorithm 1 presents the NHC process.

Algorithm 1: Noise Hierarchical Clustering of sample points

Input: Projection results $S' = \{s'_i \mid 1 \leq i \leq n\}$, Threshold C_{Min}
Output: Clusters, noises

1. Treat each s'_i as a separate cluster c_i.
2. Calculate the distance between any two clusters and find the two clusters $c1$ and $c2$ with the smallest distance.
3. If the number of objects of $c1$ and $c2$ are both less than C_{Min}, merge them as a new cluster.
4. Repeat 2 and 3 until no clusters can be merged.
5. Mark the points belonging to the cluster whose point number is less than C_{Min} as outliers.
6. Algorithm end.

4.2.2. NHC Evaluation

Figure 5 shows a comparison between our NHC method, DBSCAN, and K-means. The colors of the points encode cluster labels, and the black points represent noises. To highlight the noises, we set a larger radius for them than other clustered points. In the NHC process, we set C_{Min} to 200; in the DBSCAN process, we set the minimum number of points required to form a dense region $minPTS$ to 4 and the radius to 0.15; and in the K-means process, we set the number of clusters to 5. From Figure 5a,b, it can be observed that our method separates the clusters more elaborately when the points are intensive. As shown in Figure 5a,c, the noises are separated from the regular patterns and highlighted in our method. Thus, NHC performs better when dealing with uneven data distributions.

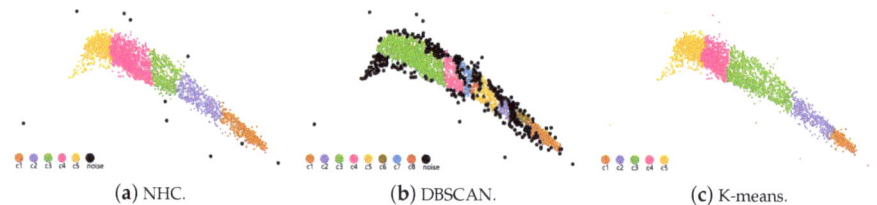

Figure 5. Results of different clustering methods.

According to Algorithm 1, C_{Min} is the threshold to control the maximum number of points in a cluster. We can adjust the parameter C_{Min} to obtain different clustering results. Figure 6 shows the results of NHC by setting C_{Min} to different values. In Figure 6a, most points are grouped into three clusters, which are marked by green, yellow, and blue. Compared with Figure 5a, in which C_{Min} is 200, we find that the green cluster in Figure 6a is a combination of three small clusters in Figure 5a.

In Figure 6b,c, the points are further divided into more clusters, and more noises are separated. Thus, we can conclude that the smaller the C_{Min} value, the more clusters and more noises we get.

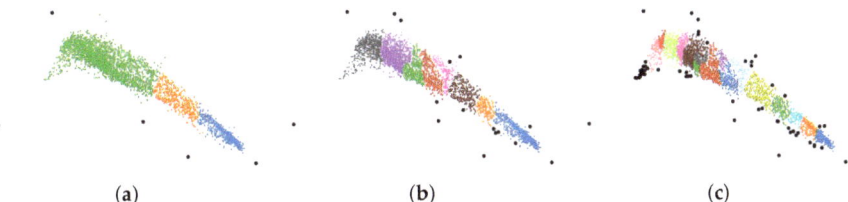

Figure 6. Results of NHC with different P_{min} values. (**a**) Cluster result by setting P_{min} to 300. (**b**) Cluster result by setting P_{min} to 100. (**c**) Cluster result by setting P_{min} to 50.

4.3. Detection of Latent Anomalies

By clustering, we can detect some noises on the basis of multivariate features. In this section, we further consider the spatiotemporal information and introduce two evaluation indices to detect potential anomalies that are mostly hidden in regular multivariate patterns.

4.3.1. Time Diversity

Typically, the air quality of a city for one month is similar to that for its neighboring months. The clustering results of Xizang for May 2015 is taken as an example; the results are divided into the same clusters for April and June 2015 and the corresponding months in 2014 and 2016. However, due to abrupt climate changes or related urban policies, the air quality of a given month may present different characteristics from its time neighborhood. To discover these kinds of anomalous events, we introduce an indicator called time diversity (TD), inspired by the work of Zhang et al. [42].

Considering periodic variations, we define the time neighborhood of sample s_i as $T_{s_i} = \{t_{s_i}^h \mid 1 \leq h \leq N_{T_{s_i}}\}$, where $N_{T_{s_i}}$ is the number of neighboring timestamps of s_i. In this paper, $N_{T_{s_i}}$ is set to 8: the previous month, the next month, and these three months in the two adjacent years. Figure 7 shows the time neighborhood of May 2015; the orange grid represents May 2015 and the blue grids represent neighboring timestamps. From the clustering results in Section 4.2, the TD of each month is computed as

$$TD(s_i) = \sum_{C_{s_i} \neq C_{t_{s_i}^h}} \left(\frac{N_{C_{t_{s_i}^h}}}{N_{T_{s_i}}}\right)^2 - \left(\frac{N_{C_{s_i}}}{N_{T_{s_i}}}\right)^2. \quad (3)$$

In Equation (3), C_{s_i} represents the cluster that sample s_i belongs to, while $C_{t_{s_i}^h}$ is the cluster label of $t_{s_i}^h$. For all samples in T_{s_i}, $N_{C_{s_i}}$ is the number of samples belonging to C_{s_i}, and $N_{C_{t_{s_i}^h}}$ is the number of samples belonging to $C_{t_{s_i}^h}$ ($C_{t_{s_i}^h} \neq C_{s_i}$). $TD(s_i)$ is a real number in the range $[-1, 1]$. The closer the value of $TD(s_i)$ is to -1, the more likely that s_i and its time neighborhood belong to the same cluster and vice versa. Hence, the higher the TD of a sample point, the more abnormal the air quality in that month.

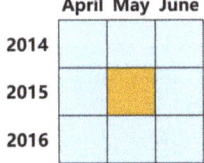

Figure 7. Neighbor timestamps of May 2015.

4.3.2. Geographic Surprise

Next, we introduce Bayesian surprise [43,44], which is used to detect geographic anomalies, and refer to hereinafter as geographic surprise (GS). Generally, the air quality data of the locations in one area have similar features in light of their similar topographic characteristics and climate conditions. This can be taken as our expectation. When we observe the data distribution of an area at a timestamp, we will not be surprised if it is consistent with that of adjacent cities. In this case, the observed data match our expectation. By contrast, if we find a unique city that possesses different air quality compared with adjacent cities, it is not in accordance with our expectation, and it can be regarded as a surprising event. Thus, the impact on expectation can be used to find abnormal cases, and we use GS to quantify this impact for every sample point.

For sample s_i, we define several expected values and an observed value. Let X be the corresponding expected data set of sample set S, and X can be written as $X = \{x_i^u \mid 1 \leq i \leq n, 1 \leq u \leq q\}$, where q is the number of expectations. $P(x_i^u)$ can be regarded as the prior probability, which is independent and artificially defined. At the same time, let Y be the observed data set and $Y = \{y_i \mid 1 \leq i \leq n\}$. After observing new data y_i, our expectation will be unmet and, as a result, change. We use $P(x_i^u|y_i)$ to model the updated likelihood of event x_i^u occurring in the face of y_i. According to Bayes' Rule, $P(x_i^u|y_i)$ is a posterior probability, and it is proportional to the product of the prior probability and standardized likelihood. It can be calculated as

$$P(x_i^u|y_i) = \frac{P(y_i|x_i^u)P(x_i^u)}{P(y_i)}. \tag{4}$$

The essence of the impact on expectation is the difference between the prior and posterior probability distributions. Thus, we use relative entropy to calculate GS:

$$GS(s_i) = KL(P(x_i|y_i)\|P(x_i)) = \sum_{u=1}^{q} P(x_i^u|y_i) \log \frac{P(x_i^u|y_i)}{P(x_i^u)}. \tag{5}$$

In this paper, we map all the sample vectors from the original mD space to $1D$ space and form the observed data set Y. In addition, two expected models, x^1 and x^2, are involved:

- x^1: at a certain timestamp, the air quality of different cities in the same area is the same.
- x^2: at a certain timestamp, the air quality of all cities is the same.

We not only specify the regional features of air quality as x^1 but also define x^2 to prevent inaccuracy caused by the artificial division of geographical areas. To balance the two expected models rationally, we define the prior probability $P(x^u)(u = 1, 2)$ by $P(x^1) = 0.8$ and $P(x^2) = 0.2$.

According to Equation (5), the value of GS is always positive. The closer the value is to 0, the more likely it is that the sample is consistent with adjacent cities. Thus, the higher the GS value of the corresponding sample, the more abnormal the related city at a particular timestamp.

4.3.3. Abnormity Classification

Using the above indices, we designed an abnormity classification view that provides an overview of abnormal cases and divides them into four categories according to the evaluation indices. As shown in Figure 8, the horizontal axis indicates TD, and the vertical axis indicates GS. Each sample is represented by a circle, whose size is proportional to the sum of the absolute values of TD and GS, so users can easily locate representative abnormal samples. Using the air quality data presented in this paper, we obtain result ranges for TD and GS of $[-1, 1]$ and $[0, 0.3]$, respectively. Furthermore, we set the classifying thresholds of GS and TD to the mean value of the maximum and minimum, respectively. On the basis of these different ranges, we define four kinds of samples:

1. **Insusceptible samples**. These are in the top-left corner (Figure 8a), with a low value of TD and a high value of GS. This combination means that these samples remain stable and different from

adjacent cities for long periods. It is important to analyze these samples and understand why they have unique features and are entirely unaffected by their neighboring areas.

2. **Accidental samples.** These are in the top-right corner (Figure 8b), with high values of both TD and GS. These samples possess entirely different features both temporally and spatially. One of them can indicate an accidental event.

3. **Ordinary samples.** These are in the bottom-left corner (Figure 8c), with low values of both TD and GS. These samples enjoy long-term stability and high similarity compared with adjacent cities. Each sample can guide users in finding a specific case that covers large areas and long periods.

4. **Susceptible samples.** These are in the bottom-right corner (Figure 8d), with a high value of TD and a low value of GS. This means that the samples change abruptly and become consistent with adjacent cities. It can be inferred that these samples may be affected by other cities.

From Figure 8, we find that most data are ordinary samples or susceptible samples, and there exist a few insusceptible samples that are worth further exploration. From the abnormity classification view, users can quickly locate unusual samples with specific spatiotemporal characteristics and further trace the detailed contextual information through other views.

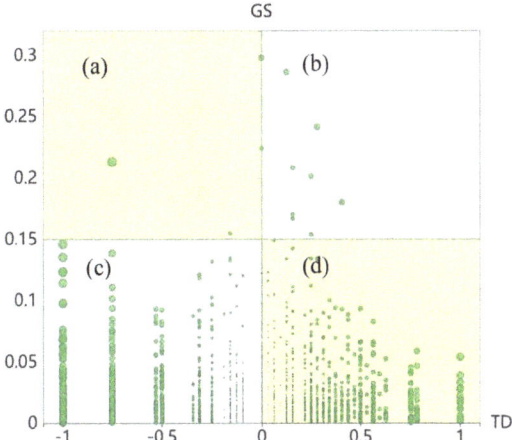

Figure 8. Abnormity Classification view. (**a**) Insusceptible block. (**b**) Accidental block. (**c**) Ordinary block. (**d**) Susceptible block.

4.4. Visual Analytic System

Integrating the above analysis methods leads to the proposed visual analytic system, AirInsight (Figure 9), which consists of three main views: (a) projection view, (b) trend view, and (c) abnormity classification view. These three views can facilitate the analyses of most requirements. Further, (d) map view and (e) radar view are also provided to display supporting information. We also provide a control panel to manage color mapping schemes and filter interesting data points. In this section, we describe the designs of the three main views, as well as the rich interactions provided in AirInsight.

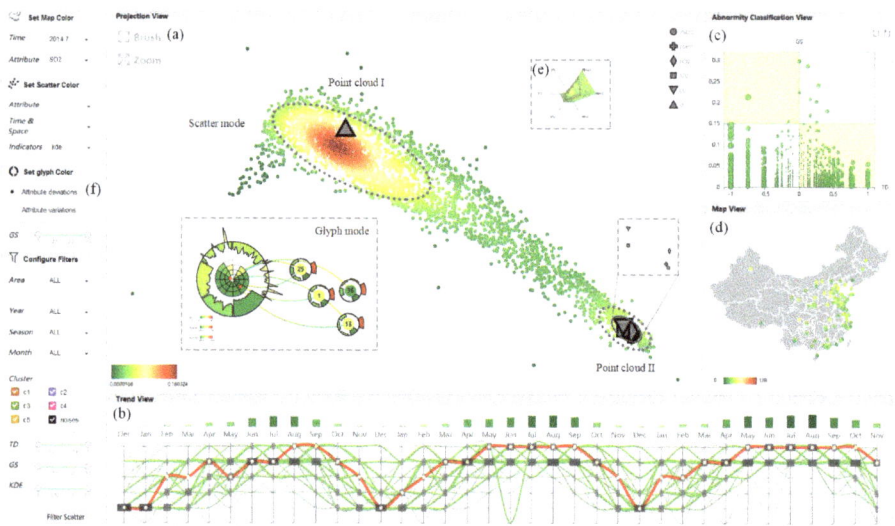

Figure 9. Analyzing regular patterns and anomalies in air quality data using AirInsight. (**a**) Projection view. (**b**) Trend view. (**c**) Abnormity classification view. (**d**) Map view. (**e**) Radar view. (**f**) Control panel.

4.4.1. Projection View

The design of the projection view is based on the layout described in Section 4.1. It includes two modes: (1) scatter mode, which is devoted to providing an overview of data and attributes, and (2) glyph mode, which contains multiple linked glyphs to show the time-varying process of a chosen city with rich context.

Scatter Mode: As shown in Figures 4b and 9a, we use large gray symbols with different shapes to represent attribute points, while the remaining small round points represent sample points. For the scatter diagram, color is an essential visual encoding channel. Our design includes three color mapping schemes for sample points:

1. **Attribute values**, such as $PM_{2.5}$ and PM_{10}, which assist in the in-depth exploration of a particular attribute's features.
2. **Spatiotemporal contextual information**, including geographic and time labels with different granularities. This information is critical for analyzing associations between spatiotemporal patterns and multiple variables.
3. **Additional evaluation indicators**: (1) The densities of overlapping scatterplots (Figure 9a, Scatter mode), computed by kernel density estimation (KDE); [45] this information strengthens the abilities to distinguish scatter distributions and observe patterns. (2) Clustering results, discussed in Section 4.2, which exhibit regular patterns and outliers. (3) Values of TD and GS, described in Section 4.3, which facilitate the exploration of the relationships between hidden anomalies and attributes.

Glyph Mode: To acquire a deeper insight into temporal variations in the air quality of a city of interest, we designed two artistic glyphs to visually summarize the regular patterns and emphasize the abnormal timestamps, as shown in Figure 10. These are named R-Shield (Figure 10a) and A-Shield (Figure 10c), respectively. After obtaining the clustering results, R-Shield is assigned for each cluster if the following two timestamp characteristics are present: (1) the TD value of a timestamp equals -1, as well as that of its time neighborhood; (2) the groups consist of at least two continuous timestamps. The remaining discrete timestamps and outliers extracted by the clustering process are treated as A-Shields.

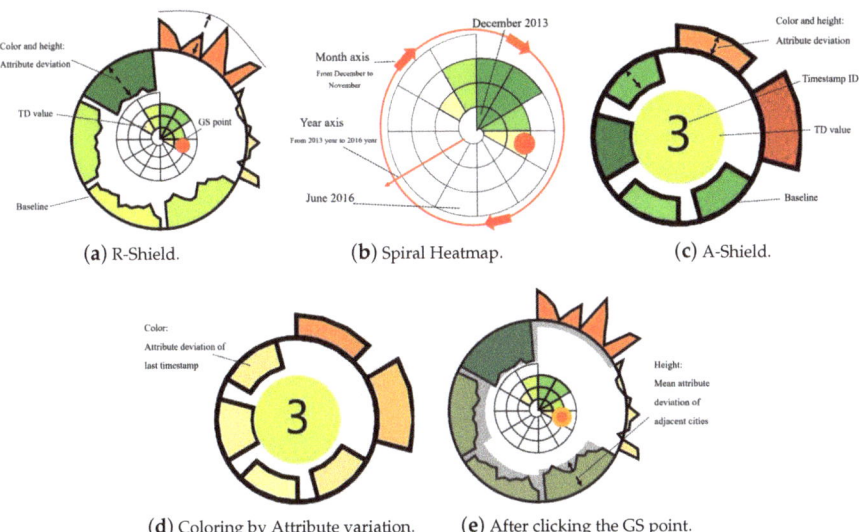

Figure 10. Design of glyphs.

The glyphs encode four fundamental metrics: attribute values, time clues, TD, and GS. A-Shield comprises two parts: the inner circle and the outer sectors (Figure 10c). The inner circle's color depicts TD, where red represents a high value and green represents a low value. The number marked in the center indicates the index of the current timestamp. At the same time, there are six outer sectors corresponding to the six kinds of pollutants, and their heights represent the deviations between the attribute values and the mean AQI of the current city. This mean value is presented as a stable circular baseline. When there is a positive deviation, the sector protrudes outwardly. Conversely, the sector is inwardly recessed if there is a negative deviation. The major pollutant can be found by comparing the sector heights and finding the most outwardly protruding sector.

R-Shield (Figure 10a) is designed by extending A-Shield, and it contains information for multiple timestamps. Its size indicates the number of the included timestamps. The interior of R-Shield is a spiral heatmap (Figure 10b), whose radial axis and angular axis represent years and months, respectively. The color of each grid encodes the corresponding TD value. In addition, the wavy outer sectors depict the attribute deviations of all the timestamps included in that specific R-Shield.

We provide two options for the color scheme of the outer sectors. One option is based on attribute deviations (Figure 10a,c). This facilitates the comparison between two glyphs and the recognition of abnormal attributes. However, it is not intuitive enough when glyphs with dissimilar sizes and scattered locations are compared only by their heights. The other option is based on the attribute variations in A-Shield compared with its last timestamp (Figure 10d), while the colors in R-shield are green by default. This mechanism can emphasize variation in an attribute over time.

Additionally, abnormal timestamps from a geographical perspective are highlighted by red dots on timestamps whose GS value exceeds a specified threshold (Figure 10e). The threshold can be set from the control panel. After clicking one red dot, additional gray sectors appear along the circular baseline; these new sectors represent the mean values of other cities in the same geographical area at the current timestamp. This function can help users to recognize the causative pollutants of the anomaly in detail.

Visual clutter is a potential drawback of this design, and it is common for glyph-based visualizations. To solve this problem, a force-directed collision detection method is implemented to separate overlapping glyphs. In addition, when the number of timestamps of a glyph exceeds a user's visual endurance, they can hover over the glyph to enlarge the spiral heatmap and bring it to the foreground.

State transitions [46–48], which are important features in visual analysis, are usually extracted and explored in the form of a node-link diagram. For example, Natalia et al. [49] designed state transition graphs for the semantic analysis of movement behaviors. In order to analyze state transitions of air quality, we use Bezier curves to connect scattered glyphs (Figure 10a, Glyph mode) on the basis of the time sequence, and a curve's color transition (from green to yellow) indicates the direction of the time flow. These curves preserve the continuity of time and show the transitions between the stable state, unstable state, recurrence state, and saltation state in a time-varying process (Figure 11).

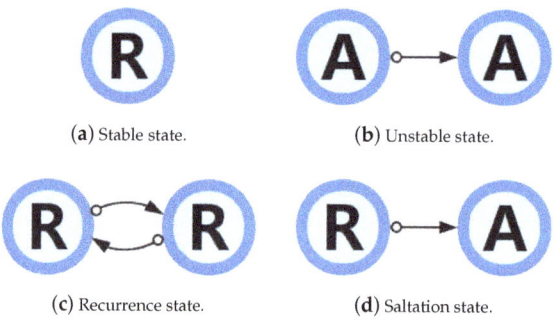

(a) Stable state.   (b) Unstable state.

(c) Recurrence state.   (d) Saltation state.

Figure 11. Typical states in a time-varying process.

The stable state (Figure 11a), which is indicated by the absence of lines in the layout, reflects a stationary time-varying process since all the timestamps belong to a single R-Shield. On the contrary, a line connecting two A-Shields indicates an unstable state (Figure 11b), which reveals that the air quality changes from one anomalous condition to another anomalous condition. Moreover, the recurrence state (Figure 11c) signifies that a loop exists between two regular patterns and indicates the periodicity rules. Dramatically changing data define the saltation state (Figure 11d), which is a noteworthy turning point that prompts analysts to look into causes.

4.4.2. Trend View

The trend view (Figure 9b) displays the temporal trend of different cities using the clustering results and the distributions of multivariate patterns among different timestamps. Similar to the traditional Parallel coordinate plot (PCP) [17], the successively placed axes represent continuous timestamps. The ticks on the axes are the cluster labels, and each line represents a city. By tracing and comparing the line trends, we can observe the temporal variations in the air quality of a city. However, when the lines become dense, it is hard to pinpoint the axis tick that contains the largest amount of data or, in other words, the tick that is representative of the major multivariate pattern at a specific timestamp. To make up for this limitation, we added a gray bar to each tick whose width encodes the number of passing lines. Therefore, by tracing the bars on the same tick of all axes, we can find the cyclical temporal rule of this pattern.

4.4.3. Interactivity

We provide the following interactive functions that allow users to switch between different temporal/spatial contexts and draw in-depth conclusions that are based on linked multiviews.

Context switching. We provide interfaces for users to switch color mapping schemes. As described in Section 4.4.1, there are various schemes for the scatters or glyphs in the projection view. In addition, the points in the map view can be colored according to the values of any attribute for a specific month; this scheme displays the geographical distribution of air quality.

Filtering. When users want to check the air quality samples for a specific situation, they can set various conditions and filter out scatters in the projection view. AirInsight offers multiple selectors and range sliders that allow the user to jointly filter the data on the basis of both spatiotemporal information and statistical indicators, such as geographic labels, clustering results, and so on.

Brushing. AirInsight supports the linkage of projection view, trend view, and map view by brushing. When sample points are brushed in the projection view, a hovering radar chart (Figure 9e) showing the attribute values of the selected samples will appear. Simultaneously, the sizes of the marks in the map view will change, along with the number of brushed samples in corresponding cities. The trend view highlights the lines and time axes of a specified city. A bar is included above each time axis, and the bar's height encodes the number of samples related to this timestamp. Apart from this, when the city lines in trend view are brushed, the projection view highlights the sample points of the selected cities, and the map view highlights the corresponding city marks.

Focusing. Users are able to focus on a city of interest and perform detailed inspections. When users click a city mark in the map view, the glyphs will appear in the projection view as time curves are drawn dynamically. At the same time, the trend view will highlight this city and erase lines that are not geographically adjacent, and circles are added to the time axes in colors that encode the GS value of the corresponding timestamps (Figure 9b).

5. Case Studies and User Evaluations

5.1. Case 1: Exploration of Multivariate Patterns

Using AirInsight, the analyst, who is an environmental expert, started by exploring the multivariate patterns of air quality data in China. To visually perceive preliminary patterns, he first looked at the projection view and employed the point densities to encode the point colors (Figure 9a, Scatter mode). After examination, he found a mass composed of points that are grouped together more tightly in the top-left corner, around the O_3 symbol (Figure 9a, Point cloud I). Also, some points are plotted closely together and far from the O_3 symbol in the bottom-right corner, where the other attribute symbols are distributed (Figure 9a, Point cloud II). He thus inferred that the above two groups of data points possess distinct multivariate features. At the same time, he realized that there is a low correlation between O_3 and the other attributes because of the enormous spatiotemporal difference.

In order to further inspect specific differences and identify more intricate patterns, the analyst set the color mapping scheme to reflect the clustering results. He quickly found that there are two clusters, C1 and C2 (Figure 12a), located in the peripheries of the attribute symbols, similar to the previous findings. Next, he used AQI values to map point colors to preliminarily distinguish these two clusters. The samples in C1 exhibit higher AQI values and more severe air pollution, while all the samples in C2 are indicative of better air quality. To further compare these two clusters in detail, the analyst successively screened out and brushed them, and he then checked other linked views. Then, the popup radar chart (Figure 12b,c), map view (Figure 12d,e), and trend view (Figure 12f,g) displayed their multivariate spatiotemporal contexts. He observed apparent distinctions between the two following clusters:

1. The values of different attributes in C1 have great disparities (Figure 12b), with $PM_{2.5}$ and PM_{10} having the largest fluctuations. Conversely, the attribute values in C2 are nearly identical (Figure 12c).
2. The multivariate pattern of C1 only appears in specific months (Figure 12f), especially in the winter months, rather than June and July, while C2 exists in every month (Figure 12g). Furthermore, the number of C1 cases decreases year by year, while the distribution of C2 cases among different months becomes more uniform; the latter pattern is a good sign that the air quality in China has generally progressively improved.
3. Spatially, C1 cases are mainly distributed in northern China (Figure 12d), while C2 cases are more common in South China and coastal areas (Figure 12e).

As an environmental expert, the analyst confirmed these findings. He explained that the production of O_3 is closely related to solar radiation, so C2 cases are more common in summer and in some sun-intensive areas. The other kinds of pollutants are mainly derived from the burning of fossil fuels and are produced in large amounts, particularly during the period in which central-heating is frequently used in cold areas. This explains why the air pollution in northern China in winter is especially serious.

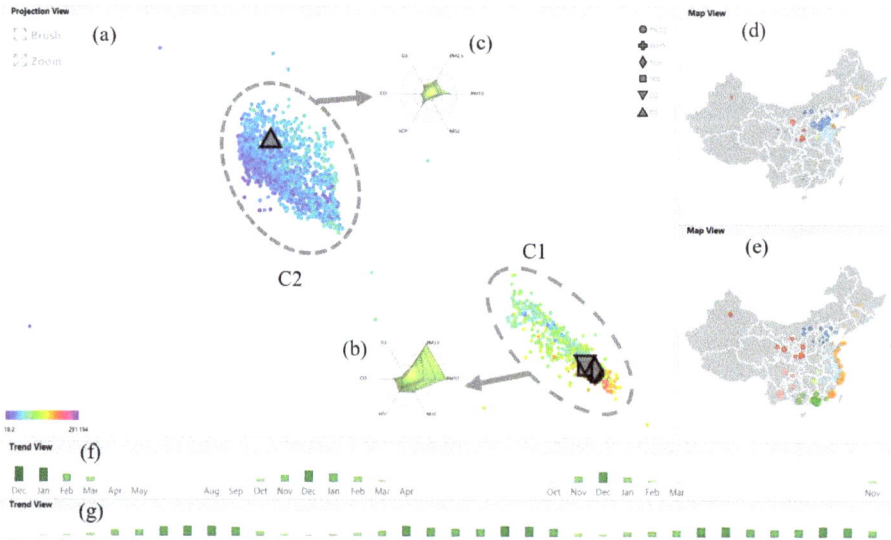

Figure 12. Multivariate patterns and corresponding spatiotemporal context. (a) Projection view after brushing C1 and C2. (b) Multivariate patterns of C1. (c) Multivariate patterns of C2. (d) Spatial context of C1. (e) Spatial context of C2. (f) Temporal context of C1. (g) Temporal context of C2.

5.2. Case 2: Finding and Understanding Temporal Anomalies

The analyst decided to identify some hidden temporally anomalous events and explore the specific difference by tracing the whole time-varying process. First, he checked the abnormity classification view (Figure 8) and found an interesting point with a high TD value. The analyst chose the point representing the 3rd timestamp of Nanning, which has a high TD value (0.565), and he then switched the projection view into glyph mode (Figure 13). At the same time, he set the colors of A-Shields to reflect the attribute variations relative to their last timestamps. From the R-shields in Figure 13, the analyst observed three regular patterns:

1. The smallest R-shield R1, located with most of the attribute symbols, only contains two timestamps that fall in winter. By comparing its outer sectors with those of other R-shields, he found that R1 has the highest $PM_{2.5}$, PM_{10}, and SO_2 values and the lowest O_3 values.
2. The biggest R-shield R2, plotted near the O_3 symbol, contains a large proportion of all timestamps, especially those that fall in spring and autumn. Except for a few timestamps, the values of $PM_{2.5}$ and PM_{10} in R2 fluctuate above and below the baseline.
3. R3, located near R2 and the O_3 symbol, contains the majority of timestamps that fall in summer. All attribute values of R3 are below the baseline, implying that it has the best air quality condition.

By tracing the temporal links, the analyst found an apparent recurrent state between R2 and R3. Combining this observation with the previous analyses, he was aware that this recurrent state is caused by the transition from spring to autumn. Since all the samples integrated into these three

R-shields have low TD and low GS values, the analyst defined them as "ordinary samples". Hence, he inferred that the cities in the same area as Nanning have similar regular patterns.

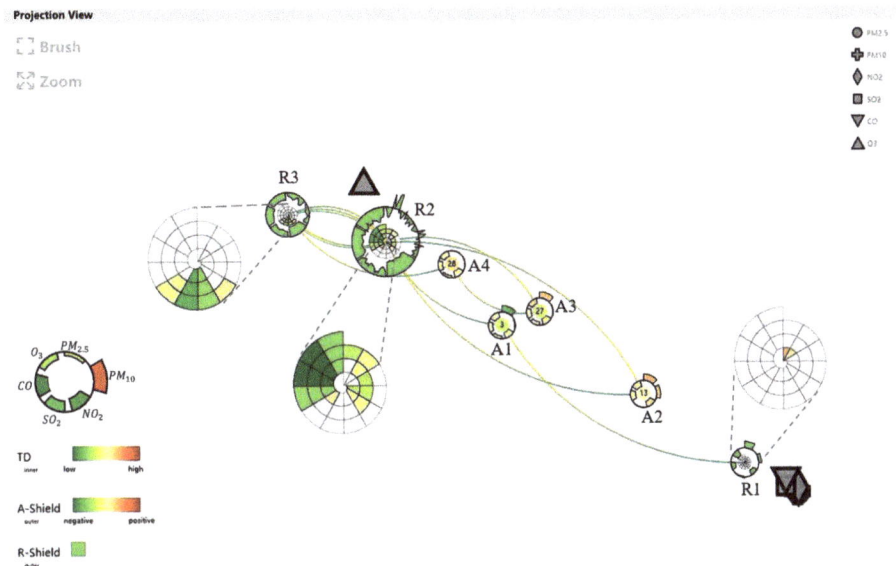

Figure 13. Projection view in glyph mode after selecting Nanning.

To locate temporal anomalies, the analyst continued his exploration by inspecting the A-Shields with high TD values, which often lead to the occurrence of saltation states and unstable states. By examining the inner color of A-Shields and sequential temporal lines, he became interested in *A1*, which has a high TD value and is linked to *R1* by a long curve. This indicates a typical saltation state in which air quality changes dramatically at the 3rd timestamp. After observing it more closely, he discovered that the color of the outer sector that represents $PM_{2.5}$ in *A1* is deep green, which means that $PM_{2.5}$ pollution decreases considerably compared with the last timestamp. By looking up the relevant climatic information, he found that there is a thicker temperature inversion layer in Nanning at the 1st and 2nd timestamps. A thick temperature inversion layer prevents atmospheric convection and can lead to air pollution. The arrival of cold air at the 3rd timestamp breaks the condition and disperses the fog and haze.

Beyond that, the analyst also found two sequential saltation states between *A2* and *R2*: the air quality changes dramatically and then immediately returns to the original condition. The outer sectors in *A2* are colored in different shades of orange, which suggests that all the attributes are elevated at the 13th timestamp, while *R2* reflects much better air conditions. From this, the analyst inferred that an unexpected pollution event occurs in short bursts at the 13th timestamp. Since this timestamp has a low GS value and is identified as a "susceptible sample", it serves as a reminder to domain experts who analyze pollution causes to not only consider Nanning's own factors but also account for the impact of surrounding cities.

One unstable state exists between *A3* and *A4*. During this period, $PM_{2.5}$ increases at the 27th timestamp, decreases at the 28th timestamp, and stabilizes after the 29th timestamp. The analyst referred to the calendar and realized that this period is around Chinese New Year, and he deduced that the observed increase in air pollution is the result of excessive burning of fireworks and firecrackers.

5.3. Case 3: Exploration of Geographic Anomalies

AirInsight also allows users to explore geographic anomalies, which can help domain experts analyze the causes of pollution in different cities from a macro perspective. The analyst continued to scrutinize the abnormity classification view (Figure 8). He was interested in the sample representing the 17th timestamp for Ordos, which is a typical "insusceptible sample" that has a high GS value of 0.21 and a low TD value of −0.75. Thus, he regenerated the projection view to focus on Ordos (Figure 14a).

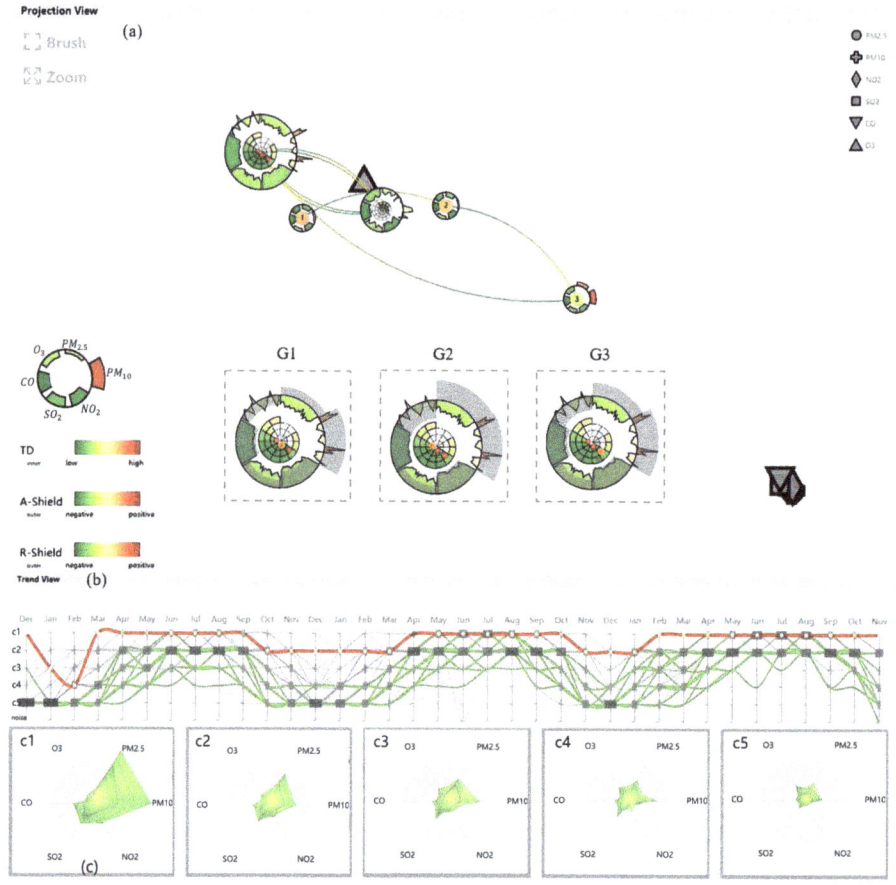

Figure 14. Projection view of glyph mode and trend view for Ordos. (**a**) Projection view; (**b**) Trend view; (**c**) Radar chart.

To investigate the reason for the unique performance of the 17th timestamp, he clicked the red point on the corresponding grid. As a result of this action, the mean condition of cities in the same area was shown as additional outer gray sectors (Figure 14 G1). By comparing the heights of the gray sectors with those of the original sectors, he realized that this geographical anomaly is caused by lower values of $PM_{2.5}$, PM_{10}, and SO_2. Then, the analyst further examined the whole view and quickly observed that most timestamps are incorporated into two nearby R-Shields. This means that the air quality in Ordos is less volatile. Hence, he surmised that the disparities between Ordos and its adjacent cities are not the result of accidental events.

To verify this hypothesis, he reduced the GS threshold to filter more samples that are less abnormal. After updating the marks of the samples that exceed the threshold, he discovered another two anomalous events (Figure 14 G2 and G3) and then clicked the red to further explore the specific abnormal manifestations. Surprisingly, adjacent cites in G2 possess more serious $PM_{2.5}$ pollution and better O_3 conditions. Meanwhile, cities in G3 have higher NO_2 and SO_2. According to the process of analysis, he conjectured that Ordos has better air quality over prolonged periods compared with its adjacent cites.

To confirm this, he brought up the highlighted trend view (Figure 14b) to explore the degree of anomalous geographical conditions over the entire timeline. Observing this view presents a satisfactory result: even though all city lines have similar variation trends, the line for Ordos is always above the others, especially in winter. He further combined the analysis with the radar chart (Figure 14c) and found that the cluster labels at the top of the trend view have higher pollution values. Therefore, he ultimately drew the conclusion that the air in Ordos remains clean in the long term and is better than that in other cities in the same area.

5.4. User Evaluations

The system received positive feedback from the environmental expert at Northeast Normal University. Among all the modules, the expert found that the linkage of the projection view, map view, and trend view was the most useful. He acknowledged that the visual analysis that fuses temporal, spatial, and multivariate perspectives was indispensable for drawing his conclusions. In addition, summarizing the multidimensional time-varying laws of an individual city by using glyphs makes the system far stronger than other general-purpose software. He also agreed that it was easy to explore the cities and months of interest using the interactive operations, especially brushing. Apart from these remarks, the expert also appreciated the effectiveness of the abnormity classification view. He believed that this is a novel direction of air quality data analysis, and it inspired him to further analyze the causes of pollution on the basis of detected anomalies.

To the best of our knowledge, a fully quantitative comparison between AirInsight and other baseline systems is not feasible because few studies [12,16] have focused on the comprehensive exploration of regular patterns and anomalies in air quality data, and these few studies have objectives that differ from the goal of AirInsight. In order to further evaluate the effectiveness and powerfulness of our visual system, we developed a simple system as a baseline to compare with AirInsight. As shown in Figure 15, the simple system integrates a map view and a line chart, both of which are common conventional visualization methods. The map view plays the same role as it does in AirInsight by showing the geographical location of the studied data. The line chart shows the temporal variation in the monthly mean values, with each line representing one pollutant in one location. After clicking a city of interest, the line chart will also focus on the selected city. As an example, Figure 16 presents the variation in air quality for Changchun.

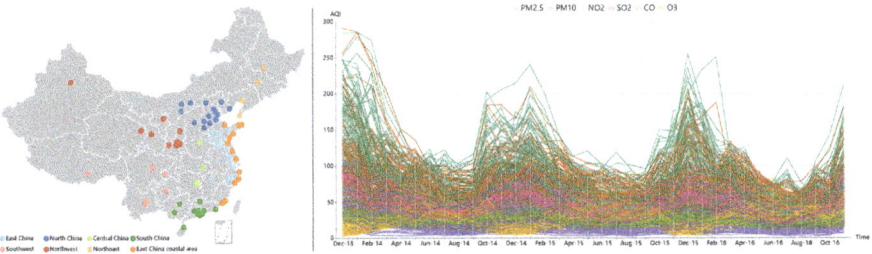

Figure 15. The simple system integrating a map and line chart.

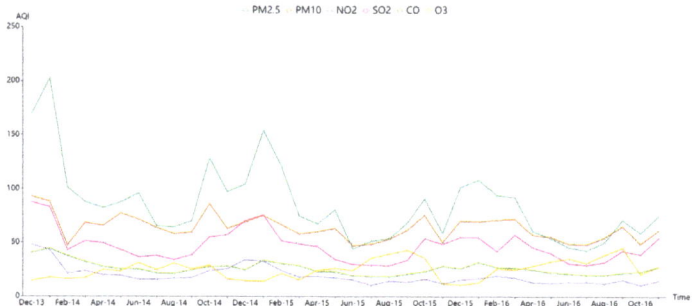

Figure 16. The line chart of Changchun.

We performed a task-oriented user study with 13 participants (5 females and 8 males). All the participants are graduate students and have little knowledge of air pollution. The tasks are as follows:

- **Task1**. Identify the pollutant that is the most distinct from others.
- **Task2**. Analyze the difference in spatiotemporal distribution when high O_3 and $PM_{2.5}$ appear.
- **Task3**. Describe the differences in air quality in different seasons in Changchun and identify the most unusual month.
- **Task4**. Compare the air quality in cities in North China and find the most distinctive city.

After a brief introduction to the AirInsight system and the simple system, the participants were asked to freely explore them individually and complete the tasks. The comparison results are as follows:

- **AirInsight**. For Task 1 and Task 2, all the participants provided the right answers in a few minutes. They all agreed that the views were legible and that the interactions were easy to learn. Most students completed Task3 and Task4 in 25 min. During the process of Task4, ten participants preferred to observe the trend view, while the others first screened the points belonging to North China in the abnormity classification view and identified the abnormal city faster than the former subjects.
- **The simple system**. For Task 1, almost all participants indicated that the line chart contained too much information and clutter. They could not identify the unique pollutant and only learned that $PM_{2.5}$ might have the highest value. For Task2, participants were forced to examine each city's line chart one by one. Although the results can be retained and compared using screenshots, they believed that the process was very boring, cumbersome, and required a good memory. For Task3, although most of the participants gave the correct answer, they said that it was difficult to observe the six pollutants at the same time. During the process of Task4, the participants indicated that the difficulty was further enhanced. They not only needed to measure six pollutants at the same time but also needed to compare different views. Only two boys insisted on completing the task. It took more than 40 min to save and compare all of the screenshots of the northern cities.

In summary, our system can help users to obtain the features of air quality data effectively.

6. Discussion

6.1. Rationale

Dimension reduction and clustering are commonly used methods to identify patterns and processes for mining big data, and many works have integrated both of them into a visual analytic system. However, there is still a question that is worth discussing: How do we choose the order of dimension reduction and clustering?. As mentioned in the literature [50], the schemes by which these processes are combined can be divided into several types and generate different results. Each scheme should be chosen on the basis of actual application requirements since they all have advantages and disadvantages. In this study, we chose to apply clustering to a data set that was already projected. The rationale of our scheme, as well as that of other applicable options, are discussed below:

Independent Algorithms: Since the dimension reduction and clustering processes are executed independently and do not affect each other, the two algorithms can optimize their results to the maximum extent. However, the clusters in the projection view may be intermingled and difficult to distinguish. It is not consistent with our goals, which included adding glyphs that display clustering information in the projection view. Independent algorithms result in overlapped glyphs, and they require users to apply more effort to trace a time-varying trend.

Clustering Preprocessing for Dimension Reduction: One possibility is to execute a clustering algorithm with high-dimensional data and then project the data into visual space using some clustering results, which can be cluster assignments or centroids. In this way, the clustering algorithm is unaffected and will get optimal results. Moreover, the found clusters can be kept together in low-dimensional space. Following this idea, we considered clustering the sample vectors first and then using the centroids in each cluster and the noises as control points for step 1 in CLSP. However, too few control points lead to inaccurate projection results because the expert often hopes to obtain fewer than 10 clusters for easy analysis. In the system proposed in this paper, the user's ability to obtain an overview of the data was an important design requirement, and it is achieved by the projection view. In order to ensure the accuracy of dimension reduction, we vetoed this scheme. Another alternative is to additionally consider the similarities among cluster labels when quantifying the diversities among sample vectors. This scheme fully emphasizes the clustering result, and the corresponding projection view can better display the found clusters. However, in contrast to the traditional dimension reduction methods, CLSP leads to a composite layout that uses nearby sample and attribute points to demonstrate the relatively high value of the sample's attribute. Additional information about cluster labels reduces the interpretability of the projection layout and makes it hard to observe the relationships between samples and attributes.

Dimension Reduction Preprocessing for Clustering: We finally chose to perform dimension reduction and then cluster the samples in low-dimensional space. This scheme leads to accurate projection results since the dimension reduction is not affected by the clustering process. However, one of the main disadvantages is that it results in potentially misleading clustering results. Since the information will be inevitably lost during the projection, the clustering results cannot fully reflect the data relationship in high-dimensional space. As mentioned above, in this study, the projection layout is the basis for most analyses, and the number of clusters required is relatively small. After balancing, we finally chose this way to get the results that are most applicable to our goal.

6.2. Scalability

The scalability of AirInsight is also an issue worthy of discussion. As a web-based system, it is easy for users to access and migrate new data. In this study, AirInsight was applied to air quality data that contains six kinds of pollutants in 88 cities over 3 years; however, it can be easily extended to the analysis of more samples and even more general problems related to multivariate spatiotemporal data.

AirInsight does not limit the geographic scale of data. Users can study large-scale urban agglomeration, as well as analyze the data from several locations or even one location. For air pollution, the system is also suitable for further analysis of the monitoring stations.

In this work, each timestamp is a month, and the combination of DTW and SSIM is applied to measure their distance. Actually, when the granularity of time is smaller or even when s_i is no longer a time series, the method of quantifying diversity can be replaced by methods that only consider the multivariate features, such as the commonly used Euclidean distance. As the number of timestamps increases, the trend view adds a scroll bar to expand the screen and display more time axes. Further, for the spiral heatmap in glyphs, focus+context techniques give users the ability to observe more time grids. However, when the number of timestamps increases to an unacceptable level and the temporally sequential lines are cluttered, the time-varying process is hard to identify. The animation supported in AirInsight can mitigate this problem. In the future, we will introduce line-simplified visualization techniques, such as edge-bundling technology [51].

For the multivariate features of the data, the higher the number of attributes, the more display space required. In the system, both glyphs and radar charts can be enlarged to show more multivariate information. However, after testing, we found that when the data exceed 30 dimensions, the observation power is significantly reduced. Also, in the projection view, we use different symbols that represent attributes. When the number of symbols exceeds the range that humans can remember and identify, new visual metaphors that are more intuitive and distinguishable are needed.

In addition to our final visualization system, several proposed methods can independently meet more requirements of other application fields. CLSP can be used to create an interpretable dimensional reduction layout, NHC can be used to analyze clusters and noises, and the anomaly detection strategy can be used to detect and classify spatiotemporal anomalies.

As an interdisciplinary application involving environmental science and visual analysis, our work applies data mining algorithms and statistical analysis indicators to extract and present hidden patterns and anomalies in big air quality data. For air quality experts, we provide the possibility to analyze correlations among multiple pollutants and find differences in pollutants among different regions or at different times. At the same time, users can diagnose cities with long-term stability, cities with dramatic changes, and urban groups with similar patterns, our system is also friendly to users without a professional background since visualization technology makes huge amounts of data readable and straightforward. For example, media reporters who want to summarize the air quality of a city over a given time span can find the city of interest from the map view and click it. From the obtained glyph view, they can define the most common air condition according to the R-Shield with the maximum radius and inspect the trend view to compare it with other cities in the same area.

6.3. Limitations

Although we received positive feedback from users, there are still some limitations that need to be discussed.

One is the size of the data that the system can manage to ensure a good analytical experience. We tested the system on an Intel Core 3.6 GHz computer with 16 GB RAM. On the basis of this implementation, we recorded the running time required for the data studied in this paper. As shown in Table 3, we divided the preprocessing stage into several subprocesses, including constructing the difference matrix (CLSP), projecting (CLSP), NHC, and computing TD and GS. The most time-consuming part is constructing the difference matrix, whose computational complexity is $O((n+m)^2)$. In other words, the running time of this process is closely related to the total number of samples and attributes, and it will grow exponentially as the size of the data increases. In the future, we will aim to design a parallel computing algorithm to reduce time costs. Another time-consuming part is projecting; the time-intensiveness of this step is primarily due to the selection of control points by SF-Kmedoids, which can be optimized by improved methods. Aside from the limitations of preprocessing, we further tested interactivity performance with different data sizes. We randomly generated three sizes of projected samples: 5000, 10,000, and 20,000. The experimental results do not reveal any delays, and the linkage between views by brushing or clicking is not affected when using a sample number of 5000 or 10,000. When the data size reaches 20,000, the initial rendering of all views takes about 3 s, and the linkage between views by brushing had some delays. Thus, we regard 20,000 as the data size limit that our system can support. In summary, our system can support the exploration of 20,000 data items with real-time response, although users need to perform preprocessing with an acceptable runtime when they analyze a new data set.

Table 3. Running time of preprocessing stage.

	Constructing the Difference Matrix (CLSP)	Projecting (CLSP)	NHC	TD	GS
Running time (sec.)	1554.054	777.396	6.771	0.007	32.189

Our users also raised some issues worth mentioning after they used AirInsight. Four participants reported that the glyphs showed rich information when they first saw them, and although they were useful and intuitive, it took some effort to fully understand the details when they first accessed them. In addition, one user pointed out that our work lacked an analysis of the sensitivity of anomalies in different temporal and spatial scales. This is a significant issue that can be further studied in the future. After brushing the projection view, the map view and trend view can only display statistics separately, rather than spatiotemporal joint distribution. They fail to solve more complex problems, such as brushing samples and comparing the most common month in each location. Also, bivariate color scales that are green and red at their extremes are not friendly to color-blind users. In the future, more accessible methods of visual mapping should be considered in AirInsight, such as mapping values in grayscale, to meet the needs of different kinds of users.

7. Conclusions

The problem of analyzing multivariate spatiotemporal laws of air quality data is challenging due to the innate data complexity and latent associations. In this paper, we have presented our design of an innovative visual analysis system, AirInsight, to address this problem. Our system supports multivariate spatiotemporal pattern exploration and abnormal case analysis. A visual analysis framework and a spatiotemporal anomaly detection strategy are designed. In the analysis process, we also propose an interpretable dimensionality reduction algorithm CLSP and a clustering algorithm NHC that can diagnose noises. Several coordinated views and novel intuitive glyph designs are included in this system to provide rich contextual information. We also described three case studies and user evaluations to demonstrate that our work enables the user to explore multivariate patterns, trace time-varying processes, compare different cities, and find abnormal timestamps and cities.

As a wider variety of big data are collected, artificial intelligence provides an effective way to handle interdisciplinary issues. Automated algorithms can give users answers to complex questions. However, finding out what causes such results is not an easy task, which often requires integrating contextual information, triggering a wide use of visualization. Based on this, we propose the visual analysis system that combines both the automation algorithms and the interactive visual representations to mine and interpret the potential features in big data. In the future, we will further explore the effective combination of artificial intelligence and visual analysis, such as developing more interpretable automation algorithms, assisting users in adjusting model parameters through visualization, and so on.

Author Contributions: conceptualization, H.Z.; methodology, K.R.; software, Y.L. and Z.L.; writing–original draft preparation, D.Q.

Funding: This research was funded by National Natural Science Foundation of China under Grant grant number 41671379.

Acknowledgments: Thanks to the experts who provided requirements and user feedback for our work, as well as the participants who actively participated in the evaluation of the system.

Conflicts of Interest: The authors declare no conflict of interest.

References

1. Ma, Z.; Hu, X.; Sayer, A.M.; Levy, R.; Zhang, Q.; Xue, Y.; Tong, S.; Bi, J.; Huang, L.; Liu, Y. Satellite-based spatiotemporal trends in PM2.5 concentrations: China, 2004–2013. *Environ. Health Perspect.* **2015**, *124*, 184–192. [CrossRef] [PubMed]
2. Yang, Y.; Cao, Y.; Li, W.; Li, R.; Wang, M.; Wu, Z.; Xu, Q. Multi-site time series analysis of acute effects of multiple air pollutants on respiratory mortality: A population-based study in Beijing, China. *Sci. Total Environ.* **2015**, *508*, 178–187. [CrossRef]
3. Liu, J.; Han, Y.; Tang, X.; Zhu, J.; Zhu, T. Estimating adult mortality attributable to PM2.5 exposure in China with assimilated PM2.5 concentrations based on a ground monitoring network. *Sci. Total Environ.* **2016**, *568*, 1253–1262. [CrossRef] [PubMed]
4. Liao, Z.; Peng, Y.; Li, Y.; Liang, X.; Zhao, Y. A web-based visual analytics system for air quality monitoring data. In Proceedings of the 2014 22nd International Conference on Geoinformatics, Kaohsiung, Taiwan, 25–27 June 2014; pp. 1–6.
5. Chen, Y.; Wang, L.; Li, F.; Du, B.; Choo, K.K.R.; Hassan, H.; Qin, W. Air quality data clustering using EPLS method. *Inf. Fusion* **2017**, *36*, 225–232. [CrossRef]
6. Gutiérrez, L.; Mena, R.H.; Ruggiero, M. A time dependent Bayesian nonparametric model for air quality analysis. *Comput. Stat. Data Anal.* **2016**, *95*, 161–175. [CrossRef]
7. Lomotey, R.K.; Pry, J.C.; Chai, C. Traceability and visual analytics for the Internet-of-Things (IoT) architecture. *World Wide Web* **2018**, *21*, 7–32. [CrossRef]
8. Zheng, Y.; Wu, W.; Chen, Y.; Qu, H.; Ni, L.M. Visual analytics in urban computing: An overview. *IEEE Trans. Big Data* **2016**, *2*, 276–296. [CrossRef]
9. Miller, C.; Nagy, Z.; Schlueter, A. A review of unsupervised statistical learning and visual analytics techniques applied to performance analysis of non-residential buildings. *Renew. Sustain. Energy Rev.* **2018**, *81*, 1365–1377. [CrossRef]
10. Di Lorenzo, G.; Sbodio, M.; Calabrese, F.; Berlingerio, M.; Pinelli, F.; Nair, R. Allaboard: Visual exploration of cellphone mobility data to optimise public transport. *IEEE Trans. Vis. Comput. Graph.* **2016**, *22*, 1036–1050. [CrossRef] [PubMed]
11. Du, Y.; Ma, C.; Wu, C.; Xu, X.; Guo, Y.; Zhou, Y.; Li, J. A visual analytics approach for station-based air quality data. *Sensors* **2017**, *17*, 30. [CrossRef] [PubMed]
12. Li, J.; Xiao, Z.; Zhao, H.Q.; Meng, Z.P.; Zhang, K. Visual analytics of smogs in China. *J. Vis.* **2016**, *19*, 461–474. [CrossRef]
13. Zhou, Z.; Ye, Z.; Liu, Y.; Liu, F.; Tao, Y.; Su, W. Visual Analytics for Spatial Clusters of Air-Quality Data. *IEEE Comput. Graph. Appl.* **2017**, *37*, 98–105. [CrossRef]
14. Guo, F.; Gu, T.; Chen, W.; Qu, H. Visual Exploration of Air Quality Data with A Time-Correlation Partitioning Tree Based on Information Theory. *ACM Trans. Interact. Intell. Syst.* **2018**, in press. [CrossRef]
15. Qu, H.; Chan, W.Y.; Xu, A.; Chung, K.L.; Lau, K.H.; Guo, P. Visual analysis of the air pollution problem in Hong Kong. *IEEE Trans. Vis. Comput. Graph.* **2007**, *13*, 1408–1415. [CrossRef] [PubMed]
16. Li, J.; Chen, S.; Zhang, K.; Andrienko, G.; Andrienko, N. COPE: Interactive Exploration of Co-occurrence Patterns in Spatial Time Series. *IEEE Trans. Visual. Comput. Graph.* **2018**. [CrossRef] [PubMed]
17. Heinrich, J.; Weiskopf, D. State of the Art of Parallel Coordinates. In *Eurographics (STARs)*; 2013; pp. 95–116. Available online: http://joules.de/files/heinrich_state_2013.pdf (accessed on 15 May 2019).
18. Mayr, G.V. *Die Gesetzmäßigkeit im Gesellschaftsleben*; Oldenbourg: Berlin, Germany, 1877; p. 78. (In German)
19. Pearson, K. LIII. On lines and planes of closest fit to systems of points in space. *Lond. Edinb. Dublin Philos. Mag. J. Sci.* **1901**, *2*, 559–572. [CrossRef]
20. Cox, T.F.; Cox, M.A. *Multidimensional Scaling*; Chapman and Hall/CRC: London, UK, 2000.
21. Maaten, L.V.D.; Hinton, G. Visualizing data using t-SNE. *J. Mach. Learn. Res.* **2008**, *9*, 2579–2605.
22. Hoffman, P.; Grinstein, G.; Marx, K.; Grosse, I.; Stanley, E. DNA visual and analytic data mining. In Proceedings of the Visualization'97 (Cat. No. 97CB36155), Phoenix, AZ, USA, 24 October 1997; pp. 437–441.
23. Lehmann, D.J.; Theisel, H. Orthographic star coordinates. *IEEE Trans. Vis. Comput. Graph.* **2013**, *19*, 2615–2624. [CrossRef]
24. de Carvalho Pagliosa, L.; Telea, A.C. RadViz: Improvements on Radial-Based Visualizations++. *Informatics* **2019**, *6*, 16. [CrossRef]

25. Cheng, S.; Mueller, K. The data context map: Fusing data and attributes into a unified display. *IEEE Trans. Vis. Comput. Graph.* **2016**, *22*, 121–130. [CrossRef]
26. Wilkinson, L. Visualizing Big Data Outliers through Distributed Aggregation. *IEEE Trans. Vis. Comput. Graph.* **2018**, *24*, 256–266. [CrossRef] [PubMed]
27. Muelder, C.; Zhu, B.; Chen, W.; Zhang, H.; Ma, K.L. Visual analysis of cloud computing performance using behavioral lines. *IEEE Trans. Vis. Comput. Graph.* **2016**, *22*, 1694–1704. [CrossRef] [PubMed]
28. Xu, P.; Mei, H.; Ren, L.; Chen, W. ViDX: Visual diagnostics of assembly line performance in smart factories. *IEEE Trans. Vis. Comput. Graph.* **2017**, *23*, 291–300. [CrossRef] [PubMed]
29. Shi, L.; Liao, Q.; He, Y.; Li, R.; Striegel, A.; Su, Z. SAVE: Sensor anomaly visualization engine. In Proceedings of the 2011 IEEE Conference on Visual Analytics Science and Technology (VAST), Providence, RI, USA, 23–28 October 2011; pp. 201–210.
30. Cao, N.; Shi, C.; Lin, S.; Lu, J.; Lin, Y.R.; Lin, C.Y. Targetvue: Visual analysis of anomalous user behaviors in online communication systems. *IEEE Trans. Vis. Comput. Graph.* **2016**, *22*, 280–289. [CrossRef] [PubMed]
31. Thom, D.; Bosch, H.; Koch, S.; Wörner, M.; Ertl, T. Spatiotemporal anomaly detection through visual analysis of geolocated twitter messages. In Proceedings of the 2012 IEEE Pacific Visualization Symposium (PacificVis), Songdo, Korea, 28 February–2 March 2012; pp. 41–48.
32. Chae, J.; Thom, D.; Bosch, H.; Jang, Y.; Maciejewski, R.; Ebert, D.S.; Ertl, T. Spatiotemporal social media analytics for abnormal event detection and examination using seasonal-trend decomposition. In Proceedings of the 2012 IEEE Conference on Visual Analytics Science and Technology (VAST), Seattle, WA, USA, 14–19 October 2012; pp. 143–152.
33. Cao, N.; Lin, C.; Zhu, Q.; Lin, Y.R.; Teng, X.; Wen, X. Voila: Visual anomaly detection and monitoring with streaming spatiotemporal data. *IEEE Trans. Vis. Comput. Graph.* **2018**, *24*, 23–33. [CrossRef] [PubMed]
34. Pearson, K. Note on regression and inheritance in the case of two parents. *Proc. R. Soc. Lond.* **1895**, *58*, 240–242.
35. Keogh, E.; Ratanamahatana, C.A. Exact indexing of dynamic time warping. *Knowl. Inf. Syst.* **2005**, *7*, 358–386. [CrossRef]
36. Wang, Z.; Bovik, A.C.; Sheikh, H.R.; Simoncelli, E.P. Image quality assessment: From error visibility to structural similarity. *IEEE Trans. Image Process.* **2004**, *13*, 600–612. [CrossRef]
37. Paulovich, F.V.; Nonato, L.G.; Minghim, R.; Levkowitz, H. Least square projection: A fast high-precision multidimensional projection technique and its application to document mapping. *IEEE Trans. Vis. Comput. Graph.* **2008**, *14*, 564. [CrossRef]
38. Park, H.S.; Jun, C.H. A simple and fast algorithm for K-medoids clustering. *Expert Syst. Appl.* **2009**, *36*, 3336–3341. [CrossRef]
39. MacQueen, J. Some methods for classification and analysis of multivariate observations. In Proceedings of the Fifth Berkeley Symposium on Mathematical Statistics and Probability, Oakland, CA, USA, 21 June–18 July 1965; Volume 1, pp. 281–297.
40. Ester, M.; Kriegel, H.P.; Sander, J.; Xu, X. A Density-Based Algorithm For Discovering Clusters in Large Spatial Databases With Noise. Available online: https://www.aaai.org/Papers/KDD/1996/KDD96-037.pdf (accessed on 21 May 2019).
41. Sibson, R. SLINK: An optimally efficient algorithm for the single-link cluster method. *Comput. J.* **1973**, *16*, 30–34. [CrossRef]
42. Zhang, Y.; Luo, W.; Mack, E.A.; Maciejewski, R. Visualizing the impact of geographical variations on multivariate clustering. *Comput. Graph. Forum* **2016**, *35*, 101–110. [CrossRef]
43. Correll, M.; Heer, J. Surprise! Bayesian Weighting for De-Biasing Thematic Maps. *IEEE Trans. Vis. Comput. Graph.* **2017**, *23*, 651–660. [CrossRef] [PubMed]
44. Itti, L.; Baldi, P. Bayesian surprise attracts human attention. *Vis. Res.* **2009**, *49*, 1295–1306. [CrossRef] [PubMed]
45. Van Kerm, P. Adaptive kernel density estimation. *Stata J.* **2003**, *3*, 148–156. [CrossRef]
46. Bach, B.; Shi, C.; Heulot, N.; Madhyastha, T.; Grabowski, T.; Dragicevic, P. Time curves: Folding time to visualize patterns of temporal evolution in data. *IEEE Trans. Vis. Comput. Graph.* **2016**, *22*, 559–568. [CrossRef]

47. Hadlak, S.; Schumann, H.; Cap, C.H.; Wollenberg, T. Supporting the visual analysis of dynamic networks by clustering associated temporal attributes. *IEEE Trans. Vis. Comput. Graph.* **2013**, *19*, 2267–2276. [CrossRef] [PubMed]
48. van den Elzen, S.; Holten, D.; Blaas, J.; van Wijk, J.J. Reducing snapshots to points: A visual analytics approach to dynamic network exploration. *IEEE Trans. Vis. Comput. Graph.* **2016**, *22*, 1–10. [CrossRef] [PubMed]
49. Andrienko, N.; Andrienko, G. State transition graphs for semantic analysis of movement behaviours. *Inf. Vis.* **2018**, *17*, 41–65. [CrossRef]
50. Wenskovitch, J.; Crandell, I.; Ramakrishnan, N.; House, L.; Leman, S.; North, C. Towards a Systematic Combination of Dimension Reduction and Clustering in Visual Analytics. *IEEE Trans. Visual. Comput. Graph.* **2018**, *24*, 131–141. [CrossRef]
51. David, S.; Brandon, H.; Jeffrey, H. Divided edge bundling for directional network data. *IEEE Trans. Vis. Comput. Graph.* **2011**, *17*, 2354–2363.

© 2019 by the authors. Licensee MDPI, Basel, Switzerland. This article is an open access article distributed under the terms and conditions of the Creative Commons Attribution (CC BY) license (http://creativecommons.org/licenses/by/4.0/).

Article

Decision-Making Method based on Mixed Integer Linear Programming and Rough Set: A Case Study of Diesel Engine Quality and Assembly Clearance Data

Wenbing Chang [1,†], Xinglong Yuan [1], Yalong Wu [2], Shenghan Zhou [1,†], Jingsong Lei [1] and Yiyong Xiao [1,*]

1. School of Reliability and Systems Engineering, Beihang University, Beijing 100191, China; changwenbing@263.net (W.C.); yuanxl@buaa.edu.cn (X.Y.); zhoush@buaa.edu.cn (S.Z.); ljsdekey1949@126.com (J.L.)
2. Henan Diesel Engine Industry Co., Luoyang 471039, China; 15896551993@163.com
* Correspondence: xiaoyiyong@buaa.edu.cn; Tel.: +86-10-82317804
† These two authors contributed equally to this work.

Received: 19 December 2018; Accepted: 22 January 2019; Published: 24 January 2019

Abstract: The purpose of this paper is to establish a decision-making system for assembly clearance parameters and machine quality level by analyzing the data of assembly clearance parameters of diesel engine. Accordingly, we present an extension of the rough set theory based on mixed-integer linear programming (MILP) for rough set-based classification (MILP-FRST). Traditional rough set theory has two shortcomings. First, it is sensitive to noise data, resulting in a low accuracy of decision systems based on rough sets. Second, in the classification problem based on rough sets, the attributes cannot be automatically determined. MILP-FRST has the advantages of MILP in resisting noisy data and has the ability to select attributes flexibly and automatically. In order to prove the validity and advantages of the proposed model, we used the machine quality data and assembly clearance data of 29 diesel engines of a certain type to validate the proposed model. Experiments show that the proposed decision-making method based on MILP-FRST model can accurately determine the quality level of the whole machine according to the assembly clearance parameters.

Keywords: data mining; decision-making system; rough set; mixed integer linear programming; assembly clearance; diesel engine quality

---

1. Introduction

Diesel engine is the power core of the ship. In the manufacturing process of the diesel engine, the assembly quality affects the performance indexes of the diesel engine, which is an important factor to measure the quality of the whole engine. Previous studies on the relationship between assembly clearance and machine quality have mainly focused on the mechanical principle, while the data mining method is still less used to mine the relationship between assembly clearance and machine quality. With the development of data mining technology and the accumulation of a large number of raw data, it is possible to apply data mining methods to solve this problem.

With the development of computers and the internet, the amount of data is increasing. Data always contain noise; therefore, it is necessary to handle noisy data to obtain accurate results. Some researchers have put forward methods to address this issue. Among these methods, the two classic methods are fuzzy set [1] and evidence theory [2]. However, these methods sometimes require additional information or prior knowledge, such as fuzzy membership functions, basic probability assignment functions and statistical probability distributions, which are not always easy to obtain.

Rough set theory provides a new way to address vagueness and uncertainty [3]. The core concept of rough set theory is to deduce imprecise data, or to find the correlation between different data by representing the given finite set as an upper approximation set or a lower approximation set.

Despite the advantages of rough set theory, some challenges need to be overcome in practical applications. These problems can be classified into two categories: (1) There are certain limitations of a rough set in practical applications. Many extension and correction theories to the classical rough set have been developed. For example, a model integrating distance and partition distance with a rough set on the basis of a rough set based on a similarity relation was proposed [4]. This model also provided a new understanding of the classification criteria of rough set equivalence classes. Φ-Rough set, another extension of the rough set theory based on the similarity relation, was proposed [5]. Φ-Rough set replaces the indiscernibility relation of the crisp rough set theory by the notion of the Φ-approximate equivalence relation. Use of dynamic probabilistic rough sets with incomplete data addressed the challenge of processing such dynamic and incomplete data [6]. Based on a three-way classification of attributes into the pair-wise disjoint sets of core, marginal, and non-useful attributes, the relationships between the corresponding classes of classification-based and class-specific attributes were examined [7]. (2) A rough set is sensitive to noisy data. The accuracy of a decision-making model based on a rough set is low when applied to the analysis of datasets containing noisy data [8]. To strengthen its ability to resist noisy data, the variable precision rough set (in short, VPRS) was proposed [9]. VPRS has been applied in several fields, such as data mining [10], decision systems [11], and expert systems [12], and provides satisfactory results. Similarly, knowledge reduction is an important research direction of VPRS. However, the related methods and theories are not mature. The most popular study based on VPRS is attribute reduction. In addition, variable precision threshold beta is usually determined by experts. Hence, some researchers have proposed the selection method of beta, which can reduce the difficulty of beta determination due to a lack of prior knowledge [13,14]. Zavareh M. and Maggioni V. proposes an approach to analyze water quality data that is based on rough set theory [15]. Bo C. studies multigranulation neutrosophic rough sets (MNRSs) and their applications in multi-attribute group decision-making [16]. Akram M., Ali G. and Alsheh N. O. introduce notions of soft rough m-polar fuzzy sets and m-polar fuzzy soft rough sets as novel hybrid models for soft computing, and investigate some of their fundamental properties [17]. Jia X. et al. propose an optimization representation of decision-theoretic rough set model. An optimization problem is proposed by considering the minimization of the decision cost [18]. Cao T. et al. discusses the use of parallel computation to obtain rough set approximations from large-scale information systems where missing data exist in both condition and decision attributes [19].

The linear programming method is a classical mathematical method, and its principle is to solve a series of linear constraint equations or inequalities on the premise of satisfying the method of solving linear functions of extreme objectives. Though its mathematical model is simple, it is widely used in various fields, such as location problems, route planning problems, manufacturing problems, marketing problems, and resource allocation problems. Application of the linear programming method can provide an effective and feasible decision-making basis for the aforementioned problems.

The linear programming problem (LP) is a problem of solving the maximum or minimum value of a linear function under a set of linear equality and inequality constraints [20]. The general linear programming model is composed of the following elements parameters and variables, objective functions, and constraint conditions.

There has been much research on optimization problems based on linear programming theory, such as the theory of linear programming and establishment of a mathematical model [21], as well as the combination of practical production, and enterprise and establishment of a linear programming model to solve the problem of allocating enterprise production resources [22]. Linear programming methods have also been used to optimize input–output models, and to establish a multi-objective linear programming model to maximize economic benefits and to minimize resource utilization [23]. One of the most important application fields of linear programming are location problems. A mixed integer linear programming model has been built to select the location of renewable energy facilities [24], and to study a multi-stage facility location problem [25]. To solve the vehicle routing problem of a distribution center, a two-stage solution was proposed.

One of the preprocessing methods of noisy data is regression. Hence, it is obvious that the linear programming model has a strong ability to resist noisy data, and designing a decision-making model based on rough set achieves the ideal accuracy. The integration of the rough set with the linear programming model will not only improve the inadequacies of the rough set, but will also make the decision-making model reach optimal accuracy, theoretically. There are a few studies on the integration of the rough set and linear programming model so far. Zhang et al. proposed a multi-objective linear programming method based on the rough set, to develop a classification for data mining. Based on their model, an improved model to predict hot spots of protein interactions was proposed [26]. However, among all of the above studies, the rough set was only used to reduce the attribute set. Because nonlinear models are considered to be the only way to describe the rough set, there are no studies on the application of linear programming methods to optimize decision-making models based on the rough set.

The biggest weakness of the decision model based on the rough set is its sensitivity to noisy data. VPRS only broadens the requirement of the upper and lower approximations in the definition, and the selection of precision often has strong subjectivity and lacks scientific evidence. VPRS can only be used as an auxiliary method to improve the resistance of the rough set model to noisy data, rather than the main method. Therefore, in this study, we extend the rough set theory via mixed-integer linear programming and we propose a model called the mixed-integer linear programming model for rough set-based classification with flexible attribute selection (in short, MILP-FRST). This model includes the advantages of MILP in resisting noisy data, and it has the ability to select attributes flexibly and automatically. MILP-FRST is able to divide the universe by attribute sets, calculate the lower approximation set under the condition of the presupposed variable precision and the minimum support number, and calculate the decision accuracy and screen out attributes. We set the maximum number of elements in the determination area as the objective function of the model. The processing of attribute selection, and partitioning of the attribute set for the universe are maximized by the objective function. During implementation, attributes that have a significant influence on the accuracy of the decision system will be selected, and the attribute set partition scheme is calculated to achieve the highest accuracy of the decision-making system. In addition, rough set models are often considered to be nonlinear. This paper first describes the related concepts and theories using linear models, which are an extension of rough set theory.

Next, we use the model to mine the correlation between the assembly clearance of diesel engine and the quality of the whole engine based on the dataset, which contains 28 attributes of the assembly clearance parameters and the whole machine quality of 29 diesel engines. Before applying the model, we carry out data pretreatment, and we screen out 15 principal components. These components cover the vast majority of information on the assembly clearance parameters of all diesel engines. Then, we input these data into the model. The experimental results verified the effectiveness and advantages of MILP-FRST.

The rest of the paper is organized as follows. In Section 2, we introduce the concept of the rough set and functional dependence. In Section 3, we build a mixed-integer linear programming model for rough set-based classification with flexible attribute selection. In Section 4, we use the clearance parameter data of 29 diesel engines and the quality data of the whole engine to verify the validity and accuracy of the model. Finally, in Section 5, conclusions are presented.

2. Rough Set Theory

2.1. Concepts and Definitions of Rough Sets

Consider a rough set based on an information system [27]: $IS = (I, A)$, where I is the universe; A is the attribute set. Both I and A are nonempty finite sets.

If the information system meets the conditions that $A = C \cup D \neq \varnothing$, this information system can be called a decision-making system $DS = (I, C \cup D)$, where C is the conditional attribute set, and D is the decisive attribute set.

Definition 1. *Indiscernibility relations [27]: In an information system $IS = (I, A)$, set B is a subset of the attribute set A, binary relation $IND(B) = \{(x,y) \in I \times I : \forall a \in B, a(x) = a(y)\}$ is the indiscernibility relation of IS, recorded as $IND(B)$, where x and y are elements of the universe; a is an attribute of the attribute set; and $a(x)$ is the value of the element x in attribute a.*

Definition 2. *Equivalence class [27]: In an information system $IS = (I, A)$, set B is a subset of the attribute set A. The indiscernibility relation $IND(B)$ divides the universe I into several equivalence classes, where $I/IND(B)$ is the set of all equivalence classes, and $[x]_{IND(B)}$ is the equivalence class containing element x.*

Definition 3. *Upper and lower approximation [27]: In an information system $IS = (I, A)$, set B is a subset of the attribute set A, and set X is a subset of the universe I:*

$$\underline{B}X = \{i \in I | [i]_{IND(B)} \subseteq X\} \tag{1}$$

$$\overline{B}X = \{i \in I | [i]_{IND(B)} \cap X \neq \varnothing\} \tag{2}$$

where $\underline{B}X$ is the lower approximation; $\overline{B}X$ is the upper approximation.

Definition 4. *The accuracy and membership grade [27] are:*

$$a_B = \frac{|\underline{B}X|}{|\overline{B}X|} \tag{3}$$

$$\rho_B = 1 - a_B \tag{4}$$

where a_B is the accuracy of rough set X, and ρ_B is the membership grade of rough set X.

Definition 5. *The membership function [27] is:*

$$\mu(x, X) = \frac{|[x]_B \cap X|}{|[x]_B|} \tag{5}$$

The membership function indicates the membership degree of element x to the rough set X.

Definition 6. *The accuracy of the decision-making system [27] is:*

$$\lambda = \frac{|\sum_{k=1}^{Kc} \underline{B}X_k|}{|I|} \tag{6}$$

Given that the strict definitions of the upper and lower approximations make the rough set sensitive to noisy data, the rough set cannot adapt well to all situations in practical applications. VPRS decreases the influence of missing data, incorrect data, and noisy data. In VPRS, an approximation variable precision β, which ranges from 0.5 to 1, represents the tolerance degree of the rough set to noisy data and incorrect data. β can be defined as follows:

Definition 7.

$$\underline{B}X_\beta = \left\{ i \in I \left| \frac{|[i]_{IND(B)} \cap X|}{|[i]_{IND(B)}|} \geq \beta \right. \right\} \tag{7}$$

$$\overline{B}X_\beta = \left\{ i \in I \left| \frac{|[i]_{IND(B)} \cap X|}{|[i]_{IND(B)}|} > 1 - \beta \right. \right\} \tag{8}$$

where set B is a subset of the attribute set A; set X is a subset of the universe I; β is the variable precision, which ranges from 0.5 to 1; $\underline{B}X_\beta$ is the lower approximation; and $\overline{B}X_\beta$ is the upper approximation.

Compared with the rough set, VPRS extends the range of the upper and lower approximation, thus restricting the sensitivity of the rough set model to noisy data.

The rough set uses the indiscernibility relation to classify equivalence classes, but it is unsuitable for numerical data, especially in the case of the application of big data and high accuracy. One way to overcome this difficulty is to use the similarity relation, so we can extend the rough set based on the similarity relation.

This extension essentially involves modifications of the two concepts of the rough set, the indiscernibility relation and equivalence class. The classical indiscernibility relation is more suitable for those descriptive attributes, while elements of an attribute set that satisfy the indiscernibility relation are divided into an equivalence class. However, when dealing with numeric data, the effect of this method will be considerably reduced. The rough set, based on the similarity relation extends the indiscernibility relation into a similarity relation, and the equivalence class classified by the indiscernibility relation is replaced by a similarity relation.

2.2. Rough Set and Functional Dependence

With the establishment of the rough set model with variable precision based on the similarity relation, the decision rules between approximately equivalence classes divided by the conditional attribute set and the approximate equivalence classes divided by decisive attribute set can be worked out. However, this is not enough to explain the correlation between the conditional attribute set and the decisive attribute set, and so, functional dependence is introduced. Although the rough set and functional dependence are two different fields, many concepts of functional dependence can be explained from the perspective of the rough set.

Definition 8. *Functional dependence, the complete dependence between universe I and attribute A, can be expressed as* $C \to d$*, where* $C \subseteq A, d \in A$*.*

Definition 9. *Partial dependence, the partial dependence between universe I and attribute A, can be expressed as* $C \to_p d$*, where* $C \subseteq A, d \in A$*.*

Inference 1. *Complete dependence of attribute set, any attribute* $\in D, D \subseteq A, C \to d$ *works. Accordingly, there is functional dependence between C and D, and this relationship can be expressed as* $C \to D$*, where D is an attribute set.*

Inference 2. *Partial dependence of attribute set, any attribute* $\in D, D \subseteq A, C \to_p d$ *works. Accordingly, there is partial functional dependence between C and D, and this relationship can be expressed as* $C \to_p D$*, where D is an attribute set.*

We now explain complete dependence and partial dependence from the perspective of the rough set. For a decision-making system based on the rough set, $\lambda = 1$ means that the decisive attribute set completely depends on the conditional attribute set, that is, there is complete dependence between the decisive attribute set and conditional attribute set. $0 < \lambda < 1$ means that there are some factors that affect the decisive attribute set in addition to the conditional attribute set, that is, the decisive attribute set partially depends on the conditional attribute set, so the following inferences are introduced.

Inference 3. *Complete dependence in the rough set, in a decision-making system $DS = (U, C \cup D)$, only occurs when $p\lambda = 1$, and the complete dependence $C \to D$ comes into effect.*

Inference 4. *Partial dependence in the rough set, in a decision-making system $DS = (U, C \cup D)$, $0 < \lambda < 1$ indicates that there is partial dependence $C \to {}_pD$ between C and D, and the degree of partial dependence p equals λ.*

After calculating the accuracy λ of the model, according to inference 3 and inference 4, if $\lambda = 1$, the decisive attribute set completely depends on the conditional attribute set. If $0 < \lambda < 1$, the decisive attribute set partially depends on the conditional attribute set. In other words, there is a certain correlation between the conditional attribute set and the decisive attribute set, and λ can be used as a parameter to measure the degree of correlation.

This section proposes the rough set model with variable precision, based on the similarity relation and some inferences related to functional dependence. This method will not only dig out the correlation between the conditional attribute set and the decisive attribute set, but also use accuracy λ to measure the degree of correlation.

3. A Mixed-Integer Linear Programming Model for Rough Set-Based Classification with Flexible Attribute Selection

There is no doubt that the decision-making model based on the rough set has the congenital defect of the rough set; thus, adding variable precision to extend the rough set into the rough set with variable precision is necessary while building the model. Nevertheless, adding variable precision only broadens the range of the upper and lower approximations. The choice of precision is often subjective and lacks scientific basis. Above all, variable precision can only be used as an auxiliary method to improve the ability of the rough set model to reduce noisy data's bad influence on accuracy.

In this study, we build a mixed-integer linear programming model for a rough set-based classification with flexible attribute selection, which has a strong ability to overcome the noise sensitivity of the rough set model. Meanwhile, this study explains the rough set model, which is often considered to be nonlinear, by using a linear model for the first time. It is also an extension of the rough set.

3.1. Rough Set Model Based on Mixed Integer Linear Programming

Applying mixed integer linear programming to optimize the rough set model is essentially explaining the definition that is related to the rough set by linear programming. The rough set in a linear model enables the maximum accuracy of dividing the equivalence class, so that the decision-making system based on the rough set can correctly determine the correlation between the conditional attribute set and the decisive attribute set.

This model focuses on the rough set based on the similarity relation, and compares the similarity of each attribute in the attribute set. Next, the elements that satisfy the similarity threshold on each attribute are selected as the elements to be divided into an approximate equivalence class.

This model can also screen out attributes in the attribute set and take the attribute makes a considerable impact in dividing the universe into the final attribute set to reduce the dimension of the attributes.

We use the following notations:

I: Universe of elements.

k_c: A set of approximate equivalence classes obtained by partitioning the conditional attribute set in the universe.

k_d: A set of approximate equivalence classes obtained by partitioning the decisive attribute set in the universe.

C: Conditional attribute set.

D: Decisive attribute set.

N: Minimum support number of the conditional attribute set.

β: Variable precision.

α_c: Similarity threshold of the conditional attribute set.

α_d: Similarity threshold of the decisive attribute set.

M: A large number.

Xc_i: Value of each element in each conditional attribute.

Xd_i: Value of each element in each decisive attribute.

w_c_{ij}: For any two elements i and j in universe I, if $w\_c_{ij} = 1$, i and j are in the same approximate equivalence class divided by the conditional attribute set; otherwise, $w\_c_{ij} = 0$.

sl_c: $sl_c = 1$ if attribute c will be selected as a new attribute set to divide universe; otherwise, $sl_c = 0$.

q_{ik}: For any element i in universe I and any approximate equivalence class k in the set of approximate equivalence classes divided by the conditional attribute set, $q_{ik} = 1$ if i belongs to k; otherwise, $q_{ik} = 0$.

ss_{ijc}: Any two elements i and j in universe I and any attribute c in the conditional attribute set. $ss_{ijc} = 1$ if value of i and j on attribute c satisfies the corresponding similarity threshold α_c; otherwise, $ss_{ijc} = 0$.

Q_k: Number of elements in the approximate equivalent class k, which is obtained from the partition of the conditional attribute set to the universe.

w_d_{ij}: $w\_d_{ij} = 1$ if any two elements i and j belong to the same approximate equivalence class divided by the decisive attribute set; otherwise, $w\_d_{ij} = 0$.

sl'_d: $sl'_d = 1$ if an attribute d in decisive attribute set will be selected as a new conditional attribute set to divide the universe; otherwise, $sl'_d = 0$, and d will be eliminated.

$q'_{ik'}$: $q'_{ik'} = 1$ if any element i in universe belongs to the approximate equivalent class k'; otherwise, $q'_{ik'} = 0$.

ss'_{ijd}: $ss'_{ijd} = 1$ if value of any two points i and j on attribute d satisfies the corresponding similarity threshold α_d; otherwise, $ss'_{ijd} = 0$.

$Q'_{k'}$: Number of elements in the approximate equivalent class k', which is obtained from the partition of decisive attribute set to the universe.

$e_{ikk'}$: $e_{ikk'} = 1$ if point i not only belongs to the approximate equivalent class k of the conditional attribute set but also belongs to the approximate class k' of decisive attribute set; otherwise, $e_{ikk'} = 0$.

$E_{kk'}$: The number of elements is not only the approximate equivalence class k of the conditional attribute set, but also the approximate equivalence class k' of the decisive attribute set.

f_k: $f_k = 1$ if the number of elements in the approximate equivalence class k of the conditional attribute set satisfies the minimum support threshold, so that the approximate equivalence class k can be a lower approximation set; otherwise, $f_k = 0$.

$L_{kk'}$: $L_{kk'} = 1$ if the approximate equivalence class k in k_c is the lower approximation set of the approximate equivalence class k' in k_d; otherwise, $L_{kk'} = 0$.

Y_k: If the approximate equivalence class k in k_c is the lower approximation set, Y_k is the number of elements of lower approximation set k.

The objective function and constraints of the model are as follows:

Objective function: Maximize $(\sum_{k=1}^{K_c} Y_k)$

Subject to:

1) $M * ss_{ijc} \geq \alpha_c - |Xc_i - Xc_j|, i \in I, j \in I, c \in C;$
2) $M * (1 - ss_{ijc}) \geq |Xc_i - Xc_j| - \alpha_c, i \in I, j \in I, c \in C;$

3) $w\_c_{ij} \leq ss_{ijc} + (1 - sl_c), i \in I, j \in I, c \in C;$

4) $ss_{ijc} \geq 1 - sl_c, i \in I, j \in I, c \in C;$

5) $w\_c_{ij} \geq 1 - \sum_c^C (1 - ss_{ijc}), i \in I, j \in I, c \in C;$

6) $M * ss'_{ijd} \geq \alpha_d - |Xd_i - Xd_j|, i \in I, j \in I, d \in D;$

7) $M * (1 - ss'_{ijd}) \geq |Xd_i - Xd_j| - \alpha_d, i \in I, j \in I, d \in D;$

8) $w\_d_{ij} \leq ss'_{ijd} + (1 - sl'_d), i \in I, j \in I, d \in D;$

9) $ss'_{ijd} \geq 1 - sl'_d, i \in I, j \in I, d \in D;$

10) $w\_d_{ij} \geq 1 - \sum_d^D (1 - ss'_{ijd}), i \in I, j \in I, d \in D;$

11) $q_{11} = 1;$

12) $\sum_k^{k_c} q_{ik} = 1, i \in I;$

13) $q_{ik} + q_{jk} \leq 1 + w_{c_{ij}}, i \in I, j \in I, k \in k_c;$

14) $Q_k = \sum_i^I q_{ik}, k \in k_c;$

15) $q'_{11} = 1;$

16) $\sum_{k'}^{k_d} q'_{ik'} = 1, i \in I, k' \in k_d;$

17) $q'_{ik'} + q'_{jk'} \leq 1 + w_{d_{ij}}, i \in I, j \in I, k' \in k_d;$

18) $Q'_{k'} = \sum_i^I q'_{ik'}, i \in I, k' \in k_d;$

19) $2 * e_{ikk'} \leq q_{ik} + q'_{ik'}, i \in I, k \in k_c, k' \in k_d;$

20) $E_{kk'} = \sum_i^I e_{ikk'}, k \in k_c, k' \in k_d;$

21) $N * f_k \leq N + (Q_k - N);$

22) $card(I) * L_{kk'} \leq card(I) + (E_{kk'} - Q_k * \beta), k \in k_c, k' \in k_d;$

23) $L_{kk'} \leq f_k, k \in k_c, k' \in k_d;$

24) $Y_k \leq Q_k, k \in k_c;$

25) $Y_k \leq M * \sum_{k'}^{k_d} L_{kk'}, k \in k_c.$

In MILP-FRST, the objective function and constraints are critical parts. These parts introduce the concept of the rough set and the way to complete related theories.

The objective function in the model is the number of elements that belong to the conditional attribute set and the decisive attribute set. For MILP-FRST, it is obvious that the maximum accuracy is essentially the number of elements in the maximum region by integrating the objective function with the definition of precision in the rough set. The goal of constructing this objective function is to determine the method of division to find a more accurate correlation between the conditional attribute set and decisive attribute set.

The description of concepts related to the rough set and the complement of related theories are both completed in the process of setting constraints. These descriptions and complements consist of filtering out attributes from the conditional attribute set and the decisive attribute set, dividing the universe by the decisive attribute set, dividing the universe by the conditional attribute set, calculating the lower approximation set, calculating the number of elements, and limiting the coverage of the lower approximation set. Each constraint will be explained as follows.

The process of choosing the attributes and dividing the universe will be completed in the model. $ss_{ijc} = 1$, if the distance between two elements of the attribute c is closer than the corresponding similarity threshold α_c; otherwise, $ss_{ijc} = 0$. The constraints are established as follows:

$$M * ss_{ijc} \geq \alpha_c - |Xc_i - Xc_j|, \ i \in I, j \in I, c \in C \quad (9)$$

$$M * (1 - ss_{ijc}) \geq |Xc_i - Xc_j| - \alpha_c, \ i \in I, j \in I, c \in C \quad (10)$$

where i and j are two elements of the same condition attribute c, and both i and j are natural numbers.

If attribute c is selected to divide the universe, $sl_c = 1$, we can establish constraint (11). Otherwise, $sl_c = 0$, as shown in constraint (12), and attribute c has no influence on dividing the universe, that is, the two elements have an indiscernibility relation on attribute c. Constraint (11) is defined as the necessary condition that indicates that when classifying two elements into an approximate equivalence class, it is not enough to make $w\_c_{ij} = 1$. The condition of $w\_c_{ij} = 1$ means that all of the attributes of the attribute set meet the corresponding similarity threshold, so that constraint (13) is established. Elements i and j have an indiscernibility relation under the condition that all ss_{ijc} in attribute set C are 1:

$$w\_c_{ij} \leq ss_{ijc} + (1 - sl_c), i \in I, j \in I, c \in C \tag{11}$$

$$ss_{ijc} \geq 1 - sl_c, i \in I, j \in I, c \in C \tag{12}$$

$$w\_c_{ij} \geq 1 - \sum_{c}^{C}(1 - ss_{ijc}), i \in I, j \in I, c \in C \tag{13}$$

Constraints (9)–(13) initially divide the universe by the conditional attribute set, and select attributes from the conditional attribute set. Attribute sets divide the universe in accordance with the similarity between the elements of the attribute.

The processes of dividing the universe and filtering out attributes are almost the same for the conditional attribute set and decisive attribute set. Therefore, we establish constraints (14)–(18) to divide the universe by the decisive attribute set and filter out attributes from the decisive attribute set:

$$M * ss'_{ijd} \geq \alpha_d - |Xd_i - Xd_j|, i \in I, j \in I, d \in D \tag{14}$$

$$M * (1 - ss'_{ijd}) \geq |Xd_i - Xd_j| - \alpha_d, i \in I, j \in I, d \in D \tag{15}$$

$$w\_d_{ij} \leq ss'_{ijd} + (1 - sl'_d), i \in I, j \in I, d \in D \tag{16}$$

$$ss'_{ijd} \geq 1 - sl'_d, i \in I, j \in I, d \in D \tag{17}$$

$$w\_d_{ij} \geq 1 - \sum_{d}^{D}(1 - ss'_{ijd}), i \in I, j \in I, d \in D \tag{18}$$

We can obtain w_c and w_d through constraints (9)–(18), but there is much to be done to fulfil the process of dividing the universe. Each element in the universe should be allocated into k_c or k_d.

To complete model building, we need to specify the initial element and the initial equivalence class, and set the initial element belong to the initial equivalence class. As the initial element and the initial equivalence class are only numbers, there is no specific meaning, and so this set will not affect the results of the model calculation. According to the definition of q_{ik}, $i = 1$ is the number of elements, $k = 1$ is the number of the approximation equivalence class, and $q_{11} = 1$ means dividing this element into this approximation equivalence class. We can establish constraint (19):

$$q_{11} = 1 \tag{19}$$

Each element belongs to only one approximate equivalence class. However, not every predetermined approximate equivalence class has its own elements. When the number of approximate equivalence classes is unknown, the number of approximate equivalence classes in the set of approximate equivalence classes may be redundant. If the number of the provided approximate equivalence classes is less than the number of actual approximate equivalence classes, the model will not be solvable, so we establish constraint (20):

$$\sum_{k}^{k_c} q_{ik} = 1, i \in I \tag{20}$$

Only when it is confirmed that the two elements i and j can be classified into the same approximate equivalence class can elements i and j be classified into an approximate equivalence class. The value of q_{ik} and q_{jk} can be 1 at the same time only when $\omega\_c_{ij} = 1$. We establish constraint (21):

$$q_{ik} + q_{jk} \leq 1 + \omega_{c_{ij}}, i \in I, j \in I, k \in k_c \tag{21}$$

Variable Q_k counts the number of elements allotted into each approximate equivalence class divided by the conditional attribute set. We establish constraint (22):

$$Q_k = \sum_i^I q_{ik}, k \in k_c \tag{22}$$

Similarly, constraints (23)–(18) implement the process of allotting the element of the decisive attribute set:

$$q'_{11} = 1 \tag{23}$$

$$\sum_{k'}^{k_d} q'_{ik'} = 1, i \in I, k' \in k_d \tag{24}$$

$$q'_{ik'} + q'_{jk'} \leq 1 + \omega_{d_{ij}}, i \in I, j \in I, k' \in k_d \tag{25}$$

$$Q'_{k'} = \sum_i^I q'_{ik'}, i \in I, k' \in k_d \tag{26}$$

The above constraints complete the process of selecting attributes and dividing the universe.

Constraints (27)–(31) implement the process of defining the lower approximation set and setting the minimum support threshold.

If one element belongs to the approximate equivalence class k and the approximate equivalence class k' on the basis of the definition of the lower approximate set, this element will be selected, so we establish constraint (27):

$$2 * e_{ikk'} \leq q_{ik} + q'_{ik'}, i \in I, k \in k_c, k' \in k_d \tag{27}$$

The number of elements obtained by constraint (19) should be counted, so we establish constraint (28):

$$E_{kk'} = \sum_i^I e_{ikk'}, k \in k_c, k' \in k_d \tag{28}$$

The minimum support threshold requires that the lower approximation set should meet the requirement of the minimum support number. Constraints (29) and (31) complete the limitation of the minimum support number for the lower approximate set. In constraints (29) and (31), f_k shows whether the number of elements in the corresponding approximate equivalence class satisfies the minimum support number; if $Q_k < N$, then f_k must be 0. MILP-FRST introduces variable precision as an auxiliary method of improving the ability of resisting noisy data. Constraint (30) realizes the process of defining the lower approximate set:

$$N * f_k \leq N + (Q_k - N) \tag{29}$$

$$card(I) * L_{kk'} \leq card(I) + (E_{kk'} - Q_k * \beta), k \in k_c, k' \in k_d \tag{30}$$

$$L_{kk'} \leq f_k, k \in k_c, k' \in k_d \tag{31}$$

Finally, the number of elements in the lower approximate set is counted. If the approximate equivalence class obtained by conditional attribute set does not belong to any approximate equivalence class obtained by the decisive attribute set, this approximate equivalence class will be deemed to be an uncertain region, so the number of elements in the certain region is 0. Otherwise, this approximate equivalence class is a certain region, so the number of elements in the region equals the number of element points in this approximate equivalence class. Above all, we establish constraints (32) and (33):

$$Y_k \leq Q_k, k \in k_c \qquad (32)$$

$$Y_k \leq M * \sum_{k'}^{k_d} L_{kk'}, k \in k_c \qquad (33)$$

3.2. Characteristics of the Model

Aiming at solving the problem that the rough set model has weak resistance to noisy information in a dataset, this study proposes the mixed-integer linear programming model for rough set-based classification with flexible attribute selection (MILP-FRST). This model integrates the mixed integer linear programming method with the rough set model to define the related concepts and to describe the related theories. It is not only an optimization of the original mining model, but also an extension of the rough set theory. This model has the following characteristics:

(1) The model can realize the process of filtering out attributes from the attribute set. In a practical application, the first step of analyzing a high-dimension dataset is the descending dimension. After the dimensionality reduction, the dataset can only contain partial information of the raw dataset; specifically, implementation of the dimensionality reduction process is at the expense of sacrificing the information contained in some raw datasets. MILP-FRST is able to eliminate the attributes that have little influence on the decisive accuracy, and to automatically complete the process of attribute selection. Therefore, only a simple preprocessing process based on data quality analysis needs to be performed, and the maximum extent of all of the information contained in the raw dataset is preserved.

(2) The model implements the partition of the attribute set to the universe, defines the lower approximation set and the lower approximation set, sets the variable precision, restricts the support of the lower approximation set, and calculates the determined region, and so on. All of the above are implemented in the linear model. The attribute set partitioning scheme that allows the decisive accuracy to reach the optimal value can be obtained.

(3) The model has strong extensibility. According to the specific object of this study, we can select the attribute set, and specific division of the universe and method to adapt to the dataset composed of various data types.

4. Application Study on Data from Diesel Engines

In this section, we report the results of computational experiments on an assembly clearance parameter dataset from a diesel engine to test the models and compare them. The MIP solver AMPL/CPLEX (version 12.6.0.1) was used to solve problem instances. All computational experiments were performed on a MacBook with a 2.90 GHz Intel Core i7 Processor and 8 GB memory.

This paper takes a certain type of marine diesel engine as the verification object. At present, this type of diesel engine has been put into the market for many years, and the production enterprises have accumulated a lot of valuable data. Table 1 lists the main technical parameters of this type of diesel engine.

Table 1. Main technical parameters.

Cylinder number	16
Overload capacity	110% (1 h, allowed for 12 h)
Cylinder Diameter/Stroke	175/190 (mm)
Rated power	1658~2032 kW
Exhaust backpressure	<2.5 (kPa)
Lubricating oil consumption rate	≤1.3 (g/kW·hr)
Calibrated speed	1500~1800 (r/min)
Single Cylinder Exhaust Volume	4.43 (L)
Fuel consumption ratio	≤200 + 5% (g/kW·hr)
Compression ratio	13.5:1
Explosion pressure	16.0 (MPa)

Figure 1 the side view and main view of this diesel engine.

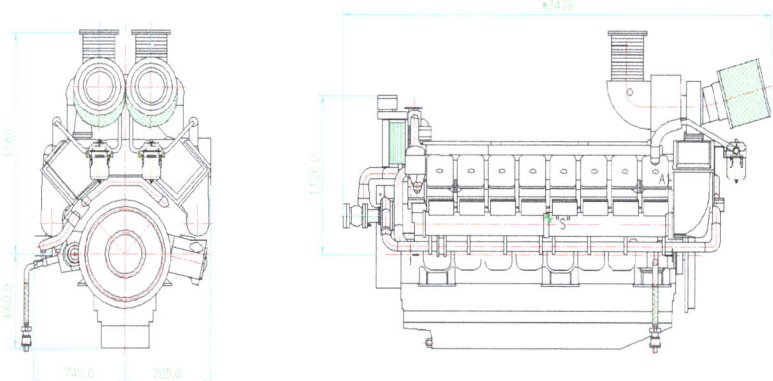

Figure 1. Side view and main view of this diesel engine.

4.1. Data Set Introduction.

The object of study is 29 16-cylinder diesel engines of the same type. The data set includes assembly clearance parameter data and quality grade data of the diesel engine. The assembly clearance parameter data of the diesel engine is numerical data, and the quality grade data of the diesel engine is classified data.

The marine diesel engine has a complex structure and many components, so there are many assembly clearance parameters. Chybowski L. and Gawdzixuska K. put forward the latest technology of component importance analysis for complex technical systems [28–30]. Choosing important components in complex systems is a key step. This type of diesel engine mainly includes four parts assembly clearance parameters: 2K, 5K, 10K and 11K. Among them, 2K refers to the mating clearance parameters of the crankshaft and the seat hole of the main bearing, 5K refers to the mating clearance parameters of the camshaft and the seat hole, 10K refers to the meshing clearance parameters of the gears, and 11K refers to the mating clearance parameters of the gear hole and the bearing. Table 2 lists the components involved in four types of assembly clearance parameters and the number of parameters.

Table 2. Assembling clearance parameters adopted.

Parameter Types	Related Components	Number of Parameters
2K	Spindle hole crankshaft and bearing seat	5
5K	Camshaft and its seat	7
10K	Gears	10
11K	Gears and bearings	6

A total of 28 assembly clearance parameters of the diesel engine were selected, that is, the experimental data set is 28-dimensional. The quality grade data comes from the test run of the diesel engine by the manufacturer before the diesel engine is delivered, including tests on flammability, diesel viscosity, and reliability. Through various test runs, the manufacturer determines the quality grade of the diesel engine. The quality grades are divided into three grades, Qualified, First grade, and High grade. Table 3 shows the part of data of the 28 assembly clearance parameters and the corresponding quality grades of the diesel engine.

Table 3. Assembly clearance data and quality grade of the diesel engine.

Diesel Engine ID	$2K_1$	$2K_2$	... ...	$11K_6$	Machine Quality Grade
1	0.193	0.176	... ...	0.11	Qualified
2	0.183	0.183	... ...	0.16	Qualified
3	0.183	0.179	... ...	0.11	First grade
4	0.174	0.164	... ...	0.18	High grade
5	0.161	0.167	... ...	0.15	Qualified
6	0.176	0.175	... ...	0.15	First grade
⋮	⋮	⋮	⋮	⋮	⋮
29	0.176	0.159	... ...	0.13	High grade

4.2. Data Pre-Treatment

After the correlation analysis of the dataset, it is obvious that there is a strong correlation between the assembly clearance parameters of the same part of the diesel engine, and this strong correlation will affect the effectiveness and efficiency of the model. Therefore, according to the correlation analysis of the assembly clearance parameters of the diesel engine, the principal component analysis method is used to reduce the dimension of the dataset. Taking all diesel engine assembly clearance parameters as the input, principal component analysis is carried out, and the cumulative variance contribution rate of each principal component is obtained.

As listed in Table 4, the cumulative variance contribution rate of the first 15 principal components is up to 89%; that is, these 15 principal components can cover most of the information of the assembly clearance parameters. A new dataset made up of these 15 principal components is presented in Table 5.

Table 4. Results of the principal component analysis.

Component	Attribute			Principal Component Contribution Rate		
	Total	Ratio of Variance (%)	Cumulative (%)	Total	Ratio of Variance (%)	Cumulative (%)
1	10.934	19.524	19.524	10.934	19.524	19.524
2	6.889	12.302	31.826	6.889	12.302	31.826
3	4.978	8.890	40.717	4.978	8.890	40.717
4	4.112	7.344	48.060	4.112	7.344	48.060
5	3.788	6.765	54.825	3.788	6.765	54.825
6	3.144	5.615	60.439	3.144	5.615	60.439
7	2.672	4.771	65.211	2.672	4.771	65.211
8	2.328	4.157	69.368	2.328	4.157	69.368
9	2.191	3.912	73.280	2.191	3.912	73.280
10	1.901	3.395	76.675	1.901	3.395	76.675
11	1.760	3.142	79.817	1.760	3.142	79.817
12	1.495	2.669	82.486	1.495	2.669	82.486
13	1.447	2.583	85.069	1.447	2.583	85.096
14	1.200	2.143	87.213	1.200	2.143	87.213
15	1.016	1.814	89.027	1.016	1.814	89.027
16	0.923	1.648	90.675			
17	0.816	1.457	92.131			
18	0.718	1.283	93.414			
19	0.664	1.186	94.600			
20	0.606	1.082	95.682			
21	0.467	0.833	96.516			
22	0.438	0.783	97.299			
23	0.432	0.772	98.071			
24	0.397	0.709	98.780			
25	0.252	0.450	99.229			
26	0.184	0.328	99.557			
27	0.164	0.292	99.850			
28	0.084	0.150	100.00			

Table 5. A new dataset made up of these 15 principal components.

ID	PC1	PC2	PC3	... ...	PC15
1	0.908	−0.379	−0.489	... ...	1.228
2	−0.560	1.453	−0.921	... ...	−0.206
... ...	... ...	... ...	... ...	... ...	... ...
13	0.339	−0.882	−0.015	... ...	0.892
14	1.509	0.454	0.669	... ...	−0.116
15	−0.297	−0.925	0.043	... ...	1.370
... ...	... ...	... ...	... ...	... ...	... ...
20	−0.295	−0.285	0.915	... ...	0.243
... ...	... ...	... ...	... ...	... ...	... ...
29	−1.782	0.146	−1.386	... ...	−0.116

The new dataset simplifies the original dataset and retains most of the information contained in the original dataset. Consequently, we can avoid a series of problems that the high-dimensional datasets creates in data mining. Simultaneously, the simplification of the original dataset can improve the efficiency of the model.

Finally, we need to integrate the assembly clearance parameters and whole-quality grades after dimension reduction, and obtain the final dataset that is directly applied to the subsequent computation (see Table 6).

Table 6. The final dataset.

ID	PC1	PC2	... ...	PC15	Level
1	0.908	−0.379	... ...	1.228	qualified
2	−0.560	1.453	... ...	0.206	qualified
... ...	... ...	... ...	... ...	...	... ...
13	0.339	−0.882	... ...	0.892	First grade
14	1.509	0.454	... ...	0.116	First grade
... ...	... ...	... ...	... ...	...	... ...
20	−0.295	−0.285	... ...	0.243	First grade
... ...	... ...	... ...	... ...	...	... ...
29	−1.782	0.146	... ...	0.116	High grade

4.3. Demonstration of the Process of the Model

Considering the specific object and dataset, the whole quality grades of diesel engine are known in this case, so that the result of partitioning the decisive attribute set to the universe is known in this instance. Therefore, we can simplify the model. We first remove the selected attributes in the decisive attribute set, and relative variables and constraints in the dividing universe. Then, we transfer the variable $q'_{ik'}$ into a parameter matrix, which is known to be a parameter that describes the result of universe partitioning by the decisive attribute set.

The model will be implemented in the MIP solver AMPL/CPLEX (version 12.6.0.1). In the operation of the model, the following parameters need to be set in advance:

1) Minimum support number of the lower approximation set $N = 3$,
2) Variable precision $\beta = 0.9$,
3) A large number $M = 999$,
4) The initial condition of the conditional attribute set partitioning universe $q_{11} = 1$,
5) List of the threshold of the similarity of the conditional attribute set $\alpha_c = [0.0495, 0.0369, \ldots, 0.099]$, where $c = 15$ is the number of assembly clearance parameters in the instance,
6) The initial number of the approximate equivalence class of the partition of the conditional attribute set to the universe is 10.

The model input consists of the principal component data of the assembly clearance parameters obtained by dimensionality reduction processing, quality grades of the diesel engine, and preset parameters described above. The output of the model includes the selection results of the principal components of the input, division results of the universe according to the conditional attribute set, calculation results of the lower approximation set, and calculation results of the number of elements in the determined region.

Fifteen principal component attributes are included in the conditional attribute set, which is composed of the assembly clearance parameters of a diesel engine. The model can filter the attributes from the attribute set to eliminate the attributes that have little impact on the accuracy of the decision system, and its filtering result are expressed by the variable sl_c. The result is:

$$sl_c = \begin{cases} 1 & c = 1 \\ 1 & c = 2 \\ 1 & c = 3 \\ 1 & c = 4 \\ 1 & c = 5 \\ 1 & c = 6 \\ 1 & c = 7 \\ 1 & c = 8 \\ 1 & c = 9 \\ 1 & c = 10 \\ 1 & c = 11 \\ 1 & c = 12 \\ 1 & c = 13 \\ 1 & c = 14 \\ 1 & c = 15 \end{cases}$$

If the sl value of attribute c is 1, this attribute will be selected; otherwise, this attribute will be eliminated. Therefore, the result shows that all 15 principal component attributes will be selected.

The conditional attribute set partitioning the universe is an important step in the calculation process of the model. Meanwhile, it is also the prerequisite for the subsequent calculation; $k = 10$ represents the 10 approximate equivalence classes. If a diesel engine belongs to an approximate equivalence class, the value of the element in the matrix is 1; otherwise, it is 0. The result is:

$$Q_k = \begin{cases} 4 & k = 1 \\ 4 & k = 2 \\ 4 & k = 3 \\ 3 & k = 4 \\ 4 & k = 5 \\ 3 & k = 6 \\ 0 & k = 7 \\ 3 & k = 8 \\ 1 & k = 9 \\ 3 & k = 10 \end{cases}$$

This result indicates the number of diesel engines in each approximate equivalence class obtained by the partitioning of conditional attribute set to the universe. Among the 10 approximate equivalence classes, one has not been allocated any element; this approximate equivalence class will be deleted. One has been allocated only one element, and its number is less than the minimum support number;

therefore, it will also be deleted. Only eight approximate equivalence classes can be regarded as the lower approximation set.

$$E = \begin{bmatrix} 0 & 0 & 4 \\ 0 & 4 & 0 \\ 0 & 4 & 0 \\ 0 & 3 & 0 \\ 4 & 0 & 0 \\ 0 & 0 & 3 \\ 0 & 0 & 0 \\ 0 & 3 & 0 \\ 0 & 0 & 1 \\ 3 & 0 & 0 \end{bmatrix}$$

The E matrix is the most important part of the model output. The E matrix represents the number of elements that not only belong to approximate equivalence class c, but also belong to one quality grade. E matrix is an important basis for solving the lower approximation set. In the E matrix for this case, the 10 lines indicates that the number of approximate equivalence classes determined by conditional attribute set partitioning of the universe is 10. Similarly, the number of approximate equivalence classes determined by decisive attribute set partitioning of the universe is 3.

$$Y_k = \begin{cases} 4 & k = 1 \\ 4 & k = 2 \\ 4 & k = 3 \\ 3 & k = 4 \\ 4 & k = 5 \\ 3 & k = 6 \\ 0 & k = 7 \\ 3 & k = 8 \\ 0 & k = 9 \\ 3 & k = 10 \end{cases}$$

Y_k is the number of elements in each lower approximation set. It can be concluded that eight approximate equivalence classes meet the condition of being members of the lower approximate set by analyzing the minimum support number and variable precision. Hence, the number of elements in the determined area is:

$$\sum_{k=1}^{15} Y_k = 28$$

The area of the model is:

$$\lambda = \frac{\sum_{k=1}^{15} Y_k}{|I|} = 0.97$$

On the basis of the inferences of the rough set and the function dependence, $0 < \lambda < 1$. Thus, there is partial dependence between the conditional attribute set and the decisive attribute set of the decision system:

$$\{\text{assembly clearance parameter}\} \rightarrow_{0.97} \{\text{quality grade}\}$$

4.4. Performance Comparison of Models

To validate the effectiveness and advantages of the model, experiments are performed to compare the accuracy of the models. The model that our model is compared to is the Φ-rough set.

As listed in Table 7, obviously, the accuracy of model MILP-FRST is higher than that of the model Φ-Rough set. The accuracy is close to one, which shows that our proposed model can establish an accurate decision-making rule between the diesel engine assembly clearance parameters and whole machine quality grades, and excavate a higher correlation between them.

Table 7. Comparison of the accuracy of the two models.

Model	λ
Φ-Rough set	0.68
MILP-FRST	0.97

MILP-FRST is an extension of the rough set. An obvious characteristic of a linear model is its ability to find the optimum solution. This characteristic enables the model to find the best way to classify attributes, even if the dataset can also obtain ideal results merely through simple data preprocessing, and it considerably increases the ability to resist noisy data.

4.5. Extension of the Model

As mentioned above, the minimum support number of the lower approximation set N and variable precision β are set in advance. The classification quality reflects the degree of dependence of decisive attribute D on the conditional attribute C and the uncertainty of decision system. The classification quality is inversely proportional to the uncertainty. In the model, the classification quality largely depends on the value of β [31]. Practically, the user does not always know how to set the value of β to obtain the maximum accuracy model. The minimum support number of the lower approximation set N also influences the accuracy of the model. Similarly, the user always sets the value of N in accordance with their experience. To determine the best value of β and N, we propose an algorithm. We set up a loop traverses all the values between 0.5–1, adding 0.01 each time. The results of the different N values are shown in Figure 2.

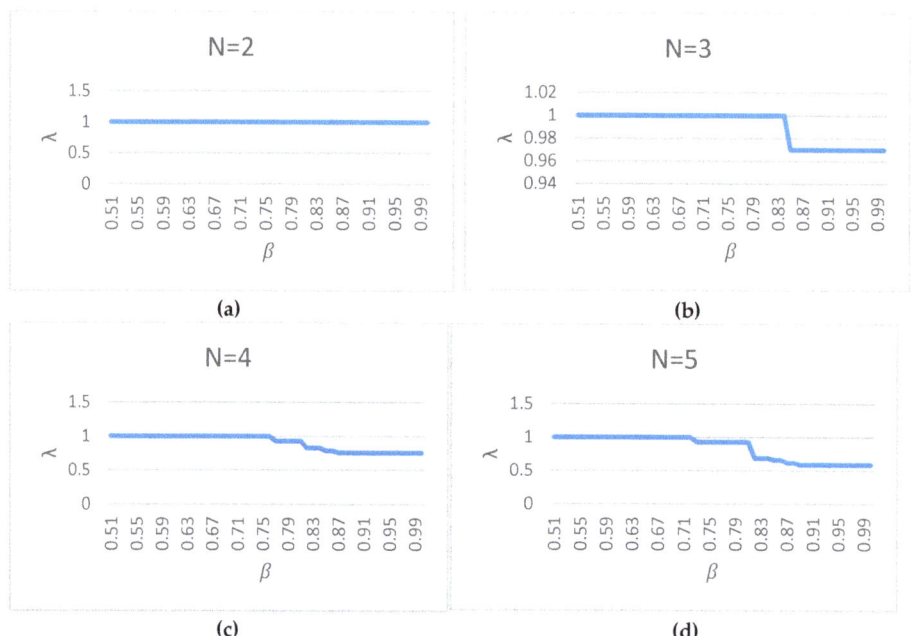

Figure 2. (a) Results when $N = 2$; (b) Results when $N = 1$; (c) Results when $N = 1$; (d) Results when $N = 1$.

As shown in Figure 3, it is obvious that with the increase in N, the average of λ decreases and the variance of λ increases.

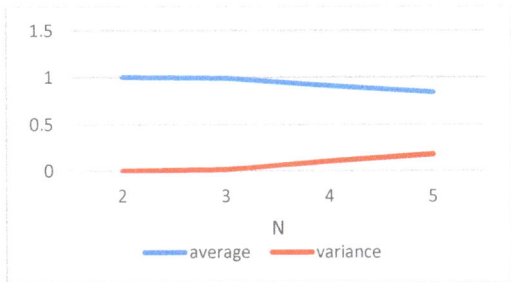

Figure 3. Comparison of the average and variance of λ.

Although the model's accuracy increases when β decreases, for this model, the smaller β does not make the model better. β represents the tolerance degree of the rough set to noisy and incorrect information in the dataset, while a smaller β tolerates more noisy data, but this violates our purpose in building MILP-FRST. Therefore, how to balance β against λ requires further research. As for the minimum support number N, our results indicate that the smaller the N, the better the λ. This rule is useful in practical applications, but when using this rule, the characteristics of the object should be considered to determine the appropriate N.

5. Conclusions

The purpose of this paper is to establish an accurate decision-making method between the quality level of the diesel engine and the parameters of assembly clearance. Therefore, a novel mixed-integer linear programming model for the rough set-based classification with flexible attribute selection, called MILP-FRST, is presented. First, the correlation between the conditional attribute set and decisive attribute set according to the inference of the rough set and function dependence is calculated. Second, by integrating the data mining model with the mixed integer linear programming theory, the optimization method is studied with regard to the sensitivity of the rough set to noisy data. Integrating the *MILP* model with the rough set model, the related theories and concepts of the rough set are implemented in the model, and the extension of the rough set research is completed. Finally, a case study on test data from a diesel engine is carried out. Experiments show that the decision-making method proposed in this paper can realize the quantitative discussion of the relationship between assembly clearance and the quality level of the whole machine. Also, the effectiveness of and the advantages of the MILP-FRST are verified. Furthermore, the extension of the MILP-FRST indicates that the usage of the minimum support number N and related topics are worthy of more in-depth study.

Author Contributions: Conceptualization, X.Y. and W.C.; methodology, Y.X. and X.Y.; software, X.Y. and J.L.; validation, X.Y. and S.Z.; formal analysis, S.Z.; investigation, J.L. and Y.W.; resources, W.C. and Y.W.; data curation, Y.X.; writing—original draft preparation, X.Y.; writing—review and editing, S.Z.; visualization, J.L.; supervision, S.Z.; project administration, W.C.; funding acquisition, W.C.

Funding: This work is supported by the National Natural Science Foundation of China (Grant No.71501007 & 71672006 & 71871003). The study is also sponsored by the Aviation Science Foundation of China (2017ZG51081), the Technical Research Foundation (JSZL2016601A004).

Conflicts of Interest: The authors declare no conflict of interest.

References

1. Zadeh, L.A. Fuzzy sets, information and control. *Inf. Control* **1965**, *8*, 338–383. [CrossRef]
2. Bundy, A.; Wallen, L. *Dempster-Shafer Theory*; Springer: Berlin/Heidelberg, Germany, 1984.

3. Pawlak, Z. Rough set. *Int. J. Comput. Inf. Sci.* **1982**, *11*, 341–356. [CrossRef]
4. Liang, J.; Li, R.; Qian, Y. Distance: A more comprehensible perspective for measures in rough set theory. *Knowl. Based Syst.* **2012**, *27*, 126–136. [CrossRef]
5. Xiao, Y.; Kaku, I.; Chang, W. Φ-Rough Sets Theory and Its Usage on Mining Approximate Dependencies; Springer: Berlin/Heidelberg, Germany, 2008; Volume 5227, pp. 922–934.
6. Luo, C.; Li, T.; Yao, Y. Dynamic probabilistic rough sets with incomplete data. *Inf. Sci.* **2017**, *417*, 39–54. [CrossRef]
7. Yao, Y.; Zhang, X. Class-specific attribute reducts in rough set theory. *Inf. Sci.* **2017**, *418*, 601–618. [CrossRef]
8. Zhang, Z.; Shi, Y.; Gao, G. A rough set-based multiple criteria linear programming approach for the medical diagnosis and prognosis. *Expert Syst. Appl.* **2009**, *36*, 8932–8937. [CrossRef]
9. Ziarko, W. Variable precision rough set model. *J. Comput. Syst. Sci.* **1993**, *46*, 39–59. [CrossRef]
10. Tao, Z.; Bao-Dong, X.U.; Wang, D.W.; Ran, L.I. Rough Rules Mining Approach Based on Variable Precision Rough Set Theory. *Inf. Control* **2004**, *33*, 17–18.
11. Beynon, M.J. Introduction and Elucidation of the Quality of Sagacity in the Extended Variable Precision Rough Sets Model. *Electron. Notes Theor. Comput. Sci.* **2003**, *82*, 30–39. [CrossRef]
12. Griffiths, B.; Beynon, M.J. Expositing stages of VPRS analysis in an expert system: Application with bank credit ratings. *Expert Syst. Appl.* **2005**, *29*, 879–888. [CrossRef]
13. Su, C.T.; Hsu, J.H. Precision parameter in the variable precision rough sets model: An application. *Omega* **2006**, *34*, 149–157. [CrossRef]
14. Wang, X.Y. New method of obtaining variable precision value based on variable precision rough set model. *Comput. Eng. Appl.* **2010**, *46*, 48–50.
15. Zavareh, M.; Maggioni, V. Application of Rough Set Theory to Water Quality Analysis: A Case Study. *Data* **2018**, *3*, 50. [CrossRef]
16. Bo, C.; Zhang, X.; Shao, S.; Smarandache, F. New Multigranulation Neutrosophic Rough Set with Applications. *Symmetry* **2018**, *10*, 578. [CrossRef]
17. Akram, M.; Ali, G.; Alsheh, N.O. A New Multi-Attribute Decision-Making MethodBased on m-Polar Fuzzy Soft Rough Sets. *Symmetry* **2017**, *9*, 271. [CrossRef]
18. Jia, X.; Tang, Z.; Liao, W.; Shang, L. On an optimization representation of decision-theoretic rough set model. *Int. J. Approx. Reason.* **2014**, *55*, 156–166. [CrossRef]
19. Cao, T.; Yamada, T.; Unehara, M.; Suzuki, I.; Nguyen, D. Parallel Computation of Rough Set Approximations in Information Systems with Missing Decision Data. *Computers* **2018**, *7*, 44. [CrossRef]
20. Zhang, J.Z. *Linear Programming*; Science Press: Beijing, China, 1990.
21. Tian, Y.P. Strengthening the Project Cost Control by Using Linear Programming Theory. *Railw. Eng. Cost Manag.* **2013**, *28*, 38–40.
22. Gu, M.C. Application of linear Programming Theory in Enterprise Production Planning. *J. Gansu Radio TV Univ.* **2010**, *20*, 40–42.
23. Gong, Q.H.; Yang, L.; Huang, G.Q. Research on Industrial Structure Adjustment Model Based on Resources and Linear Programming. *Sci. Technol. Manag. Res.* **2011**, *31*, 26–28.
24. Kelechi, O.; Tokos, H. An MILP Model for the Optimization of Hybrid Renewable Energy System. *Comput. Aided Chem. Eng.* **2016**, *38*, 2193–2198.
25. Boujelben, M.K.; Gicquel, C.; Minoux, M. A MILP model and heuristic approach for facility location under multiple operational constraints. *Comput. Ind. Eng.* **2016**, *98*, 446–461. [CrossRef]
26. Chen, R.Y.; Zhang, Z.; Wu, D.; Zhang, P.; Zhang, X.; Wang, Y.; Shi, Y. Prediction of protein interaction hot spots using rough set-based multiple criteria linear programming. *J. Theor. Biol.* **2011**, *269*, 174–180. [CrossRef] [PubMed]
27. Pawlak, Z. *Theoretical Aspect of Reasoning About Data*; Kluwer Academic Publishers: Dordrecht, The Netherlands, 1991.
28. Chybowski, L.; Gawdzińska, K. On the Present State-of-the-Art of a Component Importance Analysis for Complex Technical Systems. *Adv. Intell. Syst. Comput.* **2016**, *445*, 691–700.
29. Chybowski, L.; Gawdzińska, K. On the Possibilities of Applying the AHP Method to a Multi-criteria Component Importance Analysis of Complex Technical Objects. *Adv. Intell. Syst. Comput.* **2016**, *445*, 701–710.

30. Chybowski, L.; Gawdzińska, K. Selected issues regarding achievements in component importance analysis for complex technical systems. *Sci. J. Marit. Univ. Szcz.* **2017**, *52*, 137–144.
31. Zhang, R.; Xiong, S.; Chen, Z. Construction method of concept lattice based on improved variable precision rough set. *Neurocomputing* **2016**, *188*, 326–338. [CrossRef]

© 2019 by the authors. Licensee MDPI, Basel, Switzerland. This article is an open access article distributed under the terms and conditions of the Creative Commons Attribution (CC BY) license (http://creativecommons.org/licenses/by/4.0/).

Article

A Hybrid Unequal Clustering Based on Density with Energy Conservation in Wireless Nodes

Tao Han [1,*], Seyed Mostafa Bozorgi [2], Ayda Valinezhad Orang [3], Ali Asghar Rahmani Hosseinabadi [4], Arun Kumar Sangaiah [5] and Mu-Yen Chen [6]

1. DGUT-CNAM Institute, Dongguan University of Technology, Dongguan 523016, China
2. Department of Computer Engineering, Tehran North Branch, Islamic Azad University, Tehran 1651153311, Iran; S.M.Bozorgi@iau-tnb.ac.ir
3. Department of Computer Engineering, University of Tabriz, Tabriz 5166616471, Iran; A.Orang@gmail.com
4. Young Researchers and Elite Club, Ayatollah Amoli Branch, Islamic Azad University, Amol 4865116915, Iran; A.R.Hosseinabadi@iaubeh.ac.ir
5. School of Computing Science and Engineering, Vellore Institute of Technology (VIT), Vellore 632014, India; arunkumarsangaiah@gmail.com
6. Department of Information Management, National Taichung University of Science and Technology, Taichung 404, Taiwan; mychen.academy@gmail.com
* Correspondence: hant@dgut.edu.cn

Received: 20 December 2018; Accepted: 24 January 2019; Published: 31 January 2019

Abstract: The Internet of things (IoT) provides the possibility of communication between smart devices and any object at any time. In this context, wireless nodes play an important role in reducing costs and simple use. Since these nodes are often used in less accessible locations, recharging their battery is hardly feasible and in some cases is practically impossible. Hence, energy conservation within each node is a challenging discussion. Clustering is an efficient solution to increase the lifetime of the network and reduce the energy consumption of the nodes. In this paper, a novel hybrid unequal multi-hop clustering based on density (HCD) is proposed to increase the network lifetime. In the proposed protocol, the cluster head (CH) selection is performed only by comparing the status of each node to its neighboring nodes. In this new technique, the parameters involving energy of nodes, the number of neighboring nodes, the distance to the base station (BS), and the layer where the node is placed in are considered in CH selection. So, in this new and simple technique considers energy consumption of the network and load balancing. Clustering is performed unequally so that cluster heads (CHs) close to BS have more energy for data relay. Also, a hybrid dynamic–static clustering was performed to decrease overhead. In the current protocol, a distributed clustering and multi-hop routing approach was applied between cluster members (CMs), to CHs, and CHs to BS. HCD is applied as a novel assistance to cluster heads (ACHs) mechanism, in a way that a CH accepts to use member nodes with suitable state to share traffic load. Furthermore, we performed simulation for two different scenarios. Simulation results showed the reliability of the proposed method as it was resulted in a significant increase in network stability and energy balance as well as network lifetime and efficiency.

Keywords: Internet of things; Wireless nodes; Hybrid clustering; Multi-hop routing; Network lifetime; Artificial intelligence

1. Introduction

The Internet of Things (IoT) is based on the fact that each object or thing can use wireless communication to communicate with each other [1]. Nowadays, IoT has attracted attentions of societies, governments, and industries for a wide range of applications including smart homes, healthcare services, environmental monitoring, smart transportation, smart networks, security, fire detection, finance tracking, smart lighting, etc. [2].

In this context, wireless sensor networks (WSNs) play an important role in increasing the number of networks with low-cost smart devices which can be easily installed. WSNs are widely-used in various fields such as environment, health, military etc. Each node is composed of a sensor unit, processing unit (microcontroller), the radio communication unit, and an energy resource. Figure 1 represents these components. Examples include wildlife and environment supervision, health monitory, pediment supervision, border supervision and control, security, etc. [3–5].

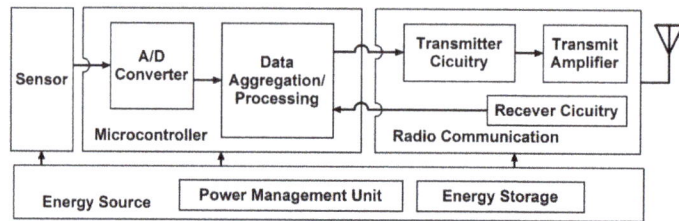

Figure 1. Components of the sensor node.

Wireless nodes typically have capabilities such as sensing, computing and self-organizing operations for routing and data transmission to a base station (BS) [6]. However, limitations of wireless nodes include short-range communications, low bandwidth, processing/storage limitation and, particularly, energy consumption [7]. One of the main problems in IoT based on wireless nodes is the energy consumption in nodes. Each node has a battery and therefore, limited energy is stored in it. Since the implemented wireless nodes are not easily accessible, it is hardly possible to access the nodes and recharge or exchange the battery. Energy consumption mainly occurs in sensing, data processing, and data transmission [7]. However, most of the mentioned energy consumption is related to data transmission. Therefore, reducing energy consumption in these networks is an ongoing research [8,9].

Routing between two nodes with the highest energy efficiency and balanced energy consumption between them are two of the factors that can affect the lifetime of a network significantly. One of the methods to reduce energy consumption in these networks is to find an optimal route by applying to cluster [7,9,10].

In the clustering method, nodes are divided into clusters and one node within a cluster is selected as a cluster head (CH). The cluster member (CMs) nodes, sensing the environment, send the data to the CH. The CH receives data from CMs and aggregates them and finally; the aggregated data is transferred directly or indirectly to a BS with the help of middle nodes. In fact, the purpose of clustering is to find an optimal route to send data to a BS [11].

Clustering protocols are usually classified into two protocols including static and dynamic protocols. In static protocols, clustering is performed once and the nodes always remain in the same cluster. Virtual concentric circle band-based clustering (VCCBC) [12] and an energy-efficient protocol with static clustering (EEPSC) [13] are two of the examples of the static clustering methods in WSNs; although, in terms purely of static protocol performance, network overhead is reduced but shows instability for a long period of time. The main disadvantage of static methods is that it results in energy depletion in several nodes [14,15]. In dynamic protocols, clustering is performed in each round, and new clusters form during each round. Low-energy adaptive clustering hierarchy (LEACH) [3] is one of the examples of the dynamic clustering methods. Dynamic performance can improve network lifetime, but usually, it has a high overhead [14,15].

Clustering is the most important energy efficient technique. In this technique, the sensor nodes are organized into groups termed as clusters. The regular nodes in the cluster are called as cluster members and a CH is selected among them [16,17]. In order to prevent the network from hot spot issue, unequal clustering techniques can be utilized for load balancing between the CHs [18,19].

Recently, hybrid static–dynamic methods have been proposed for clustering. Hybrid unequal clustering with layering protocol (HUCL) [15] is one of the examples of these clustering methods. This method is a hybrid of both static and dynamic clustering. Therefore, similar to dynamic protocols, this method performs clustering during each round and, as per static protocols, the clusters remain the same during several rounds. Within each cluster, a node is assigned as CH and remains the same until another node is selected as the new CH. After some rounds, clustering and cluster formation are performed again. This procedure always continues in the lifetime of a network. In the hybrid method, the overhead can be reduced in addition to improvement of network stability and lifetime [14,15].

Furthermore, the clustering protocols and CH selection methods in wireless nodes are typically divided into two categories: centralized and distributed clustering [10,14]. In the centralized clustering method, the BS uses the general knowledge of a network for clustering the nodes and a BS needs to collect the information about the status of the nodes within a network for clustering the nodes. This method is not applicable to large-scale networks [14]. In the distributed method, nodes perform routing in a self-organized manner and without requiring more information about the network position. In distributed algorithms, each node decides about its own CH probability based on some parameters [10]. In these algorithms, a BS has no effect on the CH selection. In contrast to centralized clustering, distributed methods are more efficient for large-scale networks. Therefore, there is less overhead in these methods due to the omission of messages transferred between nodes and a BS [14].

In this paper, given the above-mentioned advantages, the performance of a novel hybrid static–dynamic protocol is used. The current paper places emphasis on a distributed clustering algorithm. The probability of selecting a node as a CH is determined on the basis of energy level, a number of neighbors and distance to BS within each sensor and its neighbors. Moreover, CMs send a data packet to CH based on assistance to cluster heads (ACHs) mechanism and CH send packages to a BS through an energy-aware multi-hop routing method. Clustering is performed unequally. In this clustering, CHs close to the BS have smaller radius; as a result, the number of CMs are reduced and less energy is consumed for receiving data. In this way, they spend more energy to receive data from CHs far from the BS.

The remainder of this paper is organized as follows. A literature review is presented in Section 2. Section 3 gives our proposed algorithm in detail. Analysis of our proposed HCD algorithm is further discussed in Section 4. In Section 5, extensive evaluation and simulation results are given with discussion and analysis and Section 6 concludes this paper.

2. Literature Review

In the last decades, extensive research has been carried out around wireless nodes clustering. Some studies were performed on the basis of centralized clustering whilst some others presented a distributed clustering method.

A subset of widely-used clustering algorithms could be mentioned as LEACH, LEACH-centralized (LEACH-C) [3], and hybrid energy-efficient distributed clustering (HEED) [20].

One of the main distributed clustering algorithms used to reduce energy consumption in WSNs is the LEACH algorithm. In this algorithm, CH is selected based on a random rotation. Therefore, the energy consumption has been optimized and the energy load in distributed throughout the network. If fixed nodes are selected as CH, their energy will end soon, and they die earlier than other nodes. Hence, nodes are selected as a CH by a fixed probability, and they introduce themselves to the whole network. Since CH is selected in a probable manner, it is possible that they are close to each other; therefore, one of LEACH problems is the heterogeneous distribution of CH in the environment.

Another widely-used algorithm proposed is the HEED algorithm [20]. In this algorithm, each node creates a random number between zero and one. If a number smaller than CH probability is selected for the node, that node is then selected as tentative CH. If CH is equal to one, then the node becomes the final CH. Otherwise, the tentative CH remains, and finally, CH probability becomes doubled. In each ordinary node, if the CH probe is equal to one, then the node becomes final CH. Otherwise, it creates a random number between zero and one. If the number is smaller than CH probability, the node is then selected as a tentative CH, and finally, CH probability becomes double. This procedure continues until CH is selected. CH is selected according to the remaining energy of the node and they are considered as the second parameter of communication costs inside the cluster. Collectively, nodes join a CH whose distance to the related CH is smaller.

Another distributed clustering algorithm is density and distance based CH selection algorithm (DDCHS) [21]. In the clustering step, the area is virtually divided into hexagons so that circular cluster overlap is prevented and in fact, some borders are considered for clusters. For each hexagon, a CH is selected and subsequently, some subcircles are taken into account in the virtual hexagons according to the average of usual nodes distances to the cluster center. This algorithm is composed of three steps: (i) local grouping which determines a center in length and width of the clustering area. The area is divided into four equal parts, (ii) comparison of nodes density—the node density is determined in each part and one of the parts is selected as a candidate quarter. (iii) Comparing the distance between nodes by computing the distance of each node to other available nodes in candidate quarter and selecting the node with the shortest distance to other nodes as a CH.

An energy-aware distributed dynamic clustering protocol, based on fuzzy logic (ECPF) [22], is another algorithm introduced in 2012. This method performed the clustering by using the fuzzy logic and taking the energy of nodes as a nonprobabilistic parameter. The node selection was done sporadically. This protocol reduced the overhead of the network, by providing the mechanism similar to a setup phase, rather than performing the setup phase in each round. With regard to energy saving, the purpose of this algorithm was to select a set of appropriate clusters which covers the whole region selection by means of a fuzzy system. So in this fuzzy system, input parameters such as the degree and the center of the nodes were considered. The use of fuzzy logic in selecting the CH and the rule of overhead reduction contributed to improving the lifetime of the network. One of the challenges proposed in this clustering is the lack of complete coverage in the network in the time range.

Other solutions, such as energy-based clustering for WSNs lifetime optimization and balancing energy consumption in clustered WSNs (BLAC), were proposed by Ducrocq et al. [23]. BLAC used the energy level and the degree of nodes or the density of nodes for clustering. The protocol performs as distributed and dynamic. BLAC balanced the energy consumption between nodes and improved the network lifetime and stability. In order to balance the energy, the CH rotates between nodes. These methods involve overload.

Energy and coverage-aware distributed clustering (ECDC) protocol [24] was proposed in 2014. The protocol was based on two components: energy and coverage. In this protocol, nodes share their information with their neighbors for calculating a delay time. According to the calculated delay time, CH is elected to the network. ECDC protocol was able to improve the coverage. Thus, the aforementioned protocol contributed to decreased energy consumption and increased the lifespan of the network. However, this method is carried out dynamically and it involves higher overload.

Hybrid unequal clustering with layering protocol (HUCL) was presented in 2015 [15]. HUCL is a hybrid of dynamic and static clustering methods. Clusters closer to the BS were smaller. In this method, CHs are selected based on the energy status of the node, the distance to a BS and the number of neighbors. Also, data is transferred to the BS as multihops. Each node shared its own information with the size of its cluster reduces for neighbors. In the HUCL method, each node computes its own delay time and CH are selected according to the computed delay times and, therefore, the nodes join to the nearest CH. In this algorithm the CH that has no member node changes its own state to a member node and finally, it joins to the nearest CH. Data transmission step is divided into time periods. Member nodes send their own data clusters to CH and CH use multihop routing to transmit data to the BS. Simulation results show that compared to other available protocols, HUCL is able to reduce the network overhead, optimize energy consumption, and increase the network lifetime.

In this algorithm, in order to compute the cluster radius, energy consumption of nodes, and also for calculation delay time, a distance of a node to BS is not taken into account.

An improved energy aware distributed unequal clustering protocol (EADUC-II) was proposed in 2016 [25]. In this method, clusters are formed with unequal sizes and thus, clusters near to a BS have a smaller size. To determine the competition radius of cluster nodes, other parameters have been considered including node energy and to determine routing, the criterion of node energy to select the next step is taken into account for routing between CH. In this method, in order to compute the node delay time and node density, its distance to the BS is not considered. Although this method is performed in hybrid form, the improvement of overload reduction is less.

Another algorithm is an unequal multi-hop balanced immune clustering protocol (UMBIC) which was proposed in 2016 [26]. In multi-hop routing, the CH which is near to the BS loses its energy due to the relay data of the further CH. This protocol provided the WSNs with the nodes of various sizes and with a variety of homogeneous and heterogeneous nodes with distinctive densities; therefore, this method resulted in an improved network lifetime. UMBIC used an unequal clustering method to optimize the energy consumption in intra- and intercluster routing, forming the unequal clusters based on the distance of a node to BS and the energy level of the node. Also, UMBIC used the multi-objective immune algorithm to provide the routing tree with the aim of minimizing the cost of the nodes' relationship. Hence, this method could effectively reduce the network overhead and improve network lifetime.

A grid-based reliable routing protocol (GBRR) was proposed in 2016 [27]. This protocol improves the quality of the communication within the intracluster and intercluster by creating virtual clusters based on square grids and proper selection of the steps. This protocol divided the network into equally square-shaped grids so that in each grid one or more nodes might exist. According to the local information of the nodes' condition and grids, clustering was performed in a way that one cluster can occupy one or more grid. To reduce the overhead of CH, the multihop routing algorithm calculated the most efficient route between clusters; therefore, the source node does not need to transmit the data through the middle CHs to BS. In CH Competition stage of this method, it can be improved by considering the node's distance to the BS.

An energy-efficient QoS routing for WSNs using a self-stabilizing algorithm was proposed in 2015 [28]. This paper presented a self-stabilizing hop-constrained energy-efficient (SHE) clustering and a multi-hop routing algorithm for declining the delay and improving the quality of packet transmission. This protocol performs as a hybrid clustering method. CHs are determined by the BS in a definitive and offline Method and routing is done as distributed and online. The advantage of this protocol is that clustering is initialized only once at the beginning of the network. This protocol is based on TDMA schedules using the clustering algorithm for transmitting the data within the cluster in a manner that the nodes of the cluster with a tolerable delay send their own data to CH. Also, an adaptable routing protocol was proposed for data transmission between CH and the BS.

Chanak et al. [29] proposed an energy-aware distributed routing algorithm to tolerate network failure in WSNs. This protocol has specific routing schemes for better tolerating the network failure in the current position. This scheme includes three new algorithms. In a distributed energy-efficient heterogeneous clustering (DEEHC) network clustering is done according to the residual energy in order to minimize the energy required for data transmission. During clustering, each sensor node finds k-vertex disjoint paths for sending data to the CH according to the energy levels of neighbor nodes. In other words, the routing between nodes CH and BS is done based on the proposed k-vertex disjoint path routing (KVDPR) algorithm. In addition, the route maintenance mechanism (RMM) algorithm enables nodes and CH to keep a route, which is based on the neighbor nodes energy conditions and prevents failure. In DEEHC algorithm, for determining CH using computing time, distance to the BS, and node density are not considered.

Naeem et al. [30] proposed a dynamic and cooperative clustering. Furthermore, a new technique called the neighborhood formation scheme is presented. This algorithm aims to distribute energy demand among nodes and optimize a number of sensors involved in detection and report of events. This algorithm is executed distributed and dynamically. Results show that the proposed framework improved network lifetime and reliability in data transmission.

An energy-aware multi-hop routing (EAMR) protocol was proposed in 2017 [31]. This method aims to reduce overhead by reducing variations of CHs. In this method, a method similar to LEACH [3] is sued to select initial CHs to form clusters. EAMR allows a node to operate as a cluster head until its energy is not lower than a threshold; therefore, in this algorithm, CHs vary only when required. In order to improve network lifetime, this algorithm employs multi-hop routing. However, since membership of nodes in a cluster does not change until the end, in selecting the initial CHs, many of the important parameters like nodes density and distance from BS is not considered.

To sum up, the above section has summarized some clustering protocols which were provided to increase wireless node lifetime and that also reviewed recent hybrid methods to reduce the overhead and increase the lifetime of wireless nodes.

Table 1 shows a summary and comparison of some of the clustering algorithms.

Table 1. Comparison of some of the clustering algorithms.

Protocol	Cluster Size	Intracom.	Intercom.	Method	CH Election	Dynamism
LEACH [3]	equal	1-hop	1-hop	distributed	Random	dynamic
LEACH-C [3]	equal	1-hop	1-hop	centralized	deterministic by BS	dynamic
HEED [20]	equal	1-hop	k-hop	distributed	hybrid, based on Attribute	dynamic
DDCHS [21]	equal	1-hop	1-hop	distributed	based on density & distance	dynamic
VCCBC [12]	equal	1-hop	k-hop	distributed	CH rotation	static
EEPSC [13]	equal	1-hop	1-hop	distributed	selection by previous CH	static
ECPF [22]	equal	1-hop	k-hop	distributed	based on fuzzy logic	dynamic
BLAC [23]	equal	1-hop	k-hop	distributed	based on energy & degree or density	dynamic
ECDC [24]	equal	1-hop	k-hop	distributed	based on energy & coverage	dynamic
SHE [28]	equal	1-hop	k-hop	centralized	deterministic by BS	dynamic
HUCL [15]	unequal	1-hop	k-hop	distributed	hybrid, based on attribute	hybrid
GBRR [27]	equal	1-hop	k-hop	distributed	based on grid structure	dynamic
DEEHC [29]	equal	k-hop	k-hop	distributed	based on energy	dynamic
EADUC-II [25]	unequal	1-hop	k-hop	distributed	hybrid, based on attribute	hybrid
UDSC [30]	equal	1-hop	k-hop	distributed	hybrid, based on Attribute	dynamic
EMAR [31]	equal	1-hop	k-hop	distributed	at first random, then CH rotation	static
proposed alg.	unequal	k-hop	k-hop	distributed	hybrid, based on density	hybrid

The proposed protocol is an improvement of the HUCL protocol and the method is reviewed in the following sections. This improvement is due to the fact that in our protocol is a novel hybrid unequal clustering which is performed by a simple efficient algorithm for selecting CH node based on density, energy level, and distance to the BS. It also proposed a new mechanism by assisting the CH with intracluster data transmission as well as improved intercluster data transmission using layered mechanism. The main objective is to provide a high-precision clustering protocol to balance the energy consumption, decrease the overhead, substantial increase of networks' lifetime, and finally, to improve existing methods.

3. The Proposed HCD Algorithm

In this section, we introduce a hybrid unequal multi-hop clustering based on density (HCD) to improve network lifetime and throughput. HCD is performed by the distributed method. In this method, clustering is performed as a hybrid of static and dynamic methods. We assumed that nodes can detect their own distance by received signal strength indicator (RSSI) and considered CH relation according to the energy level and nodes situation in the network. Since the CH node consumes more energy, it is prevented to select the nodes having no desirable energy status as a CH and, therefore, the network stability increases. Also, the energy-aware multi-hop method was used for routing between CH.

3.1. Network Model

An IoT based on wireless nodes and a BS with an unlimited power supply connected to the network are the primary considerations in our model. Data is sampled by sensor nodes and they are routed in order to be sent to the BS. Also, each node can perform as a CH or non-CH node. Some assumptions of the network model are as follows.

- N wireless nodes are randomly distributed in M*M environment.
- Nodes are heterogeneous.
- All nodes and the BS are fixed.
- All nodes can set transfer power in terms of the distance between nodes.
- CH can aggregate data.

The first order radio model of energy consumption in this proposed method is similar to the LEACH protocol [3]. Energy consumption transfer is defined as Equation (1).

$$E_{TX}(i, K, d_{ij}) = \begin{cases} E_{elec}K + E_{fs}Kd_{ij}^2 & if \quad d_{ij} \leq d_o \\ E_{elec}K + E_{mp}Kd_{ij}^4 & if \quad d_{ij} > d_o \end{cases} \quad (1)$$

where K is the number of data bits and d_{ij} is the distance between two nodes—i and j. E_{elec} is energy consumption in sender or receiver circuit to send a data bit. E_{fs} and E_{mp} are energy consumptions in the sender amplifier for sending a data bit in terms of distance between the receiver and sender. Also, d_0 value, which is a threshold distance, is obtained from Equation (2).

$$d_0 = \sqrt{\frac{E_{fs}}{E_{mp}}} \quad (2)$$

In an energy model, a receiver energy consumption is defined as Equation (3).

$$E_{RX}(i, K) = E_{elec}K \quad (3)$$

According to the data aggregation model used in our simulation, it is assumed that the information collected by a set of N nodes can be packed in a k bit package.

3.2. Protocol Performance

After deploying nodes, a layering stage is performed. Each of the nodes computes its distance from the BS. For calculating this distance, the BS broadcast a signal which will be heard by all nodes and each node approximates its own calculated distance to the BS using the RSSI. Consequently, the node informs its position to the BS. The BS then starts layering the network. In the beginning, the BS calculates the difference between the closest and the furthest nodes to itself and experimentally defines four layers for networks. The BS sends messages within the network and assigns layer ID for each node.

All HCD operations are involved in cluster initialization stage and data transmission stage. Cluster initialization stage is composed of four phases including the delay time calculation phase, CH selection phase, cluster formation phase, and route construction phase. The data transmission stage is divided into a number of major slots. Each major slot is formed by several rounds and two substages which are called CH rotation and adjustment route. Each round involves in intercluster transmission phase and intracluster transmission phase. In a CH rotation, the role of CH is to turn between member nodes to prevent discharging of the energy in CH. The operation of HCD is displayed in Figure 2. Figure 3 also shows the flowchart of the proposed algorithm.

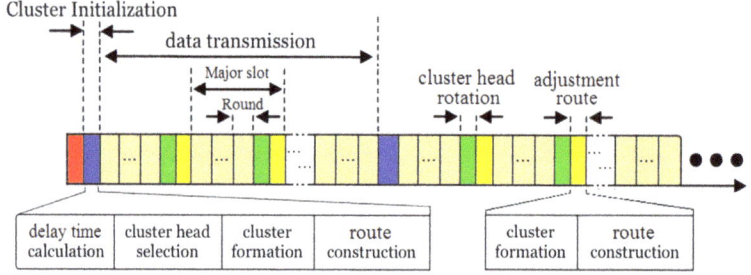

Figure 2. Hybrid unequal multihop clustering based on density (HCD) operation.

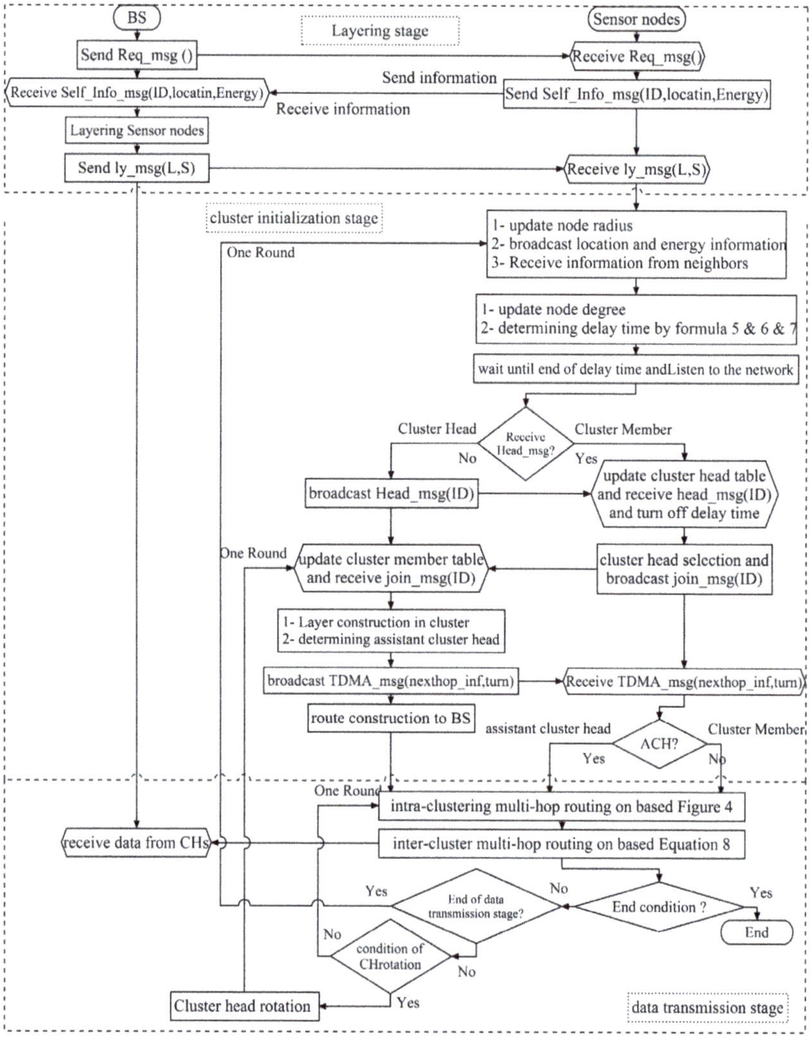

Figure 3. Flowchart of the HCD protocol.

3.2.1. Cluster Initialization

In this stage, network nodes are divided into groups to form clusters. In the first phase, when the network is operational, the probability of each node to become a CH and its cluster radius are determined based on the energy level of the node and its distance to the BS. Nodes calculate their own cluster radius according to Equation (4).

$$R_c(i) = \left[1 - \alpha\left(\frac{d_{BS,max} - d_{i,BS}}{d_{BS,max} - d_{BS,min}}\right) - \beta\left(1 - \frac{E_{rem}(i,r)}{E_{Max}}\right)\right] RL_{max} \times \lambda \qquad (4)$$

In the above-mentioned Equation, $R_c(i)$ is the radius of node i and RL_{max} is maximum competition radius for being a CH, as determined previously. $E_{rem}(i,r)$ is the remaining energy of the node i in the round r and E_{max} stands for the maximum energy capacity of the node. $d_{BS,max}$ and $d_{BS,min}$ are the maximum and minimum distance of nodes from the BS and $d_{i,BS}$ is the distance of i_{th} node from the BS. α and β are also weight factors that can vary between zero and one. λ is the weight factor associated with the layer where the nodes are located. In the lower layers RL_{max} is multiplied by a smaller coefficient to the nodes which are closer to the BS and, thus, has a smaller radius. In contrast, further clusters are multiplied by a greater coefficient to have a larger radius. Accordingly, if a node is selected as a CH it will have more energy to receive and transmit the data than the further CH to the BS.

Before computing delay time, each node shares its location information and energy level with its neighbors. All nodes, which are situated in its radio range, receive the node's message from all neighbors. After informing the nodes of their neighbors, they are able to calculate the average energy of neighbor's nodes which is calculated using Equation (5).

$$E_{Ave}(i,r) = \frac{\sum\limits_{j \in N_{nbr}(i,r)} E_{rem}(j,r)}{\max(|N_{nbr}(i,r)|, \varepsilon)} \qquad (5)$$

$N_{nbr}(i,r)$ is the number of sets of nodes of neighbors i in the round of r. $|N_{nbr}(i,r)|$ is node degree or number of neighbors for node i in the round r. The parameter ε is a very small number in order to avoid infinity caused by division by zero. Each node will give itself a scoring point parameter in order to start the routine of becoming a CH based on density. In the first cluster initialization stage, the point of CH for each node is zero. Each node considers its neighbors and if the energy level of the neighbor is smaller than its own energy level, it increases its point by one unit. The scoring point needed for each node to become a CH is updated after the computation given in Equation (6).

$$\begin{array}{ll} \forall \quad j \in N_{nbr}(i,r) & \\ if \quad E_{rem}(i,r) > E_{rem}(j,r) & then \quad p(i) = p(i) + 1 \\ if \quad |N_{nbr}(i,r)| > |N_{nbr}(j,r)| & then \quad p(i) = p(i) + 1 \\ if \quad id_{Layer}(i) < id_{Layer}(j) & then \quad p(i) = p(i) + 1 \\ if \quad d_{i,BS} < d_{j,BS} & then \quad p(i) = p(i) + 1 \end{array} \qquad (6)$$

P is the score point given to nodes. $id_{Layer}(i)$ is the id of the layer where the node is situated on. Nodes compute their own delay time to announce being a CH. In this way, nodes that have suitable energy with a higher number of neighbors in the network and are closer to the BS acquire a higher point for being a CH. It should be taken into account that in this protocol we considered the point of all alive nodes equal to zero in the initial round. Also, we applied Equation (6) in each round for i_{th}

node up to the number of $N_{nbr}(i,r)$. After computing the point of being CH, each node is computed according to Equation (7).

$$T_w(i,r) = \begin{cases} \frac{1}{p(i)} \times V_r \times T_2 & if E_{rem}(i,r) \geq E_{Ave}(i,r) \\ V_r \times T_2 & otherwise \end{cases} \quad (7)$$

In this Equation, T_w is the delay time of the node i. T_2 refers to the second phase time and V_r is a random number within the range of 0.9 to 1. Therefore, some variation occurs. In this paper, the neighbor of the node i refers to a node located in a distance smaller than the radius of the node which is calculated according to Equation (4). Since CH node consumes more energy, the chance of becoming a CH by those nodes that have undesirable status is prevented and, therefore, network stability increases.

In the second phase, each node must wait until the end of the delay time. If a node does not receive CH message from its neighbors during the delay time, it then announces being a CH after the delay time ends. It is evident that the node which has less delay time achieve a higher probability to become a CH. On the other hand, if a node receives a CH message, it stops its own timer and, thus, cannot be selected as a CH. Since CH node consumes more energy, the chance of being CH by the nodes having no desirable status is prevented; therefore, network stability increases.

After selecting a CH, next phase is cluster formation. Each node selected as a CH, broadcast head message in the network. After receiving the head messages by non-CH nodes, they join to the closest CH and transmit their joining message involving energy level and distance to the CH. The presented protocol applies an assistance node to CH mechanism that allows a CH to use member nodes to share traffic load. Each CH has intraclustering layering. Nodes having a distance less than the threshold (average distance) are placed in the first layer and nodes having distance more than the threshold are placed in the second layer. Then CH identifies nodes that their energies are more than half of the average energy and have been located in layer 1 as assistance to the CH (ACH). In contrast, if a node has been located in layer 2, CH will choose the closest ACH to the CM node and will send the packet to this node. Otherwise, if the distance between a node and CH is less than the threshold distance and is located in layer 1, it would start direct transmission. As mentioned, CH schedules clusters in a way that the farther node transmits earlier; therefore, within a cluster, when an ACH to a CH receives a packet from its neighbor it aggregates and integrates the packet into its packet and send it to the CH. If there is no assistance node to the CH node between the source node and the CH, the source node will send data directly to the CH. Subsequently, CH performs scheduling of the nodes according to the time division multiple access (TDMA) schedules and sends scheduling information to the members. Figure 4 shows the flowchart of routing intraclustering in HCD.

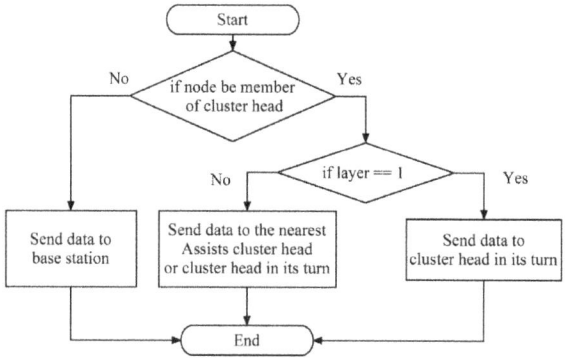

Figure 4. Routing flowchart of intraclustering in HCD.

The fourth phase is constructing a data transmission path to the BS. We use two messages involving route request and route reply to construct the route. Other member nodes will be inactive in this part. According to their distance from the BS, each CH broadcasts a route request with identification content, energy level, the count of cluster member nodes, and the distance to the BS in the network. CH receives the message and updates its routing table. The CH transmits the data packet to the BS either directly or through a multi-hop method. Following computing transmission cost to the BS and middle CH, they select the middle CH with minimum cost for multi-hop transmission. CH in layer 1 is involved in direct transmission to the BS. The value of the evaluation parameter is computed according to the following Equation (8).

$$relay(i) = \begin{cases} E_{TX}(i,l,d_{i,j}) + E_{TX}(j,l,d_{j,nexthopj}) + E_{RX}(j,l) & \text{if } \begin{array}{l} E_{rem}(i,r) \geq E_{TX}(i,l,d_{i,j}) \text{ and} \\ E_{rem}(j,r) \geq E_{TX}(j,l,d_{j,nethopj}) + (E_{RX}(j,l) \times (M(j) + R(j) + 1)) \end{array} \\ Inf & \text{Otherwise} \end{cases} \quad (8)$$

where $E_{TX}(i,l,d_{i,j})$ is the required energy for transmitting data from CH i to CH j. $E_{TX}(i,l,d_{j,nexthopj})$ is the required energy for transmitting data from CH j to the next hop. $E_{RX}(j,l)$ is the required energy for receiving data in node j. $M(j)$ is the count of member nodes of j CH. $R(j)$ is the number of CHs, for whom node j act as a relay node and receive their data. Each CH computes the cost if there is a CH between it and the BS, and if it receives a route request. After selecting CH with a minimum value, CH i sends a route reply message to the CH of the next hop.

In algorithm 1, lines 3 to 15 correspond to the first phase: the delay time calculation phase. Lines 17 to 27 and lines 28 to 46 correspond to the second and third phase, the CH selection phase and cluster formation phase, respectively. The third phase, computation of intracluster layer, is represented in lines 41. In this phase, CH divided CMs into two layers. Nodes which are in the first layer and their distance from CH is small and their energy is higher than the average energy of nodes are selected as ACH and scheduling is formulated such that further nodes transmit data sooner. Then, scheduling is broadcasted. Lines 47 to 63 represent the route construction phase.

Algorithm 1: Algorithm of cluster initialization stage in HCD.	
1.	Begin
2.	if Sensor[i].state == 'ClusterHeadP'
3.	exit
4.	else
5.	Sensor[i].state = "node"
6.	while (CT < TimePha1)
7.	V_r = rand(0.9,1)
8.	Calculate Rc by formula (4)
9.	Broadcast Neighbor_Msg;
10.	while (CT < TimeBrc)
11.	Receive Neighbor_Msg
12.	update neighbor List NL [ ]
13.	Whileend
14.	Calculate DelayTime by formula (6) & (7)
15.	whileend
16.	T = TimePh1 + DelayTime
17.	while (CT < TimePh2)
18.	if(CT > T)
19.	Sensor[i].state = 'ClusterHead'
20.	broadcast Head_Msg
21.	receive Head_Msg from competition ClusterHead
22.	store in Head_List ClusterHeadL[] along with distance
23.	elseif (received Head_Msg from any neighbor)
24.	Sensor[i].state = 'ClusterMember'

```
25.         store 'Sensor[j]' in Head_List ClusterHeadL[] along with distance
26.         end
27.     whileend
28.     while (CT < TimePh3)
29.         while (CT < TimeBrc Ph3 for Join-msg)
30.             if Sensor[i].state == 'ClusterMember'
31.                 select the nearest ClusterHead Sensor[j] from ClusterHeadL[] list
32.                 Sensor[i]. head = Sensor[j]
33.                 send JoinClusterMsg to Sensor[j]
34.             elseif Sensor[i].state == ClusterHead
35.                 Receive JoinClusterMsg from ClusterMember
36.                 store in ClusterMember[] List
37.             End
38.         Whileend
39.         If Sensor[i].state == ClusterHead
40.             Sensor[i].state = 'ClusterHeadP'
41.             Calculate Layer in Cluster & Assists CHnode
42.             send TDMA-Msg
43.         elseif
44.             Receive TDMA-Msg
45.         end
46.     Whileend
47.     while (CT < TimePha4)
48.         Broadcast Route_Msg;
49.         If layer > 1
50.             while (CT < Time_Br_RM)
51.                 Receive Route_Msg
52.                 update hopList HL [ ]
53.             Whileend
54.         End
55.         select the ClusterHead Sensor[j] from hopList HL[] by formula (8)
56.         send Rout_Replay
57.         If layer < 4
58.             while (CT < Time_Rs_RR)
59.                 Receive Route_Replay
60.                 Update RPfCH List [ ]
61.             whileend
62.         end
63.     Whileend
64.     end
65. End
```

3.2.2. Data Transmission

Data transmission stage includes several major slots. Each major slot consists of several rounds, a CH rotation, and an adjustment route. Each round is formed by two phases: (i) data transmission in intraclustering and (ii) data transmission in interclustering.

Round

In the first phase of each round, based on the schedule by the CH, nodes start to send their own data to the CH. When CH receives the packets from its own members, it starts to assemble an integration. In the second phase, after sending data by nodes to CH, CH sends their data to the BS through a path that has been created in path discovered phases. The route has been designed so that energy consumption is minimized for sending each packet. In this phase, the protocol uses the carrier-sense multiple access (CSMA) method to transfer data. Each CH sends the data to the BS through the path created in the previous section.

CH Rotation

Except for the last major slot, one part of the CH rotation was situated at the end of each major slot. In this part, each cluster member nodes send their data to their own CH. CH select a cluster member node as a CH which has more energy for the next round. After collecting the relevant information for layering in the cluster, scheduling the nodes, and constructing data transmission path to the BS, the current CH sends the aforementioned information to the new CH of the next rounds and then switches to be a member node.

Adjustment Route

After CH rotation, there will be one updated adjustment route. In this part, cluster formation phase and route construction phase in cluster initialization stage are done with slightly different runs. The only difference in cluster formation phase in this part is that CH gains the relevant information for layering and determines the assistance nodes to CH nodes from the previous CH with no changes in the other actions.

4. Analysis of HCD

Lemma 1. *Control message complexity is a clustering of type $O(N)$, and in the proposed method, in the worst case scenario, it is decreased r times.*

Proof of Lemma 1. In this protocol it is assumed that N is the number of nodes, r is the number of rounds in a major slot, M refers to the number of major slots in data transmission, and R is the number of rounds in a data transmission, which is equal to $r \times M$. □

During the layering stage BS broadcasts a message in the network. Subsequently, node N transmits self_info_msg to BS and BS broadcasts cmd_msg message in the network. Therefore, $N + 2$ messages are required for this stage. In the cluster initialization stage, node N broadcasts node_msg including information on node energy and location. Then, the K times head_msg is broadcasted by CHs and $N - k$ join_msg messages are transmitted to the CHs by CM. Consequently, K messages of TDMA_msg are broadcasted by CHs. Moreover, $2K$ control messages are required for constructing the data transmission path to the BS. Therefore, $N + K + (N - K) + K + 2K = 2N + 3K$ messages are required for clustering. In total, $3N + 3K + 2$ messages are required during the above-mentioned stages. Therefore, in the worst case scenario, the control message complexity is of type $O(N)$.

In hybrid performance, it is not necessary to perform clustering in each round and data transmission is performed with M major slot, which consists of r rounds. For CH rotation and route adjustment, maximum $(N - K) + K$ and $K + 2K$ messages are required, respectively. Therefore, in the data transmission stage, $[(M - 1) \times ((N - k) + k + k + 2k)] = (M - 1) \times (N + 3k)$ messages are needed.

Lemma 2. *If there is a node within the competition radius area of another node, then the presence of two CHs is impossible.*

Proof of Lemma 2. According to Equation (7), each node has a unique delay time. If a node has a lesser delay time, it transmits head_msg with $Rc(i)$ radius and all other nodes with this radius change their own position to CM. Therefore, if there are two nodes located within competition radius, it is not possible to have more than two CHs. □

Lemma 3. *After performing HCD, whole network space is covered by CHs; in other words, a node (either CH or CM) will be in the same cluster.*

Proof of Lemma 3. If a node such as A is neither a CH nor a CM after performing HCD, node A will have two positions before executing the algorithm: (1) it does not have any neighbors and (2) has a neighbor. In the first case, according to the algorithm, node A announces to be the cluster head at the end of the delay time. In the second position, given that node A is a CH nor a CM, none of the neighbor nodes broadcast the CH message. If one of them was CH, then A will be a CM. However, if A and some of its neighbors are not CH and they do not join to a cluster, then one of them will be converted to the CH after the end of delay time. Subsequently, a message is broadcasted and neighbor nodes receiving the message will change their positions to the CMs. Therefore, node A will be either a CH or will join another CH before the end of the algorithm. Hence, it can be said that the network is completely covered by CHs. □

Lemma 4. *The HCD guarantees the load balancing of CHs in intracluster and intercluster multihop routing.*

Proof of Lemma 4. According to the Equation (4), it can be demonstrated that the node radius depends on its distance to the BS and its remaining energy. Therefore, CHs having more distance to BS and higher remaining energy make larger clusters and they have more CMs. Hence, it consumes more energy to receive and collect data from CMs. Moreover, ACH nodes are applied to maximize the stability and balanced energy consumption of CMs during data transmission to the CH and also to balance CH energy consumption for receiving the data. On the other hand, CHs close to the BS with less energy have a smaller radius and less CMs. Therefore, they save more energy for receiving and collecting data from the CMs, and they guarantee the load balancing of the HCD protocol. □

5. Simulation Results

The main purpose of this research was to reduce energy consumption and increase the network life time. In order to achieve this purpose, simulations were performed in MATLAB programming environment. Furthermore, to evaluate network stability, efficiency, and throughput of the proposed algorithm, this algorithm was compared to ECDC (2013) [24], HUCL (2015) [15], and EADUC-II (2016) [25] algorithms.

5.1. Simulation Scenarios

We also performed simulations for two different states shown in Table 2. In the first scenario, there are 100 nodes in 200 × 200 spaces and the BS is located outside the network space and located at 100 × 250. In the second scenario, the location of the BS has changed to the network center and 100 × 100 location.

Table 2. Scenarios.

Network	BS	Number of Node	Network Space
scenarios #1	(100,250)	100	200 × 200
scenarios #2	(100,100)	100	200 × 200

In the proposed algorithm the count of alive nodes, the average of network energy and network stability, first node death (FND), half node death (HND), death of 10% and 20% of nodes (PND), and last node death (LND) during the whole simulation time were evaluated. The simulation was performed in 50 periods.

Definitions of some important concepts:

- Network lifetime: the time interval from the start of network operations to LND.

- Network stability: the time interval from the start of the network operations to FND.
- Throughput or efficiency: the number of data packets sent by a network to the BS. Efficiency improvement has a direct co-relation with increased network stability and the network lifetime.
- Load balancing: traffic load distribution. Its advantage is that when the load is well-distributed throughout the nodes, it results in balanced energy consumption. It also prevents the sudden death of the nodes caused by overusing them and increases the network stability.

5.2. Simulation Parameters

Simulation parameters are displayed in Table 3. The optimum values of some of the parameters (for example RL_{max}) were determined from various simulation results.

Table 3. Parameters used in the simulation.

Parameters	The Amount
E_{elec}	50 nJ/bit
E_{fs}	10 pJ/bit/m^2
E_{mp}	0.0013 pJ/bit/m^4
E_{DA}	5 nJ/bit/message
Data packet size	1000 byte
Packet header size	25 byte
Control message size	50 byte
RL_{max}	10–160 m
α, β	0.333
Initial energy	0.5–1.5 j
Number of rounds in a Major slot	6
Number of Major slots in the data transmission stage	7

We performed simulations several times to determine the round numbers in a major slot (Figure 2) and major slot in data transmission stage (Figure 2). Simulation parameters, such as the nodes locations, are considered to be the same for all the nodes so that the results are reliable and solid. This simulation plays a crucial role in the proposed protocol. In this protocol, by decreasing the number of rounds, we can more accurately simulate a dynamic method which results in increased overhead and energy consumption and declined the network life span. In contrast, by increasing the number of rounds the proposed protocol gets closer to the static methods and, therefore, leads to a decrease is overhead and loss of energy in CH and, subsequently, the stability and throughput of the network reduced. Since the main aim of the proposed protocol was to increase the maximum lifetime of the network by eliminating maximum control messages and reducing overhead which leads to the reduced energy consumption of networks nodes. The number of rounds in a major slot and the number of major slots in data transmission should be optimized. In order to determine the abovementioned optimized numbers, the simulation was performed several times. Considering the structure of the proposed method, we preferred to set the amount of the mentioned parameter to the highest value of FND. According to Figures 5 and 6 we considered the count of rounds as 6 and the count of the major slot as 7. The optimum FND average was obtained in different simulations. According to the simulation results, it can be seen that each data transmission stage consists of 7 portions of the major slot including 6 rounds, one CH rotation, and one adjustment route. Overall, during the data transmission stage, data was transmitted in 42 rounds and we aimed to remove the majority of the network overhead.

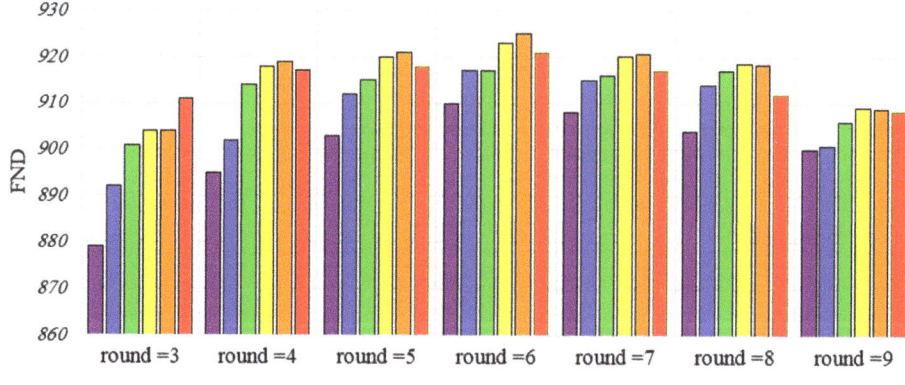

Figure 5. Network lifetime under different rounds in different major slots at data transmission stage for scenario #1 with Rl_{max} = 100 and initial energy = 1 J.

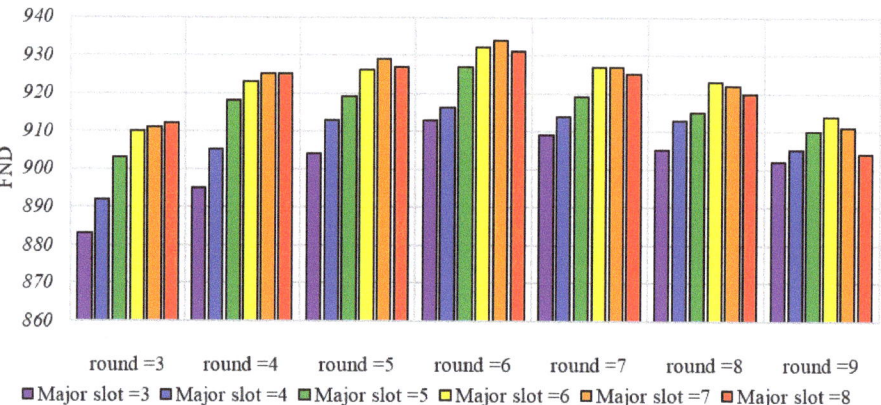

Figure 6. Network lifetime under different rounds in different major slots at data transmission stage for scenario #2 with Rl_{max} = 100 and initial energy = 1 J.

For results and considered parameters refer to Figure 2. Figure 2 demonstrates the protocol performance considering the number of rounds and major slots. According to the results of Figure 5, we set the number of rounds and a major slot in Figure 2.

One of the most important parameters in clustering is to determine the radius. The radius of the nodes in each layer of the proposed protocol is intentionally considered as different sizes. Thus, the value of λ in Equation (4) in the first layer is equal to 1, in the second and third layers is 1.25, and in the fourth layer is 1.75. Thus, the clusters which are closer to the BS are smaller and the CH can have more energy for relaying and routing other CH packets to the BS. To determine the RL_{max} parameter in the Equation (4) we carried out various simulation runs with different RL_{max} values to obtain the optimum value for RL_{max} parameter. Two of the important factors in IoT-based wireless nodes are the number of CH and the size of clusters, which are dependent on the radius of the nodes. The simulation results for different scenarios are shown in Figure 7.

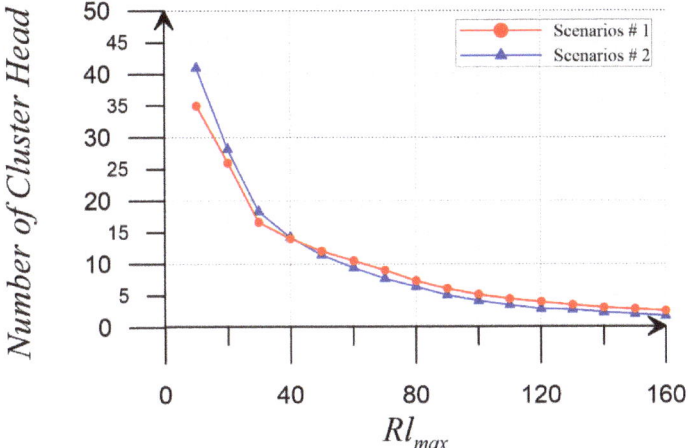

Figure 7. CH generated in two scenarios.

The radius of each node must be so that the number of cluster nodes in the network is reasonable. In the paper, the number of optimal CH was considered equal to 5% of the total number of nodes in the network. In our proposed protocol, we assumed that the value of RL_{max} parameter is equal to 100 m which makes the number of CH approximately equal to 5 based on [3].

Figures 8 and 9 demonstrate the routing and clustering graph formed in one of the simulations for scenarios 1 and 2. Green nodes display CM nodes, turquoise color indicates ACH nodes, and CHs are indicated in blue color. According to these figures, clusters close to BS are smaller and as a result, they have more energy for distant CH data relay. In addition, ACH nodes cooperate with CH in data transmission. If the network area is larger, and the distance of nodes are farther, then the role of these nodes will be more effective.

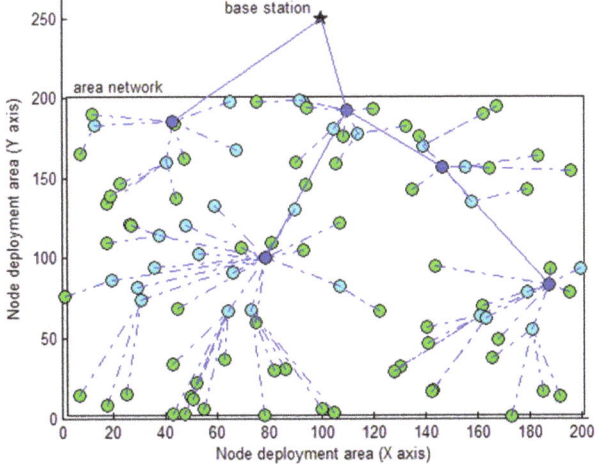

Figure 8. Routing and clustering graph for scenario 1.

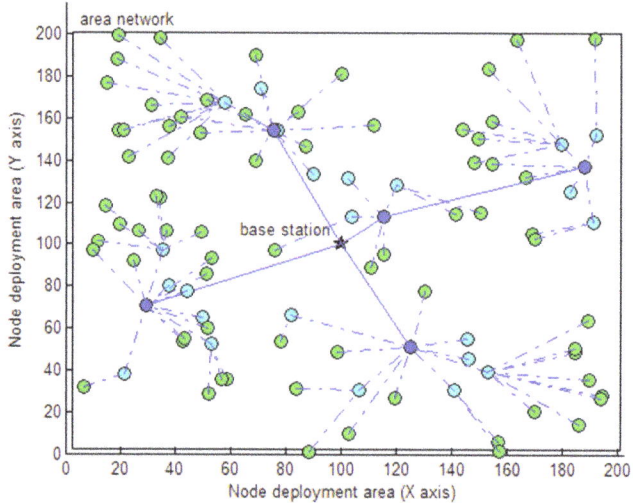

Figure 9. Routing and clustering graph for scenario 2.

5.3. Network Stability and Network Lifetime

In order to increase efficiency and throughput, we must transmit more data to the BS and, in this case, it is necessary to prevent node death. Therefore, efficiency and throughput can be improved by increasing network stability. In Tables 4 and 5, the performance of the stability period and the network lifetime involving FND, 10% PND, 20% PND, HND, and LND of the protocols was determined for the first and second scenarios. In both scenarios, the proposed protocol had better performance compared to ECDC, HUCL, and EADUC-II algorithms. Our proposed method had significantly improved performance with very high stability in two different spaces. HCD gets help from the information of neighbor nodes for clustering and uses intercluster and intracluster as well as multihop transmission appropriately. In Tables 4 and 5, the obtained results indicate that the proposed protocol could improve some parameters and be able to transmit more packets in the event of these parameters occurrence. It was emphasized that these nodes that do not have suitable energy status should not become a CH. Since CH node consumes more energy emphasizing this idea resulted in dividing energy consumption equally between the nodes during simulation time. The presented protocol helped reducing energy consumption in the network by deleting unusual control messages and reducing overhead; therefore, it resulted in a prolonged network lifetime.

Table 4. Simulation results of stability period and lifetime for scenario 1.

Protocol	FND (100 Nodes)		10% PND (90 Nodes)		20% PND (80 Nodes)		HND (50 Nodes)		LND (0 Nodes)	
	Time	Packets	Time	Packets	Time	Packets	Time	Packets	Time	Packets
ECDC	251.6	25156	465.7	45795	541.6	52307	648.8	59245	1133.8	65685
HUCL	273.7	27367	524.7	51201	638.4	60591	737.9	66555	866	68843
EADUC-II	394.2	39422	608.8	60138	662.1	64636	691.3	66365	719.4	66685
HCD	702.2	70205	881.9	86164	918.3	88646	964	90641	1047.3	91263

Table 5. Simulation results of stability period and lifetime for scenario 2.

Protocol	FND (100 Nodes)		10% PND (90 Nodes)		20% PND (80 Nodes)		HND (50 Nodes)		LND (0 Nodes)	
	Time	Packets	Time	Packets	Time	Packets	Time	Packets	Time	Packets
ECDC	345.2	34515	569.1	56204	644.9	62693	743.5	6900.7	1283.6	7620.3
HUCL	205.2	20518	489.8	47679	617.4	58584	736.8	66323	856.9	68948
EADUC-II	358.1	35808	590.5	58125	667.9	65680	712.4	67864	742.5	68265
HCD	863.5	86348	966.7	96087	983.4	97222	1013.6	98538	1088.3	99168

Table 6 shows the performance of the proposed protocol in comparison to the other three protocols. In order to evaluate it better, we showed the improvement percentage of above-mentioned criteria in Table 6. The measurement showed that the presented protocol increased network stability considerably. The ECDC protocol acts as distributed and dynamic, but the protocols of HUCL, EADUC-II, and the proposed protocol act as hybrid and distributed. When HCD was compared to HUCL, it increased the network stability to 156.5% and 320.8% in the first and second scenarios, respectively. We compared the proposed protocol with EADUC-II and noticed that this protocol had increased the network stability to 78.1% and 141.1% in the first and second scenarios, respectively.

Table 6. HCD protocol improvement in comparison with other protocols in simulation scenarios.

The Network	Parameters	HCD V ECDC	HCD V HUCL	HCD V EADUC-II
Scenarios 1	FND	179.30%	156.50%	78.10%
	10%PND	89.30%	68%	44.80%
	20%PND	69.50%	43.80%	38.60%
	HND	48.50%	30.60%	39.40%
	LND	% −7.6	20.90%	45.50%
Scenarios 2	FND	150.10%	320.80%	141.10%
	10%PND	69.80%	97.30%	63.70%
	20%PND	52.40%	59.20%	47.20%
	HND	36.30%	37.50%	42.20%
	LND	% −15.2	27%	46.50%

5.4. Number of Nodes Alive

In Table 7, the average number of live nodes is displayed. As it can be concluded from the Table 7, the average number of live nodes was more than 30% of all node counts which confirmed the maintained network stability as it was proposed by our algorithm. Figures 10 and 11 demonstrate the number of live nodes during simulation. The results showed that HCD had better performance compared to other protocols and increased the number of live nodes during simulation. It was due to the balance between the energy consumption of different nodes as it was proposed by the presented protocol and therefore, could prevent node death.

Table 7. The average number of live nodes.

Protocol	Scenario 1	Scenario 2
ECDC	20.9	24.4
HUCL	22.6	22.8
EADUC-II	21.4	21.9
HCD	30.7	32.7

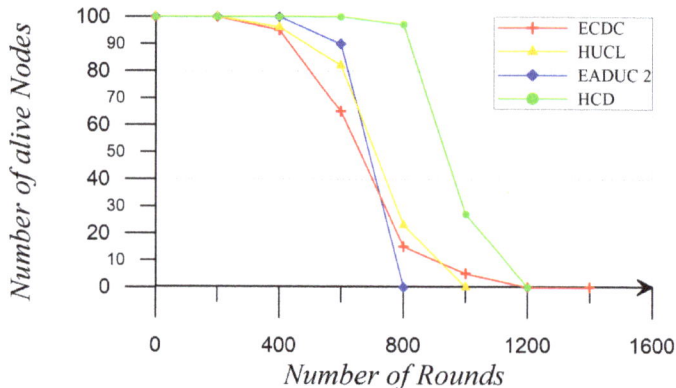

Figure 10. The average of the number of alive nodes for scenario 1.

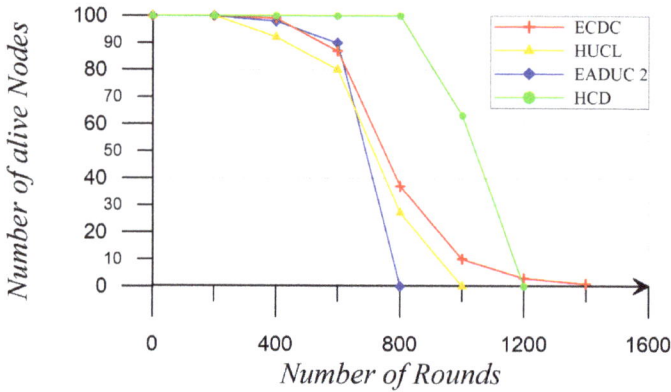

Figure 11. The average of the number of alive nodes for scenario 2.

5.5. The Average of the Energy of Alive Nodes

As it was assumed, the network is formed by heterogeneous nodes which have an energy between 0.5 to 1.5 *j*. Figure 12 illustrate the energy consumption of each node in the proposed algorithm and in scenario 1. Figures 12 and 13 compare the amount of energy in each node in HCD for scenarios 1 and 2, at the beginning of the network and during the rounds 250, 500, and 750. The proposed protocol has excellent load balancing. At first, due to the assumption of heterogeneous nodes, an energy difference between the nodes is observed. However, gradually in a period of 250, and particularly 500, during the performance of our proposed protocol, it can be seen that the energy difference between nodes is reduced. This indicates that in the proposed protocol we have high load balancing. The proposed protocol is able to distribute the energy consumption between all nodes and pave the way for increasing the load balancing by selecting the proper CH. In addition, by determining the suitable CH, the presented protocol divided the energy consumption among nodes and it helped reducing energy consumption by multihop transmission. In this type of transmission distance is short, and hence, less energy is required for transmission. Accordingly, the presented protocol prevented the immediate reduction of energy in nodes by selecting appropriate CH and avoiding direct transmission to distant nodes. Consequently, the close and distant nodes consumed energy in a balanced way, the stability was increased and the throughput was improved.

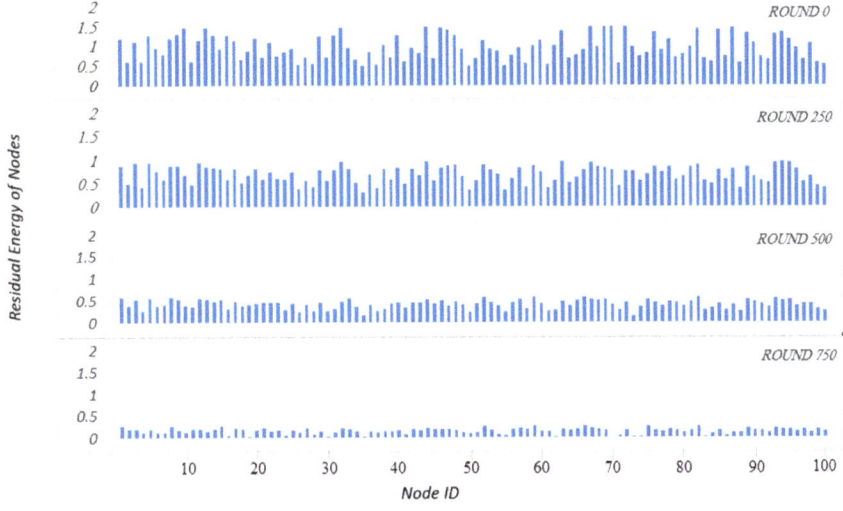

Figure 12. Energy consumption of HCD for scenario 1.

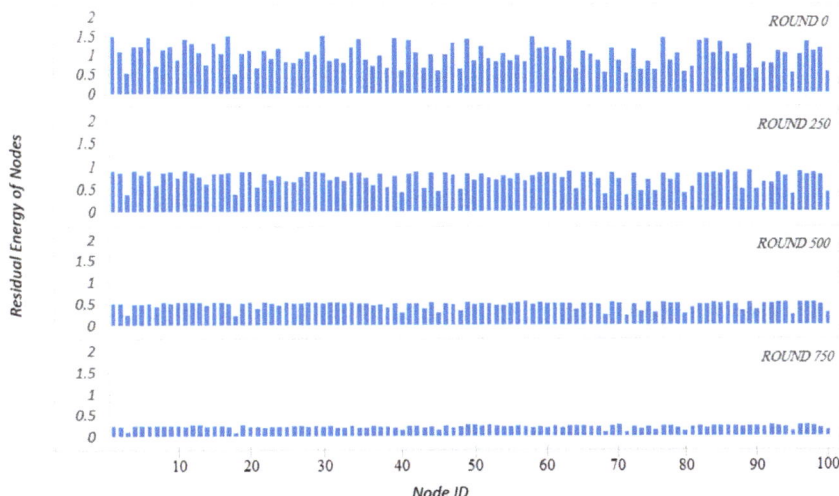

Figure 13. Energy consumption of HCD for scenario 2.

One of the important reasons in the proposed protocol which contributed to the increased network lifetime is that it omitted the maximum control messages in the network. Figures 14 and 15 show the energy consumption for control messages in the proposed protocol and other protocols. The proposed protocol decrease energy consumption in terms of control messages to 300% in comparison to EDCD and EADUC-II and 100% in comparison to HUCL.

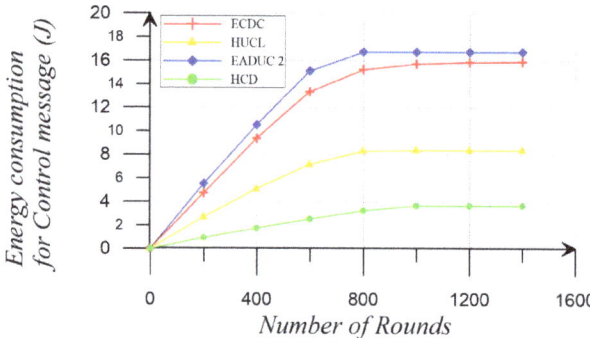

Figure 14. Total energy consumption for control message in scenario 1.

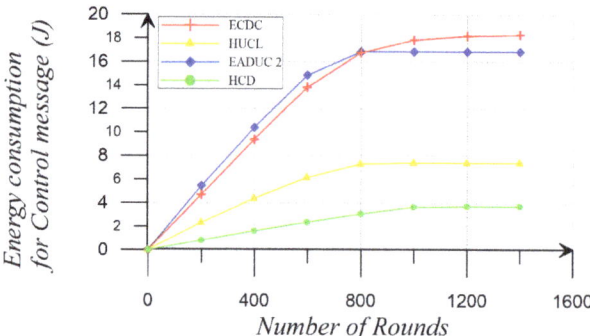

Figure 15. Total energy consumption for control message in scenario 2.

Given that in our proposed protocol there were 6 rounds of data transmission per each major slot without the overhead control message, and since the protocol had 42 rounds of data transmission to the BS per each transmission stage, this protocol was able to optimize the energy consumption by reducing the overhead. This led to an increase in average energy of nodes. Figures 16 and 17 show the average energy of alive nodes during the simulation.

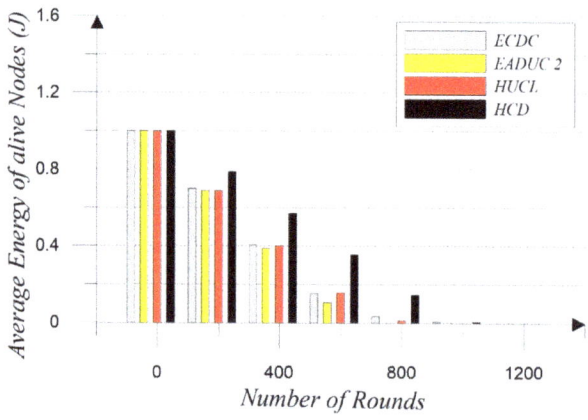

Figure 16. The average energy of alive nodes for scenario 1.

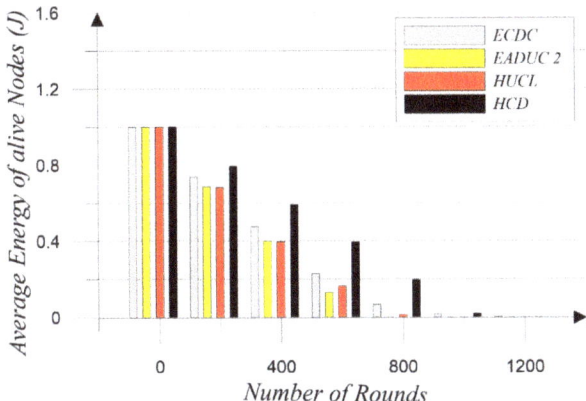

Figure 17. The average of the energy of alive nodes for scenario 2.

According to the results, it can be concluded that in the proposed method by reducing the network overhead, the energy consumption has been reduced.

5.6. Throughput

Figures 18 and 19 demonstrate packet production in relation to the round indicating an increased efficiency of the proposed protocols. This method was able to produce and transmit more packets during the simulation, increase the throughput due to the balanced energy consumption, increased stability and improved number of available nodes. The proposed protocol increases throughout to 40%, 33%, and 37% in the first scenario and 30%, 43%, and 45% in the second scenarios in comparison to ECDC, HUCL, and EADUC-II, respectively.

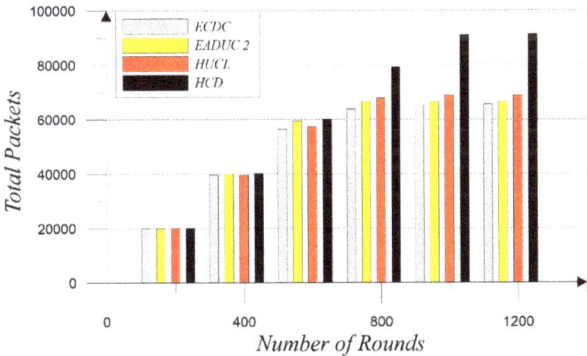

Figure 18. Throughput for scenario 1.

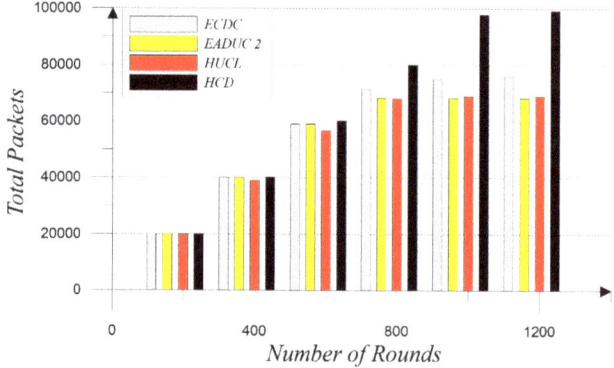

Figure 19. Throughput for scenario 2.

5.7. Simulation in Other Scenarios and Parameters

Based on the reliability of our proposed protocol in this section, we have compared this protocol with simulation scenarios of EADUC-II [25]. Therefore, the simulation parameters reported in [25] were considered. According to their first scenario, 100 nodes were distributed uniformly within an area of 200 × 200 m² and the location of the BS was set at 250 × 100. The size of the packets and control massage was 500 byte and 25 bytes, respectively. The results, as shown in Figure 20, indicated an improvement in the average number of alive nodes in comparison with the previous protocols.

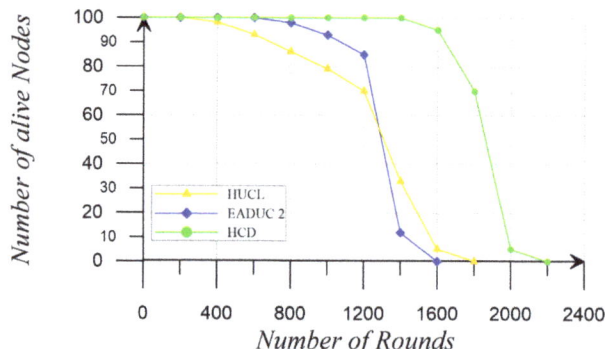

Figure 20. The average of the number of alive nodes for our Simulation.

Our simulation results with the parameters of the article [25], also confirm the simulation of the EADUC-II and the results showed that the proposed protocol had better performance compared to other protocols.

6. Conclusions

In recent years, the development of technology, IoT has been used over sensor networks in various fields. Wireless nodes have some limitation in case of energy sources since energy consumption is highly related to sending and receiving waves. Optimization of energy consumption in routing protocols is one of the main methods of increase the network lifetime. In this paper, we proposed a new and efficient clustering protocol based on density as a hybrid of static and dynamic as well as multi-hop routing for IoT based on wireless nodes. We considered a distributed clustering method and performed routing between CH and BS on the basis of multi-hop routing. The proposed method significantly reduced the network overhead and energy consumption by deleting unusual control messages. The results showed that HCD can effectively improve network stability and lifetime. Compared to EDCD [24], HUCL [15], and EADUC-II [25], the network stability increased to 179%, 156%, and 78% and to 150%, 320%, and 141% in the first and second scenarios, respectively. In addition, HCD increased throughput to 40%, 33%, and 37% in the first scenario and 30%, 43%, and 45% in the second scenarios in comparison to EDCD, HUCL, and EADUC-II. Furthermore, it is able to balance energy consumption in the network and improve efficiency and throughput.

Author Contributions: T.H. and S.M.B. prepared the literature review and performed the experiments and composed the manuscript, A.V.O., A.A.R.H., A.K.S. scrutinized the data, developed Methods and Experiments, T.H. and M.-Y.C., compiled the experimental results, A.K.S. supervised the research activities and devised the systematic plans for this study.

Acknowledgments: This work was supported in part by International Scientific and Technological Cooperation Project of Dongguan (2016508102011), in part by Science and Technology Planning Project of Guangdong Province (2016A020210142) and in part by Guangdong provincial key platform and major scientific research projects (2017GXJK174).

Conflicts of Interest: The authors declare no conflict of interest.

References

1. Machado, K.; Rosário, D.; Cerqueira, E.; Loureiro, A.; Neto, A.; de Souza, J. A Routing Protocol Based on Energy and Link Quality for Internet of Things Applications. *Sensors* **2013**, *13*, 1942–1964. [CrossRef] [PubMed]
2. Abdul-Qawy, A.S.H.; Srinivasulu, T. SEES: A scalable and energy-efficient scheme for green IoT-based heterogeneous wireless nodes. *J. Ambient Intell. Hum. Comput.* **2018**. [CrossRef]
3. Heinzelman, W.B.; Chandrakasan, A.P.; Balakrishnan, H. An application-specific protocol architecture for wireless microsensor networks. *IEEE Trans. Wirel. Commun.* **2002**, *1*, 660–670. [CrossRef]
4. Zhang, W.; Wei, X.; Han, G.; Tan, X. An Energy-Efficient Ring Cross-Layer Optimization Algorithm for Wireless Sensor Networks. *IEEE Access.* **2018**, *6*, 16588–16598. [CrossRef]
5. Xiao, F.; Liu, W.; Li, Z.; Chen, L.; Wang, R. Noise-Tolerant Wireless Sensor Networks Localization via Multinorms Regularized Matrix Completion. *IEEE Trans. Veh. Technol.* **2018**, *67*, 2409–2419. [CrossRef]
6. Qiao, J.; Zhang, X. Polar Coordinate-Based Energy-Efficient-Chain Routing in Wireless Sensor Networks Using Random Projection. *IEEE Access* **2018**, *6*, 21275–21286. [CrossRef]
7. Bozorgi, S.M.; Rostami, A.S.; Hosseinabadi, A.A.R.; Balas, V.E. A new clustering protocol for energy harvesting-wireless sensor networks. *Comput. Electr. Eng.* **2017**, *64*, 233–247. [CrossRef]
8. León, O.; Hernández-Serrano, J.; Soriano, M. Securing cognitive radio networks. *Int. J. Commun. Syst.* **2010**, *23*, 633–652. [CrossRef]
9. Wang, J.; Li, B.; Xia, F.; Kim, C.S.; Kim, J.U. An Energy Efficient Distance-Aware Routing Algorithm with Multiple Mobile Sinks for Wireless Sensor Networks. *Sensors* **2014**, *14*, 15163–15181. [CrossRef]
10. Yan, J.; Zhou, M.; Ding, Z. Recent Advances in Energy-Efficient Routing Protocols for Wireless Sensor Networks: A Review. *IEEE Access* **2016**, *4*, 5673–5686. [CrossRef]
11. Wang, J.; Cao, J.; Li, B.; Lee, S.; Sherratt, R.S. Bio-inspired ant colony optimization based clustering algorithm with mobile sinks for applications in consumer home automation networks. *IEEE Trans. Consum. Electron.* **2015**, *61*, 438–444. [CrossRef]
12. Kumar, A.; Kumar, V.; Chand, N. Energy Efficient Clustering and Cluster Head Rotation Scheme for Wireless Sensor Networks. *Int. J. Adv. Comput. Sci. Appl.* **2011**, *3*, 129–136. [CrossRef]
13. Chaurasiya, S.K.; Pal, T.; Bit, S.D. An Enhanced Energy-Efficient Protocol with Static Clustering for WSN. In Proceedings of the International Conference on Information Networking 2011 (ICOIN2011), Barcelona, Spain, 26–28 January 2011; pp. 58–63.
14. Zanjireh, M.M.; Larijani, H. A Survey on Centralised and Distributed Clustering Routing Algorithms for WSNs. In Proceedings of the 2015 IEEE 81st Vehicular Technology Conference (VTC Spring), Glasgow, UK, 11–14 May 2015; pp. 1–6.
15. Malathi, L.; Gnanamurthy, R.K.; Chandrasekaran, K. Energy efficient data collection through hybrid unequal clustering for wireless sensor networks. *Comput. Electr. Eng.* **2015**, *48*, 358–370. [CrossRef]

16. Rostami, A.S.; Badkoobe, M.; Mohanna, F.; Hosseinabadi, A.; Hosseinabadi, A.R.; Sangaiah, A.K. Survey on Clustering in Heterogeneous and Homogeneous Wireless Sensor Networks. *J. Supercomput.* **2018**, *74*, 277–323. [CrossRef]
17. Bozorgi, S.M.; Amiri, M.G.; Rostami, A.S.; Mohanna, F. A novel dynamic multi-hop clustering protocol based on renewable energy for energy harvesting wireless sensor networks. In Proceedings of the 2015 2nd international conference on knowledge-based engineering and innovation (KBEI), Tehran, Iran, 5–6 November 2015; pp. 619–624.
18. Rostami, A.S.; Bernety, H.M.; Hosseinabadi, A.R. A Novel and Optimized Algorithm to Select Monitoring Sensors by GSA. In Proceedings of the IEEE International Conference on Control, Instrumentation and Automation (ICCIA), Shiraz, Iran, 27–28 December 2011; pp. 829–834.
19. Ruiz, M.T.; Lytras, M.D.; Mathkour, H. Innovative services and applications of wireless sensor networks: Research challenges and opportunities. *Int. J. Distrib. Sens. Netw.* **2018**, *14*, 1–4.
20. Younis, O.; Fahmy, S. HEED: A hybrid, energy-efficient, distributed clustering approach for ad hoc sensor networks. *IEEE Trans. Mob. Comput.* **2004**, *3*, 366–379. [CrossRef]
21. Lee, K.; Lee, J.; Lee, H.; Shin, Y. A Density and Distance based Cluster Head Selection algorithm in Sensor Networks. In Proceedings of the 2010 The 12th International Conference on Advanced Communication Technology (ICACT), Phoenix Park, Korea, 7–10 February 2010; pp. 162–165.
22. Taheri, H.; Neamatollahi, P.; Younis, O.M.; Naghibzadeh, S.; Yaghmaee, M.H. An energy-aware distributed clustering protocol in wireless sensor networks using fuzzy logic. *Ad Hoc Netw.* **2012**, *10*, 1469–1481. [CrossRef]
23. Ducrocq, T.; Mitton, N.; Hauspie, M. Energy-based clustering for wireless sensor network lifetime optimization. In Proceedings of the 2013 IEEE Wireless Communications and Networking Conference (WCNC), Shanghai, China, 7–10 April 2013; pp. 968–973.
24. Gu, X.; Yu, J.; Yu, D.; Wang, G.; Lv, Y. ECDC: An energy and coverage-aware distributed clustering protocol for wireless sensor networks. *Comput. Electr. Eng.* **2014**, *40*, 384–398. [CrossRef]
25. Gupta, V.; Pandey, R. An improved energy aware distributed unequal clustering protocol for heterogeneous wireless sensor networks. *Eng. Sci. Technol.* **2016**, *19*, 1050–1058. [CrossRef]
26. Sabor, N.; Abo-Zahhad, M.; Sasaki, S.; Ahmed, S.M. An Unequal Multi-hop Balanced Immune Clustering protocol for wireless sensor networks. *Appl. Soft Comput.* **2016**, *43*, 372–389. [CrossRef]
27. Meng, X.; Shi, X.; Wang, Z.; Wu, S.; Li, C. A grid-based reliable routing protocol for wireless sensor networks with randomly distributed clusters. *Ad Hoc Netw.* **2016**, *51*, 47–61.
28. Chen, D. An energy-efficient QoS routing for wireless sensor networks using self-stabilizing algorithm. *Ad Hoc Netw.* **2015**, *37*, 240–255. [CrossRef]
29. Chanak, P.; Banerjee, I.; Sherratt, R.S. Energy-Aware Distributed Routing Algorithm to Tolerate Network Failure in Wireless Sensor Networks. *Ad Hoc Netw.* **2016**, *56*, 158–172.
30. Naeem, M.K.; Patwary, M.; Abdel-Maguid, M. Universal and Dynamic Clustering Scheme for Energy Constrained Cooperative Wireless Sensor Networks. *IEEE Access* **2017**, *5*, 12318–12337. [CrossRef]
31. Cengiz, K.; Dag, T. Energy Aware Multi-Hop Routing Protocol for WSNs. *IEEE Access* **2018**, *6*, 2622–2633. [CrossRef]

© 2019 by the authors. Licensee MDPI, Basel, Switzerland. This article is an open access article distributed under the terms and conditions of the Creative Commons Attribution (CC BY) license (http://creativecommons.org/licenses/by/4.0/).

Article

Development of Output Correction Methodology for Long Short Term Memory-Based Speech Recognition

Recep Sinan Arslan [1,*] and Necaattin Barışçı [2]

1. Department of Computer Programming, Vocational School of Technical Science, Yozgat Bozok University, 66200 Yozgat, Turkey
2. Department of Computer Engineering, Faculty of Technology, Gazi University, 06560 Ankara, Turkey
* Correspondence: sinanarslanemail@gmail.com

Received: 17 June 2019; Accepted: 5 August 2019; Published: 6 August 2019

Abstract: This paper presents a correction methodology for Long Short Term Memory (LSTM) based speech recognition. A strategy that validates with a reference database was developed for LSTM. It is conceptually simple but requires a large keyword database to match test templates. The correction method is based on the "most matching method" that is finding the word in which the system output is closest among the "Referenced Template Database". Each LSTM model recognition output was corrected with the proposed new concept. Thus, system recognition performance was improved by correcting faulty outputs. The effectiveness, efficiency, and contribution of this approach to system performance were demonstrated by experiments. Tests carried out using different speech-text datasets and LSTM models yielded an average performance increase of 2.25%. With some advanced models, this ratio rises to 3.84%.

Keywords: speech recognition; Long Short Term Memory (LSTM); speech output correction; most-matching

1. Introduction

Speech is the most effective means of communication among people and is the most natural way of exchanging information. Therefore, the desire of people to interact vocally with computers is increasing day by day. To meet this desire, studies are being conducted in a number of fields intended for the simulation of humans' ability to talk, from carrying out of simple tasks by computers through machine-human interaction, to turning speech to text through Automatic Speech Recognition (ASR) systems [1]. In recent years, signal processing and recognition have been utilized in many areas such as human activity tracking and detection [2,3], computer engineering [4], physical sciences, health-related applications [5], and natural science and industrial [6]. Speech sounds may get mixed with another speaker's speech in the background, in a room with TV sound or with an external voice. All sounds except the speech signal are called noise. Therefore, it is necessary to filter this noise in speech recognition systems [7]. In order to reduce noise in the recording stage of speech, the environment and the sensors are very important. Many different sensor-based technologies have been proposed for signal capturing and processing [8–11].

Along with the developments in speech modelling, ASR systems have begun to be used in many different areas such as voice processing at call centers, tasks requiring human-machine interface, travel information, stock-exchange transactions, quotations, weather reports, data entry, speech dictation, and access to information. Although there has been considerable progress in ASR systems over the last 60 years, there are still many problems that need to be solved and many particulars to be improved [12]. In the modelling of speech recognition systems, the flow-chart given in Figure 1 is generally followed. Accordingly, after the input signal is received into the system via the microphone, extracting the samples of the sound, digitizing, putting through various filters, in some necessary cases, labelling and transforming into a format that can be modelled are all carried out at pre-processing stage. Here, the aim is to produce a state of sound that is less simple, and free of speech variations and noise. In the next step, the parameters of the sampled audio signal obtained are captured and calculations are made to extract the remaining properties of the sound at certain time intervals. Feature extraction operations are used in many applications such as Real-time feature extraction of large size satellite images [13], activity tracking applications [14], face recognition [15], real-time motion capture [16], as well as human detection and activity tracking [17]. Therefore, the data obtained in feature extraction are critical values for speech recognition and provide important clues. In the next step, the comparison of the estimated word from the parameters with the language models is performed. The outputs produced after the acoustic model is compared with the outputs of the language model and a search is performed on the language model. Thus, it is aimed to find the right word to correct the acoustic model outputs. A kind of forecasting process is operated. Therefore, the correct word is obtained by making the most appropriate selection for the acoustic output from the text data that were created with the help of the word log [2].

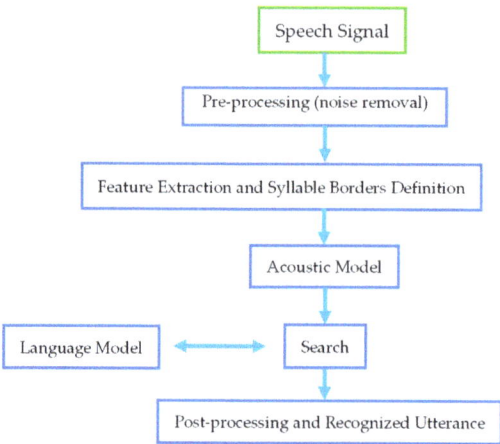

Figure 1. Basic flow of speech recognition systems.

This is the most basic flow of voice recognition techniques. Differences arise from the approaches used to create acoustic and language models.

In this study, a new method is proposed to improve the performance of Long Short Term Memory (LSTM) based Recurrent Neural Network (RNN)-trained speech recognition systems. The system is based on the principle of correcting recognition outputs with minimal increase in runtime.

Similar to the proposed method in this study, many different hybrid studies have been published in recent years. In the study [18] in which the Gaussian model was used with LSTM, a performance increase of approximately 0.5% to 0.2% was achieved compared to standard LSTM models. In the study [19], where a talking facial expression was intended to contribute to speech recognition performance, a certain increase was achieved for all situations. In the study by Kowari et al. [20], Deep Neural Network (DNN), Recurrent Neural Network (RNN) and Convolutional Neural Network (CNN) were used in combination. An increase in performance was achieved.

In Section 2 of this study, the working method of RNN-LSTM structure is explained, and, the structure of the proposed model and the working process are explained in Section 3 in detail. The comparative representation of the experiments performed to observe the contribution of the model and its results are described in Section 4. The evaluation of the results, some of the problems encountered and the studies that can be carried out for on the solving of these issues are presented in Sections 5 and 6.

2. Recurrent Neural Networks and Long Short Term Memory

Artificial neural network is a computation model based on the structure and functions of biological neural networks. It is like an artificial nerve used to receive process and transmit information. It is basically consists of 3 layers. The input layer communicates with the environment for values to be input to the neural network. The output layer is used to provide information out of the network. It collects and transmits the required information. The hidden layer is the layer that contains neurons with the activation function located on the input and output layer. It extracts and uses the properties of inputs coming from the previous layer. It can consist of multiple layers in itself. An artificial neural network includes an input layer, a certain number of hidden layers depending on the problem and an output layer. People produce new ideas by using their previous thoughts. Thus, the permanence of information is provided. Traditional neural network models, the first systems in which this type of thinking was model, cannot totally provide this idea. This forgotten old information constitutes a serious problem in the training of the network. RNN models were proposed to produce a solution to this problem. These models have loops that allow information to persist.

As shown in Figure 2, schema shows a chunk of neural network, Xn input value and y_k output value. A loop allows the information to be transmitted to the next step of the network.

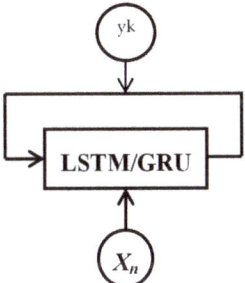

Figure 2. RNN give permission to recursion [21,22].

These loop system is not different from that of the classical neural network. It can be thought of as an architecture that includes multiple copies of a neural segment and receives messages from the previous step in each step. They work in the same way as arrays or lists. RNN structure has been applied to many problems such as speech recognition, language modelling, translation and image analysis in recent years and very successful results has been achieved.

The most important idea of RNN is that the previous data can be used in the next steps of the network. The amount of previous data is an important consideration for RNN structures. This structure is well suited for problems where recent information is sufficient to make prediction about the future. However, more information may be needed to solve some problems. For example, consider a language model that tries to predict the next word using previous words. This prediction requires subjects or verb given previously than the last word of the sentence. RNN structures cannot provide learning in cases where addiction is increased. The most important reason for this is the theoretically limited number of nodes in the network.

LSTM based RNN networks have been proposed to solve this problem. Long Short Term Memory (LSTM) is an RNN network that can learn long-term dependencies. This model was firstly proposed by Hochriter and Schmidhuber in 1997 [4]. Its popularity has increased over time and achieved very good results for many problems. It is well suited for avoiding long-term dependence problems. It is an idea that long-term recall of knowledge is a natural behavior for people (Figure 3).

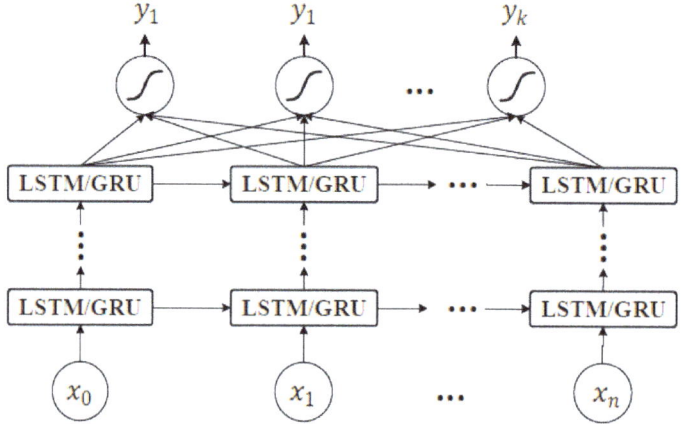

Figure 3. An Unrolled Recurrent Neural Network [21,22].

A standard RNN network is very simple and each layer can contain only one "tanh" function. However, in LSTM networks, this layer has a slightly different structure as shown in Figure 4.

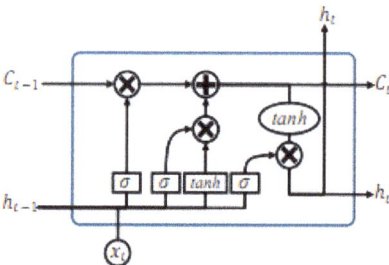

Figure 4. The repeating module in an LSTM contains four interacting layers [3].

The key structure of the LSTM is the line that runs over the diagram and works with small linear interactions. It is capable of adding and deleting information with the help of logic gates. LSTM works in a structure consisting of 6 steps.

Forget Gate Activation	$f_t = \sigma(W_f \cdot [h_{t-1}, x_t] + b_f)$	(1)
Input Gate:	$i_t = \sigma(W_i \cdot [h_{t-1}, x_t] + b_i)$	(2)
Candid Memory Cell Value:	$\check{C}_t = tanh(W_c \cdot [h_{t-1}, x_t] + b_c)$	(3)
New Memory Cell Value	$C_t = (f_t * C_{t-1} + i_t * \check{C}_t)$	(4)
Final Output Gate Values:	$o_t = \sigma(W_o \cdot [h_{t-1}, x_t] + b_o)$	(5)
Final Output Gate Values:	$h_t = (o_t * tanh(C_t))$	(6)

In the above formulas, each b is a bias vector, W is a weight matrix, and x_t is the input to the memory cell. i,c,f,o indices refer to input, cell memory, forget and output gates respectively.

The Step (1) is to decide which information is thrown away from the cell state. This decision is made using the sigmoid layer called the forget gate layer. It looks at h_{t-1} and x_t and generates an output of 0–1 for each c_{t-1} cell state. If it is 1, it means to completely keep it and 0 is to completely get rid of it.

Step (2) is to decide what new information to be kept in memory. It has two steps. First one is, decide which values to update with the sigmoid layer. Then, the tanh layer generates a vector for new candidate values(C~) in step (3).

It is necessary to update the old C_{t-1} status with the new C_t status. To forget the previous decision, it is multiplied by the f_t value and a new candidate value is created by i_t value in step (4).

Finally, it is necessary to decide what the cell output will be. This output depends on the current state of the cell but is a filtered version. Using the sigmoid function, the data to be extracted from the cell is selected in step (5). Then, the data is normalized with the tanh function in step (6). So the values between −1 and 1 are pushed. and multiplied by the output of the sigmoid function. Thus, only the part of the data that is decided is produced as output [21,22].

Using LSTM with RNN, remarkable results were obtained for many different problems. The next step from this stage is the structures that allow much larger data to be learned in each learning step. Many studies were carried out in relation to LSTM and derivatives and successful results were obtained on better learning systems [23–29]. Similar to LSTM structure, The Gated Recurrent Unit (GRU) is preferable for this study, as well. In the study of [30], comparing the LSTM and GRU approach, both models were compared and reported to produce similar results. When LSTM and GRU trainings were performed for the model proposed in this study, it was observed that more successful results could be obtained with LSTM. For this reason, the success of the hybrid model was demonstrated by creating a model with LSTM structure.

3. Proposed Correction Approaches for LSTM Speech Recognition

The LSTM based RNN structure can perform speech recognition with a certain level of performance on a test data. There are many factors such as dataset, model complexity, and the training time that affects this recognition process. For this reason, it is generally not possible to maintain satisfactory levels of system performance. Many different approaches have been proposed in the literature to improve the level of performance [31–35]. In addition to speech signal, features of human activities contribute to recognition processes. With these models, it is aimed to achieve significant increases such as our proposed model.

Using the comparison method with reference words together with the LSTM structure, an increase in performance can be achieved. Figure 5 shows the structure of proposed model.

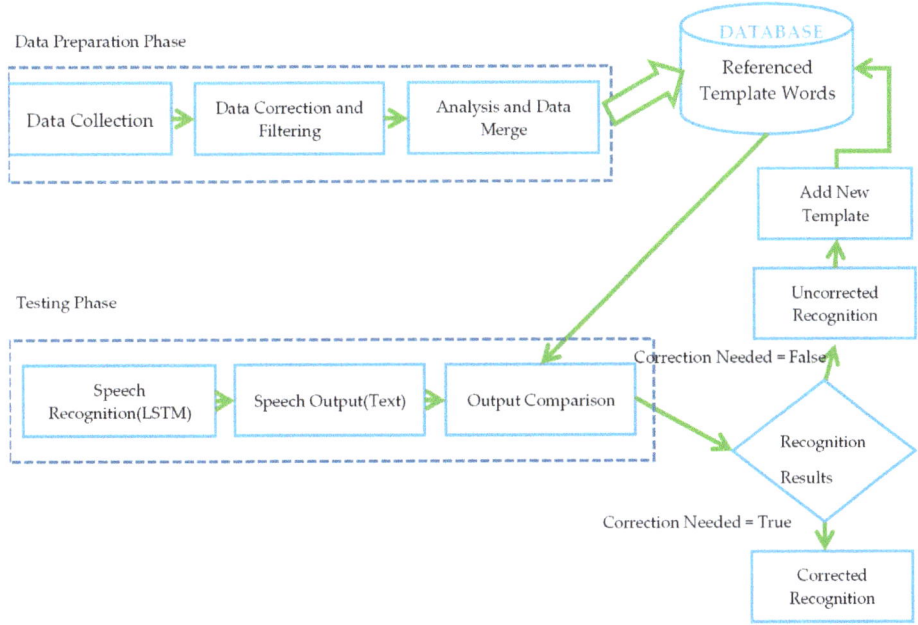

Figure 5. Framework of Speech Recognition with Correction Methodology.

There are basically two phases in this model. The creation of a database of "Referenced Template Words" is the first phase. Then, in the second phase, this database is compared with the LSTM system outputs and the correction of the system outputs is performed.

3.1. Data Preparation Phase

In the data preparation phase of the model proposed, primarily Turkish data collection process was performed. For this, 3 distributed datasets in Turkish were used. All of these datasets are created for different purposes. Therefore, in order to be used in this model, data correction and filtering operations are required. For instance, many editing procedures are needed, such as deleting schemas showing the suffix and roots of the words or correcting Turkish character problems. After these operations, 3 datasets were combined, the whole data were analyzed and the duplicated words were deleted and the type conversions were made to keep them in the same database tables. As a result, a "Referenced Template Words" database containing approximately 3 million unique Turkish words was created.

After the preparation of the text dataset, it is necessary to prepare an audio dataset. In this study, audio data of Middle East Technical University Microphone Speech v 1.0 [36,37] was used. It is a dataset prepared in Turkish language. Turkish is a phoneme based agglutinative language. Each letter is represented by a phoneme. However, in some cases, vowels and consonants may vary depending on where they are produced. Twenty letters in Turkish alphabet are represented by 45 phonetic symbols. In this dataset, a 193 speaker audio corpus and a pronunciation lexicon were developed. A new corpus and audio tools were created to ensure the accuracy of phonetic alignment and phoneme recognition. 91.2% of the automatically labelled phoneme boundaries are placed within 20 ms of hand-labelled locations for the Turkish audio corpus. The corpus is about the size of 600 Mbytes. The data has been digitally recorded with a Sound Balaster sound card on a PC at a 16 KHz sampling rate. The first 2000 sentences of the TIMIT [38] dataset were translated into Turkish. Afterwards, some studies aimed to improving the dataset yielded 2462 sentences with 9165 different words.

3.2. Testing Phase

In testing phase, an exemplary speech recognition model in RNN-LSTM structure was created. METU 1.0 Turkish speech set, which was suggested in the studies [36,37] and distributed over Linguistic Data Consortium (LDC) [39], was used for training of the model. The outputs of the standard recognition model were subjected to the comparison model process, of which the details are in Figure 5, and an increase in system performance was intended to be achieved.

The procedure for correcting the output of the LSTM speech recognition model within the proposed new model is shown in Figure 6. Accordingly, all outputs are subjected to a verification and correction process. Firstly, the outputs are checked for any corrections. If results are generated with 0% error rate, recognition process is terminated and system output is generated. In addition, this output is added into the database as a new "Referenced Template" if the word does not exist in the database. Moreover, if the recognition output is produced with uncorrected characters, it is ensured that these outputs are subjected to a correction process. "Referenced Template DB" that was previously prepared is used for this correction. Each output is subjected to different string distance calculation algorithms, some tests are subjected to 1 and some others to 11 different algorithms, in order to find the closest word in the database. Each output is subjected to this search and distance calculation process without exception and it is ensured that the closest reference word is found. This reference word is used as the system output instead of the incorrectly generated word. That is, instead of the text output generated using audio data, the new referenced word found by matching the incorrect outputs in the database is used.

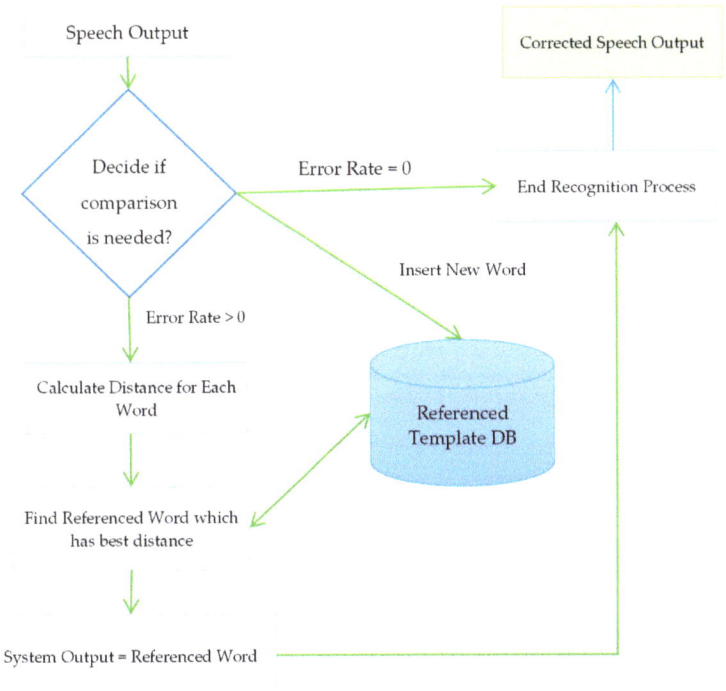

Figure 6. The proposed correction method for LSTM speech recognition.

The purpose of this proposed model is to correct system outputs with a few character errors and thereby improve system recognition performance. The pseudo code version of the algorithm is also presented in Figure 7. In the first step of this method, it is very important to reset the output value to be produced by LSTM model and the values that keep the distance of the words between LSTM model output and reference words. The LSTM-based speech recognition system is then performed and the output is produced. This output is checked for error rate is equal to 0%. This control has been put in order to contribute to a faster operation. The results that have 0% error rate, are not included the process. However, if recognition is performed incorrectly, all words in the reference table are sequentially compared and the distance of each word to the LSTM model output is calculated. After this calculation, an index with the minimum distance is determined and the related word is generated as a system output. A type of output correction is performed.

There are many different distance calculation algorithms for finding the nearest word. Although each algorithm has a different approach, the main goal is to make the correct estimation. At this stage, the most accurate approach would be to calculate each word with more than one distance algorithm and get the best value. However, it is natural that this is reflected in the process time as a significant increase. Therefore, it this study, the most suitable distance algorithm for the dataset was determined firstly by the tests and this method was used in the comparison process. The reference word closest to the recognition output with some errors is found by searching with the code given above.

```
Procedure Correction_Most_Matching_Method();
Output=""
Bestindex=0
If(Recognition Error Rate >0) then
    /*Start Find Best Distance Word*/
        For each word of references template db
            Calculate distance with word and system output
        End For
        For each n
            /*n is the number of distance with word*/
            Search the best distance index(i)
        End For
        /*output correction process*/
        output = word(i)
Else
    /* End of learning process(No correction needed)*/
End If
```

Figure 7. PSEUDOCODE: The pseudo code of most-matching learning.

3.3. Datasets, Tools and Algorithms Used For Testing Proposed Model

In order to test the model proposed in different ways, audio data, text data, database tools, LSTM model and other libraries were needed.

LSTM models require audio data for training. In this study, audio data of "Middle East Technical University Turkish Microphone Speech v. 1.0" [36,37] audio data, which contain a comprehensive data that can be used in Turkish speech recognition studies, were used. 120 speakers (60 males and 60 females) speak 40 sentences each (approximately 300 words per speaker), which makes approximately 500 min of speech in total. The 40 sentences are selected randomly for each speaker from a triphone-balanced set of 2,462 Turkish sentences. The ages range from 19 to 50 years, with an average of 23.9 years.

It is essential to create a text data set that can be used as a template for the correction of LSTM speech recognition outputs. It needs to be able to cover almost all words in Turkish. For this purpose, 3 commonly used Turkish data group were preferred. These are Zemberek [40], BOUN Corpus [41] and METU 1.0 Speech Dataset [36,37]. Zemberek, published in 2010, is an open source library containing grammatical features specific to Turkish language and can be used in Natural Language Processing (NLP) studies. It contains approximately 1.15 million unique Turkish words. BOUN Corpus, published in 2008, is a Project to create a Turkish language resource. It contains approximately 1.4 million unique Turkish words. METU 1.0 audio data set was prepared for use in speech recognition studies and published in 2002. This data set contains approximately 7 thousand unique Turkish words.

The PostGreSql database tool [42] was used to store "Referenced Template Words" and perform a quick search. Python [43] programming language was used for training of LSTM speech recognition system and Java libraries were used for testing. Dill [44], librosa [45], namedtupled [46], numpy [47], python_speech_features [48], tensorflow [49] libraries were used for speech recognition with Python.

There are many algorithms available for string comparison of the model. In this work, 11 different distance calculation algorithm were used to test the system performance in a different ways, which are Levenshtein [50], Damerau Levenshtein [51], Jaro Winkler [52,53], Longest Common Subsequence [54], Metric LCS [54], Normalized Levenshtein [50], Optimal String Alignment [51], Precomputed Cosine [55],

Qgram [56], Sift4 [57] and Weighted Levenshtein [24]. Thus, it was possible to observe the effects of different algorithms on the proposed model and make comparison in order to contribute to performance improvements.

4. Experiment and Results

In order to test the proposed data correction model, a medium scale Turkish training set was prepared. An LSTM RNN based model was prepared using an acoustic model with using Connectionist Temporal Classification (CTC) and deep learning. METU 1.0 audio dataset was used to test the application. The audio data were recorded in a quiet studio. The speech signal was recorded as a single channel at 16 Khz 16 bit resolution. The analysis frames are 20 ms wide and there is a 10 ms overlap. Different sample sets were created and the model proposed was tested. Three different text set were used for the tests. Zemberek Library [40], Boun Text Corpus [41] and Metu 1.0 text data [36,37] were preferred. All these datasets were examined and a text dataset containing more than 2M different Turkish words was obtained by combining them. For training and testing of the model, multiple training and test sets were prepared from audio dataset and the results were observed comparatively.

Two different methods were used to evaluate the proposed model in this paper. Firstly, the method was applied on more than one test, and as a result, the average contribution to system performance was observed. In the second method, the original sentence was compared with the LSTM model output and the model proposed output at each step of the 10000 Epoch tests, and the number of sentences were closer to the original sentence was counted. Thus, although the average value of the increase is important. How many sentences the proposed model had produced better results for in 10000 tests was also evaluated. Figure 8 shows the process of second method as an example.

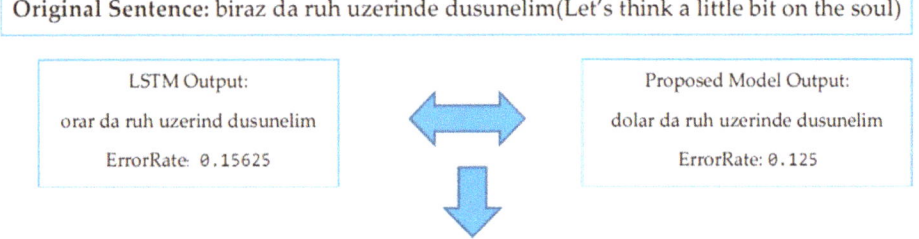

Figure 8. Sample test scheme of the proposed model.

Table 1 shows the test results of different distance algorithms. These results were obtained as a result of 10000 Epoch tests. When the results are examined, it is seen that different increase values in performance are obtained when different algorithms are used. This is due to the fact that distance algorithms produce different results for finding the closest words. The proposed model achieved maximum 3.84% increase in overall system recognition performance. In addition, a significant contribution is the before and after correction count when a comparison is made for each test in 10000 Epochs. Accordingly, after 10000 tests performed in the best condition, the model produced better results in 7711 after correction and 2289 before correction. This shows that the correction process is very useful not only for the overall performance of the system, but also in correcting inaccurate outputs throughout the system. A proportional difference of 27.21% is achieved on average.

Table 1. Recognition Results of LSTM Speech Recognition with Different Distance Algorithm.

Distance Algorithm	Error Rate Before Correction	Error Rate After Correction	Count of Better Performance(Not Corrected-Corrected)	Difference in Success Count (%)	Overall Performance Increase (%)
NormalizedLevenstain	0.3062	0.2730	2390-7610	52.20%	3.32%
DamerauLevenstein	14.8955	14.8143	3831-6169	23.38%	0.54%
JaroWinkler	0.2315	0.2093	3499-6501	30.02%	2.22%
LongestCommonSubsequence	17.7432	17.1749	3476-6524	30.48%	3.20%
MetricLCS	0.2835	0.2558	2289-7711	54.22%	2.76%
OptimalStringAlignment	14.9061	14.8344	3831-6169	23.38%	0.46%
PrecomputedCosine	0.2860	0.2798	4397-5703	13.06%	0.6%
Qgram	27.5372	26.4720	3879-6121	22.42%	3.84%
Levensthein	14.9278	14.8536	3851-6149	22.98%	0.49%
Sift4	19.8155	19.8039	4402-5598	11.96%	0.58%
WeightedLevensthein	14.9278	14.8536	3851-6149	22.98%	0.43%

Table 2 shows the basic parameters of the test models. 10 test sets were created with these parameters but working with different data. With the proposed model, Normalized Levensthein algorithm, which is one of the distance algorithms that provide the best contribution to the overall performance of the system, was kept constant and tests were performed for the increase in system performance for 10 different test sets prepared differently from each other. The test results are presented in Table 3.

Table 2. Experiment Parameters of Designed Model for LSTM.

Test Set	Optimization Algorithm	Learning Rate	Standard Deviation	Epoch Number	Batch Size	NOE	Mean
Set 1-10	GradientDescent	0.01	0.1	10000	1	1	0

NOE: Number of Examples.

Table 3. Recognition Results of LSTM Speech Recognition with Correction Method.

Test Set	Error Rate Before Correction	Error Rate After Correction	Count of Better Performance(Not Corrected-Corrected)	Difference in Success Count (%)	Overall Performance Increase (%)
NL-Test Set1	0.3062	0.2734	2417-7583	51.66%	3.28%
NL-Test Set2	0.2717	0.2572	3504-6496	29.92%	1.45%
NL-Test Set3	0.1934	0.1677	1810-8190	63.80%	2.57%
NL-Test Set4	0.2516	0.2321	2713-7287	45.74%	2.04%
NL-Test Set5	0.3758	0.3602	3166-6834	36.68%	1.56%
NL-Test Set6	0.3074	0.2719	3040-6960	39.20%	3.55%
NL-Test Set7	0.0934	0.0789	2557-7443	48.86%	1.45%
NL-Test Set8	0.3149	0.3007	4138-5862	17.24%	1.42%
NL-Test Set9	0.4265	0.4097	3883-6117	22.34%	1.68%
NL-Test Set10	0.1461	0.1307	2463-7537	50.96%	1.54%

Average Difference in Success Count: 40.64%; Average Performance Increase: 2.25%; Maximum Performance Increase: 3.55%; Minimum Performance Increase: 1.42%.

As shown in Table 3, the proposed model produced different results for different data sets. The purpose of these tests is to observe the contribution of the proposed model to the system performance in different test environments. According to this, the change of the test sets did not cause any change in the contribution to the system, but there was a difference in the contribution rate. An average system performance increase of 2.25% was achieved. The variability of the improvement ratio is directly proportional to the output produced by the system before correction. The model offers a contribution of more than 3% in cases where there are less character errors in a word but there are character errors in more than one word in a sentence. However, the improvement level drops to around 1.5% in cases where a word has more than one character errors.

Changes in the number of Epoch and the number of hidden layers of the model lead to changes in the level of contribution.

It improves the performance of system in any case but acts at levels ranging from 0.5% to 3.55% (Figure 9). Furthermore, the proportional difference in the number of recognition's before and after correction is much higher. On average, it produces more accurate outputs at 40.64%. It is seen that it makes a significant contribution. The model makes visible corrections in each test sentence. This process fixes many character errors. Numerical difference exceeds 50% indicates situations where the LSTM model does not perform learning or overall recognition performance of model remains below 20%. With the increase Epoch number, the differences in the numbers of successes decrease to more reasonable levels. This is the case where real learning takes place and numerical success goes down to average levels. In the case of realistic and good learning, both the contribution of the system to the overall performance exceeds over 3% and the difference in the number of success reaches over 40%. This shows that the proposed model can contribute more with a good learning network.

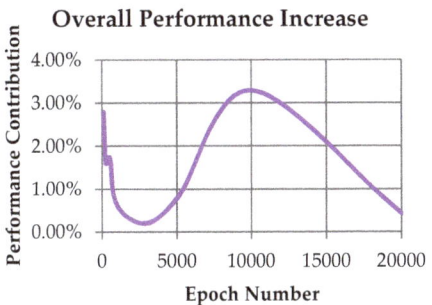
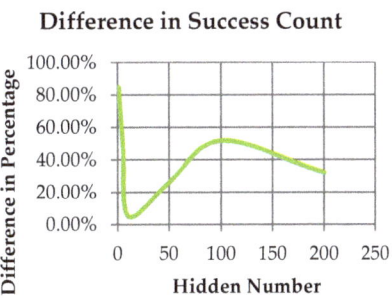
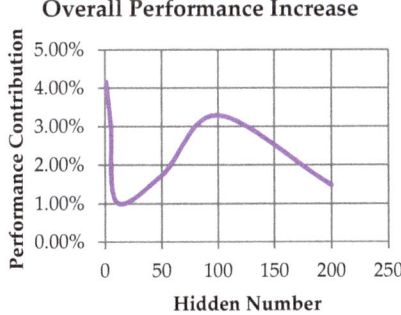
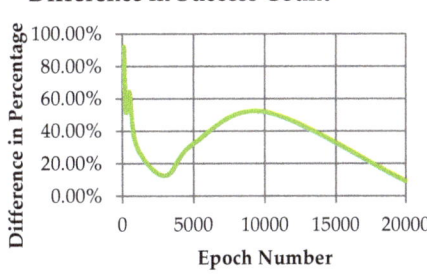

Figure 9. Effect of Epoch Number and Hidden Layer Count on Recognition Performance.

With the increase of performance, it is natural that the model proposed makes an increase in system calculation time. Since, after the system output, an output correction process is performed. After the output of the system was produced to observe how much the system was reflected as an increase of the overall runtime, we observe how long the verification method completed its operations and as a result we obtained the results as in Table 4. These results were achieved based on an Intel i5 processor and 8 GB ram memory. Approximately 0.04 s is required to correct each word during recognition. Assuming that an adult can speak an average of 200 words in 1 min, an extra 8 s is needed for a recognition model using the model proposed for creating speech data containing 1 min of continuous speech. These times are slightly longer in multiple comparison models using multiple distance calculation algorithms to find the closest word.

Table 4. Results of different recognition approach with METU 1.0.

Name of Authors	Recognition Approach	Vocabulary	Error Rate
Keser and Edizkan [58]	Common Vector Approach(CVA)	METU 1.0 Dataset	70 %
Aksoylar et al. [59]	HMM	METU 1.0 Dataset, SUVoice	Sports News: 37 %
Salor et al. [37]	HMM	METU 1.0 Dataset	29.2%
Çiloğlu et al. [60]	HMM, N-gram	METU 1.0 Dataset	35.91%
Büyük et al. [61]	HMM	METU 1.0 Dataset-2151 Test Data	3% increase performance
Proposed Model	LSTM	METU 1.0 Dataset	24.82%

Acceleration of the given processing times is possible with the necessary optimization techniques or faster computer infrastructure. However, we want to show here is that the proposed model requires an extra time in a standard speech recognition systems. It is a method that can be applied to many recognition systems with its effect on system result and run time comparison.

In this study, an LSTM based approach was preferred in speech recognition process and the proposed new approach contributed to a standard model. In addition to LSTM, many different algorithms such as Hidden Markov Model (HMM), Modified HMM, Embedded HMM, Gaussian Mixture Model (GMM), and Support Vector Machines (SVM) can be used. There have been many studies using these methods from past to present [58–65]. In order to compare the results obtained in this study, the results of the studies using modelling approaches other than LSTM and performing tests with METU 1.0 [36,37] dataset are shown in Table 4.

When the results shown in Table 4 are examined, the error rate is approximately 30%. However, small differences in the text data used in language model had effects on the results. The LSTM based model has an average error rate of 26.87%. In general, better results are produced than that of the models using HMM, CVA or N-gram. But, with the proposed new approach to reduce error rate, this performance level was further improved and reduced to 24.82%.

5. Conclusions

In this study, a viable output correction mechanism for speech recognition systems using LSTM modelling is proposed. Thus, an increase in system performance is aimed.

This proposed hybrid model provides a performance increase of approximately 2.25% with small increases in system runtime. Once the system requirements are established, it is very easy to implement.

The diversification of the audio data set and the enrichment of the word set will contribute to the performance. In addition, optimization of the distance calculation algorithms and improving database schemas would allow a considerable reduction in the processing times.

Nowadays, a speech recognition system that can operate in all situations, that has a 100% output performance and that can be used for all languages has not yet been developed. So, the model proposed can be used for many studies and structures to allow performance improvements at certain levels.

6. Future Works and Restriction

Although the new model proposed generally produces successful results, some limitations were encountered during the tests. The most important reason why the system cannot contribute more to the overall recognition performance is that the issue with the space character have not been resolved. As shown in Figure 10, the output of the system, which was made with almost 100% accuracy, is corrupted by the correction process. Solving this problem would reflect a significant increase in overall recognition performance.

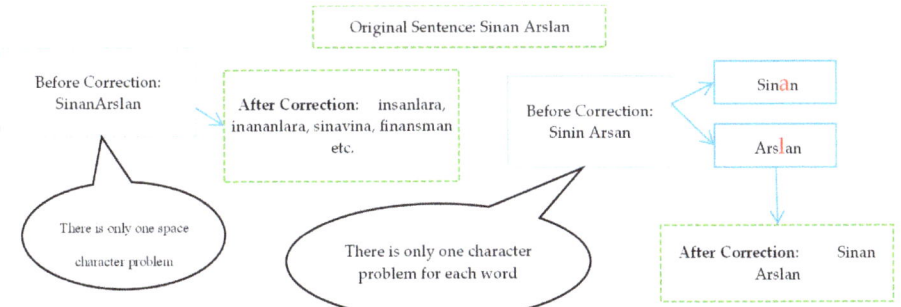

Figure 10. Restriction of Method – space character problem.

The second problem is that different distance calculation algorithms cannot be used together because of different calculation structures. If the necessary optimization and matching studies were performed on the distance values of the algorithms, it would be possible to find the correct template words. The optimization process would contribute to the system recognition performance.

Finally, the biggest problem of the system is the delays in the operating time. Since this method is a hybrid model, it requires a longer run time than that of the standard models. It is necessary to reduce this time to tolerable levels. Otherwise, it cannot be used in real-time speech recognition applications.

Author Contributions: Conceptualization, R.S.A. and N.B.; methodology, R.S.A. and N.B.; software, R.S.A.; validation, R.S.A. and N.B.; formal analysis, R.S.A. and N.B.; investigation, R.S.Arslan and N.B.; resources, R.S.A. and N.B.; data curation, R.S.A. and N.B. writing—original draft preparation, R.S.A. and N.B.; writing—review and editing, R.S.A. and N.B.; visualization, R.S.A.; supervision, N.B.; project administration, N.B."

Funding: There is no extra funding.

Conflicts of Interest: The authors declare no conflict of interest.

References

1. Tran, D.T. Fuzzy Approaches to Speech and Speaker Recognition. Ph.D. Thesis, Canberra University, Canberra, Australia, 2000.
2. Uddin, M.T.; Uddiny, M.A. Human activity recognition from wearable sensors using extremely randomized trees. In Proceedings of the International Conference on Electrical Engineering and Information Communication Technology (ICEEICT), Dhaka, Bangladesh, 13–15 September 2015; pp. 1–6.
3. Jalal, A. Human activity recognition using the labelled depth body parts information of depth silhouettes. In Proceedings of the 6th International Symposium on Sustainable Healthy Buildings, Seoul, Korea, 27 February 2012; pp. 1–8.
4. Jalal, A.; Uddin, M.Z.; Kim, J.T.; Kim, T.-S. Daily Human Activity Recognition Using Depth Silhouettes and R Transformation for Smart Home. In *International Conference on Smart Homes and Health Telematics*; Springer: Berlin/Heidelberg, Germany, 2011; Volume 6719, pp. 25–32.
5. Ahad, M.A.R.; Kobashi, S.; Tavares, J.M.R. Advancements of image processing and vision in healthcare. *J. Healthcare Eng.* **2018**, 1–3. [CrossRef] [PubMed]
6. Jalal, A.; Quaid, M.A.K.; Hasan, A.S. Wearable Sensor-Based Human Behaviour Understanding and Recognition in Daily Life for Smart Environments. In Proceedings of the International Conference on Frontiers of Information Technology (FIT), Islamabad, Pakistan, 18–20 December 2017; pp. 1–7.
7. Arora, S.J.; Singh, R.P. Automatic Speech Recognition: A Review. *Int. J. Comput. Appl.* **2012**, *60*, 34–44.
8. Chen, I.K.; Chi, C.Y.; Hsu, S.L.; Chen, L.G. A real-time system for object detection and location reminding with RGB-D camera. In Proceedings of the Conference on Consumer Electronics (ICCE), Las Vegas, NV, USA, 10–13 January 2014; pp. 1–2.
9. Kamal, S.; Jalal, A.; Kim, D. Depth Images-based Human Detection, Tracking and Activity Recognition Using Spatiotemporal Features and Modified HMM. *J. Electr. Eng. Technol.* **2016**, *11*, 1857–1862. [CrossRef]

10. Fonseca, L.M.G. Digital image processing in remote sensing. In Proceedings of the International Proceedings Conference on Computer Graphics and Image Processing, Rio de Janerio, Brazil, 11–14 October 2009; pp. 59–71.
11. Jalal, A.; Kim, Y. Ridge body parts features for human pose estimation and recognition from RGB-D video data. In Proceedings of the 5th International Conference on Computing, Communication and Networking Technologies (ICCCNT), Hefei, China, 11–13 July 2014; pp. 1–6.
12. Anusuya, M.A.; Katti, S.K. Speech Recognition by Machine: A Review. *Int. J. Comput. Sci. Inf. Secur.* **2009**, *4*, 181–205.
13. Rathore, M.M.U.; Ahmad, A.; Paul, A.; Wu, J. Real-time continuous feature extraction in large size satellite images. *J. Syst. Arch.* **2016**, *64*, 122–132. [CrossRef]
14. Farooq, A.; Jalal, A.; Kamal, S. Dense RGB-D Map-Based Human Tracking and Activity Recognition using Skin Joints Features and Self Organizing Map. *KSII Trans. Int. Inf. Syst.* **2015**, *9*, 1859–1869.
15. Jalal, A.; Kim, S. Global security using human face understanding under vision ubiquitous architecture system. *World Acad. Sci. Eng. Technol.* **2006**, *13*, 7–11.
16. Yoshimoto, H.; Date, N.; Yonemoto, S. Vision-based real-time motion capture system using multiple cameras. In Proceedings of the IEEE Conference on Multisensor Fusion and Integration for Intelligent Systems, Las Vegas, NV, USA, 7 October 2003; pp. 247–251.
17. Kamal, S.; Jalal, A. A hybrid feature extraction approach for human detection, tracking and activity recognition using depth sensors. *Arab. J. Sci. Eng.* **2016**, *41*, 1043–1051. [CrossRef]
18. Lam, M.W.; Chen, X.; Hu, S.; Yu, J.; Liu, X.; Meng, H. Gaussian process LSTM recurrent neural network language models for speech recognition. In Proceedings of the IEEE International Conference on Acoustics, Speech and Signal Processing, Brighton, UK, 12–17 May 2019; pp. 7235–7239.
19. Afouras, T. Deep audio-visual speech recognition. *IEEE Trans. Pattern Anal. Mach. Intell.* **2018**, *12*, 1–13. [CrossRef]
20. Kowsari, K.; Heidarysafa, M.; Brown, D.E.; Meimandi, K.J.; Barnes, L.E. Rmdl: Random multi model deep learning for classification. In Proceedings of the 2nd International Conference on Information System and Data Mining, Lakeland, FL, USA, 9–11 April 2018; pp. 19–28.
21. Kowsari, K.; Brown, D.E.; Heidarysafa, M.; Meimandi, K.J.; Gerber, M.S.; Barnes, L.E. Hdltex: Hierarchical deep learning for text classification. In Proceedings of the 16th IEEE International Conference on Machine Learning and Applications(ICMLA), Cancun, Mexico, 18–21 December 2017; Available online: https://arxiv.org/abs/1709.08267 (accessed on 1 February 2019).
22. Kowsari, K. Text classification algorithms: A survey. *Information* **2019**, *10*, 1–68. [CrossRef]
23. Hochreiter, S.; Schmidhuber, J. Long Short-Term Memory. *Neural Comput.* **1997**, *98*, 1735–1780. [CrossRef]
24. Kaisheng, Y. ; Deep-Gated Recurrent Neural Networks. *arXiv* **2015**, arXiv:1508.03790.
25. Koutnik, J.; Greff, K.; Gomez, F.; Schmidhuber, J. A Clockwork RNN. *arXiv* **2014**, arXiv:1402.3511.
26. Greff, K.; Srivastava, R.K.; Koutník, J.; Steunebrink, B.R.; Schmidhuber, J. LSTM: A Search Space Odyssey. *Trans. Neural Netw. Learn. Syst.* **2016**, *28*, 2222–2232. [CrossRef] [PubMed]
27. Jozefowicz, R.; Zaremba, W.; Sutskever, I. An Empirical Exploration of Recurrent Network Architectures. *Int. Conf. Mach. Learn.* **2015**, *37*, 2342–2350.
28. Gers, F.A.; Schmidhuber, J. Recurrent Nets that Time and Count. In Proceedings of the IEEE-INNS-ENNS International Joint Conference, Como, Italy, 24–27 July 2000; pp. 1–6.
29. Cho, K.; Van Merriënboer, B.; Gulcehre, C.; Bahdanau, D.; Bougares, F.; Schwenk, H.; Bengio, Y. Learning Phrase Representations using RNN Encoder-Decoder for Statistical Machine Translation. *arXiv* **2014**, arXiv:1406.1078.
30. Irie, K.; Tüske, Z.; Alkhouli, T.; Schlüter, R.; Ney, H. LSTM, GRU, Highway and a Bit of Attention: An Empirical Overview for Language Modelling in Speech Recognition. *Interspeech* **2016**, *9*, 3519–3523.
31. Piyathilaka, L.; Kodagoda, S. Gaussian mixture based HMM for human daily activity recognition using 3D skeleton features. In Proceedings of the International Conference on Industrial Electronics and Applications, Melborne, Australia, 19–21 June 2013; pp. 1–6.
32. Jalal, A.; Kamal, S.; Kim, D. A Depth Video Sensor-Based Life-Logging Human Activity Recognition System for Elderly Care in Smart Indoor Environments. *Sensors* **2014**, *14*, 11735–11759. [CrossRef] [PubMed]
33. Jalal, A.; Kim, Y.-H.; Kim, Y.-J.; Kamal, S.; Kim, D. Robust human activity recognition from depth video using spatiotemporal multi-fused features. *Pattern Recognit.* **2017**, *61*, 295–308. [CrossRef]

34. Jalal, A.; Kamal, S.; Kim, D. Individual detection-tracking-recognition using depth activity images. In Proceedings of the 12th International Conference on Ubiquitous Robots and Ambient Intelligence (URAI), Goyang City, Korea, 28–30 October 2015; pp. 450–455.
35. Wu, H.; Pan, W.; Xiong, X.; Xu, S. Human activity recognition based on the combined SVM&HMM. In Proceedings of the IEEE International Conference on Information and Automation (ICIA), Hailar, China, 28–30 July 2014; pp. 219–224.
36. Salor, Ö.; Pellom, B.; Çiloğlu, T.; Hacıoğlu, K.; Demirekler, M. On Developing New Text and Audio Corpora and Speech Recognition Tools for the Turkish Language. In Proceedings of the International Conference on Spoken Language Processing (ICSLP), Denver, CO, USA, 16–20 September 2002; pp. 1–5.
37. Salor, Ö.; Pellom, B.L.; Ciloglu, T.; Demirekler, M. Turkish speech corpora and recognition tools developed by porting SONIC: Towards multilingual speech recognition. *Comput. Speech Lang.* **2007**, *21*, 580–593. [CrossRef]
38. Garofolo, J.S.; Fisher, W.M.; Fiscus, J.G.; Pallett, D.S.; Dahlgren, N.L. *DARPA TIMIT: Acoustic-Phonetic Continuous Speech Corpus CD-ROM*; NIST: Gaithersburg, Maryland, USA, speech disc 1-1.1; 1993.
39. Liberman, M.; Cieri, C. The creation, distribution and use of linguistic data. In Proceedings of the First International Conference on Language Resources and Evaluation. European Language Resources Association, Granada, Spain, 28–30 May 1998; Available online: https://catalog.ldc.upenn.edu/ (accessed on 1 January 2017).
40. Akın, A.A.; Akın, M.D. Zemberek, an open source nlp framework for Turkic languages. *Structure* **2007**, *10*, 1–5.
41. Sak, H.; Güngör, T.; Saraçlar, M. Turkish language resources: Morphological parser, morphological disambiguator and web corpus. In *Advances in Natural Language Processing*; Springer: Berlin/Heidelberg, Germany, 2008; pp. 417–427.
42. Koopmann, J. Database Journal–The Knowledge Center for Database Professionals; 2003. Available online: https://www.postgresql.org/ (accessed on 1 January 2015).
43. Van Rossum, G. *Python*; Corporation for National Research Initiatives(CNRI): Reston, VA, USA, 1995; Available online: https://www.python.org/ (accessed on 5 January 2015).
44. McKerns, M.M.; Strand, L.; Sullivan, T.; Fang, A.; Aivazis, M.A. Building a framework for predictive science. In Proceedings of the 10th Python in Science Conference, Austin, TX, USA, 11–16 July 2011; Available online: https://pypi.org/project/dill (accessed on 10 January 2015).
45. McKerns, M.M.; Aivazis, M. Pathos: A Framework for Heterogeneous Computing. 2010. Available online: https://librosa.github.io/librosa/ (accessed on 15 January 2015).
46. Hettinger, R. Namedtuple Factory Function for Tuples with Named Fields. Available online: https://docs.python.org/2/library/collections.html (accessed on 17 January 2015).
47. Olpihant, T.E. Guide to Numpy. Ph.D. Thesis, MIT University, Cambridge, MA, USA, 2006. Available online: https://www.numpy.org/ (accessed on 15 February 2017).
48. Lyons, J. Python Speech Features. 2013. Available online: https://python-speech-features.readthedocs.io/en/latest/ (accessed on 15 February 2017).
49. Abadi, M.; Barham, P.; Chen, J.; Chen, Z.; Davis, A.; Dean, J.; Devin, M.; Ghemawat, S.; Irving, G.; Isard, M.; et al. Tensorflow: A system for large-scale machine learning. In Proceedings of the 12th USENIX Symposium on Operating Systems Design and Implementation (OSDI 16), Savannah, GA, USA, 2–4 November 2016; Available online: https://www.tensorflow.org/install/pip (accessed on 20 February 2017).
50. Levenshtein, V.I. Binary codes capable of correcting deletions, insertions, and reversals. *Sov. Phys. Dokl.* **1996**, *10*, 707–710.
51. Damerau, F.J. A technique for computer detection and correction of spelling errors. *Commun. ACM* **1964**, *7*, 171–176. [CrossRef]
52. Jaro, M.A. Advances in record linkage methodology as applied to the 1985 census of Tampa Florida. *J. Stat. Assoc.* **1989**, *84*, 414–420. [CrossRef]
53. Winkler, W.E. String Comparator Metrics and Enhanced Decision Rules in the Fellegi-Sunter Model of Record Linkage. In Proceedings of the Section on Survey Research Methods. American Statistical Association, Washington, DC, USA, 1990, 10 January 1990; pp. 354–359.
54. Aldous, D.; Diaconis, P. Longest increasing subsequences: from patience sorting to the Baik–Deift–Johansson theorem. *Bull. Am. Math. Soc.* **1999**, *36*, 413–432. [CrossRef]

55. Singhal, A. Modern Information Retrieval: A Brief Overview. *Bull. IEEE Comput. Soc. Tech. Comm. Data Eng.* **2001**, *24*, 35–43.
56. Lu, J.; Lin, C.; Wang, W.; Li, C.; Wang, H. String similarity measures and joins with synonyms. In Proceedings of the 2013 ACM SIGMOD International Conference on Management of Data, New York, NY, USA, 22–27 June 2013; pp. 373–384.
57. Siderite Zackwehdex. Super Fast and Accurate String Distance Algorithm: Sift4. Available online: https://siderite.blogspot.com/2014/11/super-fast-and-accurate-string-distance.html (accessed on 11 November 2017).
58. Keser, S.; Edizkan, R. Phonem-Based Isolated Turkish Word Recognition with Subspace Classifier. In Proceedings of the IEEE Signal Processing and Communications Applications Conference (SIU), Antalya, Turkey, 9–11 April 2009; pp. 93–96.
59. Aksoylar, C.; Mutluergil, S.O.; Erdogan, H. The Anatomy of a Turkish Speech Recognition System. In Proceedings of the IEEE Signal Processing and Communications Applications Conference (SIU), Antalya, Turkey, 9–11 April 2009; pp. 512–515.
60. Çiloğlu, T.; Çömez, M.; Şahin, S. Language Modelling for Turkish as a Agglutinative Languages. In Proceedings of the IEEE Signal Processing and Communications Applications Conference (SIU), Kuşadası, Turkey, 28–30 April 2004; pp. 1–2.
61. Büyük, O.; Erdoğan, H.; Oflazer, K. Using Hybrid Lexicon Units and Incorporating Language Constraints in Speech Recognition. In Proceedings of the IEEE Signal Processing and Communications Applications Conference, Kayseri, Turkey, 16–18 May 2005; pp. 111–114.
62. Jalal, A.; Quaid, M.A.; Sidduqi, M.A. A Triaxial Acceleration-based Human Motion Detection for Ambient Smart Home System. *Int. Conf. Appl. Sci. Technol.* **2019**, *7*, 1–6.
63. Ahmad, J. Robust spatio-temporal features for human interaction recognition via artificial neural network. In Proceedings of the IEEE Conference on International Conference on Frontiers of Information Technology, Islamabad, Pakistan, 18–20 December 2018.
64. Jalal, A.; Uddin, M.Z.; Kim, J.T.; Kim, T.S. Recognition of Human Home Activities via Depth Silhouettes and R Transformation for Smart Homes. *Indoor Built Environ.* **2012**, *21*, 184–190. [CrossRef]
65. Jalal, A.; Rasheed, Y.A. Collaboration achievement along with performance maintenance in video streaming. In Proceedings of the IEEE Conference on Interactive Computer Aided Learning, Villach, Austria, 26–28 September 2007; pp. 1–8.

© 2019 by the authors. Licensee MDPI, Basel, Switzerland. This article is an open access article distributed under the terms and conditions of the Creative Commons Attribution (CC BY) license (http://creativecommons.org/licenses/by/4.0/).

Article

LSTM-Based Deep Learning Model for Predicting Individual Mobility Traces of Short-Term Foreign Tourists

Alessandro Crivellari * and Euro Beinat

Department of Geoinformatics—Z_GIS, University of Salzburg, 5020 Salzburg, Austria; euro.beinat@sbg.ac.at
* Correspondence: alessandro.crivellari@sbg.ac.at

Received: 27 October 2019; Accepted: 26 December 2019; Published: 1 January 2020

Abstract: The increasing availability of trajectory recordings has led to the mining of a massive amount of historical track data, allowing for a better understanding of travel behaviors by revealing meaningful motion patterns. In the context of human mobility analysis, the problem of motion prediction assumes a central role and is beneficial for a wide range of applications, including for touristic purposes, such as personalized services or targeted recommendations, and sustainability studies related to crowd management and resource redistribution. This paper tackles a particular case of the trajectory prediction problem, focusing on large-scale mobility traces of short-term foreign tourists. These sparse trajectories, short and non-repetitive, lack spatial and temporal regularity, making prediction analysis based on individual historical motion data unreliable. To face this issue, we hereby propose a deep learning-based approach, taking into account the collective mobility of tourists over the territory. The underlying semantics of motion patterns are captured by means of a long short-term memory (LSTM) neural network model trained on pre-processed location sequences, aiming to predict the next visited place in the trajectory. We tested the methodology on a real-world big dataset, demonstrating its higher feasibility with respect to traditional approaches.

Keywords: deep learning; LSTM; neural networks; location prediction; trajectories; smart tourism

1. Introduction

Human mobility analysis has gained increasing popularity due to the recent growth in people's location information availability in the form of massive trajectory data sets. Motion behaviors can be passively collected by mobile phones in terms of cell tower connection or GPS signal, or even actively shared by users on social media platforms. These large volumes of geo-located data enable the opportunity to reveal and integrate motion patterns in a wide variety of contexts [1,2], from recommendation systems [3,4] to mobility modeling applications for smart city and smart enterprise [5,6].

The rise of positioning technology and motion data availability has particularly boosted location prediction analysis, which has become a very active research area in the big picture of location-based services. Location prediction is interpreted as inferring the short-term future location of an individual, leveraging his/her current place, past motion activity, and possibly additional side information. Depending on the context, it may imply very different problems and approaches, comprising motion flow modeling [7–9], individual large-scale mobility analysis [10–12], and very fine resolution systems [13–15].

While the majority of works dealing with the prediction of individual mobility traces are set in contexts with a high level of spatial and temporal regularity (e.g., motion activity of users in everyday life), our paper contributes to extend trajectory prediction analysis in the opposite direction, when individual motion regularity is lacking due to the non-repetitiveness of single mobility traces.

Our focus and intended application is related to tourists' mobility within the growing field of smart tourism. Smart tourism integrates tourism resources with information technologies to design intelligent services to provide valuable outcomes to tourists and tourism-related industries. The development of smart tourism is particularly embodied in four main aspects, namely tourism experience, tourism management, tourism service, and tourism marketing [16–19]. The tracking and recording activity of space-time paths of individual tourists is inserted in this big wave of tourism mining, not as an ultimate purpose, but as a mean of providing valuable knowledge of tourists' mobility and travel behaviors. However, although spatial-temporal trajectory data have been widely utilized in studies of tourists' behavior, their use has been mainly limited to descriptive purposes at the level of clustering and pattern analysis [20–23]. But if forestalling actions require consideration, predictive investigations become an essential tool.

Our case study targets short-term tourists in a foreign country. Foreign tourism is major source of income for the tourism industry and it is an area of investigation for public and private organizations. Most destination strategies define measures specifically designed for foreign tourists, which have different behaviors and spending patterns compared to domestic users. For this reason, the unfolding of their tourism experience is used to understand and possibly leverage the insights to improve tourism policies and decision-making.

While in everyday life a person's mobility is described by a significant probability of returning to a limited number of highly frequented locations (e.g., home and workplace) [24–26], the natural characterization of foreign tourists' motion behavior is based on short and non-repetitive trajectories of users moving in areas they have never been to. The lack of individual historical location data leads methods relying on a set of individual pre-recorded motion trajectories to performing poorly when applied to traces covering areas that are unfamiliar to the user; a prediction algorithm solely based on a sequential approximation of a single probability distribution is not effective in this case. In addition, the focus on large-scale mobility often implies a very wide territory, introducing further problems such as trajectory data sparseness and a multitude of locations, involving the curse of dimensionality.

The proposed method aims to overcome these issues with the use of a deep learning-based approach that leverages the collective mobility of users over the territory. The method consists of a long short-term memory (LSTM) neural network trained on pre-processed location sequences to learn the underlying patterns of tourists' motion activity. Original traces are first transformed into discrete location sequences, and are subsequently fed into a deep neural network model composed of embedding and LSTM layers. The model captures motion patterns directly from mobility traces, without requiring any manual feature extraction. Each individual user's mobility prediction is therefore based on the collective analysis of tourists' behavior over the territory. For a wider application in various contexts, we do not resort to any additional information besides the users' motion traces, since useful secondary information is not available in many cases. In this way, the model can be applied to a variety of geo-located data types, as long as the recorded positional data generated by users can be properly organized into mobility traces in the form of sequences of locations.

Experiments on a real-world large-scale big dataset prove the higher feasibility of our forecasting method with respect to traditional approaches in this mobility regime, standing out as a potentially beneficial methodology for many real-life applications, including touristic services for personalized recommendations, targeted advertisement, and sustainability studies related to crowd management and resource redistribution. In general, this study contributes to the expansion of tourists' mobility analysis in the direction of actively integrating artificial intelligence into the tourism sector.

2. Related Work

The rise of motion data availability has boosted the interest in human mobility analysis, establishing various methods for trajectory data mining [27,28] to either describe the observable motion behavior [29] or to predict future activities [30].

Location prediction has a central role in human mobility analysis and is applied to numerous tasks such as crowd management, congestion prediction, transportation planning, and place recommender systems [31,32]. In the past few years, plenty of predictive models have been suggested, leveraging various methods including Markov models [33,34] and data mining approaches [35–37]. Previous research on location prediction can be roughly split into two broad groups: motion regularity-based methods and multiple mobility-based methods.

The first group is based on the regularity of individual user's motion history. Since most people tend to follow regular motion patterns in daily life, often returning to the same few locations, their personal past mobility is a valuable factor to predict their future trajectories [24–26]. Therefore, the majority of works on predicting a person's next visited location rely on historical motion data collected from this person exclusively, evaluating the regularity patterns in human mobility by learning individual, frequent traveling routes [38,39]. In this sense, the most common approach is the use of Markov models, representing locations as states and movement between locations as transitions [11,12,40]. States are defined by partitioning space into grids or reference points, and transition probabilities are defined by counting each user's transitions, identifying the most likely next destinations for each current location. This type of model achieves good performances in the presence of long, pre-recorded motion trajectories of the particular user under study.

The second group comprises methodologies combining individual past locations with collective motion information from multiple users. A subgroup is represented by collaborative filtering to find similarities among users' preferences in frequently visited destinations [41]. This includes methods for classifying users' preferences into point of interest categories [42] and recommendation systems based on generic, top interesting places or personalized location matching [43]. Another subgroup focuses on geographical elements, predicting the next locations based on the definition of features for each place and the relationships between places. These methodologies do not model individual preferences or similar preferences among users, but make predictions by using geographical statistics [44,45]. A final subgroup includes motion pattern mining techniques and prediction algorithms combining individual current movements with historical collective data to find frequent patterns and co-occurrences of locations. The methods comprise ensemble probabilistic algorithms [46,47], feature-based machine learning methodologies [48,49], and deep learning models [50,51] to predict users' locations over time, based on individual and collective behaviors.

In general, when people rarely share their history of past visited places with other users, location prediction methods based on previously seen locations of an individual user are likely to be chosen over other methodologies. However, in the case of irregular individual motion patterns, short data history users, and non-repetitive mobility behaviors, prediction algorithms approximating single probability distributions are not reliable and multiple mobility-based methods may be preferred. Moreover, it is worth mentioning that a large number of methods enrich trajectories with further context data, such as prior knowledge of motion information (e.g., acceleration, orientation) [11], external data (e.g., weather, social media analysis) [52,53], or user-specific features (e.g., home and workplace, user specific preferences) [44,54–57]. In these cases, the main disadvantage is of a practical nature, since secondary information is often insufficient or not available.

Over the last decades, academics and practitioners have increasingly approached the study of tourists' movements [20,58,59] and how to guide practical measures based on these findings [60–62]. Most studies focused on mapping and modeling movements between locations [21,63], as tourist destinations are involved in a complementary relationship [64,65]. These include travel itinerary models [66] and spatial pattern examination of travel flows [67,68], often leveraging a variety of measures within the study framework [21,69]. Only few studies, however, exclusively involved international visitors [70,71]. While the interest in mining movement patterns of tourists has been prominent, and studies are developing fast for collectively estimating the overall amount of visitors within single destinations [72], the explicit prediction of individual short-term tourists' mobility traces still requires further expansion, being mainly based on Markov approaches for modeling location transitions [47,58,59].

This paper therefore introduces a deep learning model to predict individual trajectories of short-term foreign tourists. Its characteristics comprise: leveraging the collective mobility of people to predict individual traces, falling in the category of multiple mobility-based algorithms; learning mobility patterns without any manual feature extraction or secondary context data by simply feeding the model with sequences of locations, from a purely data-driven perspective; explicitly designed to predict the next location of a user, specifically when a very short data history is known about that user. The use of LSTM is tested in this particular mobility regime of short and non-repetitive traces to assess its feasibility when applied to large-scale movements of visitors in a foreign country.

3. Methodology

The proposed prediction method aims to model patterns hidden in the historical motion data of multiple people, in order to identify the most likely future movement of an individual user. Given a short mobility trace sampled at a given time step, the solution of our model consists of inferring the future visited location in the next time step. This section reports the details of the proposed methodology, from trajectory pre-processing to deep learning modeling.

3.1. Trajectory Pre-Processing

The first step of the path from original mobility traces to location prediction is characterized by trajectory discretization, a pre-processing phase transforming raw traces into the input for the neural network model.

An original mobility trace is described by a series of chronologically ordered track points $T = \{p_i | i = 1, 2, 3, \ldots, N\}$, generated by an individual user, whereby each point is defined by a coordinate pair enriched with a time stamp $p_i = (lon_i, lat_i, t_i)$. The trajectory discretization task consists of aggregating continuous values of longitude and latitude into discrete locations and transforming the continuity of time into fixed time steps. This results in a pre-processed trajectory in the form of a sequence of locations $(LOC_1, LOC_2, \ldots, LOC_N)$, where, given a time step unit t, locations refer to time $(t, 2t, \ldots, Nt)$. Time information is therefore encoded in the position along the sequence and the location associated to each time step is chosen as the one identified by the majority of track points recorded within that time period. The length of the time step is case specific, depending on the data source and the prediction problem: a short unit increases fragmentation in the presence of discontinuous traces and low time resolution data, a long unit may compromise a proper trajectory representation affecting prediction results. Moreover, even spatial resolution varies according to the data source, and may be further discretized (e.g., through clustering, reference point definition, and grid-based approaches) in relation to the time resolution and the specific purpose of different applications (e.g., prediction of motion traces over a whole country or mining city-level mobility). This is particularly suggested when trajectories are very sparse and there are many locations with only very few occurrences. In addition, because human mobility is not generally uniformly distributed over the territory, locations that are potentially inaccessible or irrelevant should be discarded; only those locations that are seen by a sufficient amount of people should be considered, avoiding bias samples in the data and worthless computational effort. The result should consist of a set of fixed points (or areas) over the territory, each of them associated with a particular unique identifier. A pre-processed trajectory is made of a sequence of these discrete locations unfolding in fixed time steps.

3.2. Deep Learning Model for Trajectory Prediction

The collection of the pre-processed trajectories from multiple users, in the form of sequences of unique location identifiers, is used as input data to the deep neural network model. The model is made of three building blocks: an embedding layer, a block of one or more LSTM layers, and a softmax layer. Each location identifier is initially associated to a particular corresponding embedding vector, encoding input trajectories into sequences of embeddings that are subsequently fed to the LSTM block, made of stacked LSTM neural network layers. The final trajectory representation, output vector of the last LSTM layer, becomes the input of a softmax layer for generating the probability distribution of the next predicted location in the trace. A graphic exemplifying overview of the whole model, with a block of two LSTM layers, is illustrated in Figure 1.

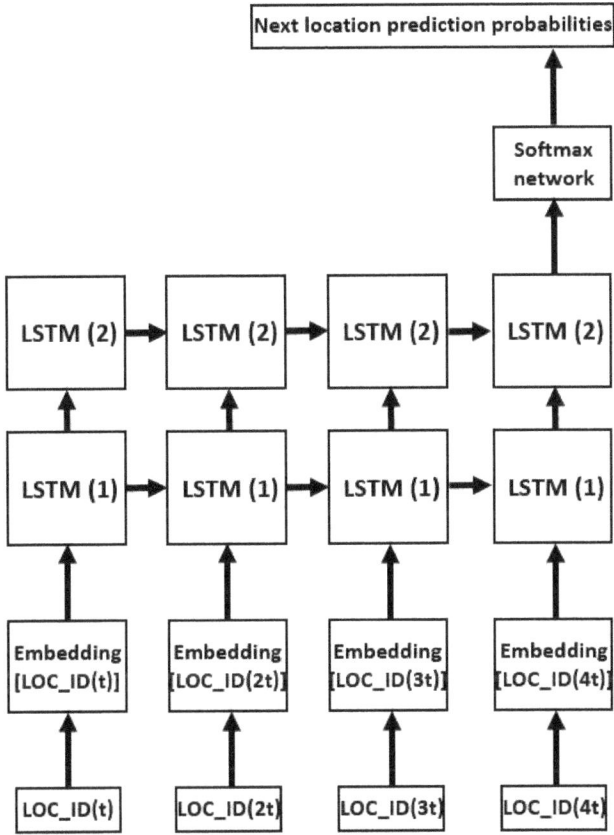

Figure 1. Exemplifying overview of the deep neural network model using a block of two long short-term memory (LSTM) layers and a four-location trajectory.

3.2.1. Embedding Layer

To limit the problems of the curse of dimensionality, trajectory sparseness, and computational inefficiency, we replace traditional representations such as one-hot by associating each discrete location with a low-dimensional dense vector (embedding). This is done by means of an embedding layer, transforming sequences of discrete location identifiers into sequences of dense vectors before they are fed to the LSTM block, as depicted in Figure 2. In particular, each location is initially defined by a random vector of a pre-defined size, whose values are updated during the training process; just like other model parameters, embeddings are tweaked, through backpropagation, on the basis of the prediction outcomes. Over training, they assume a meaningful mathematical representation as vectors of continuous values, whereby locations that are often co-occurring in the same traces share similar representations in this embedding space.

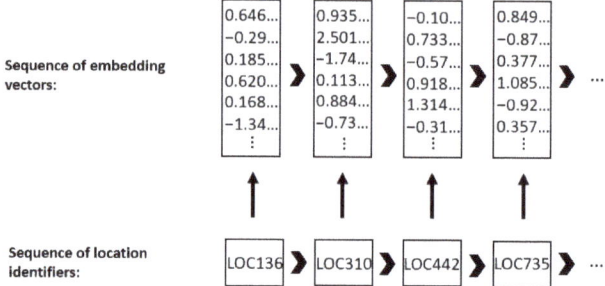

Figure 2. Embedding layer representation: from a sequence of discrete locations to a sequence of dense vectors.

3.2.2. LSTM Block

The next stage consists of the LSTM block. LSTM [73] is a complex recurrent neural network type, whose repeating module is composed of four different neural networks interacting between each other. The network processes an input sequence one element at a time, receiving, at each step, two sources of input data: the current vector of the data sequence concatenated with the output vector of the network module at the previous step. The information flows through the network modules, encoded in the cell state, and is modified by the four neural network structures until the end of the sequence is reached. The output at the last step is the final vector characterization of the sequence, which is subsequently used for the actual prediction task. If the LSTM block contains multiple LSTM layers, the final trajectory vector is represented as the output, at the last step, of the last layer. In general, the first LSTM layer is fed with the input sequence, the second layer is fed with the output of the first layer, and so on. Figure 3 displays a visual representation of the LSTM block; the example shows the last two steps of an embedding sequence and a block of two LSTM layers.

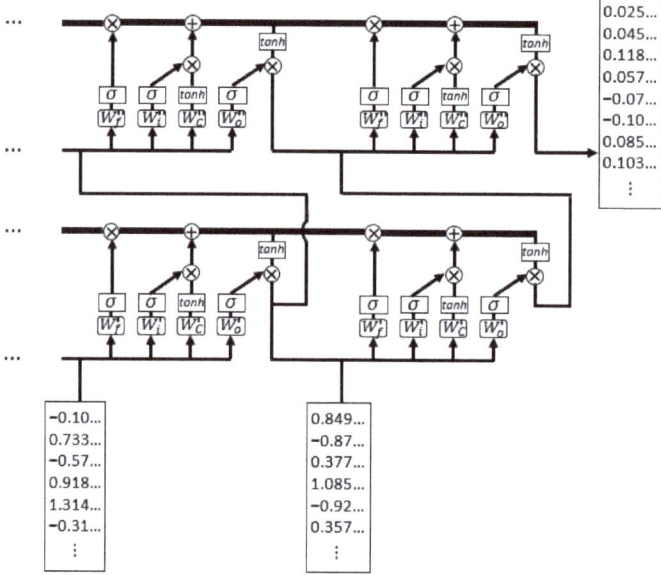

Figure 3. Visual representation of the last two steps of an LSTM block composed of two LSTM layers: the lower vectors represent the input embeddings; the vector on the upper right represents the final trajectory characterization.

Equations (1)–(6) report the formulas describing the functioning of a repeating module of LSTM, given an input vector x_t; the forget gate (1) defines the information to be deleted from the cell state; the input gate (2) decides which values to update; the tanh network (3) determines a vector of new values to be added to the state; the new cell state (4) is obtained by filtering the old cell state through the forget gate, and by adding the combination outcome between the input gate and the tanh network; the output gate (5) defines which parts of the cell state to output; and the final LSTM output (6) results from the multiplication between the output gate and the tanh of the new cell state.

$$f_t = \sigma\left(W_f \cdot [h_{t-1}, x_t] + b_f\right) \tag{1}$$

$$i_t = \sigma(W_i \cdot [h_{t-1}, x_t] + b_i) \tag{2}$$

$$\widetilde{C}_t = \tanh(W_C \cdot [h_{t-1}, x_t] + b_C) \tag{3}$$

$$C_t = f_t * C_{t-1} + i_t * \widetilde{C}_t \tag{4}$$

$$o_t = \sigma(W_o \cdot [h_{t-1}, x_t] + b_o) \tag{5}$$

$$h_t = o_t * \tanh(C_t) \tag{6}$$

3.2.3. Softmax Layer

The predicted next location is explicitly disclosed by means of a softmax layer on top of the LSTM block. The softmax layer is a simple, fully-connected neural network followed by a softmax activation function. It receives the final trajectory vector characterization as an input, and outputs the predicted probability distribution for the next potential location, as shown in Figure 4.

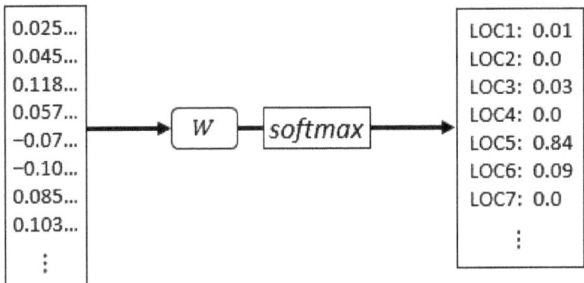

Figure 4. Softmax layer representation transforming the output vector of the LSTM block into the probability distribution of the potential predicted location.

Equation (7) reports the description of the softmax layer, where h_{last} represents the output of the last LSTM layer at the last step and n_LOC is the total number of locations.

$$(LOC = j \mid h_{last}) = \frac{\exp\left(W_j h'_{last} + b_j\right)}{\sum_{k=1}^{n\_LOC} \exp(W_k h'_{last} + b_k)} \tag{7}$$

3.2.4. Model Training

Prior to being fed into the neural network model, location sequences are scanned by a sliding window, determining the training features and the target variable. The window moves forward by one location until the end of each sequence, defining multiple segments of fixed length as input sequences to the deep learning model. The segment length represents the amount of past motion activity taken into account for learning to predict the future location (e.g., predicting the next location based on the last six hours of a user's mobility). Its choice, besides strongly depending on the applications and dataset restrictions, is closely related to the time resolution of the sequence, whereby a higher time resolution determines a larger number of locations describing the past motion activity.

The deep learning model is fed with a collection of these segments, where, for example, a window length equal to four locations would define a sequence (LOC_{t-3}, LOC_{t-2}, LOC_{t-1}, LOC_t) as input features to the model and the location LOC_{t+1} as the target variable. The model training maximizes the log probability, with respect to the weights of every layer (embedding, LSTM, and softmax), of observing the correct next location, given the sequence of past locations. The process relies on backpropagation and mini-batch stochastic training to determine in which direction the weights are adjusted.

The prediction of a location sequence is therefore based on the collective historical mobility of people, identifying the most likely next location as the one having the highest probability according to the output of the model.

4. Experiment

The current section introduces the dataset used for the prediction task and reports the description and results of the experiments conducted. A particular focus is given to the evaluation of results, which are compared to traditional approaches and are analyzed according to different motion characteristics. The proposed model was implemented and executed on TensorFlow (Google Brain, Mountain View, CA, USA), using AWS EC2 p3.2xlarge GPU instance.

4.1. Dataset

To properly describe the general large-scale motion activity of foreign tourists, we used a real-world dataset comprising seven months of anonymized mobile phone call detailed records (CDRs) of roamers in Italy. In order to present meaningful findings, it is indeed important, especially when dealing with wide territories, to make use of a sufficiently large and complete dataset, whose trajectories redundantly cover the study area. CDRs have been widely used in human mobility studies [74–77], reporting the detected mobile phone activities enriched with the time stamp and the position of the device in terms of the coverage area of the principal antenna. We only took into account short-term visitors, recorded to be located in the country for a maximum of two weeks. In addition, we discarded those users that appeared to be completely stationary. Foreign visitors' mobility was therefore represented by short traces and non-repetitive behaviors.

The erratic profile of mobile activity, represented by sparse connection events, may critically fragment mobility traces, making it difficult to create continuous location sequences. To limit the fragmentation problem and define proper trajectories, we pre-processed traces into sequences unfolded in 1 h time step; the prediction problem is formulated as predicting the location of a user in the next hour. In particular, if more than one track point was recorded in the same hour, the location associated to the majority of those recordings was chosen to identify the current position of the user. Given the wide territory, the choice of the time step unit, and our focus on large-scale movements, a minimum spatial resolution of 2 km was selected. Reference points were defined as the antennas subjected to the highest number of connections within the minimum spatial resolution, projecting the other ones to the closest reference point. Furthermore, we discarded very rare locations, identified by just a few tens of recorded events. Being mostly randomly visited, they are not significantly involved in the overall travel behavior of foreign visitors in Italy. Nevertheless, specific characteristics of different datasets may provide an influence on parameters such as time and space resolution, and a choice of different values can be suitable for different applications.

The final dataset consists of 1 h encoded sequences of 5903 possible unique locations over the Italian territory. To appropriately focus on short motion behaviors and to make complete and proper utilization of the dataset, represented by relatively short continuous traces, we set a window length equal to 6 h (6 locations), determining a total of 13 million trajectory segments (with a median displacement per segment of 36.1 km) generated by 1.4 million users. We believe this large amount of data is representative of the overall real motion behavior of foreign tourists.

4.2. Experimental Settings

We designed the neural network model using an embedding size of 100 dimensions and a block of two LSTM layers having a hidden size of 4000 neurons each. The training process was based on cross-entropy cost function, mini-batches, and Adam optimizer [78]. To evaluate the performance of the model on previously unseen data, we randomly split the dataset into a training set and a test set, containing 80% and 20% of the users, respectively.

For a better evaluation of the results, we compared the achieved prediction accuracy with traditional approaches involving the use of Markov modeling, which is widely applied in location prediction problems. Locations are represented as states and movements between locations as state transitions. The creation of a transition matrix identifies the most likely next destinations for each current location [33]. We reported three different Markov model types as comparison baselines for our methodology:

- Personal Markov model. Transition probabilities were calculated by counting each single user's transitions, modeling individual movement patterns.
- Global Markov model. First-order probability distributions were calculated by counting the collective state transitions of all users, modeling collective movement patterns.
- Variable-order global Markov model. The principle of the longest match was applied to select which global Markov model order to adopt to calculate the transition probabilities; for a given location sequence, the collective prediction probability distribution was computed on the set of training sequences matching its longest suffix.

4.3. Results

Table 1 reports the comparison results in terms of accuracy and accuracy in top 3 (if the correct label corresponds to one of the top three predicted locations, the accuracy is 1, otherwise it is 0; the result is the average for each testing trajectory). Our model (LSTM) outperformed the Markov approaches, yielding a 5% improvement compared to the best baseline, the global Markov model (GMM), 10% improvement compared to the variable-order Markov model (VGMM), and 33% to the personal Markov model (PMM). The accuracy in top 3 confirmed this trend, showing a 7% improvement of our model with respect to GMM, 8% to VGMM, and 47% to PMM.

Table 1. Overall performance comparison between our methodology (LSTM) and the Markov baseline approaches, namely personal Markov model (PMM), global Markov model (GMM), and variable-order global Markov model (VGMM).

	Accuracy	Accuracy in Top 3
PMM	0.3373	0.3717
GMM	0.4822	0.6508
VGMM	0.4553	0.6445
LSTM	0.5076	0.7013

Reasonably, PMM, which was solely based on individual mobility and ignored the collective motion behavior, had the lowest scores in this regime of short and non-repetitive traces. GMM and VGMM, which considered the collective mobility of all users, greatly improved performances, with the first-order model surpassing the variable-order model. LSTM determined a further increment, exceeding the best baseline of 2.5 percentage points in terms of accuracy and 5 percentage points in terms of accuracy in top 3.

Moreover, we analyzed how different trajectory characteristics affect prediction. The idea was to evaluate the influence of different values of motion features, such as the traveled distance and radius of gyration, on the prediction performances.

Table 2 shows the accuracy and accuracy in top 3 (in brackets) for different values of traveled distance within six hours prior to prediction. Five bins were selected: ≤10 km, 10–25 km, 25–50 km, 50–100 km, and ≥100 km. Comparing accuracy, despite an overall tendency of decreasing performance when the traveled distance increases, PMM always performed very poorly, while GMM and VGMM achieved remarkable results for mid and short distances, respectively. In particular, GMM substantially outperformed VGMM for mid-range values (10–100 km), but was overcome by the latter for very short distances (≤10 km). LSTM always exceeded every baseline, even if it only slightly outperformed GMM for mid-short distance values (10–50 km). It is worth noticing how LSTM largely overcame the other methods for very long distances (≥100 km). Moreover, its accuracy in top 3 was consistently much higher than every baseline for each distance bin.

Table 2. Accuracy (and accuracy in top 3 in brackets) comparison for different values of traveled distance.

Trav. Dist. =	≤10 km	10–25 km	25–50 km	50–100 km	≥100 km
PMM	0.4645 (0.5088)	0.4240 (0.4901)	0.3260 (0.3639)	0.2613 (0.2796)	0.1665 (0.1689)
GMM	0.5495 (0.7805)	0.5648 (0.7412)	0.4988 (0.6534)	0.4494 (0.5845)	0.3391 (0.4582)
VGMM	0.5788 (0.7945)	0.5033 (0.7201)	0.4312 (0.6270)	0.3979 (0.5656)	0.3212 (0.4630)
LSTM	0.5938 (0.8172)	0.5696 (0.7933)	0.5061 (0.7036)	0.4633 (0.6293)	0.3803 (0.5270)

Table 3 reports the accuracies for different values of radius of gyration (ROG), in bins of ≤3 km, 3–10 km, 10–32 km, and ≥32 km. These results reinforce the observations reported in the previous case, such as the general tendency of decreasing performance as the ROG value increases, the overall poor achievements of PMM, the good results of VGMM for very small values (≤3 km), and the remarkable performance of GMM for mid-range values (3–32 km). Again, LSTM always outperformed the baselines, only slightly beating the GMM accuracy for the 3–10 km bin, but greatly overcoming the other methods for very large ROG values (≥32 km). As in the traveled distance case, its accuracy in top 3 was consistently much higher than the baselines for each of the ROG bins.

Table 3. Accuracy (and accuracy in top 3 in brackets) comparison for different values of radius of gyration.

ROG =	≤3 km	3–10 km	10–32 km	≥32 km
PMM	0.4539 (0.5213)	0.3650 (0.4078)	0.2974 (0.3089)	0.1880 (0.1899)
GMM	0.5496 (0.7859)	0.5246 (0.6880)	0.4719 (0.6038)	0.3548 (0.4729)
VGMM	0.5661 (0.7923)	0.4578 (0.6668)	0.4218 (0.5846)	0.3371 (0.4781)
LSTM	0.5891 (0.8229)	0.5299 (0.7480)	0.4849 (0.6426)	0.3955 (0.5404)

In addition, we observed the prediction variability at different hours of the day. Figure 5 displays the accuracy and accuracy in top 3 of the four methods over time, starting from midnight. Rush hours in the afternoon appeared to be more predictable than the ones in the morning, while accuracies significantly increased in the evening and night due to the higher regularity of mobility patterns during these hours. LSTM was shown to outperform the baselines for every hour of the day.

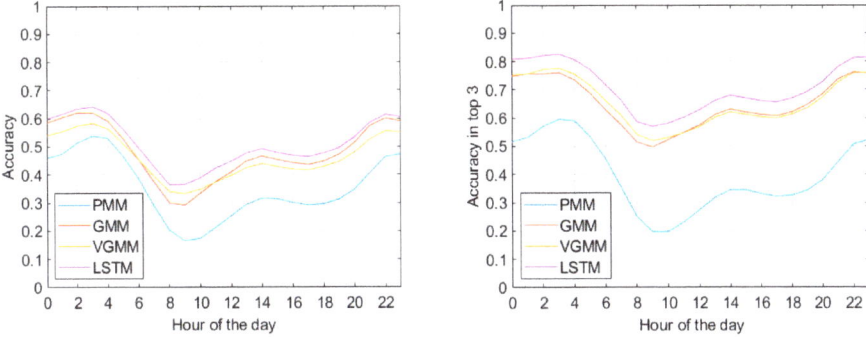

Figure 5. Prediction accuracy (on the left) and accuracy in top 3 (on the right) with respect to the hour of the day.

Performances were further explored based on the imbalance of the dataset, by evaluating results corresponding to popular and rare locations. Table 4 reports the accuracies for different ranges of location occurrences in the data, defining frequently visited locations and less visited ones. The columns from left to right identify specific groups of locations, where each location of each group represents, respectively, over 0.5% of the whole dataset, between 0.1% and 0.5%, between 0.05% and 0.1%, and less than 0.05%. As expected, there is a general drop of performance when passing from popular locations to rare ones. However, the superiority of LSTM is once again clearly exhibited.

Table 4. Accuracy (and accuracy in top 3 in brackets) comparison for visited locations in different ranges of occurrence in the data. The percentage value in the first row refers to the amount of occurrences of each location in that column with respect to the whole dataset.

Amount of Data:	≥0.5%	0.1–0.5%	0.05–0.1%	≤0.05%
PMM	0.5169 (0.5485)	0.3809 (0.4147)	0.3280 (0.3600)	0.2624 (0.2986)
GMM	0.6872 (0.9305)	0.5398 (0.7659)	0.4745 (0.6511)	0.3925 (0.5095)
VGMM	0.7172 (0.9146)	0.5448 (0.7624)	0.4462 (0.6456)	0.3336 (0.5049)
LSTM	0.7372 (0.9459)	0.6024 (0.8210)	0.5039 (0.7151)	0.3925 (0.5660)

Finally, we focused on the prediction errors to study the performance of our model in the particular case when it was not able to correctly identify the future visited location. We compared LSTM with GMM, the best baseline in terms of accuracy, to assess how their predicted locations differed when a misprediction occurred in both models. Figure 6 reports the bar graphs representing the error distance distribution of the segments that are wrongly predicted by both models. The error distance was calculated as the absolute distance between the wrongly predicted location and the real future location (to calculate the error distance of wrong predictions in top 3, we considered the predicted location, within the first three, having the shortest distance with the real location). The bar graphs highlight the overall tendency of LSTM to make mistakes with a shorter error distance than GMM.

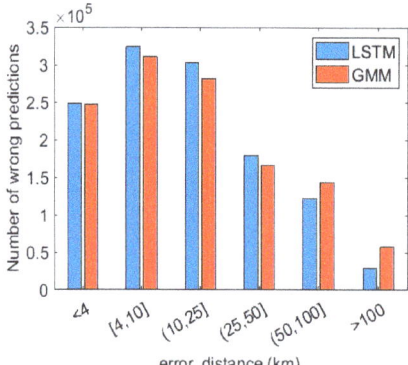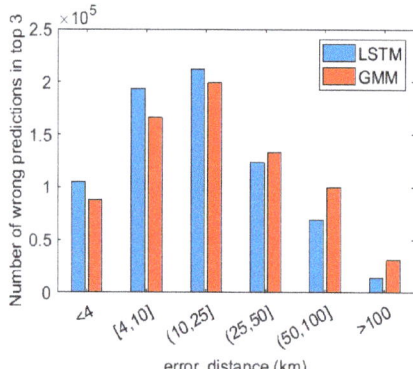

Figure 6. Bar graphs representing the error distance distribution of LSTM and global Markov model (GMM) when both models predicted wrongly (wrong predictions in the left graph, wrong predictions in top 3 in the right graph).

We also studied the difference of error distance between the two prediction models, analyzing the corresponding mispredictions on the same segment. The bar graphs in Figure 7 display the subtraction $error\_distance(GMM) - error\_distance(LSTM)$ for wrong predictions and wrong predictions in top 3; a negative value indicates that the baseline provided a shorter error distance on a wrongly predicted segment; a positive value is in favor of our model. As depicted by the high bars on the right part of both graphs, there were a remarkable number of samples on which GMM tended to make prediction mistakes in the order of a few tens of km more than LSTM. Overall, our model, besides the higher prediction accuracy, also presented better results in terms of the shortest error distance.

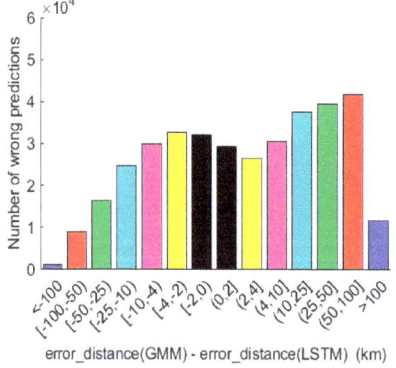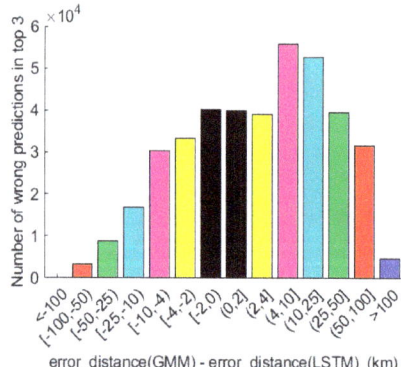

Figure 7. Bar graphs representing the difference of error distance between GMM and LSTM when both models predicted wrongly (wrong predictions in the left graph, wrong predictions in top 3 in the right graph).

4.4. Discussion

We proposed a method to predict individual mobility traces of short-term foreign tourists leveraging the collective large-scale motion behavior of people and a deep learning-based methodology adapted to process motion trajectories. The model relies on a recurrent neural network architecture composed of embedding and LSTM layers. We assessed the feasibility of such methodology on short, non-repetitive traces, revealing its potentiality for human mobility studies and applications.

In particular, our method was shown to outperform the widely used Markov model approaches based on location transition probabilities. The results reported how a probabilistic approach built on the motion behavior of a single individual performs very poorly in this mobility regime, proving the need for collective motion information. This collective mobility, however, consists of non-repetitive traces that clearly influence prediction performances; the simpler first-order Markov model generally overcame the variable-order model based on the longest common suffix. LSTM, specifically designed to find patterns along series, outperformed every baseline, demonstrating a higher capability of correctly predicting individual mobility traces, represented as ordered sequences of locations.

We also observed how predictability varied for different trajectory characteristics. Despite the general tendency of decreasing performances for longer traveled distances and larger explored areas (local movements were more predictable than long-distance movements), our model always achieved a better accuracy than the baseline approaches. Reasonably, local movements rely on a restricted set of likely future locations, whereas long-distance movements are more unpredictable since the broad explored area could determine a large number of possible future visited locations. However, our model achieved the largest accuracy gap over the baselines exactly in correspondence of very high values of traveled distance and ROG, showing a particular potential for long distances and large covered areas. Moreover, its accuracy in top 3 was always significantly higher than the other models independently from trajectory characteristics. This also includes predictability over time, where results were split on the basis of the hour of the day. Besides the fact that our methodology constantly performed better than the comparison methods, we observed that rush hours in the morning were generally less predictable than rush hours in the afternoon. This is caused by the fact that the traces preceding the early morning hours contain less meaningful past information with regard to future activities. Due to the higher stationarity and regularity (individual and collective) during the night hours, trajectories sharing the same locations during the night can easily lead to different destinations in the morning; therefore, the recent past motion activity becomes less important in predicting the next location. However, the recent past visited locations gain more importance for predicting the afternoon hours because they carry information about motion behavior in the morning, which is more often meaningful and indicative of future movements. Finally, predictability increases in the night due to the intrinsic higher regularity of mobility patterns during these hours, which is also represented by the better performance of the variable-order Markov model over the first-order model in the late night and morning hours, and in correspondence of small values of traveled distance and ROG.

Furthermore, another meaningful performance indicator was defined by assessing the results in relation to the class imbalance, to observe how the model behaves with respect to frequent locations and rare locations. While better results were expected in correspondence to those locations that are often visited, it was worth verifying that the model did not totally drop in performance for very rare locations. In general, besides a tendency to obtain very accurate predictions for popular locations, LSTM was shown to still outperform the baselines, achieving acceptable results even for very rare locations.

Another meaningful matter to mention is related to the prediction error. While the main goal is to correctly detect the next location, it is also important, when the prediction is wrong, to assess how wrong it is. Comparing our model with the best baseline, we verified that the error distance of our methodology is generally smaller, in particular a few tens of kilometers smaller for a large number of observations, whereas far more rarely the error is strongly in favor of the Markov model. This shows that LSTM implicitly makes less serious mistakes in terms of the error distance with respect to Markov, further emphasizing its superiority.

In conclusion, the presented deep learning methodology shows advantages in location prediction of non-repetitive traces generated by short-term foreign tourists. This fits in the field of deep learning-based artificial intelligence for smart city research and smart tourism, e.g., for enhancing user experiences or providing advanced decision making. In particular, this work brings a contribution to the computer science side of the variety of disciplines involved in smart city research [79], specifically falling into the field of analytics technologies, comprising decision-making oriented approaches to discover hidden patterns over big data. These approaches have recently gained critical interest and development, especially for social impact implications [80,81]. Nonetheless, their contribution is only a facet of the multi-disciplinary reality of smart city and smart tourism, and synergies with the other disciplines need to be carefully evaluated to guarantee valuable outcomes [82]. In any case, the proposed research opens a wide variety of potentially suitable applications, ranging from personalized location-based services, to crowd control, to destination planning and management. The most straightforward implementation option is related to the optimization of the quality of individual touristic experiences. Personalized information and recommendations can be provided to a specific tourist along the path, highlighting optional spots and attractions within the next visited area predicted by the model. In addition, collecting the predictions of individual spatial choices can reveal potential crowded areas, giving rise to congestion warning information for those tourists that were forecasted to visit those areas. Combining individual predictions can indeed be used to study the future spatial collective distribution of tourists, which is certainly important for several tasks, including the adjustment of supply of facilities and services, and sustainable countermeasures complying with real-time crowd control.

More broadly, this study fits in the background of trajectory prediction employing machine learning methodologies, particularly contributing to highlighting the potential of deep learning on human mobility studies, disclosing recurrent network models as a promising tool for pattern recognition in trajectory analysis.

5. Conclusions

This paper presented a deep learning model to mine human motion patterns, aimed at predicting short-term foreign tourists' next location from place-based trajectories. The model was trained on the collective behavior of users to capture the dependency of track points and infer the latent patterns of motion traces to predict individual trajectories. The process follows a purely data-driven perspective, whereby the model is able to grasp mobility patterns directly from location sequences, without requiring any manual feature extraction or external information. We initially transformed raw traces into sequences of locations unfolding in fixed time steps, and then applied a deep neural network model composed of embedding and LSTM layers to correctly predict the next location in the sequence. Adopted in the context of short non-repetitive traces, our methodology was shown to outperform traditional approaches, expressing a potential that is worth examining in depth.

Possible extensions of this paper can explore augmentation of trajectory data with further information. A research direction may consist of explicitly integrating time information in the sequence, assessing probable performance improvements. In addition, other factors can be taken into consideration, including tourist characteristics such as nationality or age. Furthermore, it could be appropriate to study tourists' mobility at a smaller scale, investigating the predictability of finer traces in time and space (e.g., in an urban environment); in this case, GPS data would allow more detailed resolutions than telecom data. Lastly, the same methodology could be tested for different use cases dealing with short and non-repetitive traces, not limited to tourism analysis.

In conclusion, the use of recurrent network architectures should be further explored in the field of human mobility, since the current promising results can potentially become successful applications in a variety of tasks related to trajectory analysis and motion behavioral studies.

Author Contributions: A.C. conceived and designed the experiments, analyzed the data and wrote the paper. E.B. supervised the work, helped with designing the conceptual framework, and edited the manuscript. All authors have read and agreed to the published version of the manuscript.

Funding: This research was funded by the Austrian Science Fund (FWF) through the Doctoral College GIScience at the University of Salzburg (DK W 1237-N23).

Acknowledgments: The authors would like to thank Vodafone Italia for providing the dataset for the case study, and the Austrian Science Fund (FWF) for the Open Access Funding.

Conflicts of Interest: The authors declare no conflict of interest.

References

1. Feng, Z.; Zhu, Y. A survey on trajectory data mining: Techniques and applications. *IEEE Access* **2016**, *4*, 2056–2067. [CrossRef]
2. Zheng, Y. Trajectory data mining: An overview. *Acm. Trans. Intell. Syst. Technol.* **2015**, *6*, 1–41. [CrossRef]
3. Bhargava, P.; Phan, T.; Zhou, J.; Lee, J. Who, what, when, and where: Multi-dimensional collaborative recommendations using tensor factorization on sparse user-generated data. In Proceedings of the 24th International Conference on World Wide Web, Florence, Italy, 18–22 May 2015; pp. 130–140. [CrossRef]
4. Cheng, C.; Yang, H.; Lyu, M.R.; King, I. Where you like to go next: Successive point-of-interest recommendation. In Proceedings of the Twenty-Third International Joint Conference on Artificial Intelligence, Beijing, China, 3–9 August 2013; pp. 2605–2611.
5. Semanjski, I.; Gautama, S. Smart city mobility application—Gradient boosting trees for mobility prediction and analysis based on crowdsourced data. *Sensors* **2015**, *15*, 15974–15987. [CrossRef] [PubMed]
6. Crivellari, A.; Beinat, E. Identifying Foreign Tourists' Nationality from Mobility Traces via LSTM Neural Network and Location Embeddings. *Appl. Sci.* **2019**, *9*, 2861. [CrossRef]
7. Litman, T.; Colman, S.B. Generated traffic: Implications for transport planning. *ITE J.* **2001**, *71*, 38–46.
8. Song, X.; Zhang, Q.; Sekimoto, Y.; Shibasaki, R. Prediction of human emergency behavior and their mobility following large-scale disaster. In Proceedings of the 20th ACM SIGKDD International Conference on Knowledge Discovery and Data Mining, New York, NY, USA, 24–27 August 2014; pp. 5–14. [CrossRef]
9. Helbing, D.; Brockmann, D.; Chadefaux, T.; Donnay, K.; Blanke, U.; Woolley-Meza, O.; Moussaid, M.; Johansson, A.; Krause, J.; Schutte, S. Saving human lives: What complexity science and information systems can contribute. *J. Stat. Phys.* **2015**, *158*, 735–781. [CrossRef]
10. Ye, M.; Yin, P.; Lee, W.-C. Location recommendation for location-based social networks. In Proceedings of the 18th SIGSPATIAL International Conference on Advances in Geographic Information Systems, San Jose, CA, USA, 2–5 November 2010; pp. 458–461. [CrossRef]
11. Cho, S.-B. Exploiting machine learning techniques for location recognition and prediction with smartphone logs. *Neurocomputing* **2016**, *176*, 98–106. [CrossRef]
12. Gambs, S.; Killijian, M.-O.; del Prado Cortez, M.N. Next place prediction using mobility markov chains. In Proceedings of the First Workshop on Measurement, Privacy, and Mobility, Bern, Switzerland, 10 April 2012. Art. No. 3. [CrossRef]
13. Miller, R.; Huang, Q. An adaptive peer-to-peer collision warning system. In Proceedings of the IEEE 55th Vehicular Technology Conference, Birmingham, AL, USA, 6–9 May 2002; pp. 317–321. [CrossRef]
14. Ammoun, S.; Nashashibi, F. Real time trajectory prediction for collision risk estimation between vehicles. In Proceedings of the 2009 IEEE 5th International Conference on Intelligent Computer Communication and Processing, Cluj-Napoca, Romania, 27–29 August 2009; pp. 417–422. [CrossRef]
15. Broadhurst, A.; Baker, S.; Kanade, T. Monte Carlo road safety reasoning. In Proceedings of the IEEE Intelligent Vehicles Symposium, Las Vegas, NV, USA, 6–8 June 2005; pp. 319–324. [CrossRef]
16. Bae, S.J.; Lee, H.; Suh, E.-K.; Suh, K.-S. Shared experience in pretrip and experience sharing in posttrip: A survey of Airbnb users. *Inf. Manag.* **2017**, *54*, 714–727. [CrossRef]
17. Towner, N. How to manage the perfect wave: Surfing tourism management in the Mentawai Islands, Indonesia. *Ocean Coast. Manag.* **2016**, *119*, 217–226. [CrossRef]
18. Atsalakis, G.S.; Atsalaki, I.G.; Zopounidis, C. Forecasting the success of a new tourism service by a neuro-fuzzy technique. *Eur. J. Oper. Res.* **2018**, *268*, 716–727. [CrossRef]
19. Albuquerque, H.; Costa, C.; Martins, F. The use of geographical information systems for tourism Marketing purposes in Aveiro region (Portugal). *Tour. Manag. Perspect.* **2018**, *26*, 172–178. [CrossRef]
20. De Cantis, S.; Ferrante, M.; Kahani, A.; Shoval, N. Cruise passengers' behavior at the destination: Investigation using GPS technology. *Tour. Manag.* **2016**, *52*, 133–150. [CrossRef]
21. Lew, A.; McKercher, B. Modeling tourist movements: A local destination analysis. *Ann. Tour. Res.* **2006**, *33*, 403–423. [CrossRef]
22. McKercher, B.; Shoval, N.; Ng, E.; Birenboim, A. First and repeat visitor behaviour: GPS tracking and GIS analysis in Hong Kong. *Tour. Geogr.* **2012**, *14*, 147–161. [CrossRef]
23. Shoval, N.; McKercher, B.; Ng, E.; Birenboim, A. Hotel location and tourist activity in cities. *Ann. Tour. Res.* **2011**, *38*, 1594–1612. [CrossRef]

24. Gonzalez, M.C.; Hidalgo, C.A.; Barabasi, A.-L. Understanding individual human mobility patterns. *Nature* **2008**, *453*, 779–782. [CrossRef]
25. Ashbrook, D.; Starner, T. Using GPS to learn significant locations and predict movement across multiple users. *Pers. Ubiquitous Comput.* **2003**, *7*, 275–286. [CrossRef]
26. Feder, M.; Merhav, N.; Gutman, M. Universal prediction of individual sequences. *IEEE Trans. Inf. Theory* **1992**, *38*, 1258–1270. [CrossRef]
27. Schneider, C.M.; Belik, V.; Couronné, T.; Smoreda, Z.; González, M.C. Unravelling daily human mobility motifs. *J. R. Soc. Interface* **2013**, *10*, 20130246. [CrossRef]
28. Mazimpaka, J.D.; Timpf, S. Trajectory data mining: A review of methods and applications. *J. Spat. Inf. Sci.* **2016**, *13*, 61–99. [CrossRef]
29. Jonietz, D.; Bucher, D. Continuous trajectory pattern mining for mobility behaviour change detection. In Proceedings of the LBS 2018: 14th International Conference on Location Based Services, Zurich, Switzerland, 15–17 January 2018; pp. 211–230. [CrossRef]
30. De Brébisson, A.; Simon, É.; Auvolat, A.; Vincent, P.; Bengio, Y. Artificial neural networks applied to taxi destination prediction. *arXiv* **2015**, arXiv:1508.00021.
31. Etter, V.; Kafsi, M.; Kazemi, E. Been there, done that: What your mobility traces reveal about your behavior. In Proceedings of the Mobile Data Challenge by Nokia Workshop, in Conjunction with Int. Conf. on Pervasive Computing, Newcastle, UK, 18–19 June 2012.
32. Gomes, J.B.; Phua, C.; Krishnaswamy, S. Where will you go? mobile data mining for next place prediction. In Proceedings of the International Conference on Data Warehousing and Knowledge Discovery, Prague, Czech Republic, 26–29 August 2013; pp. 146–158. [CrossRef]
33. Dong, M.; He, D. Hidden semi-Markov model-based methodology for multi-sensor equipment health diagnosis and prognosis. *Eur. J. Oper. Res.* **2007**, *178*, 858–878. [CrossRef]
34. Lin, L.-Z.; Yeh, H.-R. Analysis of tour values to develop enablers using an interpretive hierarchy-based model in Taiwan. *Tour. Manag.* **2013**, *34*, 133–144. [CrossRef]
35. Chen, L.; Lv, M.; Ye, Q.; Chen, G.; Woodward, J. A personal route prediction system based on trajectory data mining. *Inf. Sci.* **2011**, *181*, 1264–1284. [CrossRef]
36. Vu, T.H.N.; Ryu, K.H.; Park, N. A method for predicting future location of mobile user for location-based services system. *Comput. Ind. Eng.* **2009**, *57*, 91–105. [CrossRef]
37. Yavaş, G.; Katsaros, D.; Ulusoy, Ö.; Manolopoulos, Y. A data mining approach for location prediction in mobile environments. *Data Knowl. Eng.* **2005**, *54*, 121–146. [CrossRef]
38. Liao, L.; Patterson, D.J.; Fox, D.; Kautz, H. Building personal maps from GPS data. *Ann. N. Y. Acad. Sci.* **2006**, *1093*, 249–265. [CrossRef]
39. Lee, S.; Lim, J.; Park, J.; Kim, K. Next place prediction based on spatiotemporal pattern mining of mobile device logs. *Sensors* **2016**, *16*, 145. [CrossRef]
40. Alvarez-Garcia, J.A.; Ortega, J.A.; Gonzalez-Abril, L.; Velasco, F. Trip destination prediction based on past GPS log using a Hidden Markov Model. *Expert Syst. Appl.* **2010**, *37*, 8166–8171. [CrossRef]
41. Yuan, Q.; Cong, G.; Ma, Z.; Sun, A.; Thalmann, N.M. Time-aware point-of-interest recommendation. In Proceedings of the 36th international ACM SIGIR conference on Research and development in information retrieval, Dublin, Ireland, 28 July–1 August 2013; pp. 363–372. [CrossRef]
42. Liu, X.; Liu, Y.; Aberer, K.; Miao, C. Personalized point-of-interest recommendation by mining users' preference transition. In Proceedings of the 22nd ACM International Conference on Information & Knowledge Management, San Francisco, CA, USA, 27 October–1 November 2013; pp. 733–738. [CrossRef]
43. Zheng, Y.; Xie, X. Learning travel recommendations from user-generated GPS traces. *ACM Trans. Intell. Syst. Technol. (TIST)* **2011**, *2*, 2. [CrossRef]
44. Noulas, A.; Scellato, S.; Lathia, N.; Mascolo, C. Mining user mobility features for next place prediction in location-based services. In Proceedings of the 2012 IEEE 12th International Conference on Data Mining, Brussels, Belgium, 10–13 December 2012; pp. 1038–1043. [CrossRef]
45. Noulas, A.; Shaw, B.; Lambiotte, R.; Mascolo, C. Topological properties and temporal dynamics of place networks in urban environments. In Proceedings of the 24th International Conference on World Wide Web, Florence, Italy, 18–22 May 2015; pp. 431–441. [CrossRef]

46. Chen, M.; Liu, Y.; Yu, X. Nlpmm: A next location predictor with markov modeling. In Proceedings of the Pacific-Asia Conference on Knowledge Discovery and Data Mining, Tainan, Taiwan, 13–16 May 2014; pp. 186–197.
47. Hawelka, B.; Sitko, I.; Kazakopoulos, P.; Beinat, E. Collective prediction of individual mobility traces for users with short data history. *PLoS ONE* **2017**, *12*, e0170907. [CrossRef]
48. Do, T.M.T.; Gatica-Perez, D. Where and what: Using smartphones to predict next locations and applications in daily life. *Pervasive Mob. Comput.* **2014**, *12*, 79–91. [CrossRef]
49. Urner, J.; Bucher, D.; Yang, J.; Jonietz, D. Assessing the influence of spatio-temporal context for next place prediction using different machine learning approaches. *ISPRS Int. J. Geo-Inf.* **2018**, *7*, 166. [CrossRef]
50. Liu, Q.; Wu, S.; Wang, L.; Tan, T. Predicting the next location: A recurrent model with spatial and temporal contexts. In Proceedings of the Thirtieth AAAI Conference on Artificial Intelligence, Phoenix, AZ, USA, 12–17 February 2016; pp. 194–200.
51. Wu, F.; Fu, K.; Wang, Y.; Xiao, Z.; Fu, X. A spatial-temporal-semantic neural network algorithm for location prediction on moving objects. *Algorithms* **2017**, *10*, 37. [CrossRef]
52. Hoang, M.X.; Zheng, Y.; Singh, A.K. FCCF: Forecasting citywide crowd flows based on big data. In Proceedings of the 24th ACM SIGSPATIAL International Conference on Advances in Geographic Information Systems, San Francisco, CA, USA, 31 October–3 November 2016. Art. No. 6. [CrossRef]
53. Gunduz, S.; Yavanoglu, U.; Sagiroglu, S. Predicting next location of Twitter users for surveillance. In Proceedings of the IEEE 2013 12th International Conference on Machine Learning and Applications (ICMLA), Miami, FL, USA, 4–7 December 2013; Volume 2, pp. 267–273. [CrossRef]
54. Siła-Nowicka, K.; Vandrol, J.; Oshan, T.; Long, J.A.; Demšar, U.; Fotheringham, A.S. Analysis of human mobility patterns from GPS trajectories and contextual information. *Int. J. Geogr. Inf. Sci.* **2016**, *30*, 881–906. [CrossRef]
55. Yuan, Y.; Raubal, M. Spatio-temporal knowledge discovery from georeferenced mobile phone data. In Proceedings of the 2010 Movement Pattern Analysis, Zurich, Switzerland, 14 September 2010; Volume 14.
56. Zheng, Y.; Zhang, L.; Xie, X.; Ma, W.Y. Mining interesting locations and travel sequences from GPS trajectories. In Proceedings of the ACM 18th International Conference on World Wide Web, Madrid, Spain, 20–24 April 2009; pp. 791–800. [CrossRef]
57. Quercia, D.; Lathia, N.; Calabrese, F.; Di Lorenzo, G.; Crowcroft, J. Recommending social events from mobile phone location data. In Proceedings of the 2010 IEEE international Conference on Data Mining, Sydney, Australia, 13–17 December 2010; pp. 971–976. [CrossRef]
58. Xia, J.; Zeephongsekul, P.; Arrowsmith, C. Modelling spatio-temporal movement of tourists using finite Markov chains. *Math. Comput. Simul.* **2009**, *79*, 1544–1553. [CrossRef]
59. Xia, J.; Zeephongsekul, P.; Packer, D. Spatial and temporal modelling of tourist movements using Semi-Markov processes. *Tour. Manag.* **2011**, *32*, 844–851. [CrossRef]
60. Xia, J.C.; Evans, F.H.; Spilsbury, K.; Ciesielski, V.; Arrowsmith, C.; Wright, G. Market segments based on the dominant movement patterns of tourists. *Tour. Manag.* **2010**, *31*, 464–469. [CrossRef]
61. Xiao-Ting, H.; Bi-Hu, W. Intra-attraction tourist spatial-temporal behaviour patterns. *Tour. Geogr.* **2012**, *14*, 625–645. [CrossRef]
62. McKercher, B.; Shoval, N.; Park, E.; Kahani, A. The [limited] impact of weather on tourist behavior in an urban destination. *J. Travel Res.* **2015**, *54*, 442–455. [CrossRef]
63. McKercher, B.; Lau, G. Movement Patterns of Tourists within a Destination. *Tour. Geogr.* **2008**, *10*, 355–374. [CrossRef]
64. Ben-Akiva, M.E.; Lerman, S.R.; Lerman, S.R. *Discrete Choice Analysis: Theory and Application to Travel Demand*; MIT Press: Cambridge, MA, USA, 1985; Volume 9.
65. Lue, C.-C.; Crompton, J.L.; Fesenmaier, D.R. Conceptualization of multi-destination pleasure trips. *Ann. Tour. Res.* **1993**, *20*, 289–301. [CrossRef]
66. Oppermann, M. A model of travel itineraries. *J. Travel Res.* **1995**, *33*, 57–61. [CrossRef]
67. Li, X.; Meng, F.; Uysal, M. Spatial pattern of tourist flows among the Asia-Pacific countries: An examination over a decade. *Asia Pac. J. Tour. Res.* **2008**, *13*, 229–243. [CrossRef]
68. Yang, Y.; Fik, T.; Zhang, J. Modeling sequential tourist flows: Where is the next destination? *Ann. Tour. Res.* **2013**, *43*, 297–320. [CrossRef]

69. Fennell, D.A. A tourist space-time budget in the Shetland Islands. *Ann. Tour. Res.* **1996**, *23*, 811–829. [CrossRef]
70. Hwang, Y.-H.; Gretzel, U.; Fesenmaier, D.R. Multicity trip patterns: Tourists to the United States. *Ann. Tour. Res.* **2006**, *33*, 1057–1078. [CrossRef]
71. Tideswell, C.; Faulkner, B. Multidestination travel patterns of international visitors to Queensland. *J. Travel Res.* **1999**, *37*, 364–374. [CrossRef]
72. Chang, Y.-W.; Tsai, C.-Y. Apply deep learning neural network to forecast number of tourists. In Proceedings of the 2017 31st International Conference on Advanced Information Networking and Applications Workshops (WAINA), Taipei, Taiwan, 27–29 March 2017; pp. 259–264. [CrossRef]
73. Hochreiter, S.; Schmidhuber, J. Long Short-Term Memory. *Neural Comput.* **1997**, *9*, 1735–1780. [CrossRef]
74. De Montjoye, Y.-A.; Quoidbach, J.; Robic, F.; Pentland, A. Predicting Personality Using Novel Mobile Phone-Based Metrics. In Proceedings of the Social Computing, Behavioral-Cultural Modeling and Prediction, Washington, DC, USA, 2–5 April 2013; pp. 48–55. [CrossRef]
75. Lu, X.; Bengtsson, L.; Holme, P. Predictability of population displacement after the 2010 Haiti earthquake. *Proc. Natl. Acad. Sci. USA* **2012**, *109*, 11576–11581. [CrossRef]
76. Crivellari, A.; Beinat, E. From Motion Activity to Geo-Embeddings: Generating and Exploring Vector Representations of Locations, Traces and Visitors through Large-Scale Mobility Data. *ISPRS Int. J. Geo-Inf.* **2019**, *8*, 134. [CrossRef]
77. Sundsøy, P.; Bjelland, J.; Reme, B.A.; Iqbal, A.M.; Jahani, E. Deep learning applied to mobile phone data for individual income classification. In Proceedings of the 2016 International Conference on Artificial Intelligence: Technologies and Applications, Bangkok, Thailand, 24–25 January 2016. [CrossRef]
78. Kingma, D.P.; Ba, J. Adam: A method for stochastic optimization. *arXiv* **2014**, arXiv:1412.6980.
79. Lytras, M.D.; Visvizi, A.; Sarirete, A. Clustering smart city services: Perceptions, expectations, responses. *Sustainability* **2019**, *11*, 1669. [CrossRef]
80. Lytras, M.D.; Raghavan, V.; Damiani, E. Big data and data analytics research: From metaphors to value space for collective wisdom in human decision making and smart machines. *Int. J. Semant. Web Inf. Syst. (IJSWIS)* **2017**, *13*, 1–10. [CrossRef]
81. Angelidou, M.; Psaltoglou, A.; Komninos, N.; Kakderi, C.; Tsarchopoulos, P.; Panori, A. Enhancing sustainable urban development through smart city applications. *J. Sci. Technol. Policy Manag.* **2018**, *9*, 146–169. [CrossRef]
82. Lytras, M.; Visvizi, A. Who uses smart city services and what to make of it: Toward interdisciplinary smart cities research. *Sustainability* **2018**, *10*, 1998. [CrossRef]

© 2020 by the authors. Licensee MDPI, Basel, Switzerland. This article is an open access article distributed under the terms and conditions of the Creative Commons Attribution (CC BY) license (http://creativecommons.org/licenses/by/4.0/).

Article

Comparative Analysis between International Research Hotspots and National-Level Policy Keywords on Artificial Intelligence in China from 2009 to 2018

Jie Gao [1,2], Xinping Huang [1,2,*] and Lili Zhang [1,2]

[1] School of Public Policy and Management, Tsinghua University, Beijing 100084, China; littlehope@mail.tsinghua.edu.cn (J.G.); zhangll18@mail.tsinghua.edu.cn (L.Z.)
[2] Center for Science, Technology & Education Policy, Tsinghua University, Beijing 100084, China
* Correspondence: huangxinping@mail.tsinghua.edu.cn; Tel.: +86-132-5181-8511

Received: 6 October 2019; Accepted: 20 November 2019; Published: 21 November 2019

Abstract: In the last decade, artificial intelligence (AI) has undergone many important developments in China and has risen to the level of national strategy, which is closely related to the areas of research and policy promotion. The interactive relationship between the hotspots of China's international AI research and its national-level policy keywords is the basis for further clarification and reference in academics and political circles. There has been very little research on the interaction between academic research and policy making. Understanding the relationship between the content of academic research and the content emphasized by actual operational policy will help scholars to better apply research to practice, and help decision-makers to manage effectively. Based on 3577 English publications about AI published by Chinese scholars in 2009–2018, and 262 Chinese national-level policy documents published during this period, this study carried out scientometric analysis and quantitative analysis of policy documents through the knowledge maps of AI international research hotspots in China and the co-occurrence maps of Chinese policy keywords, and conducted a comparative analysis that divided China's AI development into three stages: the initial exploration stage, the steady rising stage, and the rapid development stage. The studies showed that in the initial exploration stage (2009–2012), research hotspots and policy keywords had a certain alienation relationship; in the steady rising stage (2013–2015), research hotspots focused more on cutting-edge technologies and policy keywords focused more on macro-guidance, and the relationship began to become close; and in the rapid development stage (2016–2018), the research hotspots and policy keywords became closely integrated, and they were mutually infiltrated and complementary, thus realizing organic integration and close connection. Through comparative analysis between international research hotspots and national-level policy keywords on AI in China from 2009 to 2018, the development of AI in China was revealed to some extent, along with the interaction between academics and politics in the past ten years, which is of great significance for the sustainable development and effective governance of China's artificial intelligence.

Keywords: artificial intelligence; international research; knowledge map visualization; policy documents quantification; research hotspot; policy keyword

1. Introduction

What is artificial intelligence (AI)? There is no direct definition of AI or a consensus thereon, and AI is often understood as a set of techniques designed to use machines to approximate certain aspects of human or animal cognition. Early theorists believed that the symbolic system (the organization of abstract symbols using logical rules) was the most productive way to pursue a computer that could "think"; however, as originally unimagined by Turing and others, the strategy of constructing an inference engine did not achieve the initial cognitive tasks, and it seemed that the theoretically possible concepts had not produced many feasible applications in practice [1]. Li and Wang gave five common definitions of artificial intelligences (AI) in their book *Artificial Intelligence*: (1) AI is a computer program which makes people feel inconceivable; (2) AI is a computer program similar to human thinking; (3) AI is a computer program similar to human behavior; (4) AI is a computer program that can learn; (5) AI is a computer program that can make reasonable actions according to the perception of the environment and obtain the most profitable benefits [2]. They believe that the fifth definition relates to the comprehensive definition used by Wikipedia, which offers a relatively recognized, textbook-like definition of the academic world, and it is comprehensively balanced and emphasized. The first few definitions are from the perspective of public, pragmatism, or machine learning. The perspective of trends it is not comprehensive enough and slightly biased; of course, AI is a field with a wide range of meaning and rich enrichment, and it is necessary for the scientific community and society to continue to extend, expand, and apply its connotations and denotations [2]. Some scholars believe that AI is the intelligent simulation of human behavior through the use of advanced technology, and that the process involves extremely complex human–machine relationships; from the perspective of information perception, data management, deep learning, bionic behavior, and language interaction, AI includes five core elements: cross media perceptual computing, autonomous deep learning, big data intelligent management, virtualized bionics, and simulated language interaction [3].

The research of artificial intelligence has attracted the attention of many scholars, and many fields involves the application of artificial intelligence, machine learning, and pattern recognition, etc. There are published studies and applications involving data transmission, pattern recognition, behavioral research, robotics, and computer engineering [4–8], as well as research and applications in physical sciences, health-related issues, natural sciences, and industrial academic areas [9–11]. Furthermore, there have also been some studies related to applications of different sensors, such as binary, digital cameras, depth data, and wearable sensors, that use AI and data classification fields [12–18].

The latest *China AI Development Report 2018* proposed that the two main lines of development of AI core technologies are brain science and brain-like intelligence technology, and machine learning represented by deep neural networks; currently, brain science and brain-like intelligence technology research progress is limited. Machine learning is developing rapidly, and has become the mainstream paradigm of AI technology today; people often even equate the concepts of "AI" and "machine learning"; in general, the AI we know today is based on modern algorithms and supported by historical data to form artificial programs or systems that can perceive, recognize, make decisions, and execute actions like human beings [19].

Discussions and studies on AI were published in *Sciences, Artificial Intelligence*, and other important academic journals in 1980s and 1990s. At that time, most of them discussed the relationship between AI and computer information processing, and the significance of AI for future innovation and new ideas [20,21]. Boden believed that AI could simulate and realize the creativity of human intelligence in the future [21]. Since the beginning of the new century, research into and application of AI has become more and more abundant, rapid, and in-depth, and it has played an increasingly obvious role in promoting scientific and technological innovation and economic and social development; especially in the past decade, artificial intelligence has garnered a considerable amount of attention from academia and governments of many countries and regions. Scholars' research keeps pace with contemporary trends and benefits from the government's policy guidance and promotion; meanwhile, the research and application of new technology and AI has a significant role in promoting the development of countries and societies [22–26].

A considerable number of scholars have been engaged in research on big data, data mining, smart city, education, knowledge management, innovation network, policy-making, and other areas related to AI, as well as many journal articles, research topics, and research conferences on AI [25–35]. The special issue on "Human Centered Web Science" from the journal *World Wide Web* is to explore how humans could keep up with the current trend toward authorizing users to collectively decide on the usage of web-based information and services in the new era of Internet and AI, and to study and discuss how to master human-driven features of Web-based systems, conduct high-level governance policies and so on [36]. These studies discuss how to adapt to the new era and new trends, and explore the corresponding ideas and solutions. The special issue "Knowledge Management, Innovation and Big Data: Implications for Sustainability, Policy Making and Competitiveness" of the journal *Sustainability* is another typical representation [37]. A considerable number of articles have explored the new era of big data, knowledge management, and innovation. Integration would result in policy driven at a higher level of abstraction; many related scholars believe that the diffusion and development of these multidisciplinary characters and innovations will be based on critical and radical diffusions of smart machines and AI. This research was based on the special issue "Artificial Intelligence and Cognitive Computing: Methods, Technologies, Systems, Applications and Policy Making", and explored the interactive relationship between the hotspots of China's AI international research and national-level policy keywords.

Many scholars have explored the diverse effects, problems, and implications of AI. From the perspective of social science, Miller combed and proposed the development of interpretable artificial intelligence [38]. Lytras, Hassan, and Aljohani believed that in a new era of collective human wisdom, the intelligent library would be one of the important representations and composition systems of AI and the smart city; this kind of personalized and intelligent service and technology-integrated data mining, scientometrics, computer science, AI, and other technologies, and, in the future, library and information science, combined with AI, smart cities and other concepts could help humans to better make scientific and sensible decisions in the face of complex networks and big data [39]. Rajan and Saffiotti discussed the development status and practice of the emerging field of integrated AI and Robotics [40]. Chui, Lytras, and Visvizi discussed the various ways in which AI and big data could offer important support during the process of attaining energy sustainability in smart cities [41].

Some scholars have discussed the impact of AI on scientific research, the expansion of scientific discoveries, and the economic impact of AI in last few years [42,43]. Visvizi, Lytras, and co-workers conducted research on smart cities, big data, education, knowledge management, and AI, explored the comprehensive impact of related technology and service, and discussed the relationship between policy-making and academic research, focusing on existing research and technological innovation [44–47]. In recent years, AI has gradually become a national strategy in China, and relevant policies and designs at the central and local levels have been introduced. Chinese scholars' research on domestic and international AI applications has gradually deepened and expanded. This research includes not only the comprehension of relevant policies and industrial trends of AI in China [19,48–51] and the comparative analysis of AI development strategies and situations domestically and abroad [52–54], but also the discussion of AI development and application to specific fields [55–57]. Over the past five years, more articles have been published on the internal and external governance, construction path and social impact of AI [58–60]; meanwhile, more and more econometric analyses have been conducted in certain fields of AI [61–63].

In general, there are two parts to the research into China's AI policy and China's AI research hotspot. The first part is the research on AI policy. For example, some scholars have discussed the policy quantification of AI [63,64], and there are studies on the development policy and strategic layout of China and other countries in the overall field or specific field of AI [53,65–67]. The other part is research on the field and hotspots of artificial intelligence research in China, such as the analysis of the academic pedigree of scholars in the field of AI research [63], and the comparative study of research hot spots and frontier trends between China and other countries [68], but the comparative study of Chinese academic research hotspots and political policy priorities has been relatively sparse.

As some members of the China AI Development Report 2018 research group, the team of this research participated in the sorting and analysis of the policy part of the report. After the completion of the report, the team members wanted to further explore the relationships and interactions between the content of China's AI policy concerns and Chinese scholars' research concerns, hoping to further enrich such comparative studies and provide corresponding suggestions to political and academic circles.

This research was based on Chinese scholars' international research on artificial intelligence and the relevant hotspots, keywords in English articles, and the comparison of hotspots and keywords in Chinese government policy literature. By tracing the hot topics and key words of Chinese scholars' international studies and domestic political circles, this study was able to track the interaction between domestic policies and international research, and then provide certain implications, references, and theoretical bases for the internationalization of AI research in China, the internationalization of relevant domestic policies, and the relationship between academia and policies.

2. Knowledge Map Visualization Analysis of International Research Evolution of Artificial Intelligence in China

A knowledge map is an image of a knowledge domain and shows the relationship between the development process and structure of scientific knowledge. Citespace visualization software is one of the representative tools used for the visualization of scientometrics and knowledge map [69–71]. Through an international analysis of Chinese scholars in the field of artificial intelligence and visual analysis of the knowledge maps of English articles, this study explored the network structure and evolution of related research hotspots and keywords of Chinese scholars in the field of AI [69–72]. By analyzing the hotspots and keywords of international research in a certain field, scholars can provide necessary reference and identify implications for the development direction, policy formulation, knowledge base, and frontier trends of the field [73–76]. In addition to scientometrics and knowledge mapping, many scholars and experts also use other algorithms and technologies to study AI, such as data extraction, features fusion, and classification and recognition technologies [77–84]. Based on these studies, from the perspective of evolution and cooperation, this study used the methods of scientometrics and knowledge map visualization to research, which is helpful for further enrichment of the field and gives this research a certain uniqueness and novelty.

We chose to download and obtain the corresponding literature data from the "Web of Science Core Collection" of ClarivateAnalytics's Web of Science database (http://www.isiknowledge.com/). Most of the research team members were members of the China AI Development Report 2018 report research group for policy analysis, and they were not very familiar with many specific AI technologies due to the wide range of artificial intelligence research. To ensure that the literature was pertinent and reflected the targeted situation, this study only selected "Artificial Intelligence" as "Topic", "China" as "Address", and "2009–2018" as "Timespan" in the research literature in the Web of Science Core Collection, so as to carry out a comparative analysis of China's national-level AI policies between 2009 and 2018. Therefore, the sample selection of this study had certain limitations, and the literature trend chart (Figure 1) had a certain one-sidedness and misleading nature; it only showed that the research on AI by Chinese scholars is increasing year by year, and that research literature presents a certain significant growth trend with policy encouragement and financial support.

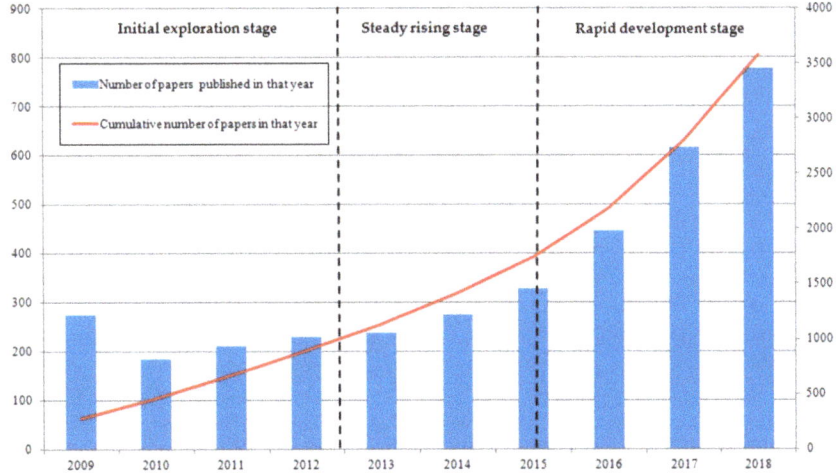

Figure 1. The annual number and stage distribution of China's international artificial intelligence (AI) research (2009–2018).

As mentioned above, this paper selectd the relevant papers of Chinese scholars from the core collection of ClarivateAnalytics's Web of Science database from 2009 to 2018, and used "Artificial Intelligence" and its key keywords for searching and selecting. A total of 3746 related papers were collected, and the three types of papers (1762 articles, 1830 proceedings papers, and 112 review; 3577 in total) which best reflected the international research of artificial intelligence were selected and served as samples for data and visualization analysis in this study. After sorting and screening, 3577 articles were collected for further analysis.

2.1. Distribution of AI International Research Results

The growth regularity and trend of papers published in international high-level journals as well as conferences are important indicators of knowledge accumulation or change in research fields [26]. After screening the topic paper data of China's AI international research, classifying and sorting them by year, the number and change trend of Chinese research papers on AI in 2009–2018 was obtained, as shown in Figure 1. Figure 1 has two coordinate systems. The left coordinate system corresponds to the blue column (number of papers published in that year), and the right coordinate system corresponds to the red curve (cumulative number of papers in that year).

It can be seen from Figure 1 that although the publication of international AI research papers fluctuates, in general, the growth with time showed a trend of increasing year by year. The cumulative number of papers over the year showed a very stable year-on-year growth trend, and the growth process was divided into three stages: (1) Stage 1 is the initial exploration stage (2009–2011). The number of relevant papers in this stage was around 100–200, among which the number of papers in 2009 was relatively large, and the overall situation was relatively stable. (2) Stage 2 is the steady rising stage (2012–2015). The number of papers was growing at this stage, fluctuating slightly, and the number of papers gradually increased from more than 200 to more than 300. (3) Stage 3 is the rapid development stage (2016–2018). The number of papers in this stage grew relatively rapidly, from 300 or 400 in 2015–2016 to 777 in 2018.

Regarding the division of the literature into these three stages: on the one hand, the division was based on the sorting and growth trend of the literature in the studied years, and, on the other hand, it was based on the three-stage division of China's national-level policy in 2009–2018 in the China AI

Development Report 2018 [19], so as to use the keywords of the three-stage literature and the keywords of the three-stage policy documents for comparative analysis.

2.2. Distribution of High-Yield Countries/Regions and Institutions with AI International Research Cooperation

Based on the relevant international research articles on AI, the refinement statistics of "Countries/Regions" represented the countries and regions that have cooperated with Chinese institutions or scholars to conduct AI research. The number and percentage of total publications from these countries or regions in cooperation with Chinese scholars is shown in Table 1. From Table 1, the top 15 aside from China were the United States (250 articles, accounting for 6.99%), the United Kingdom (82 articles, accounting for 2.99%), Australia (68, 1.90%), Canada (62, 1.73%), Singapore (52, 1.45%), Japan (42, 1.17%), France (24, 0.67%), Iran (23, 0.64%), India (19, 0.53%), Italy (18, 0.50%), Spain (16, 0.45%), Saudi Arabia (15, 0.42%), South Korea (15, 0.42%). Among them, the United States was the first group, with 250 papers in cooperation; the second group was concentrated in other developed countries and regions in the field of AI in other continents, such as the United Kingdom (traditional powers), Australia in Oceania, Canada in North America, Singapore in Southeast Asia, etc.

Table 1. The high-yield countries/regions distribution of China's AI international research cooperation (2009–2018).

No.	Country/Region	Paper Number	Percentage
1	China	3572	99.86%
2	USA	250	6.99%
3	UK	82	2.99%
4	Australia	68	1.90%
5	Canada	62	1.73%
6	Singapore	52	1.45%
7	Japan	42	1.17%
8	Taiwan	34	0.95%
9	France	24	0.67%
10	Iran	23	0.64%
11	India	19	0.53%
12	Italy	18	0.50%
13	Spain	16	0.45%
14	Saudi Arabia	15	0.42%
15	Korea	15	0.42%

Based on the relevant international research articles on AI, the refined statistics of "Organizations" were calculated for countries and regions that cooperate with China, as shown in Table 2. The first 15 universities in the first group began with the Chinese Academy of Sciences (331 articles), in which research benefits from the Chinese Academy of Sciences' long-standing research in this field, and the huge research institutes under the Chinese Academy of Sciences. The second group included China's Ministry of Education and China's high level universities, such as the Ministry of Education of China (140 articles), Tsinghua University (111 articles), the University of Chinese Academy of Sciences (101 articles), the Hong Kong Polytechnic University (99 articles), Beihang University (96 articles), Zhejiang University (81 articles), Wuhan University (76 articles), Huazhong University of Science and Technology (73 articles), and Shanghai Jiaotong University (72 articles), which were all over 70. Among them, traditional science and engineering and defense science colleges had an advantage, and many other comprehensive universities also had good performance.

Table 2. The high-yield institution distribution of China's international AI research (2009–2018).

No.	Organization	Paper Number	Percentage
1	Chinese Academy of Science	331	8.37%
2	Ministry of Education China	140	3.54%
3	Tsinghua University	111	2.81%
4	University of Chinese Academy of Science CAS	101	2.56%
5	Hong Kong Polytechnic University	99	2.50%
6	Beihang University	96	2.43%
7	Zhejiang University	81	2.05%
8	Wuhan University	76	1.92%
9	Huazhong University of Science Technology	73	1.85%
10	Shanghai Jiao Tong University	72	1.82%

2.3. Research Hotspots of China's AI International Research

In this study, the topics and keywords in the literature were used to explore the hot topics and hotspots of Chinese scholars in the field of AI in 2009–2018. It is generally believed that keywords are highly condensed and concise in the topic and research hotspots; with the assistance of the knowledge map of co-occurrence keywords drawn by CiteSpace software, this study quickly elucidated the structure, network distribution, and frequency of co-occurrence of related articles keywords, so as to clarify the research hotspots in the field [73–76]. Through the visualization analysis of 3577 related papers collected in this paper, a knowledge map of the international research hotspots of China's AI by node type and time-zone type was obtained. The two maps are shown in Figures 2 and 3.

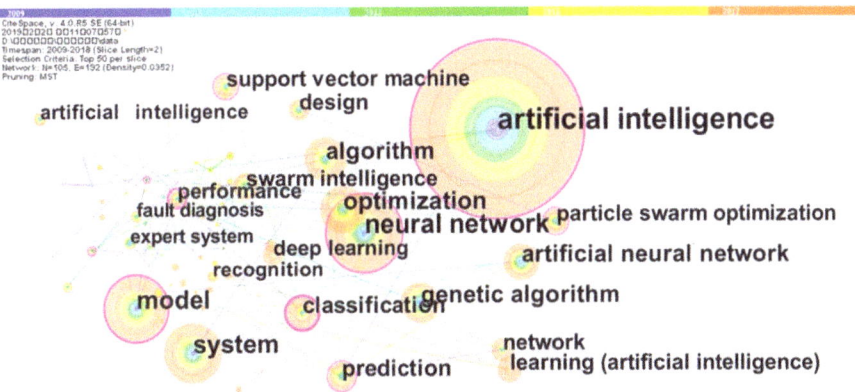

Figure 2. The knowledge map of China's international AI research hotspots (node type) (2009–2018).

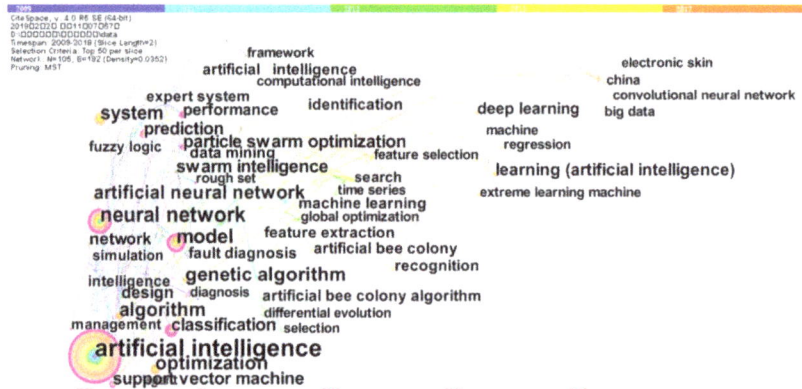

Figure 3. The knowledge map of China's international AI research hotspots (time-zone type) (2009–2018).

The keywords in the knowledge maps shown in Figures 2 and 3 represent the nodes in the network, and the connections between the network nodes represent their co-occurrence relationships. The larger the nodes, the more rings, indicating that the co-occurrence frequency of the keywords is higher. Figure 2 shows that besides the node of "artificial intelligence" (673 times), the nodes with high frequency were "neural network" (307 times), "model" (261 times), "system" (244 times), "optimization" (202 times), "genetic algorithm" (172 times), and "cloud computing" (97 times), etc. Furthermore, new keywords and research hotspots of "China" (32 times), "extreme learning machine" (29 times), "big data" (29 times), "face recognition" (25 times), "electronic skin" (28 times) and other nodes emerged 2015. By reviewing the keywords and subject words that have appeared over the years, the hotspots and interests of Chinese scholars' research on AI can be understood. In the initial exploration stage of AI, Chinese scholars relied on "artificial neural networks" and "genetic algorithms" to conduct research and gradually formed models and systems, and then transferred focus to "cloud computing" and "data sharing" in the steady rising stage. In recent years, hot topics such as "China", "big data", "face recognition", and "electronic skin" have been closely related to the frontier areas of AI, or closely related to current policies and social concerns. In addition, some experts mentioned new functions of AI applications in different fields, such as pattern tracking, data classicization, neural network, deep mining, etc. [85–91], which are worthy of further attention in this study. The organic connection and quantitative comparative analysis between the hot spots of AI international research in the past ten years and policy keywords at the national level is discussed in the following sections.

3. Quantification Analysis of China's AI National-Level Policy Documents

3.1. Stage Division of China's AI National-Level Policy

The quantification analysis of policy documents is based on the analysis of policy documents; on the basis of collecting policy documents and constructing subject words, it further integrates the information contained in the documents, and carries out co-occurrence analysis, clustering analysis, and trend evolution analysis of relevant information, keywords and subject words from multiple dimensions and multiple angles. Starting from the quantitative law of inductive document attributes, it puts forward deeper policy suggestions and reflections based on the combination of qualitative and quantitative research [92–95].

This study established a dataset of AI policy analysis. First, based on the word frequency statistics of AI documents, it identified and constructed the list of initial AI keywords, which were mainly about "AI", and "deep learning", "big data", and "cloud computing", etc. The research team further asked experts in the corresponding field to judge and screen the keywords. Based on the keywords, the pre-search was conducted in the Government Documents Information System (GDIS) of the School of Public Policy and Management of Tsinghua University, and the title and text of policy documents containing the above-mentioned search terms were selected and screened. A total of 262 pieces of China's central-level or national AI policy documents were retrieved. The relevant policy documents were initially sorted and classified according to their years of publication, and the policy trend as well as a stage division map was drawn (shown in Figure 4).

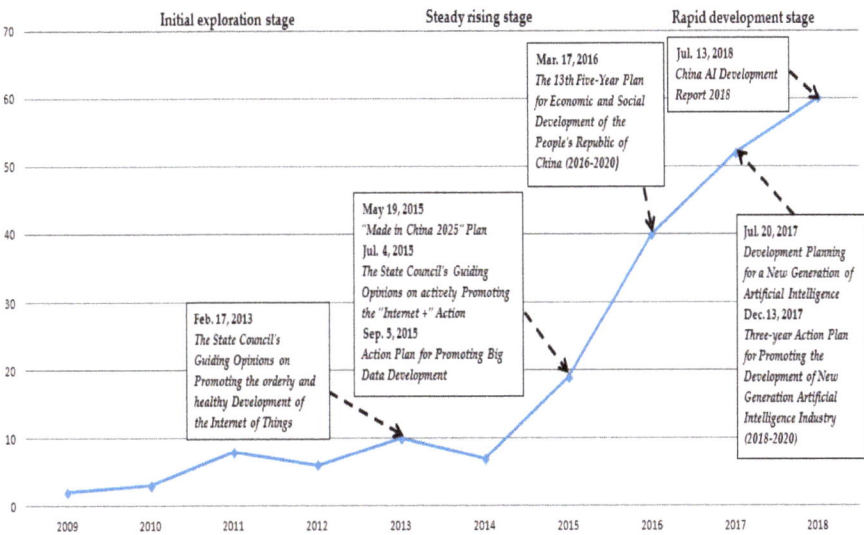

Figure 4. The trends and stages of China's national-level AI policy (2009–2018). Source: According to References [19,51].

The collection of policy documents and reports, especially the China AI Development Report 2018 and Domestic and Foreign AI Policy Analysis Report 2018 was combined with the three-stage distribution of AI international research hotspots discussed in Section 2. In order to maintain the consistency and contrast of the analysis, this study roughly sorted the national AI policy into three groups: (1) the initial exploration stage of 2009–2012, where there were fewer national-level policies for AI; (2) the steady rising stage of 2013–2015, when the development of AI gradually increased to the level of national strategy, and policy documents were issued more quickly and steadily; and (3) the rapid development stage of 2016–2018, representing the upsurge of AI development, in which the national-level AI policies became more comprehensive, the top-down design was further enhanced, and the follow-up policies and plans at all levels in various fields were more targeted and specific.

3.2. Quantification Analysis of National-Level Policy Documents on AI and Comparative Analysis between International Research Hotspots and Policy Keywords

Word co-occurrence is one of the most commonly used analytical methods for bibliometrics. Two keywords appear in one document and are recorded as one co-occurrence of the topic. The more co-occurrences, the closer the relationships between the two words and the stronger the correlations; analyzing the co-occurrence relationships of keywords in existing policy documents can cluster the subject words and identify the core theme of the field; thus, the co-occurrence network of the keywords in each period and stage can be constructed, and the stages can be identified [19,51]. After integrating and modifying the co-occurrence map of AI reports, a three-stage theme co-occurrence map of AI development was obtained, as shown in Figures 5–7.

Sustainability **2019**, *11*, 6574

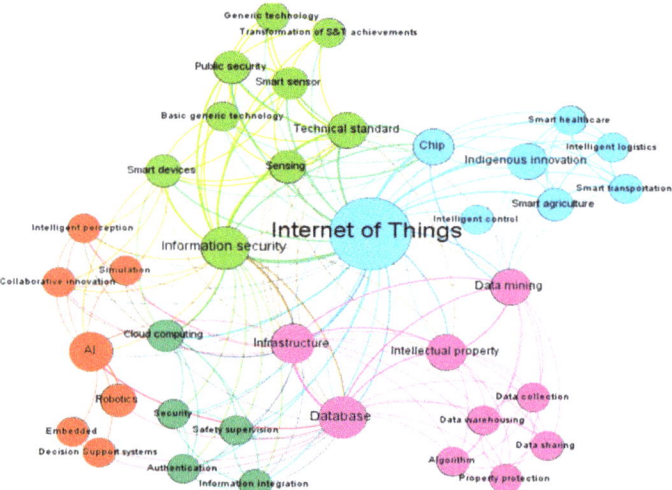

Figure 5. The initial exploration stage keywords co-occurrence map of China's national AI policy (2009–2012). Source: According to References [19,51].

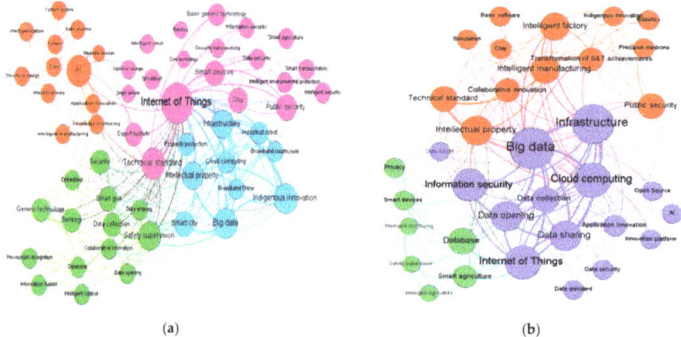

Figure 6. The steady rising keywords co-occurrence map of China's national AI policy (2013–2015). (**a**) (2013–2014); (**b**) (2014–2015). Source: According to References [19,51].

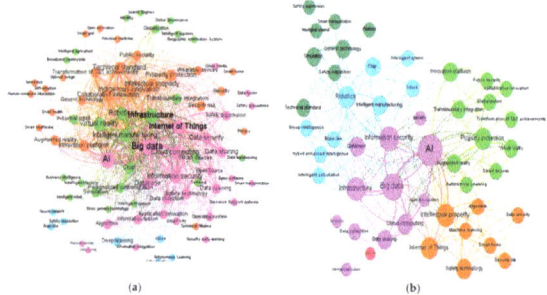

Figure 7. The rapid development keywords co-occurrence map of China's national AI policy (2016–2018). (**a**) (2016–2017); (**b**) (2017–2018). Source: According to References [19,51].

In the initial exploration stage of AI policy (2009–2012), as shown in the co-occurrence map of policy keywords in Figure 5, "AI", "infrastructure", "information security", "technical standards", and "Internet of Things" were the core themes of relevant policies. These were closely related to the social development at that time. During this period, the Internet of Things was just beginning to emerge, and infrastructure construction about AI was ineffective, especially in some aspects such as data collection, data mining, and database construction. However, at this stage, national-level and central-level policies directly related to AI and the Internet of Things had not yet been introduced, resulting in drawbacks in intellectual property rights, property rights protection, technical standards, information security, and public safety.

At this stage, the hotspots of international research on AI in China were "artificial intelligence", "artificial neural network", "genetic algorithm", "group intelligence", "return", "model", "system", "standard", "recognition", "predict", "data mining", and others. It can be seen that there are differences between the two. For example, many hotspots of international research focused on specific technique and frontier exploration of AI (such as "artificial neural network", "genetic algorithms", "recognition", etc.), while policy keywords and hotspots were "Internet of Things", "Infrastructure", "Information Security", and so on. However, there were subtle similarities and connections, such as "data mining", "identification", "prediction", and so on, which were the foundation and prototype of policy keywords in terms of "infrastructure", "Internet of Things", "database construction" and "intelligent industry chain". The exploration of "model" and "system" in research hotspots is the exploration and foundation of future policies on "technical standards". It can be seen that in the initial exploration stage of 2009–2012, the hotspots of international research on AI in China had a certain alienation from the AI policy at the national level, because at this time, there were not many national-level policies on AI. At the same time, international research hotspots and policy keywords had a certain degree of connection. The research hotspots contained the technical basis and prototypical exploration of the current and future policies.

In the steadily rising stage of AI policy (2013–2015), as shown in the co-occurrence maps of policy keywords in Figure 6a (2013–2014) and Figure 6b (2014–2015), "AI", "Internet of Things", "big data", "infrastructure", and "information security" were the core keywords of relevant policies. In this period, China had a certain foundation in the application of big data technology and the development of the internet of things industry, and the knowledge of AI had become more and more mature, and then turned to the basic technology of AI and related practical applications. In 2015, "Made in China 2025" was released, deploying "intelligent manufacturing" in a holistic way and implementing the strategy of manufacturing power; in the same year, the guidelines for the "Internet +" Action were released, clarifying that AI was one of the 11 key development areas for the formation of the new industrial model, promoting the development of AI to the national strategic level. During this period, the hotspots of international research on AI in China were "deep learning", "feature selection", "face recognition", "artificial bee colony algorithm", "time series", "regression", "China", "strategy", and so on. From a macro perspective, the international research on AI in China gradually increased the research and analysis of "China" and "strategy" level; at the micro level, the discussions on the technology and application of AI were more specific and cutting-edge, being inseparable from the policy promotion and keywords of this period, and many specific technologies were built on the basis of AI infrastructure, big data, and databases deployed in China. Compared with the alienation relationship in the initial exploration stage of the previous period, the specific technology and application of AI in this period began to be reflected in policy formulation and social life, that is to say, the hotspots of AI international research began to be closely integrated with the keywords of national policy, but research hotspots focused more on the exploration and application of technology, and national policy was more macroscopic, representing the overall embodiment of hotspots and technologies.

In the rapid development stage of AI policy (2016–2018), as shown in the co-occurrence maps of policy keywords in Figure 7a (2016–2017) and Figure 7b (2017–2018), "AI" became the largest keyword in this stage, while "big data", "infrastructure", "Internet of Things", and "technical standards" were still relevant policy keywords. It should be noted that the keywords such as "robot", "intelligent manufacturing", and "deep learning" also appeared and increased, and the related words of "intellectual property" and "property rights protection" also began to appear. In 2016, the National 13th Five-Year

Plan of China proposed to break through AI technology. During this period, the development of virtual technology, intelligent commerce, industrial robots, and other fields marked the gradual establishment and improvement of the AI industry system, and the state began to attach importance to the intellectual property rights and property rights protection of AI. The release of the New Generation Artificial Intelligence Development Plan in 2017 marked the beginning of the new era of AI in China. At present, China has systematically arranged AI from the national level, and the Report of 19th National Congress of China put forward "promoting the deep integration of the Internet, big data, AI and the real economy" and strengthened the comprehensive support of AI for science and technology, economy, social development, and national security [4,36]. During this period, the hotspots of international research on AI in China focused on specific frontier technologies and practical commercial application technologies such as "big data", "convolution neural network", "electronic skin", "image classification", "sensors", "movies", "electronic games", and "applications", which is in line with the current policy advocating integration of artificial intelligence and the real economy at the national level. At the same time under the promotion and accumulation of previous research hotspots, current research hotspots began to closely integrate with current policy topics. There are two reasons for this: on the one hand, the planning and top-down design of policies are constantly strengthened, and the contents and keywords of policy documents often cover most of the hotspots and keywords of AI research; on the other hand, the hotspots of AI international research in this period also indicate that more scholars began to pay attention to expanding their research topics and directions to cover policy strategies and commercial applications. Therefore, in this period, the international research hotspots of AI in China were closely integrated with the characteristics of national policies, and they were deeply integrated with and covered by with each other.

In this part, some experts suggested that the research team could continue to use new algorithms and systems to further enhance performance values, e.g., HMM, modified HMM, embedded HMM, GMM, etc. [96–101], and these need to be further expanded upon by the research team in follow-up studies.

4. Discussion and Conclusions

First, this paper adopted the methods of mathematical statistics to carry out simple historical statistics and stage division of relevant Chinese scholars' papers on China's international AI research downloaded and screened from Web of Science database. According to the number and growth trend of articles published, the international research on AI in China was roughly divided into three stages, namely the initial exploration stage (2009–2012), the steady rising stage (2013–2015), and the rapid development stage (2016–2018). Subsequently, the high-yielding countries/regions and institutions of AI international research were analyzed, and the CiteSpace software was used to process related papers. Hotspot knowledge maps of international AI research were drawn, the relevant research topics, keywords, and hotspots are found, and the network results and distribution of research hotspots were obtained. Hotspots and keywords included "artificial intelligence", "neural network", "model", "system", "optimization", "genetic algorithm", "cloud computing", and so on according to the frequency. In the past three years, new hot topic words have included "China", "extreme learning machine", "face recognition", and "electronic skin", etc.

Based on the theory and method of quantitative analysis of policy documents, 262 central-level AI policy documents were collected and screened from the Government Document Information System (GDIS); the documents were also sorted by quantity and distributed into stages. Based on the documents themselves and the previous division of research hotspot stages, the documents were also divided into three stages according to the time of publication: the initial exploration stage (2009–2012), the steady rising stage (2013–2015), and the rapid development stage (2016–2018), which were the same as the research hotspot stage for comparative analysis. On the three-stage co-occurrence maps of China's national-level policy keywords, this study made a preliminary quantitative analysis of policy documents and carried out a comparative analysis of the evolution of AI international research hotspots.

In terms of stages, in the initial exploration stage (2009–2012), China's international AI research hotspots and national-level policy keywords had a somewhat alienated relationship; research hotspots were more frontier, while national level policies were few, but research hotspots formed the technical basis and embryonic exploration of the current and future policy keywords. In the steady rising stage (2013–2015), the AI research hotspots were more closely related to the national level policy keywords; the research hotspots focused more on the exploration and application of technology, and the national level policy was the overall collection of hotspots and technologies. In the rapid development stage (2016–2018), the characteristics of China's international AI research hotspots and national level policies were closely integrated, and they were deeply integrated and covered.

In general, research hotspots often focus on exploring the frontiers and technologies of AI. With the development of the times and the progress of policies, research hotspots gradually began to integrate with policies: research hotspots expanded from frontier exploration to the applications of technology and attention was paid to strategies and policies, while policies at the national level began to pay more attention to top-down design and bottom-level promotion, and the overall strategy and planning layout of research hotspots and technological frontiers were also relatively in place, being more targeted strategically and overall.

Although this research had a certain novelty in comparing and analyzing the hot spots and keywords of policy and academic circles, and involved scientometrics and knowledge map visualization analysis of relevant academic literature and policy documents, there are still many limitations and weaknesses related to the opinions of some experts and reviewers. First, the selection of academic literature and policy documents had certain limitations and could be misleading. This study only shows the general situation of China's AI research and policy-making from one side or one general trend. It is possible that different sample selections would reflect different situations and outcomes, clarification of which will require greater sample sizes in the future or more sample selections from other perspectives. Secondly, experts also suggested some novel algorithms and systems in AI, which the research team need to further study, reference, and apply to enrich the research on AI development. Future studies need to select samples scientifically, and use more new algorithms, new systems, and a variety of research methods to comb and study the development and research of AI in China and the world.

Author Contributions: Conceptualization, J.G. and X.H.; Methodology, J.G. and X.H.; Software, J.G. and L.Z.; Validation, J.G., X.H. and L.Z.; Formal analysis, J.G. and X.H.; Investigation, J.G. and L.Z.; Data Curation, J.G. and X.H.; Visualization, J.G., X.H. and L.Z.; Writing—Original Draft Preparation, J.G., X.H. and L.Z.; Writing—Review & Editing, J.G., X.H. and L.Z.; Funding Acquisition, X.H. and J.G.

Funding: This research was funded by [The National Natural Science Foundation of China] grant number [71904101, 71801169], [China Postdoctoral Science Foundation] grant number [2018M640150, 2019M650754], and [The National Social Science Foundation of China] grant number [18ZDA075, 18CTQ040].

Conflicts of Interest: The authors declare no conflict of interest.

References

1. Calo, R. Artificial Intelligence Policy: A Prime and Roadmap. 2017. Available online: https://ssrn.com/abstract=3015350 (accessed on 8 August 2017).
2. Li, K.; Wang, Y. *Artificial Intelligence*; Culture Development Press: Beijing, China, 2017; pp. 24–37.
3. Chen, M.; Zhang, Y. Practice Innovation and Thinking of Library Service Base on Artificial Intelligence. *Library* **2018**, *12*, 8–16.
4. Bakli, M.S.; Sakr, M.A.; Soliman, T.H.A. A spatiotemporal algebra in Hadoop for moving objects. *Geogr. Inf. Sci.* **2018**, *21*, 102–114. [CrossRef]
5. Jalal, A.; Quaid, M.A.K.; Kim, K. A wrist worn acceleration based human motion analysis and classification for ambient smart home system. *J. Electr. Eng. Technol.* **2019**, *14*, 1733–1739. [CrossRef]
6. Jalal, A.; Mahmood, M. Students' behavior mining in e-learning environment using cognitive processes with information technologies. *Educ. Inf. Technol.* **2019**, *24*, 2797–2821. [CrossRef]

7. Li, T.; Zhou, J.; Tuya, N.; Du, C.; Chen, Z.; Liu, S. Recognize facial expression using active appearance and neural network. In Proceedings of the International Conference on Cyber-Enabled Distributed Computing and Knowledge Discovery (CyberC), Nanjing, China, 12–14 October 2017; pp. 182–185.
8. Jalal, A.; Mahmood, M.; Hasan, A.S. Multi-features descriptors for human activity tracking and recognition in Indoor-outdoor environments. In Proceedings of the IEEE International Conference on Information Technology (ICIT 2019), Saratov, Russia, 7–8 February 2019. [CrossRef]
9. Jalal, A.; Quaid, M.A.K.; Sidduqi, M.A. A Triaxial acceleration-based human motion detection for ambient smart home system. In Proceedings of the IEEE International Conference on Information Technology (ICIT 2019), Saratov, Russia, 7–8 February 2019. [CrossRef]
10. Hsu, F.S.; Lin, W.Y.; Tsai, T.W. Automatic facial expression recognition for affective computing based on bag of distances. In Proceedings of the IEEE 2013 Asia-Pacific Signal and Information Processing Association Annual Summit and Conference (APSIPA), Kaohsiung, Taiwan, 29 October–1 November 2013. [CrossRef]
11. Jalal, A.; Kamal, S. Improved Behavior Monitoring and Classification Using Cues Parameters Extraction from Camera Array Images. *Int. J. Interact. Multimed. Artif. Intell.* **2018**, *5*, 1–8. [CrossRef]
12. Koller, D.; Klinker, G.; Rose, E.; Breen, D.E.; Whitaker, R.T.; Tuceryan, M. Real-time vision-based camera tracking for augmented reality applications. In Proceedings of the Symposium on Virtual Reality Software and Technology (VRST-97), Lausanne, Switzerland, 15–17 September 1997; pp. 87–94.
13. Mahmood, M.; Jalal, A.; Evans, H.A. Facial expression recognition in image sequences using 1D transform and gabor wavelet transform. In Proceedings of the 2018 International Conference on Applied and Engineering Mathematics (ICAEM), Taxila, Pakistan, 15–17 September 2018; pp. 1–6.
14. Jalal, A.; Kamal, S.; Kim, D. A Depth Video-based Human Detection and Activity Recognition using Multi-features and Embedded Hidden Markov Models for Health Care Monitoring Systems. *Int. J. Interact. Multimed. Artif. Intell.* **2017**, *4*, 54–62. [CrossRef]
15. Sony, A.; Ajith, K.; Thomas, K.; Thomas, T.; Deepa, P.L. Video summarization by clustering using euclidean distance. In Proceedings of the 2011 International Conference on Signal Processing, Communication, Computing and Networking Technologies, Thuckalay, India, 21–22 July 2011. [CrossRef]
16. Jalal, A.; Kamal, S.; Kim, D. Facial Expression recognition using 1D transform features and Hidden Markov Model. *J. Electr. Eng. Technol.* **2017**, *12*, 1657–1662.
17. Kamal, S.; Jalal, A.; Kim, D. Depth images-based human detection, tracking and activity recognition using spatiotemporal features and modified HMM. *J. Electr. Eng. Technol.* **2016**, *11*, 1921–1926. [CrossRef]
18. Jalal, A.; Kamal, S.; Kim, D. Individual detection-tracking-recognition using depth activity images. In Proceedings of the 2015 12th International Conference on Ubiquitous Robots and Ambient Intelligence (URAI), KINTEX, Goyang, Korea, 28–30 October 2015; pp. 450–455.
19. China Institute for Science and Technology Policy at Tsinghua University. China AI Development Report 2018. Available online: http://www.sppm.tsinghua.edu.cn/eWebEditor/UploadFile/20180712001.pdf (accessed on 13 July 2018).
20. Waldrop, M.M. Artificial Intelligence Moves into Mainstream. *Science* **1987**, *237*, 484–485. [CrossRef]
21. Boden, M.A. Creativity and artificial intelligence. *Artif. Intell.* **1998**, *103*, 347–356. [CrossRef]
22. Hovy, E.; Navigli, R.; Ponzetto, S.P. Collaboratively built semi-structured content and Artificial Intelligence: The story so far. *Artif. Intell.* **2013**, *194*, 2–27. [CrossRef]
23. Russell, S.J.; Norvig, P. Artificial intelligence: A modern approach. *Appl. Mech. Mater.* **2010**, *263*, 2829–2833.
24. Mccarthy, J. Generality in artificial intelligence. *Resonance* **2014**, *19*, 283–296.
25. Wang, K.; Wan, X. Automatic generation of sentimental texts via mixture adversarial networks. *Artif. Intell.* **2019**, *275*, 540–558. [CrossRef]
26. Mu, K. Measuring inconsistency with constraints for propositional knowledge bases. *Artif. Intell.* **2018**, *259*, 52–90. [CrossRef]
27. Zhuhadar, L.; Marklin, S.; Thrasher, E.; Lytras, M.D. Is there a gender difference in interacting with intelligent tutoring system? Can bayesian knowledge tracing and learning curve analysis models answer this question? *Comput. Hum. Behav.* **2016**, *61*, 198–204. [CrossRef]
28. Zhang, X.; Jiang, S.; Pablos, P.O.D.; Lytras, M.D.; Sun, Y. How virtual reality affects perceived learning effectiveness: A task–technology fit perspective. *Behav. Inf. Technol.* **2017**, *36*, 548–556. [CrossRef]
29. Lytras, M.D. From the special issue editor: Information systems research for a sustainable knowledge society. *J. Inf. Syst. Manag.* **2010**, *27*, 196–197. [CrossRef]

30. Hassan, S.U.; Visvizi, A.; Waheed, H. The 'who' and the 'what' in international migration research: Data-driven analysis of Scopus-indexed scientific literature. *Behav. Inf. Technol.* **2019**, *38*, 924–939. [CrossRef]
31. Davis, E.; Marcus, G. The scope and limits of simulation in automated reasoning. *Artif. Intell.* **2016**, *233*, 60–72. [CrossRef]
32. Lytras, M.D.; Raghavan, V.; Damiani, E. Big data and data analytics research: From metaphors to value space for collective wisdom in human decision making and smart machines. *Int. J. Semant. Web Inf. Syst.* **2017**, *13*, 1–10. [CrossRef]
33. Lytras, M.D.; Mathkour, H.I.; Abdalla, H.; Al-Halabi, W.; Yanez-Marquez, C.; Siqueira, S.W.M. Enabling technologies and business infrastructures for next generation social media: Big data, cloud computing, internet of things and virtual reality. *J. Univ. Comput. Sci.* **2015**, *21*, 1379–1384.
34. Lytras, M.D.; Mathkour, H.I.; Abdalla, H.; Al-Halabi, W.; Yanez-Marquez, C.; Siqueira, S.W.M. An emerging–Social and emerging computing enabled philosophical paradigm for collaborative learning systems: Toward high effective next generation learning systems for the knowledge society. *Comput. Hum. Behav.* **2015**, *51*, 557–561. [CrossRef]
35. Lytras, M.D.; Mathkour, H.I.; Torres-Ruiz, M. Innovative Mobile Information Systems: Insights from Gulf Cooperation Countries and All over the World. *Mob. Inf. Syst.* **2016**, *2016*, 2439389. [CrossRef]
36. Damiani, E.; Lytras, M.D.; Cudre-Mauroux, P. Guest Editorial: Special Issue on Human-Centered Web Science. *World Wide Web* **2010**, *13*, 1–2. [CrossRef]
37. Pablos, P.O.D.; Lytras, M.D. Knowledge Management, Innovation and Big Data: Implications for Sustainability, Policy Making and Competitiveness. *Sustainability* **2018**, *10*, 2073. [CrossRef]
38. Miller, T. Explanation in artificial intelligence: Insights from the social sciences. *Artif. Intell.* **2019**, *267*, 1–38. [CrossRef]
39. Lytras, M.D.; Hassan, S.U.; Aljohani, N.R. Linked open data of bibliometric networks: Analytics research for personalized library services. *Libr. Hi Tech* **2019**, *37*, 2–7. [CrossRef]
40. Rajan, K.; Saffiotti, A. Towards a science of integrated AI and Robotics. *Artif. Intell.* **2017**, *247*, 1–9. [CrossRef]
41. Chui, K.T.; Lytras, M.D.; Visvizi, A. Energy Sustainability in Smart Cities: Artificial Intelligence, Smart Monitoring, and Optimization of Energy Consumption. *Energies* **2018**, *11*, 2869. [CrossRef]
42. Gil, Y.; Greaves, M.; Hendler, J.; Hirsh, H. Artificial intelligence: Amplify scientific discovery with artificial intelligence. *Science* **2014**, *346*, 171–172. [CrossRef] [PubMed]
43. Parkes, D.C.; Wellman, M.P. Economic reasoning and artificial intelligence. *Science* **2015**, *349*, 267–272. [CrossRef] [PubMed]
44. Visvizi, A.; Lytras, M.D. Rescaling and refocusing smart cities research: From mega cities to smart villages. *J. Sci. Technol. Policy Mak.* **2018**, *9*, 134–145. [CrossRef]
45. Lytras, M.D.; Aljohani, N.R.; Visvizi, A.; Pablos, P.O.D.; Gasevic, D. Advanced decision-making in higher education: Learning analytics research and key performance indicators. *Behav. Inf. Technol.* **2018**, *37*, 937–940. [CrossRef]
46. Visvizi, A.; Lytras, M.D.; Damiani, E.; Mathkour, H. Policy making for smart cities: Innovation and social inclusive economic growth for sustainability. *J. Sci. Technol. Policy Manag.* **2018**, *9*, 126–133. [CrossRef]
47. Pablos, P.O.D.; Lytras, M.D.; Visvizi, A.; Zhang, X. Opportunities for information technologies and knowledge management to answer emerging challenges for manufacturing and services industries in the digital economy. *Hum. Factors Ergon. Manuf. Serv. Ind.* **2019**, *29*, 3–4. [CrossRef]
48. Cai, Z. 40 Years of Artificial Intelligence in China. *Sci. Technol. Rev.* **2016**, *34*, 12–32.
49. Pan, Y. Heading toward Artificial Intelligence 2.0. *Engineering* **2016**, *2*, 409–413. [CrossRef]
50. Jia, K.; Jiang, Y. Three Fundamental Issues of Artificial Intelligence Governance: Principle, Challenge and Public Policy. *Chin. Public Admin.* **2017**, *10*, 40–45.
51. Center for Science, Technology & Education Policy at Tsinghua University. *Domestic and Foreign AI Policy Analysis Report 2018*; CSTEP: Beijing, China, 2018; pp. 1–19.
52. Jia, K.; Guo, Y.; Lei, H. International Comparative Study of AI Public Policy: History, Characteristics and Enlightenment. *E-Government* **2018**, *9*, 78–86.
53. Tang, H. Main policy orientation and development trends of artificial intelligence at home and abroad. *China Radio* **2018**, *5*, 45–46.
54. Wang, Y.; Chen, D. Rising Sino-U.S. Competition in Artificial Intelligence. *China Q. Int. Strateg. Stud.* **2018**, *4*, 241–258. [CrossRef]

55. Zhang, Y.; Agarwal, P.; Bhatnagar, V.; Balochian, S.; Zhang, X. Swarm Intelligence and Its Applications. *Sci. World J.* **2014**, *2013*, 1–3. [CrossRef]
56. Li, R.; Zhao, Z.; Zhou, X.; Ding, G.; Chen, Y.; Wang, Z.; Zhang, H. Intelligent 5G: When Cellular Networks Meet Artificial Intelligence. *IEEE Wirel. Commun.* **2017**, *24*, 2–10. [CrossRef]
57. Yang, T.; Asanjan, A.A.; Welles, E.; Gao, X. Developing reservoir monthly inflow forecasts using artificial intelligence and climate phenomenon information. *Water Resour. Res.* **2017**, *53*, 2786–2812. [CrossRef]
58. Liu, J.; Kong, X.; Xia, F.; Bai, X.; Wang, L.; Qing, Q.; Lee, I. Artificial Intelligence in the 21st Century. *IEEE Access* **2018**, *6*, 34403–34421. [CrossRef]
59. Gao, S.; Liu, J. The impact of artificial intelligence on enterprise management theory and its countermeasures. *Stud. Sci. Sci.* **2018**, *36*, 2004–2010.
60. Ou, Y.; Wei, Q.; Xiao, X. Knowledge Management under Artificial Intelligence in Organizations: Change and System Framework. *Libr. Inf.* **2017**, *6*, 104–111.
61. Vincent, C.; Tuomas, S. Expressive Markets for Donating to Charities. *Artif. Intell.* **2011**, *175*, 1251–1271.
62. Yuan, Y.; Yu, M.; Tao, Y.; Gong, Z.; Liu, J. Quantitative Research on China's Artificial Intelligence Industry Policy Based on Text Mining. *J. China Acad. Electron. Inf. Technol.* **2018**, *13*, 663–668.
63. Wang, S.; Zhao, X.; Pan, Y.; Wang, Y.J. Growth of Talent from the Perspective of Academic Genealogy: Taking the Laureates of Turing Award Artificial Intelligence Field for Example. *China Soc. Sci. Tech. Inf.* **2018**, *37*, 1232–1240.
64. Liu, H.; Lin, B. The Value Orientation, Issue Construction and Path Choice of China's Artificial Intelligence Development: Quantitative Research Based on Policy Texts. *E-Government* **2018**, *11*, 47–58.
65. Song, W.; Xia, H. A Quantitative Study on the Text of Local Government Artificial Intelligence Industry Policy. *Sci. Technol. Manag. Res.* **2019**, *39*, 192–199.
66. Chen, X.; Liu, Z.; Wei, L.; Yan, J.; Hao, T.; Ding, R. A comparative quantitative study of utilizing artificial intelligence on electronic health records in the USA and China during 2008–2017. *BMC Med. Inform. Decis.* **2018**, *18*, 117. [CrossRef]
67. Gao, J.; Xie, Q.; Huang, C.; Su, J. Comparative Study on the Development Policy and Strategic Layout of Artificial Intelligence between China and Germany. *Sci. Technol. Manag. Res.* **2019**, *39*, 206–209.
68. Sun, B.; Dong, Z. Comparative Study on the Academic Field of Artificial Intelligence in China and Other Countries. *Wirel. Pers. Commun.* **2018**, *102*, 1879–1890. [CrossRef]
69. Gao, J.; Ding, Y. Visualization Analysis of Cooperation Network Configuration of Creative Research Group based on Scientometrics. *Sci. Technol. Program Policy* **2018**, *35*, 9–17.
70. Chen, Y.; Chen, C.; Liu, Z.; Hu, Z.; Wang, X. The methodology function of Cite Space mapping knowledge domains. *Stud. Sci. Sci.* **2015**, *33*, 242–253.
71. Li, J.; Chen, C. *CiteSpace: Text Mining and Visualization in Scientific Literature*; Capital University of Economics and Business Press: Beijing, China, 2016; pp. 149–152.
72. Chen, C. Science Mapping: A Systematic Review of the Literature. *J. Data Inf. Sci.* **2017**, *2*, 1–40. [CrossRef]
73. Li, M.; Wang, M.; Qi, H.; Qi, Y. Evolution of international research on science and technology policy. *Stud. Sci. Sci.* **2018**, *36*, 1565–1574.
74. Hu, Z.; Lin, A.; Willett, P. Identification of research communities in cited and uncited publications using a co-authorship network. *Scientometrics* **2019**, *118*, 1–19. [CrossRef]
75. Cui, T.; Zhang, J. Bibliometric and review of the research on circular economy through the evolution of Chinese public policy. *Scientometrics* **2018**, *116*, 1013–1037. [CrossRef]
76. Zhu, J.; Hua, W. Visualizing the knowledge domain of sustainable development research between 1987 and 2015: A bibliometric analysis. *Scientometrics* **2017**, *110*, 893–914. [CrossRef]
77. Singh, D.; Mohan, C.K. Graph formulation of video activities for abnormal activity recognition. *Pattern Recognit.* **2017**, *65*, 265–272. [CrossRef]
78. Kim, K.; Jalal, A.; Mahmood, M. Vision-Based Human Activity Recognition System Using Depth Silhouettes: A Smart Home System for Monitoring the Residents. *J. Electr. Eng. Technol.* **2019**, *9*, 1–7. [CrossRef]
79. Ahmed, A.; Jalal, A.; Rafique, A.A. Salient Segmentation based Object Detection and Recognition using Hybrid Genetic Transform. In Proceedings of the International Conference on Applied and Engineering Mathematics (ICAEM), Taxila, Pakistan, 27–29 August 2019. [CrossRef]

80. Nguyen, T.N.; Ly, N.Q. Abnormal Activity Detection based on Dense Spatial-Temporal Features and Improved One-Class Learning. In Proceedings of the Eighth International Symposium on Information and Communication Technology, Nha Trang City, Vietnam, 7–8 December 2017; pp. 370–377.
81. Batool, M.; Jalal, A.; Kim, K. Sensors Technologies for Human Activity Analysis Based on SVM Optimized by PSO Algorithm. In Proceedings of the International Conference on Applied and Engineering Mathematics (ICAEM), Taxila, Pakistan, 27–29 August 2019. [CrossRef]
82. Jalal, A.; Mahmood, M.; Sidduqi, M.A. Robust spatio-temporal features for human interaction recognition via artificial neural network. In Proceedings of the 2018 International Conference on Frontiers of Information Technology (FIT), Islamabad, Pakistan, 17–19 December 2018. [CrossRef]
83. Jalal, A.; Kamal, S.; Azurdia-Meza, C.A. Depth maps-based human segmentation and action recognition using full-body plus body color cues via recognizer engine. *J. Electr. Eng. Technol.* **2019**, *14*, 455–461. [CrossRef]
84. Luo, X.; Tan, H.; Guan, Q.; Liu, T.; Zhuo, H.; Shen, B. Abnormal activity detection using pyroelectric infrared sensors. *Sensors* **2016**, *16*, 822. [CrossRef]
85. Huang, Q.; Yang, J.; Qiao, Y. Person re-identification across multi-camera system based on local descriptors. In Proceedings of the 2012 Sixth International Conference on Distributed Smart Cameras (ICDSC), Hong Kong, China, 30 October–2 November 2012; pp. 1–6.
86. Jalal, A.; Kim, Y.; Kamal, S.; Farooq, A.; Kim, D. Human daily activity recognition with joints plus body features representation using Kinect sensor. In Proceedings of the 2015 International Conference on Informatics, Electronics & Vision (ICIEV), Fukuoka, Japan, 15–18 June 2015. [CrossRef]
87. Jalal, A.; Uddin, M.Z.; Kim, J.T.; Kim, T.S. Daily Human Activity Recognition Using Depth Silhouettes and R Transformation for Smart Home. In Proceedings of the 9th International Conference on Smart Homes and Health Telematics (ICOST 2011), Montreal, QC, Canada, 20–22 June 2011; pp. 25–32.
88. Yoshimoto, H.; Date, N.; Yonemoto, S. Vision-based real-time motion capture system using multiple cameras. In Proceedings of the IEEE International Conference on Multisensor Fusion and Integration for Intelligent Systems (MFI2003), Tokyo, Japan, 30 July–1 August 2003; pp. 247–251.
89. Jalal, A.; Kamal, S. Real-time life logging via a depth silhouette-based human activity recognition system for smart home services. In Proceedings of the 2014 11th IEEE International Conference on Advanced Video and Signal Based Surveillance (AVSS), Seoul, South Korea, 26–29 August 2014; pp. 74–80.
90. Jalal, A.; Kim, S.; Yun, B.J. Assembled algorithm in the real-time H. 263 codec for advanced performance. In Proceedings of the 7th International Workshop on Enterprise networking and Computing in Healthcare Industry (HEALTHCOM 2005), Busan, Korea, 23–25 June 2005; pp. 295–298.
91. Jalal, A.; Zeb, M.A. Security and QoS optimization for distributed real time environment. In Proceedings of the 7th IEEE International Conference on Computer and Information Technology (CIT 2007), Aizu-Wakamatsu, Fukushima, Japan, 16–19 October 2007; pp. 369–374.
92. Huang, C.; Ren, T.; Zhang, J. Policy Documents Quantitative Research: A New Direction for Public Policy Study. *J. Public Manag.* **2015**, *12*, 129–137.
93. Huang, C. *Quantitative Research on Policy Literature*; Science Press: Beijing, China, 2016; pp. 3–46.
94. Huang, C.; Yue, X.; Yang, M.; Su, J.; Chen, J. A quantitative study on the diffusion of public policy in china: Evidence from the S&T finance sector. *J. Chin. Gov.* **2017**, *2*, 235–254.
95. Huang, C.; Wang, S.; Su, J.; Zhao, P. A Social Network Analysis of Changes in China's Education Policy Information Transmission System (1978–2013). *High. Educ. Policy* **2018**, *3*, 1–23. [CrossRef]
96. Piyathilaka, L.; Kodagoda, S. Gaussian mixture based HMM for human daily activity recognition using 3D skeleton features. In Proceedings of the 2013 IEEE 8th conference on industrial electronics and applications (ICIEA), Melbourne, VIC, Australia, 19–21 June 2013; pp. 567–572.
97. Jalal, A.; Kamal, S.; Kim, D. A depth video sensor-based life-logging human activity recognition system for elderly care in smart indoor environments. *Sensors* **2014**, *14*, 11735–11759. [CrossRef]
98. Jalal, A.; Kim, Y.H.; Kim, Y.J.; Kamal, S.; Kim, D. Robust human activity recognition from depth video using spatiotemporal multi-fused features. *Pattern Recognit.* **2017**, *61*, 295–308. [CrossRef]
99. Jalal, A.; Kamal, S.; Kim, D. Shape and motion features approach for activity tracking and recognition from kinect video camera. In Proceedings of the 2015 IEEE 29th International Conference on Advanced Information Networking and Applications Workshops, Gwangju, Korea, 24–27 March 2015; pp. 445–450.

100. Jalal, A.; Quaid, M.A.K.; Hasan, A.S. Wearable Sensor-Based Human Behavior Understanding and Recognition in Daily Life for Smart Environments. In Proceedings of the 2018 International Conference on Frontiers of Information Technology (FIT), Islamabad, Pakistan, 17–19 December 2018; pp. 105–110.
101. Wu, H.; Pan, W.; Xiong, X.; Xu, S. Human activity recognition based on the combined svm&hmm. In Proceedings of the 2014 IEEE International Conference on Information and Automation (ICIA), Hailar, China, 28–30 July 2014; pp. 219–224.

© 2019 by the authors. Licensee MDPI, Basel, Switzerland. This article is an open access article distributed under the terms and conditions of the Creative Commons Attribution (CC BY) license (http://creativecommons.org/licenses/by/4.0/).

Article

A Hybrid Model for Addressing the Relationship between Financial Performance and Sustainable Development

Yanfang Zhang [1,2] and Mushang Lee [3,*]

[1] Straits Institute of Minjiang University, Fuzhou 350108, China; yanfang825@163.com
[2] Institute of Higher Education Cooperation and Exchange across the Taiwan Strait, Minjiang University, Fuzhou 350108, China
[3] Department of Accounting, Chinese Culture University, Taipei 11114, Taiwan
* Correspondence: leemushang@gmail.com; Tel.: +88-62-2861-0511 (ext. 35501)

Received: 28 February 2019; Accepted: 15 May 2019; Published: 22 May 2019

Abstract: Measuring financial performance has become an essential topic due to the potential decimating impacts on the corporation itself as well as to whole societies during financial turmoil. In order to provide an overarching description of the multidimensional nature for measuring a corporation's operations, it is preferable to employ data envelopment analysis (DEA). Different from prior research that merely focuses on a singular DEA performance rank, this study extends it to multiple DEA specifications (i.e., it combines inputs and outputs in several different ways) so as to make judgments more complete and robust. We also execute fuzzy visualization technique (i.e., nonlinear fuzzy robust principal component analysis, NFRPCA) to represent the main characteristics of data so that non-specialists can have better access to the results. The analyzed result is then fed into the restricted Boltzmann machine (RBM) to establish a model to forecast a firm's operating performance. Even a fraction of accuracy improvement can result in considerable future savings to a firm and investors. When examined using real cases, the model is a promising alternative for operating performance forecasting and can assist both internal and external market participants.

Keywords: data envelopment analysis; decision making; artificial intelligence; performance

1. Introduction

The financial distress of 2007 started in the U.S., promptly took the form of full-blown systematic risk in the U.S., and rapidly spread to other developed countries to become a serious global economic crisis [1–5]. Because the resultant financial distress had enormous impacts on firms and economies, such as impacting the stability of stock markets, decimating the values of corporations, and impeding the circulation of resources, financial distress prediction is gaining considerably greater interest. If the constructed prediction model is trustworthy and reliable, then managers can initiate some treatments to avoid further deterioration, before financial trouble erupts, and reach the goal of sustainable development, and market participants can adjust their investment strategy to maximize profitability under anticipated risk exposure [6–9].

From the seminal work done by Altman [10], which is grounded on multivariate discriminant analysis (MDA), a large volume of statistical-based techniques and operation research approaches have been consecutively implemented to deal with both credit risk and financial distress prediction. However, the aforementioned techniques have to satisfy some strict statistical assumptions, such as linear separability, multivariate normality, and independence of predictors, which are often violated in real-life applications [11–13]. With the rapid improvement of innovative data-driven technologies, computational intelligence (such as neural network (NN), decision tree (DT), and support vector machine (SVM)) not only has the ability to cope with non-linearity, but can also extract meaningful information from vague, imprecise data as well as identify implicit trends that are too complicated to be discovered by either users or traditional systems [7,8]. This study adopts computational intelligence due to its (1) superior generalization capability and (2) it does not obey statistical assumptions.

Compared with the well-established research studies in the literature on financial distress and credit risk prediction, works on performance forecasting are quite rare, even as it is widely recognized that the critical trigger for financial distress is bad operating performance [14–16]. Kamei [17] also indicated that bad operating performance is responsible for many financial distress cases (almost 99%). In other words, events such as firm insolvency and defaults on promissory notes do not just happen by coincidence. Instead, there are notable root causes that precede corporate financial distress, and it is the inability to deal with such events properly at an early stage that triggers the demise of these corporations [18]. In short, bad operating performance is not only an inevitable prior stage before financial distress erupts, but also ruins the goal of corporate sustainable development. This is because the corporation with good financial performance normally poses superior operating efficiency. A corporation's operating efficiency increase (such as initiatives to improve energy efficiency, reduce CO_2 emissions in production and transportation, reduce water use, eliminate the utilization of virgin materials, and reuse waste) means that it can reduce the operational costs so as to increase its profitability [19]. For example, Coca-Cola established a monitoring and targeting system in its plant to control and evaluate energy and water use, leading to a 15% reduction in water use, with a 6% increase in production. The solar park of Volkswagen AG in North America is expected to provide the electricity to all the plants when the manufacturing line is not ruining. Furthermore, Wanger and Bloom [20] identified the relationship between financial performance and sustainability. They divided their samples into two different subgroups based on their financial performance. Their finding showed that financially good-performing corporations have more resources to invest in sustainability, which, in return, lead to better financial results. Eccles et al. [21] also indicated that good financial performance corporations outperform bad financial performance corporations in terms of sustainable initiatives and accounting rate of return. That is, the corporation with good financial performance has a greater possibility to implement social and environmental sustainability so as to reach the goal of sustainable development.

How to evaluate and appropriately determine corporate operating performance is an attractive research topic. Past studies mainly focused on analyzing financial ratios such as return on assets (ROA) and return on investment (ROI), but these measures belong to the category of one-input and one-output techniques. However, merely implementing a one-input and one-output measurement to describe the whole facets of a corporation's inherent operations is not reliable. In order to provide an overarching assessment to determine the corporation's inherent operating performance, one can adopt data envelopment analysis (DEA), which handles multiple inputs and multiple outputs simultaneously without a pre-defined production function (e.g., profit maximization or cost minimization) [22,23].

In today's big data environment, users gather and disseminate data from so many different resources, but too much data without proper handling will confuse the users and push them to maybe even make an inappropriate decision. This is called the curse of dimensionality. DEA has the advantage of handling multiple inputs and multiple outputs simultaneously, but it comes with a weakness in that too much data will deteriorate its discriminant ability—that is, it cannot tell the difference between superior and inferior operating performances. To overcome this challenge, a novel dimensionality reduction technique, named the non-linear fuzzy robust principal component analysis (NFRPCA), was initiated. The analyzed outcome can then be fed into the restricted Boltzmann machine (RBM) to construct a model for corporate operating performance forecasting.

There is a clear requirement for precise decision-making support for both investments and the ongoing monitoring of the health of corporations. Even a fraction of forecasting accuracy improvement can translate into a tremendous amount of future savings [24]. An ensemble learning architecture is a set of individual classifiers whose predictions are integrated, leading to superior forecasting performance versus those from individual classifiers [25]. The fundamental idea of ensemble learning is to complement the error made by the individual model, which is widely recognized as one of the most efficient ways to improve the performance and robustness of the forecasting problem. Thus, the study used an ensemble learning strategy.

Managers can view the model as a decision support system (DSS) to assist them in forming better decisions under an anticipated risk level as well as reaching the goal of sustainable development. Investors can take the model as an investment guideline to modify their financing strategy and investment portfolio with the target of profit maximization. Policy makers can consider the potential implication of this research outcome and formulate future policies so as to solidify the stability of financial markets and upgrade a nation's industrial level.

The aim of this study was therefore four-fold as follows:

- To provide a sophisticated corporate operating performance forecasting model for managers to reach the goal of sustainable development, this study combined the utilization of financial ratios with a variety of DEA specifications;
- To eliminate the curse of dimensionality as well as enhance the discriminant ability of DEA, this study performed a novel dimensionality reduction technique (NFRPCA);
- To make the analysis outcome more accessible to non-specialists, this study executed a visualization technique to represent the main structure of the data; and
- To improve the model's forecasting quality as well as eliminate risk exposure to investors, this study adopted an ensemble learning strategy.

The rest of this study is organized as follows. Section 2 expresses the literature review. Section 3 briefly describes the implemented methodologies. Section 4 conducts some experiments to examine and compare the performance of the proposed model. Finally, Section 5 offers conclusions and some future work ideas.

2. Literature Review

How to diagnose the nature of financial distress is still an open topic in the domain of corporate finance and accounting. As it is widely acknowledged that bad operating performance is the main trigger for financial distress, performance assessment has therefore become an important issue for the business world and academics for several decades. The three most commonly used criteria to describe corporate operating performance are return on assets (ROA), return on investment (ROI), and return on equity (ROE), but they are solely derived from financial statements that could hide some essential information about true financial troubles through different estimation methods and selective accounting principles. Moreover, these criteria belong to the category of one-input and one-output measurement. Merely utilizing these simple criteria to depict the whole structure of a corporation's operation is not reliable and trustworthy. DEA can deal with this obstacle by simultaneously handling multiple inputs and multiple outputs, and providing a final performance rank for each decision-making unit (DMU). However, the performance rank determined by DEA is affected by the inclusion or exclusion of an input or an output [26,27]—that is, the utilization of different inputs or outputs will lead to different performance ranks. Rather than employ a single DEA specification, this study preferred to go beyond a single performance rank and extended into multiple DEA specifications (i.e., it combined inputs and outputs in several dissimilar ways). By doing so, we achieved two objectives at the same time: (1) the assessment mechanism is useful for examining the robustness of the results, and (2) a bundle of performance ranks yields comprehensive information for classifying the units of observations [28].

Although multiple DEA specifications can provide overarching information for decision makers to form appropriate decisions, they still come with some challenges as too much information will confuse the decision makers and too much data fed into DEA will deteriorate its discriminant ability. To overcome this challenge, one can utilize NFRPCA (i.e., one of the dimensionality reduction techniques). The original data going through the NFRPCA procedure not only can facilitate the decision-making process of the users, but also can enhance DEA's discriminant ability. By combining the utilization of DEA specifications, financial indicators, and dimensionality reduction technique, we were able to classify corporations into four different categories and designated those that have superior operating performance and those that have inferior operating performance. In other words, we transformed the performance assessment task into a conventional binary classification task. The determined results were then fed into the restricted Boltzmann machine (RBM) to construct the model for corporate operating performance forecasting.

3. Methodology

Restricted Boltzmann Machine Ensemble (RBME)

The restricted Boltzmann machine (RBM), a probabilistic graphical mechanism that can be deemed as a stochastic neural network, has gained considerable attention in the artificial intelligence (AI) community due to its remarkable advantages, such as outstanding representation capability, fast extraction of helpful information from a complex dataset, and quick identification of abstract features [29–32]. Furthermore, with the great improvement and advancement in computing power and the development of efficient learning algorithms (i.e., contrastive divergence), the RBM has demonstrated its effectiveness in numerous forecasting tasks [29].

The RBM has a two-layer architecture with a set of visible units **v** of dimension G depicting the observable data, and a set of binary hidden units **h** of dimension B that learn to express features that capture the higher-order correlation in the observed data. These two layers are linked together by means of the symmetrical weight matrix $E \in R^{G \times B}$, whereas there are no linkages within the same layer. The conceptual architecture of the two-layer RBM is represented in Figure 1. The RBM initially introduced the utilization of visible and hidden binary units, but it can also be extended to adopt numerous dissimilar sorts of units, such as Gaussian units, binominal units, softmax units, and so forth [30].

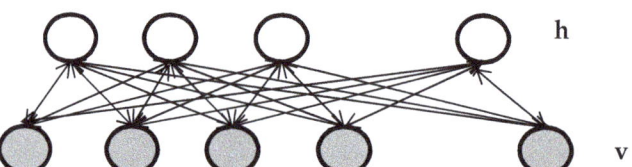

Figure 1. The conceptual structure of restricted Boltzmann machine (RBM).

The RBM, in reality, can be deemed as a Markov random field that attempts to express input data with hidden units. The weights between two layers are encoded by a statistical relationship. Given the energy function $K(\mathbf{v},\mathbf{h})$ of the state $(\mathbf{v},\mathbf{h})$, the joint distribution over the visible units and hidden units is described in Equation (1):

$$P(\mathbf{v},\mathbf{h}) = \frac{1}{Z}\exp(-K(\mathbf{v},\mathbf{h})), \qquad (1)$$

where Z denotes the normalization constant. The binary visible and hidden units are depicted in Equation (2):

$$Z = \sum_{\mathbf{v}}\sum_{\mathbf{h}}\exp(-K(\mathbf{v},\mathbf{h})). \qquad (2)$$

For the real-valued visible units and binary units, the normalization constant Z can be determined by Equation (3):

$$Z = \int_{\mathbf{v}}\sum_{\mathbf{h}}\exp(-K(\mathbf{v},\mathbf{h}))d\mathbf{v}. \qquad (3)$$

The visible units are binary-valued, and the energy function can be shown in Equation (4):

$$K(\mathbf{v},\mathbf{h}) = -\sum_{i=1}^{G}\sum_{j=1}^{B} v_i E_{ij} h_j - \sum_{j=1}^{B} m_j h_j - \sum_{i=1}^{G} n_i v_i, \quad (4)$$

where the biases of the hidden and visible units are depicted as m_j and n_i, respectively. If the visible units are real-valued, then the energy function $K(\mathbf{v},\mathbf{h})$, incorporated with a quadratic term, can be expressed in Equation (5):

$$K(\mathbf{v},\mathbf{h}) = \frac{1}{2}\sum_{i=1}^{G} v_i^2 - \sum_{i=1}^{G}\sum_{j=1}^{B} v_i E_{ij} h_j - \sum_{j=1}^{B} m_j h_j - \sum_{i=1}^{G} n_i v_i. \quad (5)$$

According to the abovementioned energy function, we can see that the hidden units h_j are independent of each other when conditioned on $\mathbf{v}$, since there are no direct linkages among all hidden units. In the same vein, the visible units v_i are also independent of each other when conditioned on $\mathbf{h}$. Conditioning on the visible layer, the units of a binary hidden layer are independent Bernoulli random variables. The probability of binary state h_j of each hidden unit j is set to 1, and seen in Equation (6):

$$p(h_j = 1 | \mathbf{v}) = \rho(\sum_i E_{ij} v_i + m_j), \quad (6)$$

where $\rho(q) = 1/(1 + \exp(-q))$ denotes the sigmoid activation function.

The visible units conditioned on the hidden layer are independent Bernoulli random variables under the situation of visible units having binary values. The probability of the binary state v_i of each visible unit i is set to 1, and depicted in Equation (7):

$$p(v_i = 1 | \mathbf{h}) = \rho(\sum_j E_{ij} h_j + n_i). \quad (7)$$

The visible units conditioned on the hidden layer are independent Gaussian random variables for the case of visible units having real values, and the mathematical formulation can be represented in Equation (8):

$$p(v_i | \mathbf{h}) = D(\sum_j E_{ij} h_j + n_i, \ 1 \ ), \quad (8)$$

where $D()$ expresses the Gaussian distribution function.

The RBM is a generative model, and the inherent parameters can be determined by implementing a stochastic gradient descent algorithm. By aggregating all possible hidden vectors, the probability that the network assigns to a visible vector can be decided:

$$p(\mathbf{v}) = \frac{1}{Z}\sum_h \exp(-K(\mathbf{v},\mathbf{h})) \quad (9)$$

The weight of the derivative of the log probability of a training vector can be decided by Equation (10):

$$\frac{\partial \log p(\mathbf{v})}{\partial E_{ij}} = [v_i h_j]_{data} - [v_i h_j]_{model}, \quad (10)$$

where the bracket expresses expectations under the distribution determined by the subscript follows. The subscripts data and model in Equation (10) depict the distribution of the data and the equilibrium distribution decided by the RBM, respectively. Based on this concept, we updated the learning rule of the weight very easily, represented in Equation (11):

$$\Delta E_{ij} = \lambda[(v_i h_j)_{data} - (v_i h_j)_{model}], \quad (11)$$

where λ depicts the learning rate.

How to get a precise sample of $(v_i h_j)_{model}$ under the situation of calculating the exact gradient of the log probability of training data is very complicated. In order to solve this obstacle, an efficient and faster learning rule, called contrastive divergence (CD), was introduced:

$$\Delta E_{ij} = \lambda[(v_i h_j)_{data} - (v_i h_j)_{recon}], \quad (12)$$

where recon describes a distribution decided by implementing alternative Gibbs sampling for 1 step, and Gibbs sampling is initialized with the data.

According to a similar concept for the learning rule of E_{ij}, the biases of hidden and visible units (i.e., m_j and n_i) can be updated by the following equations:

$$\Delta m_j = \lambda[(h_j)_{data} - (h_j)_{recon}] \text{ and} \quad (13)$$

$$\Delta n_i = \lambda[(v_i)_{data} - (v_i)_{recon}]. \quad (14)$$

Ensemble learning is an active research field in AI owing to its great potential to enhance the forecasting quality of a singular classifier. Even a fraction of improvement in forecasting accuracy can translate into a considerable amount of future monetary savings. Due to the urgent requirement for forecasting quality improvement, this study extended the singular classifier to an ensemble one (i.e., RBM ensemble: RBME) by implementing the bagging and random subspace method (RSM). By doing so, decision makers can receive much more accurate and unbiased forecasting outcomes as well as protect their personnel or investment wealth.

4. Research Design and Analysis

4.1. The Data

The capital-intensive electronics industry in Taiwan has gained considerable attention due to its great impact and influence on the global supply chain. The Taiwan government has also allocated considerable resources and provided numerous financing incentives to upgrade this sector's industrial level. Electronics firms in Taiwan make up an important capital market for global investors/market participants, as related listed firms typically make up over 60% of the domestic stock market turnover. Therefore, we chose the electronics industry in Taiwan from 2016 to 2018 as our research sample. After deleting the missing and extreme data, 1200 samples were preserved. All the data were collected from public websites, such as Taiwan Economic Journal Data Bank (TEJ), Taipei Exchange (TE), and Taiwan Stock Exchange Corporation (TSEC) from the period of 2015–2017.

4.2. The DEA Specifications and Predictors

By executing DEA to determine corporate operating performance, the informative input and output variables can be decided. In accordance with prior work done by Xu and Wang [31], total assets (TA), total liability (TL), and the cost of goods sold (COGS) were identified as input variables, and earnings before interest and tax (EBIT) and total sales (TS) were decided as output variables. In order to examine the representativeness of the chosen variables, we conducted the Pearson correlation (Table 1). A higher correlation coefficient implies a closer relation between two variables, while a lower correlation coefficient implies less correlation. The results in Table 1 state that all the selected variables show significant positive correlation. Obviously, it is not necessary to remove any of the selected variables.

Table 1. The Pearson correlation results.

	I1: TA	I2: TL	I3: COGS	O1: EBIT	O2: TS
I1: TA	1				
I2: TL	0.953 **	1			
I3: COGS	0.866 **	0.866 **	1		
O1: EBIT	0.877 **	0.877 **	0.877 **	1	
O2: TS	0.903 **	0.903 **	0.903 **	0.903 **	1

Note: TA: total assets, TL: total liabilities; COGS: cost of goods sold; EBIT: earnings before interest and tax; TS: total sales. * denotes $p < 0.1$; ** denotes $p < 0.05$; *** denotes $p < 0.01$.

It is necessary, however, to look beyond a singular DEA score so as to provide an overarching consideration of corporate operating assessment. To deal with this challenge, we implemented a variant of DEA specifications (i.e., three input variables and two output variables can generate 14 different combinations) that combined input and output variables in several dissimilar ways. Table 2 shows all DEA specifications.

Table 2. The modules of each data envelopment analysis (DEA) specification.

Module	Input	Output
DEA specification 1	I1:TA	O1:EBIT
DEA specification 2	I1:TA	O1:EBIT, O2:TS
DEA specification 3	I2:TL	O1:EBIT
DEA specification 4	I2:TL	O1:EBIT, O2:TS
DEA specification 5	I3:COGS	O1:EBIT
DEA specification 6	I3:COGS	O1:EBIT, O2:TS
DEA specification 7	I1:TA, I2:TL	O1:EBIT
DEA specification 8	I1:TA, I2:TL	O1:EBIT, O2:TS
DEA specification 9	I1: TA, I3: COGS	O1:EBIT
DEA specification 10	I1:TA, I3:COGS	O1:EBIT, O2:TS
DEA specification 11	I2:TL, I3:COGS	O1:EBIT
DEA specification 12	I2:TL, I3:COGS	O1:EBIT, O2:TS
DEA specification 13	I1:TA, I2:TL, I3:COGS	O1:EBIT
DEA specification 14	I1:TA, I2:TL, I3:COGS	O1:EBIT, O2:TS

Note: TA: Total assets, TL: total liabilities, COGS: cost of goods sold, EBIT: earnings before interest and tax, TS: total sales.

The corporate operating performance forecasting is highly related to the issue of corporate financial distress prediction, whereby the selected predictors are designated as the condition variables in this study. Table 3 shows the descriptive statistics of selected predictors.

Table 3. The predictors.

Predictors	Description	Mean	Variance
X1: NI/TA	Net income to total assets	0.05	0.01
X2: TL/TA	Total liability to total assets	0.41	0.03
X3: S/TA	Sales to total assets	0.89	0.31
X4: TL/TE	Total liability to total equity	0.99	3.44
X5: WC/TA	Working capital to total assets	0.31	0.04
X6: NI/(TA-TL)	Net income to (total assets—total liability)	0.05	0.20
X7: LTL/TA	Long-term liability to total assets	0.06	0.01
X8: OI/TA	Operating income to total assets	0.04	0.01

4.3. The Assessment Criteria

Assessment criteria have dissimilar influences on financial risk prediction. For example, false negative (FN) is the amount of positive or abnormal cases that is misclassified as normal cases. Since positive cases are distressed, inefficient, or fraudulent accounts in financial risk prediction, a forecasting mechanism with a higher FN rate can lead to tremendous losses for stock market participants as well as negatively influence the stability of the economy and stock market. Therefore, compared with a false positive (FP) rate, the FN rate should have higher importance in a forecasting task. One of the most commonly executed assessment criteria is overall accuracy/error rate. However, merely relying on one assessment criterion to determine the appropriate forecasting mechanism is not reliable and trustworthy. To yield a more comprehensive measurement, we utilized three other assessment criteria: recall, precision, and F-measure. The mathematical formulations are depicted as follows, and the confusion matrix is shown in Table 4 [32–35].

Overall accuracy (OA): this criterion is the percentage of a precisely classified module:

$$OA = \frac{(TN + TP)}{(TP + FP + FN + TN)}.$$

Precision (Pre): this criterion is the amount of predicted fault-prone modules that precisely are fault-prone modules:

$$Pre = \frac{TP}{(TP + FP)}.$$

Recall (Rec): this criterion is the number of fault-prone modules that are precisely predicted:

$$Rec = \frac{TP}{(TP+FN)}.$$

F-measure: this criterion is the harmonic mean of precision and recall that has been widely implemented in AI fields:

$$F = \frac{2 \times Pre \times Rec}{(Pre + Rec)}.$$

Table 4. The confusion matrix.

Actual (↓)/Predicted (→)	Predicted Positive	Predicted Negative
Positive case	True positive (TP)	False negative (FN)
Negative case	False positive (FP)	True negative (TN)

4.4. The Forecasting Outcome

To provide a more sounded measurement, two types of information are considered: 5 indicators derived from financial statements (i.e., gross profit ratio, sales growth rate, inventory turnover rate, earnings per share, and net profit margin) and a performance score obtained from 14 possible DEA specifications (see Table 2). To be much more understandable to non-specialists, visualization technique, one of the dimensionality reduction architecture, namely NFRPCA was conducted. The first component was by far the most essential, accounting for 65.84% of the variability in the data. The addition of the second component increased this percentage to 85.16% (see Table 5). The first two components provided an adequate representation of the data. According to the data structure, we can classify the data into four categories. The data located in quadrant I are designated as having superior operating performance, and the data located in quadrant III are deemed as having inferior operating performance. The analyzed results are fed into the RBME to construct the forecasting model. We conducted five-fold cross-validation (CV) to eliminate the influence of over-fitting. To test the usefulness of NFRPCA, the experiments were separated into two dissimilar scenarios: (1) with principal component analysis (PCA) and (2) with nonlinear fuzzy robust principal component analysis (NFRPCA). To ensure the result did not happen by coincidence, a statistical examination was implemented. Table 6 shows the result. This finding is in accordance with Luukka [36] who indicated that the NFRPCA can project the data sets into a more feasible form. Furthermore, the introduced model not only can be represented in a singular structure, it also can be extended to an ensemble structure.

To examine the effectiveness of ensemble strategies, the experiments were divided into two different scenarios: (1) with ensemble strategies and (2) without ensemble strategies. Table 7 presents the result. We can see that the model with ensemble strategies can not only attain superior forecasting quality under all assessment criteria, but can also facilitate decision-makers to form an appropriate judgment [37]. This finding is in line with prior work done by Wozniak et al. [38] who indicated that an ensemble structure can achieve enhanced forecasting performance by integrating many singular classifiers and using their strengths. The result also can be explained by the famous "no free lunch" theorem introduced by Wolpert [39], which indicated that there is no specific classifier modelling method that is optimal for all forecasting tasks, as each method has its specific competitive edge.

Table 5. Non-linear fuzzy robust principal component analysis (NFRPCA) results.

Component	% of Variance	Cumulative %
PC1	65.84	65.84
PC2	19.32	85.16
PC3	8.92	94.08

Table 6. The forecasting result (PCA vs. NFRPCA).

Assessment Criteria	RBM		Statistical Result
	With NFRPCA	With PCA	
OA	72.56	68.26	0.000 ***
Pre	64.60	60.40	0.000 ***
Rec	66.15	62.03	0.000 ***
F	65.32	61.12	0.000 ***

Note: OA: overall accuracy; Pre: precision; Rec: recall; F: F-measure. * denotes $p < 0.1$; ** denotes $p < 0.05$; *** denotes $p < 0.01$.

Table 7. The forecasting result (With ensemble strategy vs. Without ensemble strategy).

Assessment Criteria	RBM		STATISTICAL RESULT
	With ENSEMBLE	Without Ensemble	
OA	86.48	72.56	0.000 ***
Pre	82.40	64.60	0.000 ***
Rec	83.60	66.15	0.000 ***
F	82.99	65.32	0.000 ***

Note: OA: overall accuracy; Pre: precision; Rec: recall; F: F-measure. * denotes $p < 0.1$; ** denotes $p < 0.05$; *** denotes $p < 0.01$.

To reach a more reliable research finding, this study took the introduced model as a benchmark and compared it with another four different AI-based techniques: decision tree (DT), rough set theory (RST), random forest (RF), and extreme learning machine (ELM). However, it is widely recognized that there is no individual forecasting mechanism that performs the best under all assessment criteria (see Table 8). Rokach [40] stated that the classifier selection can be transformed into a multiple criteria decision analysis (MCDA) task. Before executing the MCDA algorithm, the competitive score of each classifier under different assessment criteria should be decided. The competitive score is computed by utilizing a paired t-test for each classifier at the 5% significance level. The purpose of the paired t-test is to assess whether the superior or inferior competitive score of one classifier over another is statistically significant. We conducted one of the MCDA algorithms, called TOPSIS, to solve this task, because it poses a straightforward computational process, has easy-to-understand decision logics, and the mathematical formulation is rational and understandable. Table 9 shows the competitive score of each classifier and Figure 2 represents the ranking priority of each classifier. We can see that the proposed model reached the 1st rank, meaning that the proposed model outperformed the other four models.

Table 8. The forecasting result under four different assessment criteria.

Model	Assessment Criteria (Avg.)			
	OA	Pre	Rec	F
Proposed model	86.48	82.40	83.60	82.99
ELM	85.28	72.20	88.93	79.67
RST	81.20	76.60	76.47	76.52
RF	84.08	70.80	87.15	78.03
DT	78.56	66.60	77.10	71.26

Note: ELM: extreme learning machine; RST: rough set theory; RF: random forest; DT: decision tree; OA: overall accuracy; Pre: precision; Rec: recall; F: F-measure.

Table 9. The competitive score.

Model	Assessment Criteria (Avg.)			
	OA	Pre	Rec	F
Proposed model	2	3	1	2
ELM	2	−2	3	1
RST	−2	2	−3	0
RF	0	−1	2	−1
DT	−3	−2	−3	−2

Figure 2. The ranking priority of each classifier. (Note: ELM: extreme learning machine; RST: rough set theory; RF: random forest; DT: decision tree.)

4.5. Robustness Test

Most parts of previous works only utilized one pre-decided database to reach a final conclusion that cannot necessarily be fully trusted in today's highly fluctuating business environment. To prevent users from reaching a biased outcome, we tested our introduced model with another two databases: (1) Condition 1: the performance rank is decided by a traditional financial ratio (i.e., ROA); and (2) Condition 2: the performance rank is determined by a singular DEA score. The results are shown in Figures 3 and 4. We can see that the proposed model performed better in the two different databases.

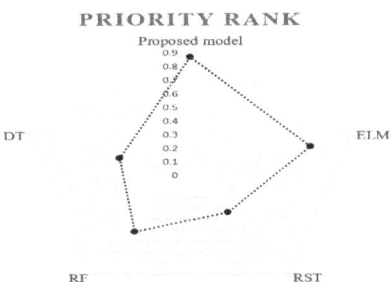

Figure 3. The ranking priority of each classifier in Condition 1: the performance rank is decided by a traditional financial ratio.

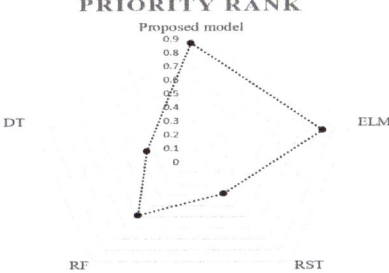

Figure 4. The ranking priority of each classifier in Condition 2: the performance rank is determined by a singular DEA score.

To ensure that the selected performance measure was fairly representative, we considered each corporation's credit rating status. The corporate credit rating status is evaluated by an independent institution that aims to find out how a corporation is able to meet its financial obligation and specifically relies on a detailed and comprehensive analysis of all the risk factors of the measure object [41]. The usage of credit rating status is widely taken as a measure of corporation's risk and creditworthiness [42,43]. The rating status can be divided into 10 ranks, ranging from best to worst (ranks from 1 to 4 express low risk; from 5 to 6 express middle risk; and from 7 to 10 express high risk). The results under three different performance measures are shown in Figure 5. We can see that the corporation with superior performance derived from multiple DEA specifications has better credit rating status. In contrast, most corporations with good ROA performance still have bad credit rating status. That is, the discriminant ability of multiple DEA specifications outperforms that of the other two measures.

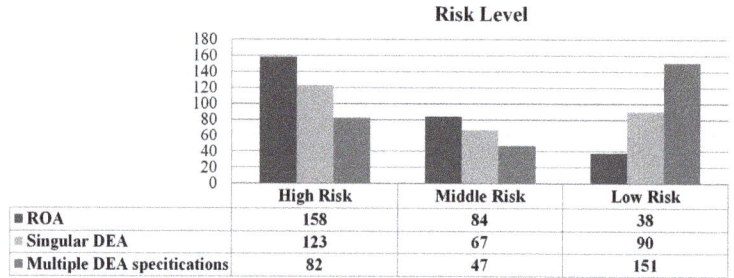

	High Risk	Middle Risk	Low Risk
ROA	158	84	38
Singular DEA	123	67	90
Multiple DEA specifications	82	47	151

Figure 5. The discriminant ability of each performance measure.

Corporations should realize how corporate sustainability is established in s specific context and how the concept of sustainable development can be implemented to the business level and what corporations should do when they intend to reach the goal of sustainability [44]. For example, efficient utilization of the corporation's valuable resources, handling the requirements of all the stakeholders appropriately, maximizing the corporation's long term profitability, and so on, should be covered in the domain of corporate governance [45]. When integrating sustainability with corporate governance, the corporation should propose an avenue that will result in the creation of social, environmental, and economic value [46]. It is an urgent and required task to establish corporate governance that incorporates a positive response to the corporation's social, economic, and environmental risk, and chances that have the potential to affect the financial outcome of the corporations [47,48]. So, the corporate governance can be viewed as the integral part of sustainability. We divided our research samples into two different subgroups based on their corporate governance performance. The corporations with strong corporate governance normally perform better than the corporations with weak corporate governance in terms of financial performance (see Table 10). The finding is in accordance with the work done by Eccles et al. [21]. That is, the corporations with superior financial performance has higher potential to invest in sustainability.

Table 10. The comparison results (Average).

Condition	Corporation with Strong Corporate Governance	Corporation with Weak Corporate Governance
ROA	0.07	−0.09
Singular DEA	0.62	0.41
Multiple DEA specifications	0.53	0.34

5. Conclusions

Compared with thoroughly studied projects on financial distress prediction, works on performance forecasting are quite rare, even as it is widely acknowledged that a corporation's bad operating performance is the critical trigger for financial distress. Thus, this study introduced a novel hybrid mechanism that combined different technologies—as financial indicators and efficiency scores—in order to present a comprehensive description of corporate operating performance evaluation for users to make reliable judgments. The financial indicators were collected from financial statements, and the efficiency scores were obtained from 14 different DEA specifications (i.e., inputs and outputs are combined in several dissimilar ways). It has been demonstrated that there are numerous advantages from computing efficiency scores under all possible specifications of the DEA model [49]. While it is obvious that such a mechanism generates much redundancy, it does provide valuable and useful information. In order to make the outcome accessible to non-specialists, we employed a data reduction technique, called NFRPCA, to visualize the data's main characteristics. By doing so, we can determine which corporation belongs to the efficient group and which corporation belongs to the inefficient group.

We then sequentially fed the analyzed outcome into the RBME to construct the model for corporate operating performance forecasting. To enhance the model's forecasting quality, the introduced model was extended to an ensemble structure. Even a fraction of improvement in forecasting accuracy can be converted into tremendous future savings. However, no specific model can attain the best forecasting outcome under all assessment criteria. Model selection is a classical MCDA task, which can be handled through an MCDA algorithm. The model herein, examined by real cases, is a promising alternative for corporate operating performance forecasting. Corporate managers can take this model as a guideline to adjust their firm's financial structure so as to reduce the cost of capital as well as enhance its profit margin. A corporation with greater profits implies that it has higher risk-absorbing ability to survive in this highly turbulent business environment and greater possibility to reach the goal of sustainable development. Investors can view the model as a roadmap to modify their investment portfolio to maximize personal wealth under anticipated risk level. Policy makers can consider the potential implication of the research outcome and formulate future policies to strengthen financial markets as well as reach the goal of efficient markets.

Future works can consider two potential research directions. First, we worked on the target sample of Taiwan's electronics industry, which suggests that the ability to generalize the results is limited. Future studies can look into other industries or conduct cross-country analyses. Second, future direction can enhance the model's forecasting quality by considering much more sophisticated information, such as R&D expenditure and innovation capability. This is because innovation capability has been widely viewed as an essential element for sustainable economic growth as well as for representing the corporation's competitive advantage [50–54].

Author Contributions: The following statements should be used "conceptualization, Y.Z. and M.L.; methodology, M.L.; software, M.L.; validation, Y.Z. and M.L.; formal analysis, Y.Z. and M.L.; investigation, Y.Z. and M.L.; resources, M.L.; data curation, M.L.; writing—original draft preparation, Y.Z. and M.L.; writing—review and editing, Y.Z. and M.L.; visualization, M.L.; supervision, Y.Z. and M.L., please turn to the CRediT taxonomy for the term explanation. Authorship must be limited to those who have contributed substantially to the work reported.

Funding: This research was funded by Straits Institute of Minjiang University and Institute of Higher Education Cooperation and Exchange across the Taiwan Strait, Minjiang University.

Conflicts of Interest: No conflict of interest exists in the submission of this manuscript.

References

1. Ciani, M.; Gagliardi, F.; Riccarelli, S.; Betti, G. Fuzzy Measures of Multidimensional Poverty in the Mediterranean Area: A Focus on Financial Dimension. *Sustainability* **2019**, *11*, 143. [CrossRef]
2. Dinçer, H.; Yüksel, S.; Şenel, S. Analyzing the Global Risks for the Financial Crisis after the Great Depression Using Comparative Hybrid Hesitant Fuzzy Decision-Making Models: Policy Recommendations for Sustainable Economic Growth. *Sustainability* **2018**, *10*, 3126. [CrossRef]
3. Lane, P.R. The European sovereign debt crisis. *J. Econ. Perspect.* **2012**, *26*, 49–67. [CrossRef]
4. Covitz, D.; Liang, N.; Suarez, G.A. The evolution of a financial crisis: Collapse of the asset-backed commercial paper market. *J. Financ.* **2013**, *68*, 815–848. [CrossRef]

5. Grout, P.A.; Zalewska, A. Stock market risk in the financial crisis. *Int. Rev. Financ. Anal.* **2016**, *46*, 326–345. [CrossRef]
6. Geng, R.; Bose, I.; Chen, X. Prediction of financial distress: An empirical study of listed Chinese companies using data mining. *Eur. J. Oper. Res.* **2015**, *241*, 236–247. [CrossRef]
7. Liang, D.; Lu, C.C.; Tsai, C.F.; Shih, G.A. Financial ratios and corporate governance indicators in bankruptcy prediction: A comprehensive study. *Eur. J. Oper. Res.* **2016**, *252*, 561–572. [CrossRef]
8. Hsu, M.F.; Yeh, C.C.; Lin, S.J. Integrating dynamic Malmquist DEA and social network computing for advanced management decisions. *J. Intell. Fuzzy Syst.* **2018**, *35*, 231–241. [CrossRef]
9. Lin, S.J.; Hsu, M.F. Decision making by extracting soft information from CSR news report. *Technol. Econ. Dev. Econ.* **2018**, *24*, 1344–1361. [CrossRef]
10. Altman, E.I. Financial ratios, discriminant analysis and the prediction of corporate bankruptcy. *J. Financ.* **1968**, *23*, 589–609. [CrossRef]
11. Zhang, L.; Zhou, W.D. Fisher-regularized support vector machine. *Inf. Sci.* **2016**, *343*, 79–93. [CrossRef]
12. Ju, H.; Hou, Q.; Jing, L. Select this result for bulk action Fuzzy and interval-valued fuzzy nonparallel support vector machine. *J. Intell. Fuzzy Syst.* **2019**, *36*, 2677–2690. [CrossRef]
13. Wang, G. Safety evaluation model for smart driverless car using support vector machine. *J. Intell. Fuzzy Syst.* **2019**. [CrossRef]
14. Hajek, P.; Olej, V.; Myskova, R. Forecasting corporate financial performance using sentiment in annual reports for stakeholders' decision-making. *Technol. Econ. Dev. Econ.* **2014**, *20*, 721–738. [CrossRef]
15. Lin, R.; Chen, Z. Modified super-efficiency DEA models for solving infeasibility under non-negative data set. *INFOR Inf. Syst. Oper. Res.* **2018**, *56*, 265–285. [CrossRef]
16. Zhu, W.; Sun, P.; Zhang, Q. Context-dependent data envelopment analysis with common set of weights. *INFOR Inf. Syst. Oper. Res.* **2018**, *56*, 286–297. [CrossRef]
17. Kamei, T. *Risk Management*; Dobunkan: Tokyo, Japan, 1997. (In Japanese)
18. Shirata, C.Y.; Sakagami, M. An analysis of the "going concern assumption": Text mining from Japanese financial reports. *J. Emerg. Tech. Account.* **2008**, *5*, 1–16. [CrossRef]
19. Soytas, M.A.; Denizel, M.; Usar, D.D. Addressing endogeneity in the causal relationship between sustainability and financial performance. *Int. J. Prod. Econ.* **2019**, *210*, 56–71. [CrossRef]
20. Wagner, M.; Blom, J. The reciprocal and non-linear relationship of sustainability and financial performance. *Bus. Eth.* **2011**, *20*, 418–432. [CrossRef]
21. Eccles, R.G.; Ioannou, I.; Serafeim, G. The impact of corporate sustainability on organizational processes and performance. *Manag. Sci.* **2014**, *60*, 2835–2857. [CrossRef]
22. Basso, A.; Casarin, F.; Funari, S. How well is the museum performing? A joint use of DEA and BSC to measure the performance of museums. *Omega* **2018**, *81*, 67–84. [CrossRef]
23. Li, Z.; Crook, J.; Andreeva, G. Dynamic prediction of financial distress using Malmquist DEA. *Expert. Syst. Appl.* **2017**, *80*, 94–106. [CrossRef]
24. West, D.; Dellana, S.; Qian, J. Neural network ensemble strategies for financial decision applications. *Comput. Oper. Res.* **2005**, *32*, 2543–2559. [CrossRef]
25. Jurek, A.; Hong, J.; Chi, Y.; Liu, W. A novel ensemble learning approach to unsupervised record linkage. *Inf. Syst.* **2017**, *71*, 40–54. [CrossRef]
26. Parkin, D.; Hollingsworth, B. Measuring production efficiency of acute hospitals in Scotland, 1991–1994: Validity issues in data envelopment analysis. *Appl. Econ.* **1997**, *29*, 1425–1433. [CrossRef]
27. Sagarra, M.; Mar-Molinero, C.; Agasisti, T. Exploring the efficiency of Mexican universities: Integrating data envelopment analysis and multidimensional scaling. *Omega* **2017**, *67*, 123–133. [CrossRef]
28. Raveh, A. Co-plot: A graphic display method for geometrical representations of MCDM. *Eur. J. Oper. Res.* **2000**, *125*, 670–678. [CrossRef]
29. Xie, C.; Lv, J.; Li, X. Finding a good initial configuration of parameters for restricted Boltzmann machine pre-training. *Soft Comput.* **2017**, *21*, 6471–6479. [CrossRef]
30. Welling, M.; Rosen-Zvi, M.; Hinton, G. Exponential family harmoniums with an application to information retrieval. *NIPS* **2005**, *17*, 1481–1488.
31. Xu, X.; Wang, Y. Financial failure prediction using efficiency as a predictor. *Expert Syst. Appl.* **2009**, *36*, 366–373. [CrossRef]

32. Peng, Y.; Wang, G.; Wang, H. User preferences based software defect detection algorithms selection using MCDM. *Inf. Sci.* **2012**, *191*, 3–13. [CrossRef]
33. Kou, G.; Peng, Y.; Wang, G. Evaluation of clustering algorithms for financial risk analysis using MCDM methods. *Inf. Sci.* **2014**, *275*, 1–12. [CrossRef]
34. Chang, T.M.; Hsu, M.F.; Lin, S.J. Integrated news mining technique and AI-based mechanism for corporate performance forecasting. *Inf. Sci.* **2018**, *424*, 273–286. [CrossRef]
35. Hsu, M.F. Integrated multiple-attribute decision making and kernel-based mechanism for risk analysis and evaluation. *J. Intell. Fuzzy Syst.* **2019**, *36*, 2895–2905. [CrossRef]
36. Luukka, P. A new nonlinear fuzzy robust pca algorithm and similarity classifier in classification on medical data sets. *Int. J. Fuzzy Syst.* **2011**, *13*, 153–162.
37. Zhang, C.X.; Zhang, J.S.; Ji, N.N.; Guo, G. Learning ensemble classifiers via restricted Boltzmann machines. *Pattern Recognit. Lett.* **2014**, *36*, 161–170. [CrossRef]
38. Wozniak, M.; Graña, M.; Corchado, E. A survey of multiple classifier systems as hybrid systems. *Inf. Fusion* **2014**, *16*, 3–17. [CrossRef]
39. Wolpert, D. William Dembski's treatment of the No Free Lunch theorems is written in jello. *Math. Rev.* **2003**. Available online: http://www.talkreason.org/articles/orr.cfm (accessed on 20 May 2019).
40. Rokach, L. Ensemble-based classifiers. *Artif. Intell. Rev.* **2012**, *33*, 1–39. [CrossRef]
41. Hájek, P. Municipal credit rating modelling by neural networks. *Decis. Support Syst.* **2011**, *51*, 108–118. [CrossRef]
42. Lin, S.J.; Chang, C.; Hsu, M.F. Multiple extreme learning machines for a two-class imbalance corporate life cycle prediction. *Knowl. Based Syst.* **2013**, *39*, 214–223. [CrossRef]
43. Lin, S.J. Integrated artificial intelligence-based resizing strategy and multiple criteria decision making technique to form a management decision in an imbalanced environment. *Int. J. Mach. Learn. Cybern.* **2017**, *8*, 1981–1992. [CrossRef]
44. Dyllick, T.; Hockerts, K. Beyond the business case for corporate sustainability. *Bus. Strateg. Environ.* **2002**, *11*, 130–141. [CrossRef]
45. Sustentare. Sustainability Governance. 2010. Available online: http://www.sustentare.pt/pdf/doc.suste+sam(ENG1).pdf (accessed on 20 May 2019).
46. Krechovska, M.; Prochazkova, P.T. Sustainability and its integration into corporate governance focusing on corporate performance management and reporting. *Procedia Eng.* **2014**, *69*, 1144–1151. [CrossRef]
47. Zheng, J.; Wang, Y.M.; Chen, L.; Zhang, K. A new case retrieval method based on double frontiers data envelopment analysis. *J. Intell. Fuzzy Syst.* **2019**, *36*, 199–211. [CrossRef]
48. Hsu, M.F. A fusion mechanism for management decision and risk analysis. *Cybern. Syst.* **2019**. [CrossRef]
49. Cinca, C.S.; Molinero, C.M. Selecting DEA specifications and ranking units via PCA. *J. Oper. Res. Soc.* **2004**, *55*, 521–528. [CrossRef]
50. Lytras, M.D.; Raghavan, V.; Damiani, E. Big data and data analytics research: From metaphors to value space for collective wisdom in human decision making and smart machines. *Int. J. Semant. Web Inf. Syst.* **2017**, *13*, 1–10. [CrossRef]
51. Lytras, M.D.; Visvizi, A. Who uses smart city services and what to make of it: Toward interdisciplinary smart cities research. *Sustainability* **2018**, *10*, 1998. [CrossRef]
52. Visvizi, A.; Lytras, M.D. Rescaling and refocusing smart cities research: From mega cities to smart villages. *J. Sci. Technol. Policy Manag.* **2018**, *9*, 134–145. [CrossRef]
53. Visvizi, A.; Lytras, M.D.; Damiani, E.; Mathkour, H. Policy making for smart cities: Innovation and social inclusive economic growth for sustainability. *J. Sci. Technol. Policy Manag.* **2018**, *9*, 126–133. [CrossRef]
54. Hou, J.; Meng, J.; Zhu, L. Empirical analysis of corporate innovation, investor focus and stock slumps risk based on fuzzy mathematics and function optimization. *Int. J. Fuzzy Syst.* **2019**. [CrossRef]

© 2019 by the authors. Licensee MDPI, Basel, Switzerland. This article is an open access article distributed under the terms and conditions of the Creative Commons Attribution (CC BY) license (http://creativecommons.org/licenses/by/4.0/).

Article

Entropy-Based Face Recognition and Spoof Detection for Security Applications

Francisco A. Pujol [1,*], María José Pujol [2], Carlos Rizo-Maestre [3] and Mar Pujol [4]

1. Department of Computer Technology, University of Alicante, 03690 San Vicente del Raspeig-Alicante, Spain
2. Department of Applied Mathematics, University of Alicante, 03690 San Vicente del Raspeig-Alicante, Spain; mjose@ua.es
3. Department of Architectural Constructions, University of Alicante, 03690 San Vicente del Raspeig-Alicante, Spain; carlosrm@ua.es
4. Department of Computer Science and Artificial Intelligence, University of Alicante, 03690 San Vicente del Raspeig-Alicante, Spain; mar@dccia.ua.es
* Correspondence: fpujol@ua.es

Received: 24 October 2019; Accepted: 16 December 2019; Published: 20 December 2019

Abstract: Nowadays, cyber attacks are becoming an extremely serious issue, which is particularly important to prevent in a smart city context. Among cyber attacks, spoofing is an action that is increasingly common in many areas, such as emails, geolocation services or social networks. Identity spoofing is defined as the action by which a person impersonates a third party to carry out a series of illegal activities such as committing fraud, cyberbullying, sextorsion, etc. In this work, a face recognition system is proposed, with an application to the spoofing prevention. The method is based on the Histogram of Oriented Gradients (HOG) descriptor. Since different face regions do not have the same information for the recognition process, introducing entropy would quantify the importance of each face region in the descriptor. Therefore, entropy is added to increase the robustness of the algorithm. Regarding face recognition, our approach has been tested on three well-known databases (ORL, FERET and LFW) and the experiments show that adding entropy information improves the recognition rate significantly, with an increase over 40% in some of the considered databases. Spoofing tests has been implemented on CASIA FASD and MIFS databases, having obtained again better results than similar texture descriptors approaches.

Keywords: face recognition; security; spoofing; histogram of oriented gradients; smart cities

---

1. Introduction

Biometrics relies on measuring different human characteristics and matching them to previously collected measurements in a database. Biometric features are "built-in" the body so they cannot be shared or subtracted. Even though these systems seem to be extremely reliable, it is always possible to capture a legitimate biometric trait from a user, copy it and replicate it later by someone else. The act of using an artifact to fool a biometric system, where someone pretends to be another person, is known as spoof attack [1].

Nowadays, fingerprint hardware systems represent more than 92% of the total biometric features market [2]. With the rise of facial identification in mobile systems, experts forecast that annual facial recognition devices and licenses will increase from $28.5 mn in 2015 to more than $122.8 mn worldwide by 2024. During that period, annual revenue for facial biometrics, including both visible light facial recognition and infrared-based facial thermography, will increase from $149.5 mn to $882.5 mn, at a compound annual growth rate (CAGR) of 22% [3].

In the last few years, technology regarding image capturing has evolved, allowing consumers to buy high resolution cameras at a very low cost, specially with the use of billions of smartphones that allow users to have a digital camera on their hand constantly. Taking advantage of this situation, it seems straightforward to prevent spoofing by authenticating using biometric sensors such as fingerprints, iris or facial features. The annual revenue from mobile biometrics systems and applications is expected to grow from $6.5 bn in 2016 to $50.6 bn in 2022, with a compound annual growth rate of 41% [4].

Biometric systems can be compromised and are vulnerable to a wide range of attacks. Among all these potential attacks, the one with the greatest practical relevance is the spoof attack. As mentioned before, it consists of submitting a stolen or copied biometric trait to the sensor in order to defeat the biometric system and access the system in an unauthorized way. These attacks don't need any knowledge about the security system itself because, if the authorized user is able to access, the attacker just needs to simulate the biometric trait of that user. Because of this, most security systems provide some kind of protection such as hashing, digital signature or encryption that are ineffective in spoof attacks [5]. In the last few years there has been an intensive research to provide reliable anti-spoofing systems for biometric traits, including fingerprints [6,7], face [8–10], and other biometric features [11–13].

Spoofing attacks have grown exponentially in the last few years [14–16]. Among other areas, social networks have recently reported serious privacy and security issues [17–19]. Therefore, to ensure a higher security level in social networks it would be convenient to implement some kind of spoofing detector. However, using a supervised control of all the information on a social network is unfeasible due to the huge amount of data that can be produced at any given time. One of the most common ways cyberbullying develops is through identity spoofing. In this case, false user profiles attributed to the victim can be created. It may also be possible to access the user's profile or personal account on different social networks in such a way that the identity is spoofed by contacting others or making comments on behalf of the victim of bullying.

Consequently, the main objective of this work is to propose and develop a face recognition and spoof detection method that can be applied on social media by means of a novel entropy-based system. Entropy has been used in face recognition in recent years [20,21]. Thus, as different areas of a face image contribute in a different way to the global recognition, entropy on each area is introduced to construct a new version of the Histogram of Oriented Gradients (HOG) descriptor. As a result, the main contribution of this paper is the introduction of this new HOG-based descriptor, which makes use of entropy to code each area in a face image. To do this, after the Entropy-Based Histogram of Oriented Gradients descriptor is computed, Support Vector Machines are used for the classification process. Our system has been tested with three face recognition databases (Olivetti Research Laboratory: ORL, FERET and Labeled Faces in the Wild: LFW) and two face spoof detection datasets (CASIA Face Anti-Spoofing Database:FADS and Makeup Induced Face Spoofing: MIFS dataset), obtaining reliable results and outperforming other recent works using texture descriptors on the same databases.

This paper is organized as follows: Section 2 summarizes some related works; Section 3 explains our proposal of face detection, recognition and spoofing detection, introducing the Entropy-Based Histogram of Oriented Gradients (EBHOG) descriptor; Section 4 describes the experimental setup and the set of experiments completed with different databases; and finally, conclusions and some future works are discussed in Section 5.

2. Related Work

On social networks, a great amount of pictures and videos are uploaded and shared every day, where users can post an image where someone else appears without his/her consent. A face detection and recognition system would act before the image is published, identifying the people appearing in the image and notifying those users to give consent, protecting their privacy and increasing security by reporting potential cases of spoofing.

In order to simulate the authorized user, some face recognition systems can be spoofed by showing a photograph, video or even a face model of the user. Spoofing attacks can be detected using several methods. When detection and recognition are required to work in real-time, they must be computationally inexpensive. Most of the recognition methods are not fast enough or use non-conventional images [22]. Moreover, due to social image sharing and social networking websites, personal facial photographs of many users are usually accessible to the public. For instance, an impostor can obtain the photographs of genuine users from a social network, and submit them to a biometric authentication system to fool it [23].

Over the last few years, a wide variety of feature representation methods have been proposed to help describe scenes, objects and biometric features in different images. The particularities of each of these methods describe different aspects of visual features, each being best suited to certain particular conditions. Some of these methods focus on local information, others on holistic descriptors. Among all local feature descriptors, the most commonly used are SIFT (Scale-Invariant Feature Transform) [24,25], HOG (Histogram of Oriented Gradients) [26,27], SURF (Speeded-up Robust Features) [28,29] and LBP (Local Binary Patterns) [30,31], which are used to address variability in the image caused by changes in perspective, occlusions and variation in brightness.

As in many other machine learning applications, deep learning methods have proven to be an effective way to detect spoofing attacks. Many related works have considered face spoofing as a binary classification problem, where the system classifies a face as belonging to either a legitimate user or a fake user [32,33]. Thus, in [34] authors use CaffeNet and GoogLeNet convolutional neural networks (CNNs) models and perform a texture analysis. Alotaibi and Mahmood [35] presented a nonlinear diffusion to distinguish a fake image from a real image, which is the applied to a CNN for face liveness detection. Finally, an LBP network for face spoofing detection is proposed in [36], where LBP features are combined with deep learning. In spite of the immense potential of deep learning methods, they are computationally expensive, they need extremely large datasets for training and their internal complexity makes it difficult in some applications to interpret the results or to understand the algorithm mechanism [37–39].

The HOG descriptor is one of the most popular approaches for object detection. It is invariant to illumination and geometric transformations and it has been successfully applied to many security applications, such as privacy in image feature extraction using homomorphic encryption [40], phishing detection [41], classification of sensitive information embedded within uploaded photos [42], handwritten digits recognition [43], facial expression recognition with CNNs [44] and, particularly, to face spoofing detection [11,45–48]. Due to its popularity in anti-spoofing detection, in this work a variant of the HOG descriptor will be presented and experimentally validated.

3. Materials and Methods

The proposed system will detect and extract faces in a set of images, recognize extracted faces by matching them against the ones stored in a database and perform experimental proofs of the proposed method to enhance security. In order to validate the system, images with only one face will be considered. A description of the developed system is in Figure 1.

The whole process consists of the following stages:

- Image acquisition: image retrieval from a still photo.
- Face detection: detection of some patterns in the image in order to locate a face.
- Image pre-processing: crop the image to remove irrelevant parts and, if needed, apply image processing (change color space, filtering, etc.) to enhance some parameters to be measured in the next stage.
- Identifiers extraction: calculation of coefficients or identifying characteristic values.
- Face recognition: comparison of coefficients of the faces in the database and a new input image to verify identity.

Let us explain next the key features of our proposal.

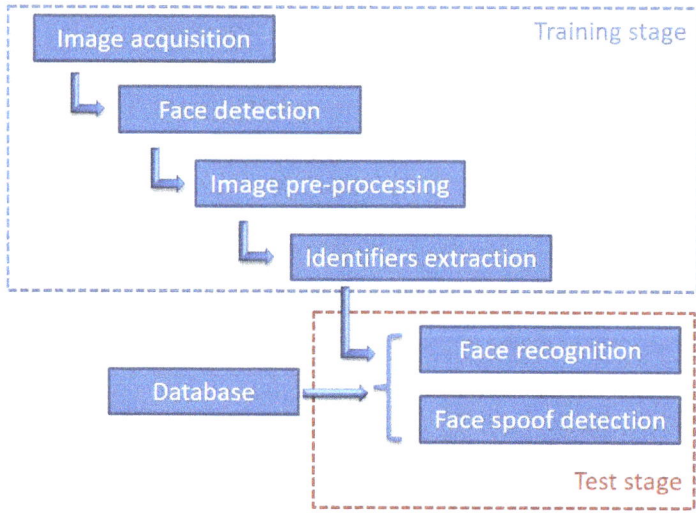

Figure 1. System overview.

3.1. Detection Framework

Regarding the detection framework, we have used a well-known object detection algorithm developed by Paul Viola and Michael Jones [49]. It is a robust algorithm with a very high detection rate, suitable for real time applications that can be used for face detection. The algorithm uses four stages to enable a fast and accurate detection: Haar feature selection, the integral image for feature computation, AdaBoost for feature selection and an attentional cascade for efficient computational resource allocation [50].

After this process, original images are cropped so that only face images are taken into account in the following stages of our proposal. Then images are normalized in size and color information is removed, since our system will work with grayscale images.

3.2. Recognition Framework

For the recognition process, the Histogram of Oriented Gradients (HOG) has been considered. HOG is a well-known image descriptor based on the image's gradient orientations. HOGs are rotationally-invariant image descriptors that have been used in optimization problems as well as in computer vision. The Histogram of Oriented Gradients (HOG) method has proven to be an effective descriptor, in general, for object recognition and for face recognition in particular [27].

The method is based on evaluating local histograms of image gradient orientations in a dense grid. The basic idea is that local object appearance and shape can often be characterized by the distribution of local intensity gradients or edge directions, even without precise knowledge of the corresponding gradient or edge positions [51]. HOG counts occurrences of edge orientations in a neighborhood of an image. In practice, this is implemented by dividing the image window into small spatial regions ("cells"), and each cell accumulates a local 1-D histogram of gradient directions (or edge orientations) over the pixels of the cell. The combined histogram entries form the representation [26].

Let G_x and G_y be the horizontal and vertical gradients of the image I. They can be computed for each pixel (x, y) using simple 1-D masks as follows:

$$G_x = I(x+1, y) - I(x-1, y) \quad (1)$$
$$G_y = I(x, y+1) - I(x, y-1) \quad (2)$$

Then, the magnitude and orientation of the gradient are calculated as:

$$M(x,y) = \sqrt{G_x^2 + G_y^2} \qquad (3)$$

$$\theta(x,y) = \arctan\left(\frac{G_y}{G_x}\right) \qquad (4)$$

Histograms are then constructed with the magnitude and orientation of each pixel, so that each cell will have one histogram and they will be concatenated to obtain the feature descriptor. The procedure for the implementation of the HOG descriptor algorithm is shown in Figure 2 and can be summarized as:

- Divide input image into small connected regions (cells).
- For each cell, a histogram of edge orientations is computed for all the pixels in the cell.
- Every cell is discretized into angular bins, according to the gradient orientation.
- Calculate histograms of oriented gradients over spatial cells.
- Group adjacent cells into overlapping blocks and normalize histograms.
- Block HOGs constitute the descriptor.
- Train a classifier (by using SVM -Support Vector Machines-, for instance).
- Classify using the trained SVM.

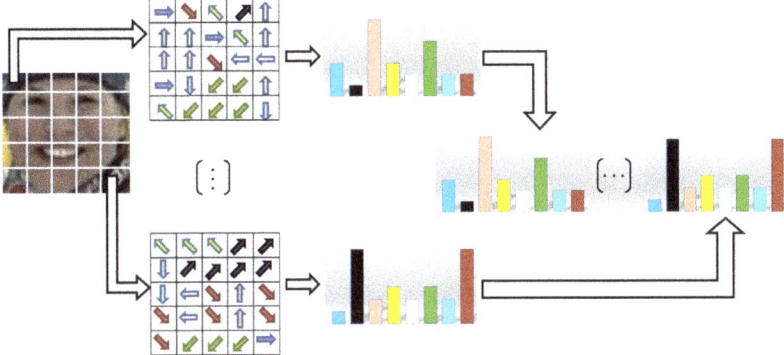

Figure 2. Histogram of Oriented Gradients (HOG) calculation. The orientation of gradients are calculated in each cell and all the histograms are concatenated to obtain the global HOG descriptor.

HOGs give the same importance (or weight) to each block in the image. However, some of these blocks contain information of the most remarkable features for face recognition, such as the eyes, the nose or the mouth [52,53], and many other blocks do not provide significant features for recognition. In other words, not all the blocks give the same information for a face recognition scheme. Shannon introduced entropy as a measure for measuring quantitatively the amount of information produced by a process [54]. Therefore, we consider that using entropy would quantify or weigh the importance of each block in the calculated HOGs, since different face regions will have different weights. Consequently, we introduce the Entropy-Based Histogram of Oriented Gradients (EBHOG) descriptor as follows:

- Divide input image into c small connected regions (cells).
- For each cell c, a histogram of edge orientations is computed for all the pixels in the cell.
- Every cell is discretized into b angular bins, according to the gradient orientation.
- Calculate histograms of oriented gradients over spatial cells.

- Group adjacent cells into overlapping blocks and normalize histograms.
- Calculate Shannon's entropy for each computed HOG. This will give a weight w_k for each block, for $k = 1, 2, \cdots, N$.
- Normalize weighted histograms.
- The weighted HOGs using entropy constitute the descriptor.
- Train a classifier by using SVM.
- Classify using the trained SVM.

The entropy for block k, H_k, is defined as:

$$H_k = -\sum_{j_k=1}^{N} P_{j_k} \log_2 P_{j_k} \tag{5}$$

where N is the number of blocks in the image and P_{j_k} is:

$$P_{j_k} = \frac{HOG_k(j)}{\sum_{i=1}^{c \times b} HOG_k(i)}. \tag{6}$$

HOG_k indicates the HOG obtained for block k in the input image.

The entropies of different regions in an image are shown in Figure 3. In this figure, it can be noticed that blocks containing key features for recognition, such as eyes, nose or mouth, have significant higher entropy values than blocks with irrelevant information for face recognition.

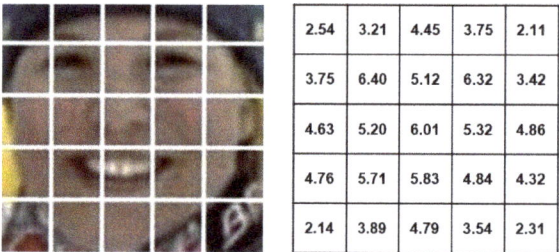

Figure 3. Entropy for different blocks in an image.

The weight w_k will then be calculated as:

$$w_k = H_{max} \cdot \left(\frac{H_k - H_{min}}{H_{max} - H_{min}} \right), \tag{7}$$

where

$$H_{max} = \max_{\forall k} H_k \tag{8}$$

$$H_{min} = \min_{\forall k} H_k \tag{9}$$

Let $W = \{w_1, w_2, \cdots, w_N\}$ be the set of weights calculated from Equation (7) and $HOG = \{HOG_1, HOG_2, \cdots, HOG_N\}$ the histograms of oriented gradients for each block. The entropy-based HOG is then calculated by multiplying each HOG_k by its corresponding weight w_k:

$$EBHOG = \{w_1 \times HOG_1, w_2 \times HOG_2, \cdots, w_N \times HOG_N\} \tag{10}$$

After weighting each HOG, the histograms must be normalized again, since the sum of all the values in each entropy weighted histogram is not 1. Thus, if $EBHOG_k = w_k \times HOG_k$ is the

k-th weighted histogram, min_k and max_k are the minimum and maximum values in $EBHOG_k$, the normalized histogram $EBHOG_k^{Norm}$ is:

$$EBHOG_k^{Norm} = \frac{EBHOG_k}{max_k - min_k} \qquad (11)$$

The whole training and testing process has been represented in Figures 4 and 5.

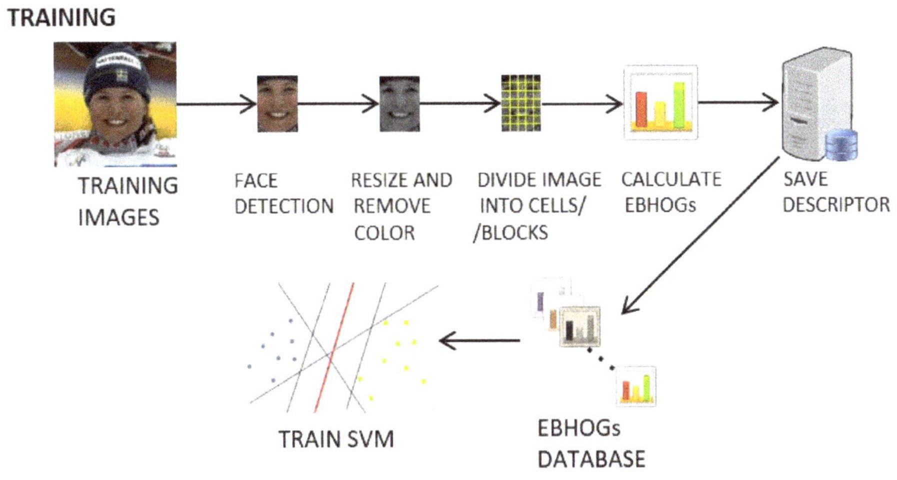

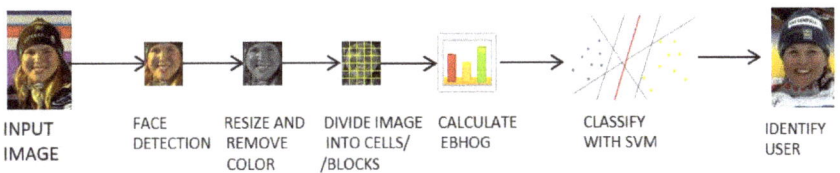

Figure 4. Diagram of the training stage for the face recognition process.

Figure 5. Diagram of the test stage for the face recognition process.

For classification, the Support Vector Machines (SVM) classifier has been chosen. Having several classes to be identified, the main idea of SVM is to select a hyperplane that is equidistant from the examples of each class to achieve the so-called maximum margin on each side of the hyperplane. To define this hyperplane, only the training data of each class next to these margins, which are called support vectors, are taken into account. The search for the separation hyperplane in these transformed spaces, usually of very high dimension, will be done implicitly using the so-called kernel functions. A kernel function $K(\mathbf{x}_i, \mathbf{x}_j)$ is a function that assigns to each pair of elements $\mathbf{x}_i, \mathbf{x}_j \in \mathbb{X}$ of an input space $\mathbb{X}$, a real value corresponding to the scalar product of the transformed version of that element in a new space. Among the most popular kernel functions, one can find:

- Linear kernel, whose expression is:

$$K(\mathbf{x}_i, \mathbf{x}_j) = \langle \mathbf{x}_i, \mathbf{x}_j \rangle \qquad (12)$$

where $\langle \cdot, \cdot \rangle$ refers to the scalar product.

- Gaussian kernel, expressed as:

$$K(\mathbf{x}_i, \mathbf{x}_j) = \exp\left(\frac{-\|\mathbf{x}_i - \mathbf{x}_j\|^2}{2\sigma^2}\right) \quad (13)$$

where σ is standard deviation.

The selection of the kernel function depends on the data to be classified and will be validated in Section 4.

3.3. Detecting Spoofing Using EBHOG

Face spoofing attacks can be performed in general terms by using still images, videos or real faces. In order to apply the EBHOG method, our proposal aims at training models with different textures to detect a real face from fake faces. It can be noticed that fake faces cause some reflections that depend on the surface from where the facial image is being projected, being non-existent if the image were real [55].

Our proposal is based on the results of [9]. In their work, authors showed that introducing color information achieves reliable results to prevent face spoofing attacks. In particular, the YCbCr color system is used, since the texture information of the chrominance components show visible differences between real and fake faces. They used LBP to validate their proposal, among other texture descriptors. We propose here to use EBHOG instead of LBP as antispoofing scheme, as shown in Figure 6.

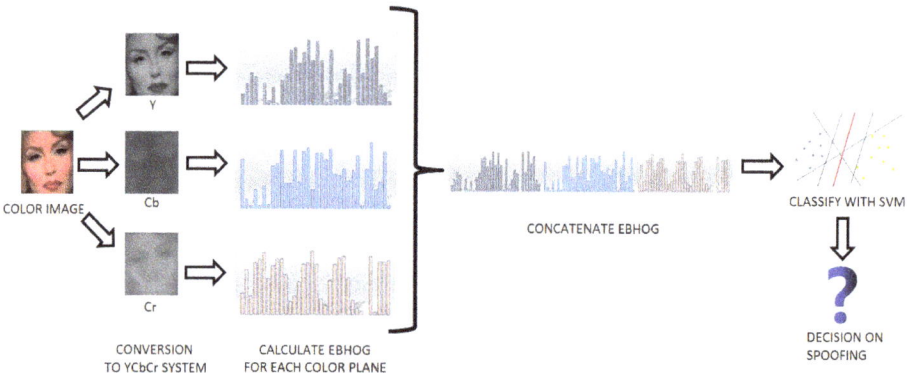

Figure 6. Proposal for face anti spoofing system based on Entropy-Based Histogram of Oriented Gradients (EBHOG).

4. Results

In this section, the datasets used to evaluate our model will be first introduced. Then, the parameters to be used in order to achieve reliable results in face recognition are calculated. After that, our approach will be compared with state-of-the-art methods on the selected databases. Finally, the results of some experiments completed to verify the suitability of our anti spoofing model are shown.

The tests for face recognition were performed using three face databases:

- The Olivetti Research Laboratory (ORL) database [56], which has 400 grayscale images of 40 persons. The images were taken at different times, with changing illumination conditions and different facial expressions. There are 10 images per person. 3 images were used for the training process in order to estimate the necessary EBHOG parameters. Then 2 images were used for the enrollment and, finally, the remaining 5 were used for the recognition stage.

- The Color FERET database [57]. It contains 11,338 pictures of 994 different individuals. The gallery set *fa* was used for the training process, with a subset of 200 users. Then, the tests were completed using gallery sets *fb*, *fc*, *dup1* and *dup2* of FERET database. Images stored in *fb* have changes in the expression from the images in subset *fa*. Images in *fc* have mainly differences in illumination. Then, *dup1* and *dup2* subsets are challenging, since images were taken on different dates from the ones in subset *fa*.
- The Labeled Faces in the Wild (LFW) dataset [58], composed of color images taken from the Internet. There are more than 13,000 photos of 5749 individuals, but for the recognition process only the users with at least two or more images per person have been considered. This reduces the bank of images to 1680 individuals. For the training process a subset of 200 users is again taken into account.

Figure 7 shows graphical examples of some images in these three databases.

Figure 7. Face examples from the databases used in the face recognition databases: first row, images from the ORL database; second row, images from the Color FERET database; third row, images from the LFW database.

On the other hand, the datasets used for face spoof detection are:

- The CASIA Face Anti-Spoofing Database (FASD) [59], which contains videos of 50 subjects with their corresponding fake faces. There are different image qualities and the face attacks are warped photo, cut photo and digital display device attacks. 20 subjects were used for training the remaining 30 for testing.
- The MIFS (Makeup Induced Face Spoofing) dataset [60], composed of face images of 107 subjects obtained from YouTube video makeup tutorials and face images of associated target subjects from the Internet. There are 4 photos per subject (2 before makeup, 2 after makeup) and 2 photos per target subject, making a total of 642 still images. This database focus specially on impersonating a target person by using makeup.

Figure 8 presents some examples of images in both CASIA FASD and MIFS datasets.

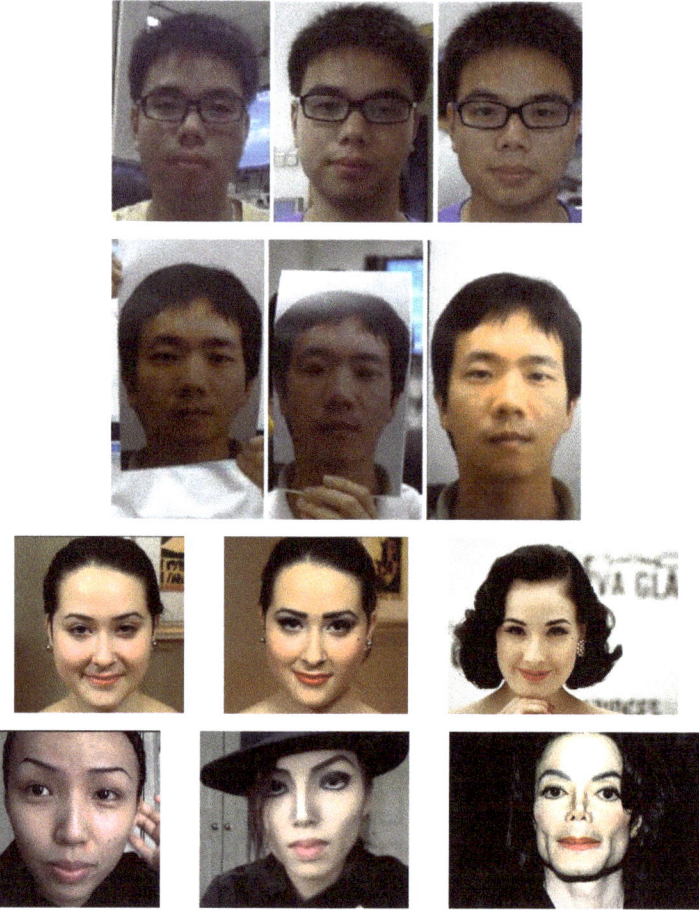

Figure 8. Some examples from the datasets used in the spoof detection: first row, images from the CASIA FASD database with different resolutions; second row, images from the CASIA FASD database with different spoofing attacks; third and fourth rows, images from the MIFS dataset, where the first image in each row is the subject before makeup, the second image is the subject after makeup and the third image is the target subject.

All the experiments have been completed in a computer using MATLAB in Windows 10, with an Intel Core i7-7500U processor @2.70 GHz and 8 GB of RAM.

4.1. Proposed System Settings and Recognition Results

As mentioned before (see Section 3.1 and Figure 4), the well-known Viola and Jones detector has been used to detect faces, and then, color information is removed from images. Finally, all the images have been normalized to 130 × 150 pixels.

Then, the parameters for the calculation of the Entropy-Based Histogram of Oriented Gradients (EBHOG) descriptor must be set. In order to choose the best cell size and the number of cells per block for our application, several tests changing the cell size of EBHOG have been performed. These calculations were performed by using 3 images per user in the ORL database. The number of orientation histogram bins (9 bins) has been the same as in [26], as well as the number of overlapping cells between adjacent blocks: half the block size. Finally, a Support Vector Machine (SVM) with a linear kernel has been chosen to classify faces [61], since it is usually suggested to use linear kernels if the number of features is much larger than the number of samples, which would happen in the original data set. The results using Receiver Operating Characteristic (ROC) curves are shown in Figure 9, where CS stands for Cell Size and BS stands for Block Size.

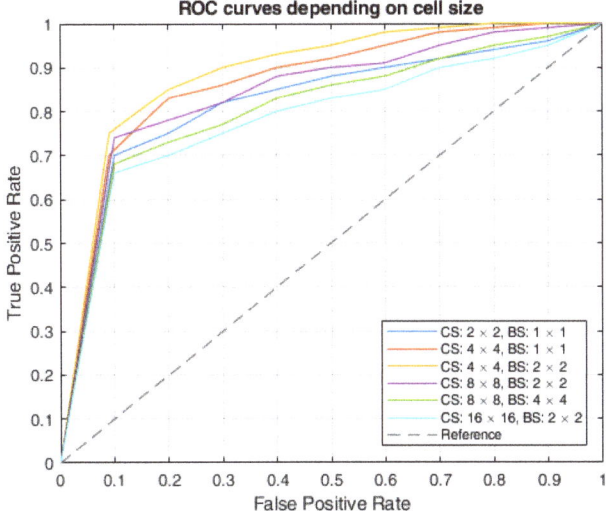

Figure 9. ROC curves depending on EBHOG cell sizes. CS stands for Cell Size, BS stands for Block Size.

To analyze these curves, the Area Under the ROC Curve (AUC) will be computed. The bigger the area, the better the classifier performs. Therefore, the results obtained regarding cell size/block size are presented in Table 1 in terms of area under the ROC curve (AUC).

Table 1. Area Under the ROC Curve (AUCs) of different cell sizes/block sizes for the considered database. The best results are highlighted in bold font.

Cell size (CS)/Block size (BS)	AUC
CS : 2 × 2, BS : 1 × 1	0.8220
CS : 4 × 4, BS : 1 × 1	0.8671
CS : 4 × 4, BS : 2 × 2	**0.8892**
CS : 8 × 8, BS : 2 × 2	0.8450
CS : 8 × 8, BS : 4 × 4	0.8090
CS : 16 × 16, BS : 2 × 2	0.7860

From these results, it becomes clear that the biggest area in Figure 9 is the one obtained with a EBHOG cell size of 4 × 4 and a block size of 2 × 2, so these are the parameters chosen to compute the histograms. To sum up, the parameters to obtain the Entropy-Based Histogram of Oriented Gradients are:

- Size of EBHOG cell: 4 × 4 pixels.
- Number of cells in block: 2 × 2 cells.
- Number of overlapping cells between adjacent blocks: 1 × 1 cells. It is calculated as half the block size.
- Number of orientation histogram bins: 9 bins.

All the experiments considered the same number of samples of a true null hypothesis and a false null hypothesis. With this, the False Rejection Rate (FRR) is defined as the probability that the system will not recognize the identity of an already enrolled person, and the False Acceptance Rate (FAR) is the probability that the system will not reject an impostor (person who is not in the database). False Rejection and False Acceptance errors happen when genuine users are denied access while impostors are accepted to the system, respectively. The experiments completed with the testing set in the ORL database give a False Rejection Rate (Number of False Rejections/Number of Enrollee Recognition Attempts) of 7% and a False Acceptance Rate (Number of False Acceptances/Number of Impostor Recognition Attempts) of just 2%.

Finally, the True Positive Rate (TPR) describes the performance of our system, since it calculates the ratio between the number of True Positives and the number of correct identification cases. In our case, with the parameters considered before we obtained a TPR of 94.4% for the ORL database. Table 2 shows the recognition rate results for the three databases considered in the experiments.

Table 2. Recognition results for the considered databases.

	ORL	FERET				LFW
		fb	fc	$dup1$	$dup2$	
TPR (%)	94.4	97.5	89.2	84.5	88.4	78.2

Note that the LFW database is commonly used for benchmarking face verification. However, in this work we consider the closed set identification protocol defined in [62–64]. The TPR is measured by the rank-1 identification accuracy, i.e., by a correct identification.

The mean computational time to extract EBHOG with the parameters set before was 12 ms for one subject on average. When using standard HOG this time was 8 ms on average.

4.2. Comparison with Other Methods and Discussion

Let us compare now the performance of our EBHOG descriptor and some other state-of-the-art descriptors for face recognition. In particular, the original Histogram of Oriented Gradients (HOG) approach has been taken into account [26], as well as other texture descriptors, such as Local Binary Patterns (LBP) [30], Patterns of Oriented Edge Magnitudes (POEM) [65], Scale-Invariant Feature Transform (SIFT) [51], Local Directional Patterns (LDP) [66], Weber Local Descriptors (WLD) [67] and recent Local Diagonal Extrema Number Patterns (LDENP) [68].

On the other hand, given their popularity and accuracy in recognition tasks, CNNs and Deep Learning represent a very successful model and they are used in many applications, particularly in computer vision tasks. One of the strategies that can be followed to apply Deep Learning is transfer learning. It consists of taking a pre-trained network and using it as a starting point to learn a new task. The advantage of this approach is that the pre-established network has already learned a broad set of features that can be applied for similar purposes. To do this, AlexNet has been selected [69]. The AlexNet architecture has eight layers with their respective learning parameters, five of which are convolutional layers and the remaining are fully connected. AlexNet was originally designed to support 1000 classes. However, in our classification problem the number of classes will be equal to the number of different users in each considered database. Thus, AlexNet was adapted to a smaller number of outputs, this being possible due to the flexibility to modify the last layer of the network.

The results the comparison between all these methods can be found in Table 3.

From these results, it becomes clear that adding entropy information to the original Histogram of Oriented Gradients descriptor improves the recognition rate significantly, with an increase over 40% in some of the databases considered for the experiments.

When working with ORL database and fb and fc sets from the FERET database, our proposal does not get the best results, although the performance is rather similar to other state-of-the-art descriptors (our recognition rate is less than 2% lower than the best method in Table 3). In particular, both the Local Diagonal Extrema Number Patterns (LDENP) method and using AlexNet with Transfer Learning achieve the highest recognition rates for these datasets, which are characterized by having different light conditions (ORL and subset fc in FERET) and different expressions (ORL and subset fb in FERET).

Table 3. Recognition rate results (%) of our method in comparison with state-of-the-art algorithms. The best results for each database are highlighted in bold font.

Method	ORL	FERET				LFW
		fb	fc	$dup1$	$dup2$	
LBP [30]	87.8	81.0	84.7	64.9	48.6	44.9
POEM [65]	94.4	97.6	86.0	77.8	76.5	74.0
SIFT [51]	92.7	95.9	66.1	65.2	55.4	69.8
LDP [66]	88.5	97.0	82.0	72.0	69.0	71.3
WLD [67]	90.0	93.0	51.0	61.0	50.0	38.0
LDENP [68]	94.6	97.7	**89.9**	82.9	86.8	58.5
AlexNet [69]	**95.5**	**99.7**	88.7	84.3	87.8	75.4
HOG [26]	93.5	90.0	74.0	54.0	46.6	48.2
EBHOG	94.4	97.5	89.2	**84.5**	**88.4**	**78.2**

On the other hand, the EBHOG descriptor has the better recognition rates for both datasets $dup1$ and $dup2$ from the FERET database and for the challenging LFW database. These datasets are characterized by including photos with temporal/age changes (subsets $dup1$ and $dup2$ in FERET) and large variations in pose, expression and illuminations (LFW). Our method achieves high recognition results for these difficult datasets, which shows again that entropy plays a major role to achieve reliable recognition rates in difficult, demanding situations.

4.3. Experiments on Detecting Spoofing and Discussion

Let us show now the results of the completed tests in order to detect face spoofing attacks. Experiments on the CASIA FASD database are strictly done with the original protocol defined by the authors. Thus, 30 face images in each of the training videos are selected randomly. Then, 30 face images from each of the testing videos are also selected randomly. The video is then classified as 'real' or 'fake' by averaging the 30 images scores. In order to compare the classification results, the Equal Error Rate (EER) is used, as suggested by the authors. The results are shown in Table 4, where a comparison with the results from [9] and from using HOG instead of EBHOG are displayed.

Table 4. Performance using Equal Error Rate (EER) (%) in the CASIA FASD database and YCbCr color system. The best results are highlighted in bold font.

Method	EER
LBP [9]	12.4
HOG [26]	21.6
EBHOG	**9.5**

As it can be seen, the proposed method improves on the original developed in [9], and it can be considered as an alternative to face spoofing detection.

In [60] authors defined two spoofing indexes. SI_1 evaluates the similarity between the after-makeup images of subject p, A_i^p, and the target images, T_j^p, for $i,j \in \{1,2\}$, with respect to two samples of the target identity, T_1^p, T_2^p. SI_2 computes the similarity between the after-makeup images A_i^p and the target images T_j^p with respect to two samples of the after-makeup images A_1^p, A_2^p:

$$SI_1 = 1 - \min_{i,j} \left| \phi\left(A_i^p, T_j^p\right) - \phi\left(T_1^p, T_2^p\right) \right| \quad (14)$$

$$SI_2 = 1 - \min_{i,j} \left| \phi\left(A_i^p, T_j^p\right) - \phi\left(A_1^p, A_2^p\right) \right| \quad (15)$$

Here $\phi(x,y)$ is the similarity match score between images x and y. Since our descriptor is based on histogram calculation, we propose to calculate the similarity between two images x and y by using the histogram intersection kernel:

$$\phi(x,y) = \sum_{i=1}^{N} \min\left(EBHOG_i^{Norm}(x), EBHOG_i^{Norm}(y)\right) \qquad (16)$$

$\phi(x,y)$ is finally normalized in the $[0,1]$ interval.

Input images are then again classified as 'real' or 'fake' and, as in the CASIA FASD database, the Equal Error Rate (EER) is calculated to compare the results. The results are shown in Table 5, where a comparison with the same methods as in Table 4 are considered. Notice that the threshold in the similarity score to consider that an image is genuine or not has been introduced, as well.

Table 5. Performance using EER (%) in the MIFS database and YCbCr color system. The best results for each database are highlighted in bold font.

Method	Similarity Threshold				
	0.75	0.8	0.85	0.9	0.95
LBP [9]	15.5	7.6	3.4	4.5	9.8
HOG [26]	22.4	16.5	9.5	12.6	18.3
EBHOG	13.8	6.8	**3.1**	3.8	7.5

The threshold for the histogram intersection similarity score that achieves better results from Table 5 is 0.85. Again, the best performance corresponds to the method proposed. As a conclusion, introducing entropy improves the results in face spoofing detection compared with similar approaches.

To sum up, the results from the experiments show that our proposal is consistently among the best local descriptors for face recognition, outperforming most of the recent approaches results in Tables 3–5. The great amount of tests implemented on several face databases have effectively shown the potential of the EBHOG approach.

5. Conclusions

In the last few years, with the increasing popularity of mobile technologies, almost all mobile phone applications have access to private data in some way. This fact is particularly vulnerable in a smart city context. Cyberattacks on social networks have become common to get profiles and hackers often use them to steal personal data or even to discredit their real user. One way to prevent spoofing is by authenticating users using biometric traits such as fingerprints, iris or facial features.

In this work, a new face recognition and spoofing detection approach using an entropy-based HOG descriptor has been presented. The results show that our method provides a reliable descriptor for different databases and, as a result, we consider that our proposal may be applied to detect possible face spoofing attacks using pictures uploaded to social media. Future works aim at applying the proposed algorithm to real situations in social networks. We are currently adapting the method to work with GPUs and parallelizing the most time-consuming steps in the algorithm.

Author Contributions: Conceptualization, F.A.P. and M.J.P.; methodology, C.R.-M.; validation, C.R.-M. and M.P.; formal analysis, M.J.P.; writing—review and editing, F.A.P. and M.P. All authors have read and agreed to the published version of the manuscript.

Funding: This research was funded by the Ministerio de Economía y Competitividad (Spain), project TIN2013-40982-R and by the Programa Redes-I³CE de Investigación en Docencia Universitaria 2016–2017, Red ICE 3701, of the Instituto de Ciencias de la Educación of the University of Alicante.

Acknowledgments: This work was partially supported by the Ministerio de Economía y Competitividad (Spain), project TIN2013-40982-R, the FEDER funds, and the "Red de Investigación en el uso del aprendizaje colaborativo para la adquisición de competencias básicas. El caso Erasmus+ EUROBOTIQUE", Red ICE 3701 curso 2016–2017.

Conflicts of Interest: The authors declare no conflict of interest.

References

1. Jain, A.K.; Flynn, P.; Ross, A.A. *Handbook of Biometrics*; Springer: Boston, MA, USA, 2008. doi:10.1007/978-0-387-71041-9.
2. Girardin, G. Consumers rule: Why the biometrics market is facing major disruption. *Biom. Technol. Today* **2017**, *2017*, 10–11. doi:10.1016/S0969-4765(17)30116-9.
3. Tractica. Global Biometrics Market Revenue to Reach $15.1 Billion by 2025 | Tractica. Available online: https://www.tractica.com/newsroom/press-releases/global-biometrics-market-revenue-to-reach-15-1-billion-by-2025/ (accessed on 8 January 2019).
4. Mobile biometrics revenues predicted to boom. *Biom. Technol. Today* **2017**, *2017*, 3–12. doi:https://doi.org/10.1016/S0969-4765(17)30161-3.
5. Nita, S.L.; Mihailescu, M.I.; Pau, V.C. Security and Cryptographic Challenges for Authentication Based on Biometrics Data. *Cryptography* **2018**, *2*, 39. doi:10.3390/cryptography2040039.
6. Chugh, T.; Cao, K.; Jain, A.K. Fingerprint Spoof Buster: Use of Minutiae-Centered Patches. *IEEE Trans. Inform. Forensics Secur.* **2018**, *13*, 2190–2202. doi:10.1109/TIFS.2018.2812193.
7. Shaju, S.; Davis, D. Haar wavelet transform based histogram concatenation model for finger print spoofing detection. In Proceedings of the IEEE 2017 International Conference on Communication and Signal Processing (ICCSP), Chennai, India, 6–8 April 2017; pp. 1352–1356.
8. Fernandez, A.; Carus, J.L.; Usamentiaga, R.; Casado, R. Face Recognition and Spoofing Detection System Adapted To Visually-Impaired People. *IEEE Lat. Am. Trans.* **2016**, *14*, 913–921.
9. Boulkenafet, Z.; Komulainen, J.; Hadid, A. Face spoofing detection using colour texture analysis. *IEEE Trans. Inform. Forensics Secur.* **2016**, *11*, 1818–1830.
10. Li, H.; Li, W.; Cao, H.; Wang, S.; Huang, F.; Kot, A.C. Unsupervised domain adaptation for face anti-spoofing. *IEEE Trans. Inform. Forensics Secur.* **2018**, *13*, 1794–1809.
11. Farmanbar, M.; Toygar, Ö. Spoof detection on face and palmprint biometrics. *Signal Image Video Process.* **2017**, *11*, 1253–1260.
12. Hsieh, S.H.; Li, Y.H.; Wang, W.; Tien, C.H. A Novel Anti-Spoofing Solution for Iris Recognition Toward Cosmetic Contact Lens Attack Using Spectral ICA Analysis. *Sensors* **2018**, *18*, 795.
13. Yu, S.; Ai, Y.; Xu, B.; Zhou, Y.; Li, W.; Liao, Q.; Poh, N. Two strategies to optimize the decisions in signature verification with the presence of spoofing attacks. *Inform. Sci.* **2016**, *352*, 188–202.
14. Dawson, M.; Omar, M.; Abramson, J. Understanding the methods behind cyber terrorism. In *Encyclopedia of Information Science and Technology*, 3rd ed.; IGI Global: Hershey PA, USA, 2015; pp. 1539–1549.
15. Patel, K.; Han, H.; Jain, A.K. Secure face unlock: Spoof detection on smartphones. *IEEE Trans. Inform. Forensics Secur.* **2016**, *11*, 2268–2283.
16. Kamble, A.; Malemath, V.S.; Patil, D. Security attacks and secure routing protocols in RPL-based Internet of Things: Survey. In Proceedings of the IEEE 2017 International Conference on Emerging Trends & Innovation in ICT (ICEI), Pune, India, 3–5 February 2017; pp. 33–39.
17. Liu, F.; Zhu, X.; Hu, Y.; Ren, L.; Johnson, H. A cloud theory-based trust computing model in social networks. *Entropy* **2016**, *19*, 11.
18. Rathore, S.; Sharma, P.K.; Loia, V.; Jeong, Y.S.; Park, J.H. Social network security: Issues, challenges, threats, and solutions. *Inform. Sci.* **2017**, *421*, 43–69.
19. van Schaik, P.; Jansen, J.; Onibokun, J.; Camp, J.; Kusev, P. Security and privacy in online social networking: Risk perceptions and precautionary behaviour. *Comput. Hum. Behav.* **2018**, *78*, 283–297.
20. Karczmarek, P.; Pedrycz, W.; Kiersztyn, A.; Rutka, P. A study in facial features saliency in face recognition: An analytic hierarchy process approach. *Soft Comput.* **2017**, *21*, 7503–7517.
21. Lu, Y.; Wang, S.; Zhao, W. Facial Expression Recognition Based on Discrete Separable Shearlet Transform and Feature Selection. *Algorithms* **2019**, *12*, 11.
22. Maatta, J.; Hadid, A.; Pietikainen, M. Face spoofing detection from single images using texture and local shape analysis. *IET Biom.* **2012**, *1*, 3–10. doi:10.1049/iet-bmt.2011.0009.
23. Chakka, M.M.; Anjos, A.; Marcel, S.; Tronci, R.; Muntoni, D.; Fadda, G. Competition on counter measures to 2-D facial spoofing attacks. In Proceedings of the International Joint Conference on Biometrics (IJCB 2011), Washington, DC, USA, 11–13 December 2011.

24. Lowe, D.G. Object recognition from local scale-invariant features. In Proceedings of the Seventh IEEE International Conference on Computer Vision, Kerkyra, Greece, 20–27 September 1999; Volume 2, pp. 1150–1157.
25. Luo, J.; Ma, Y.; Takikawa, E.; Lao, S.; Kawade, M.; Lu, B.L. Person-specific SIFT features for face recognition. In Proceedings of the IEEE International Conference on Acoustics, Speech and Signal Processing (ICASSP 2007), Honolulu, HI, USA, 15–20 April 2007; Volume 2, p. 593.
26. Dalal, N.; Triggs, B. Histograms of oriented gradients for human detection. In Proceedings of the 2005 IEEE Computer Society Conference on Computer Vision and Pattern Recognition (CVPR'05), San Diego, CA, USA, 20–25 June 2005; pp. 886–893.
27. Déniz, O.; Bueno, G.; Salido, J.; De la Torre, F. Face recognition using histograms of oriented gradients. *Pattern Recognit. Lett.* **2011**, *32*, 1598–1603.
28. Bay, H.; Tuytelaars, T.; Van Gool, L. Surf: Speeded up robust features. In *European Conference on Computer Vision*; Springer: Berlin/Heidelberg, Germany, 2006; pp. 404–417.
29. Boulkenafet, Z.; Komulainen, J.; Hadid, A. Face antispoofing using speeded-up robust features and fisher vector encoding. *IEEE Signal Process. Lett.* **2017**, *24*, 141–145.
30. Ahonen, T.; Hadid, A.; Pietikäinen, M. Face Recognition with Local Binary Patterns. In *Computer Vision—ECCV 2004*; Pajdla, T., Matas, J., Eds.; Springer: Berlin/Heidelberg, Germany, 2004; pp. 469–481.
31. Ma, Z.; Ding, Y.; Li, B.; Yuan, X. Deep CNNs with Robust LBP Guiding Pooling for Face Recognition. *Sensors* **2018**, *18*, 3876.
32. Yang, J.; Lei, Z.; Li, S.Z. Learn Convolutional Neural Network for Face Anti-Spoofing. *arXiv* **2014**, arXiv:1408.5601.
33. Rehman, Y.A.U.; Po, L.M.; Liu, M. LiveNet: Improving features generalization for face liveness detection using convolution neural networks. *Expert Syst. Appl.* **2018**, *108*, 159–169. doi:10.1016/j.eswa.2018.05.004.
34. Patel, K.; Han, H.; Jain, A.K. Cross-Database Face Antispoofing with Robust Feature Representation. In *Biometric Recognition*; You, Z., Zhou, J., Wang, Y., Sun, Z., Shan, S., Zheng, W., Feng, J., Zhao, Q., Eds.; Springer International Publishing: Cham, Switzerland, 2016; Volume 9967, pp. 611–619. doi:10.1007/978-3-319-46654-5_67.
35. Alotaibi, A.; Mahmood, A. Deep face liveness detection based on nonlinear diffusion using convolution neural network. *Signal Image Video Process.* **2017**, *11*, 713–720. doi:10.1007/s11760-016-1014-2.
36. Li, L.; Feng, X.; Xia, Z.; Jiang, X.; Hadid, A. Face spoofing detection with local binary pattern network. *J. Vis. Commun. Image Represent.* **2018**, *54*, 182–192. doi:10.1016/j.jvcir.2018.05.009.
37. Livni, R.; Shalev-Shwartz, S.; Shamir, O. On the Computational Efficiency of Training Neural Networks. In *Advances in Neural Information Processing Systems 27*; Ghahramani, Z., Welling, M., Cortes, C., Lawrence, N.D., Weinberger, K.Q., Eds.; Curran Associates Inc.: Dutchess County, NY, USA, 2014; pp. 855–863. Available online: http://papers.nips.cc/paper/5267-on-the-computational-efficiency-of-training-neural-networks (accessed on 10 December 2019).
38. Miralles-Pechuán, L.; Rosso, D.; Jiménez, F.; García, J.M. A methodology based on Deep Learning for advert value calculation in CPM, CPC and CPA networks. *Soft Comput.* **2017**, *21*, 651–665.
39. Mahmud, M.; Kaiser, M.S.; Hussain, A.; Vassanelli, S. Applications of deep learning and reinforcement learning to biological data. *IEEE Trans. Neural Netw. Learn. Syst.* **2018**, *29*, 2063–2079.
40. Yang, H.; Huang, Y.; Yu, Y.; Yao, M.; Zhang, X. Privacy-Preserving Extraction of HOG Features Based on Integer Vector Homomorphic Encryption. In Proceedings of the International Conference on Information Security Practice and Experience, Melbourne, Australia, 13–15 December 2017; Springer: Berlin/Heidelberg, Germany, 2017; pp. 102–117. Available online: https://www.semanticscholar.org/paper/Privacy-Preserving-Extraction-of-HOG-Features-Based-Yang-Huang/e286f4fb60fd819dd36db44d0f56dc76932aaee4 (accessed on 10 December 2019).
41. Bozkir, A.S.; Sezer, E.A. Use of HOG descriptors in phishing detection. In Proceedings of the 2016 IEEE 4th International Symposium on Digital Forensic and Security (ISDFS), Little Rock, AR, USA, 25–27 April 2016; pp. 148–153.
42. Chandra, D.K.; Chowgule, W.; Fu, Y.; Lin, D. RIPA: Real-Time Image Privacy Alert System. In Proceedings of the 2018 IEEE 4th International Conference on Collaboration and Internet Computing (CIC), Philadelphia, PA, USA, 18–20 October 2018; pp. 136–145.

43. Lu, W.S. Handwritten digits recognition using PCA of histogram of oriented gradient. In Proceedings of the 2017 IEEE Pacific Rim Conference on Communications, Computers and Signal Processing (PACRIM), Victoria, BC, Canada, 21–23 August 2017; pp. 1–5.
44. Alizadeh, S.; Fazel, A. Convolutional neural networks for facial expression recognition. *arXiv* **2017**, arXiv:1704.06756.
45. Schwartz, W.R.; Rocha, A.; Pedrini, H. Face spoofing detection through partial least squares and low-level descriptors. In Proceedings of the 2011 IEEE International Joint Conference on Biometrics (IJCB), Washington, DC, USA, 11–13 October 2011; pp. 1–8.
46. Komulainen, J.; Hadid, A.; Pietikainen, M. Context based face anti-spoofing. In Proceedings of the 2013 IEEE Sixth International Conference on Biometrics: Theory, Applications and Systems (BTAS), Arlington, VA, USA, 29 September–2 October 2013; pp. 1–8.
47. Kaur, S.; Sharma, R. An Intelligent Approach for Anti-Spoofing in a Multimodal Biometric System. *Int. J. Comput. Sci. Eng.* **2017**, *9*, 522–529.
48. Galdi, C.; Nappi, M.; Dugelay, J.L. Secure User Authentication on Smartphones via Sensor and Face Recognition on Short Video Clips. In Proceedings of the International Conference on Green, Pervasive, and Cloud Computing, Cetara, Italy, 11–14 May 2017; Springer: Berlin/Heidelberg, Germany, 2017, pp. 15–22. Available online: https://www.semanticscholar.org/paper/Secure-User-Authentication-on-Smartphones-via-and-Galdi-Nappi/d7936ad5e71703d3c7b686ff13eacb88f3b7dbf9 (accessed on 10 December 2019).
49. Viola, P.; Jones, M. Robust real-time face detection. *Int. J. Comput. Vis.* **2004**, *57*, 137–154. doi:{10.1023/B:VISI.0000013087.49260.fb}.
50. Wang, Y.Q. An Analysis of the Viola-Jones Face Detection Algorithm. *Image Process. Line* **2014**, *4*, 128–148. doi:10.5201/ipol.2014.104.
51. Lowe, D. Distinctive image features from scale-invariant keypoints. *Int. J. Comput. Vis.* **2004**, *60*, 91–110. doi:10.1023/B:VISI.0000029664.99615.94.
52. Karmakar, D.; Murthy, C.A. Face Recognition using Face-Autocropping and Facial Feature Points Extraction. In Proceedings of the 2nd International Conference on Perception and Machine Intelligence (PerMIn '15), Kolkata, West Bengal, India, 26–27 February 2015; ACM Press: New York, NY, USA, 2015; pp. 116–122. doi:10.1145/2708463.2709056.
53. Leung, H.Y.; Cheng, L.M.; Li, X.Y. A FPGA implementation of facial feature extraction. *J. Real-Time Image Process.* **2015**, *10*, 135–149. doi:10.1007/s11554-012-0263-8.
54. Portes de Albuquerque, M.; Esquef, I.A.; Gesualdi Mello, A.R.; Portes de Albuquerque, M. Image thresholding using Tsallis entropy. *Pattern Recognit. Lett.* **2004**, *25*, 1059–1065. doi:10.1016/j.patrec.2004.03.003.
55. Pan, G.; Wu, Z.; Sun, L. Liveness detection for face recognition. In *Recent Advances in Face Recognition*; IntechOpen: London, UK, 2008.
56. Samaria, F.S.; Harter, A.C. Parameterisation of a stochastic model for human face identification. In Proceedings of the Second IEEE Workshop on Applications of Computer Vision, Sarasota, FL, USA, 5–7 December 1994; pp. 138–142.
57. Phillips, P.J.; Moon, H.; Rizvi, S.A.; Rauss, P.J. The FERET evaluation methodology for face recognition algorithms. *IEEE Trans. Pattern Anal. Mach. Intell.* **2000**, *22*, 1090–1104.
58. Huang, G.B.; Ramesh, M.; Berg, T.; Learned-Miller, E. *Labeled Faces in the Wild: A Database for Studying Face Recognition in Unconstrained Environments*; Technical Report 07-49; University of Massachusetts: Amherst, MA, USA, 2007.
59. Zhang, Z.; Yan, J.; Liu, S.; Lei, Z.; Yi, D.; Li, S.Z. A face antispoofing database with diverse attacks. In Proceedings of the 2012 5th IAPR International Conference on Biometrics (ICB), New Delhi, India, 29 March–1 April 2012; pp. 26–31.
60. Chen, C.; Dantcheva, A.; Swearingen, T.; Ross, A. Spoofing faces using makeup: An investigative study. In Proceedings of the 2017 IEEE International Conference on Identity, Security and Behavior Analysis (ISBA), New Delhi, India, 22–24 February 2017; pp. 1–8.
61. Chang, C.C.; Lin, C.J. LIBSVM: a library for support vector machines. *ACM Trans. Intell. Syst. Technol.* **2011**, *2*, 27.
62. Best-Rowden, L.; Han, H.; Otto, C.; Klare, B.F.; Jain, A.K. Unconstrained face recognition: Identifying a person of interest from a media collection. *IEEE Trans. Inform. Forensics Secur.* **2014**, *9*, 2144–2157.

63. Taigman, Y.; Yang, M.; Ranzato, M.; Wolf, L. Web-scale training for face identification. In Proceedings of the IEEE Conference on Computer Vision and Pattern Recognition (CVPR 2015), Boston, MA, USA, 7–12 June 2015; pp. 2746–2754.
64. Pujol, F.A.; Mora, H.; Girona-Selva, J.A. A connectionist computational method for face recognition. *Int. J. Appl. Math. Comput. Sci.* **2016**, *26*, 451–465.
65. Vu, N.S.; Caplier, A. Face recognition with patterns of oriented edge magnitudes. In *European Conference on Computer Vision*; Springer: Berlin/Heidelberg, Germany, 2010; pp. 313–326.
66. Jabid, T.; Kabir, M.H.; Chae, O. Local directional pattern (LDP) for face recognition. In Proceedings of the 2010 Digest of Technical Papers International Conference on Consumer Electronics (ICCE), Las Vegas, NV, USA, 9–13 January 2010; pp. 329–330.
67. Chen, J.; Shan, S.; He, C.; Zhao, G.; Pietikainen, M.; Chen, X.; Gao, W. WLD: A robust local image descriptor. *IEEE Trans. Pattern Anal. Mach. Intell.* **2010**, *32*, 1705–1720.
68. Pillai, A.; Soundrapandiyan, R.; Satapathy, S.; Satapathy, S.C.; Jung, K.H.; Krishnan, R. Local diagonal extrema number pattern: A new feature descriptor for face recognition. *Future Gener. Comput. Syst.* **2018**, *81*, 297–306. doi:10.1016/j.future.2017.09.055.
69. Krizhevsky, A.; Sutskever, I.; Hinton, G.E. ImageNet Classification with Deep Convolutional Neural Networks. In Proceedings of the 25th International Conference on Neural Information Processing Systems (NIPS'12), Lake Tahoe, NV, USA, 3–6 December 2012; Curran Associates Inc.: Red Hook, NY, USA, 2012; Volume 1, pp. 1097–1105.

© 2019 by the authors. Licensee MDPI, Basel, Switzerland. This article is an open access article distributed under the terms and conditions of the Creative Commons Attribution (CC BY) license (http://creativecommons.org/licenses/by/4.0/).